Oh My Goddess!

ああっ女神さまっ   THE DEVIL IN MISS URD

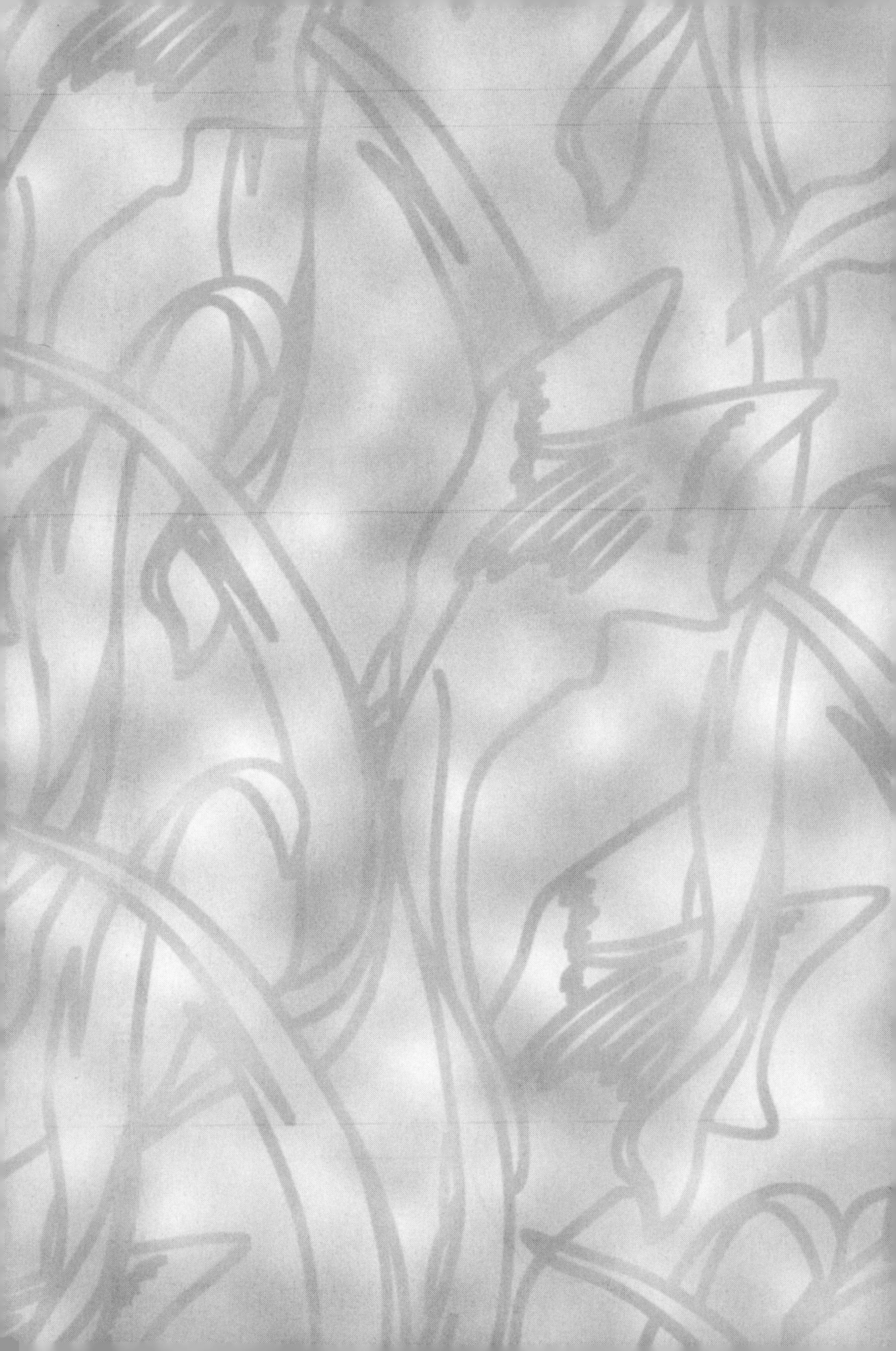

Oh My Goddess!

ああっ女神さまっ **THE DEVIL IN MISS URD**

STORY AND ART BY

Kosuke Fujishima

TRANSLATION BY

Dana Lewis & Toren Smith

LETTERING AND RETOUCH BY

Susie Lee & PC Orz

DARK HORSE COMICS®

PUBLISHER
Mike Richardson

SERIES EDITOR
Rachel Penn

COLLECTION EDITOR
Chris Warner

COLLECTION DESIGNER
Amy Arendts

ART DIRECTOR
Mark Cox

English-language version produced by Studio Proteus
for Dark Horse Comics, Inc.

OH MY GODDESS! Volume XI: The Devil in Miss Urd

This volume collects issues one through six of the Dark Horse comic-book series *Oh My Goddess!* Part VI.

Published by
Dark Horse Comics, Inc.
10956 SE Main Street
Milwaukie, OR 97222

www.darkhorse.com

To find a comics shop in your area, call the Comic Shop
Locator Service toll-free at 1-888-266-4226

First edition: June 2001
ISBN: 1-56971-540-8

3 5 7 9 10 8 6 4
Printed in Canada

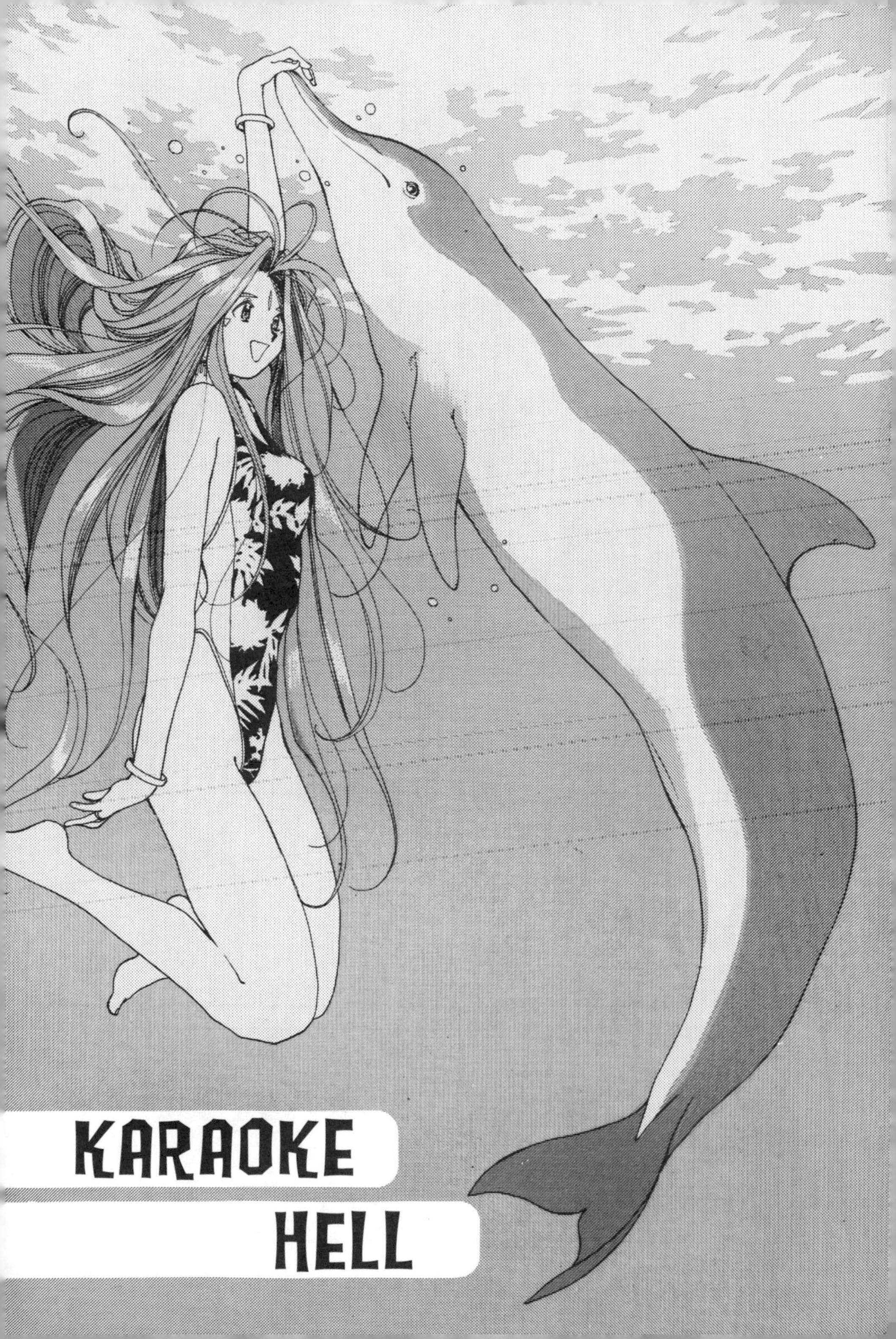
KARAOKE
HELL

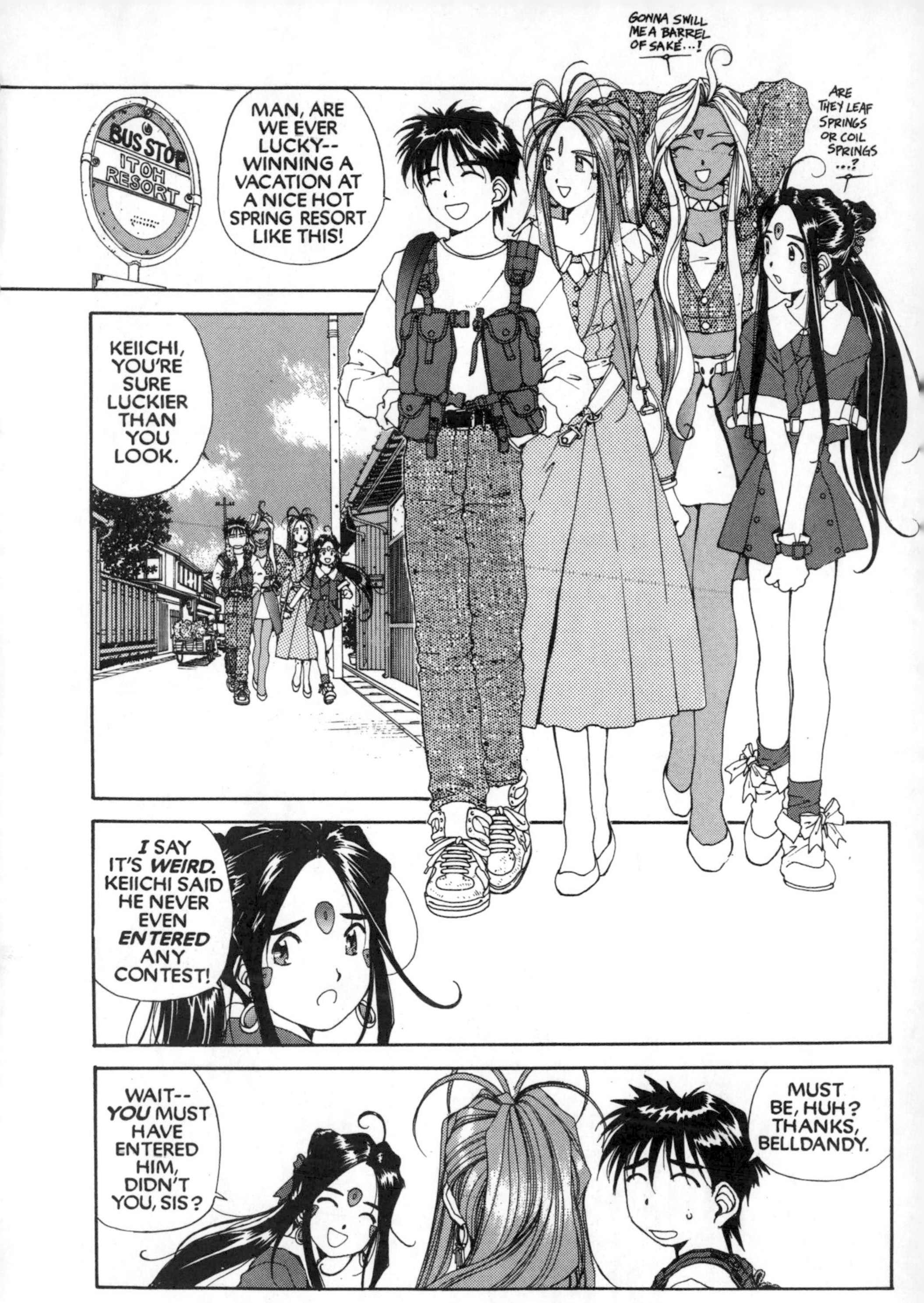
BUS STOP
ITOH RESORT
MAN, ARE WE EVER LUCKY-- WINNING A VACATION AT A NICE HOT SPRING RESORT LIKE THIS!
GONNA SWILL ME A BARREL OF SAKÉ...!
ARE THEY LEAF SPRINGS OR COIL SPRINGS ...?
KEIICHI, YOU'RE SURE LUCKIER THAN YOU LOOK.
I SAY IT'S WEIRD. KEIICHI SAID HE NEVER EVEN ENTERED ANY CONTEST!
WAIT-- YOU MUST HAVE ENTERED HIM, DIDN'T YOU, SIS?
MUST BE, HUH? THANKS, BELLDANDY.

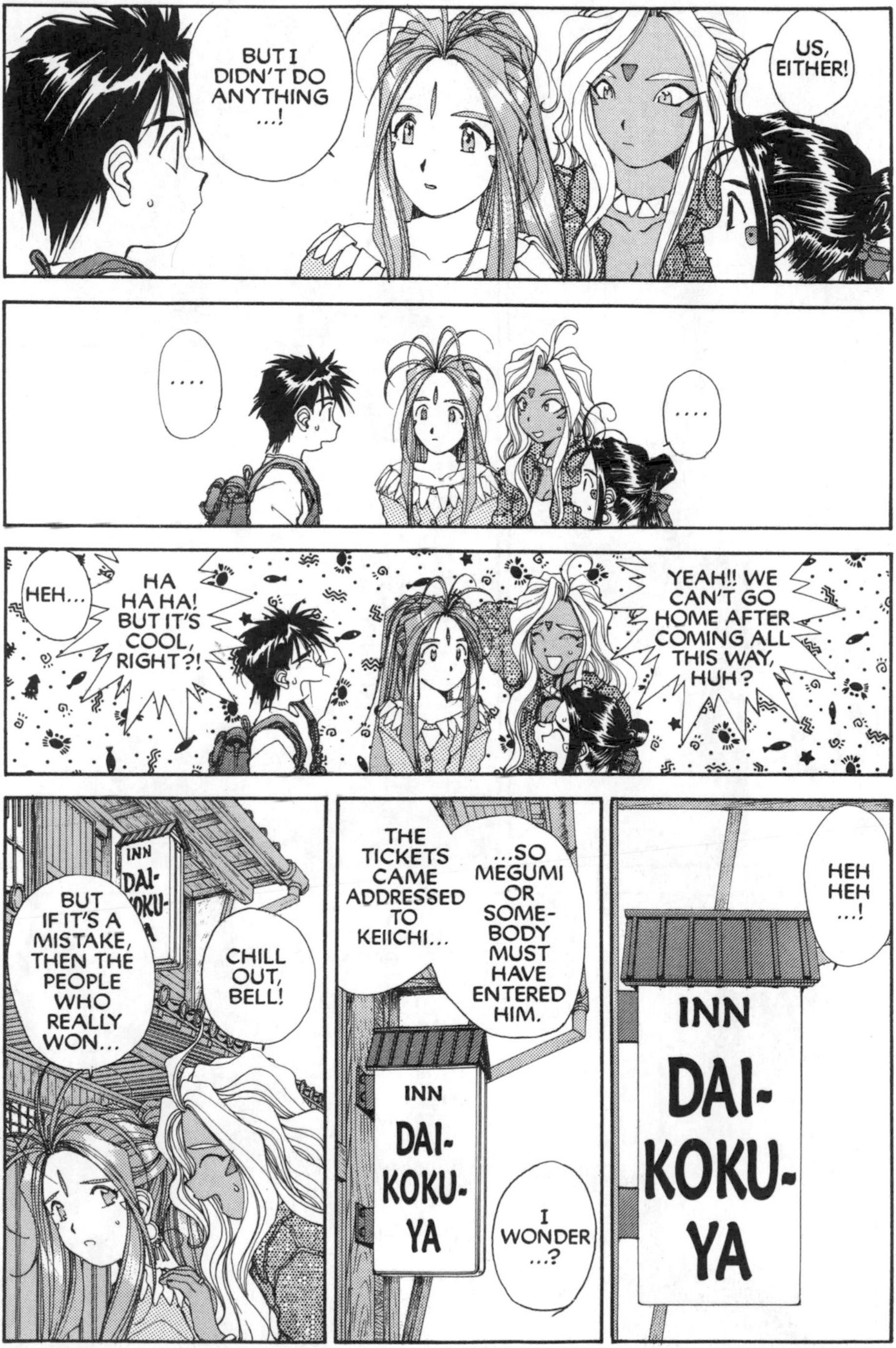
BUT I DIDN'T DO ANYTHING ...!
US, EITHER!
....
....
HEH...
HA HA HA! BUT IT'S COOL, RIGHT?!
YEAH!! WE CAN'T GO HOME AFTER COMING ALL THIS WAY, HUH?
INN DAI-KOKU-YA
BUT IF IT'S A MISTAKE, THEN THE PEOPLE WHO REALLY WON...
CHILL OUT, BELL!
THE TICKETS CAME ADDRESSED TO KEIICHI...
...SO MEGUMI OR SOME-BODY MUST HAVE ENTERED HIM.
INN DAI-KOKU-YA
I WONDER ...?
HEH HEH ...!
INN DAI-KOKU-YA

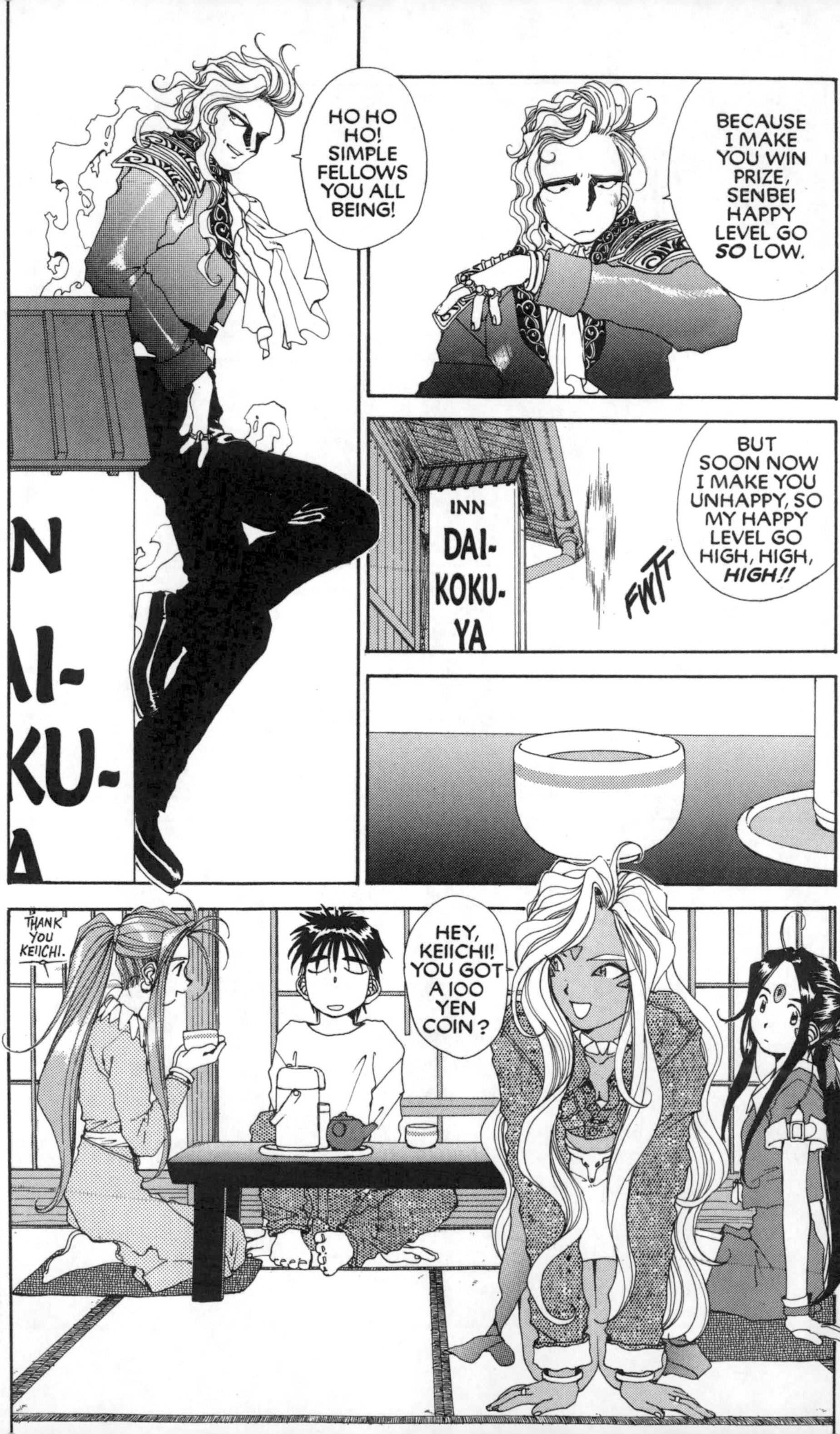
HO HO HO! SIMPLE FELLOWS YOU ALL BEING!
BECAUSE I MAKE YOU WIN PRIZE, SENBEI HAPPY LEVEL GO *SO* LOW.
INN DAI-KOKU-YA
FWTT
BUT SOON NOW I MAKE YOU UNHAPPY, SO MY HAPPY LEVEL GO HIGH, HIGH, *HIGH!!*
THANK YOU KEIICHI.
HEY, KEIICHI! YOU GOT A 100 YEN COIN?

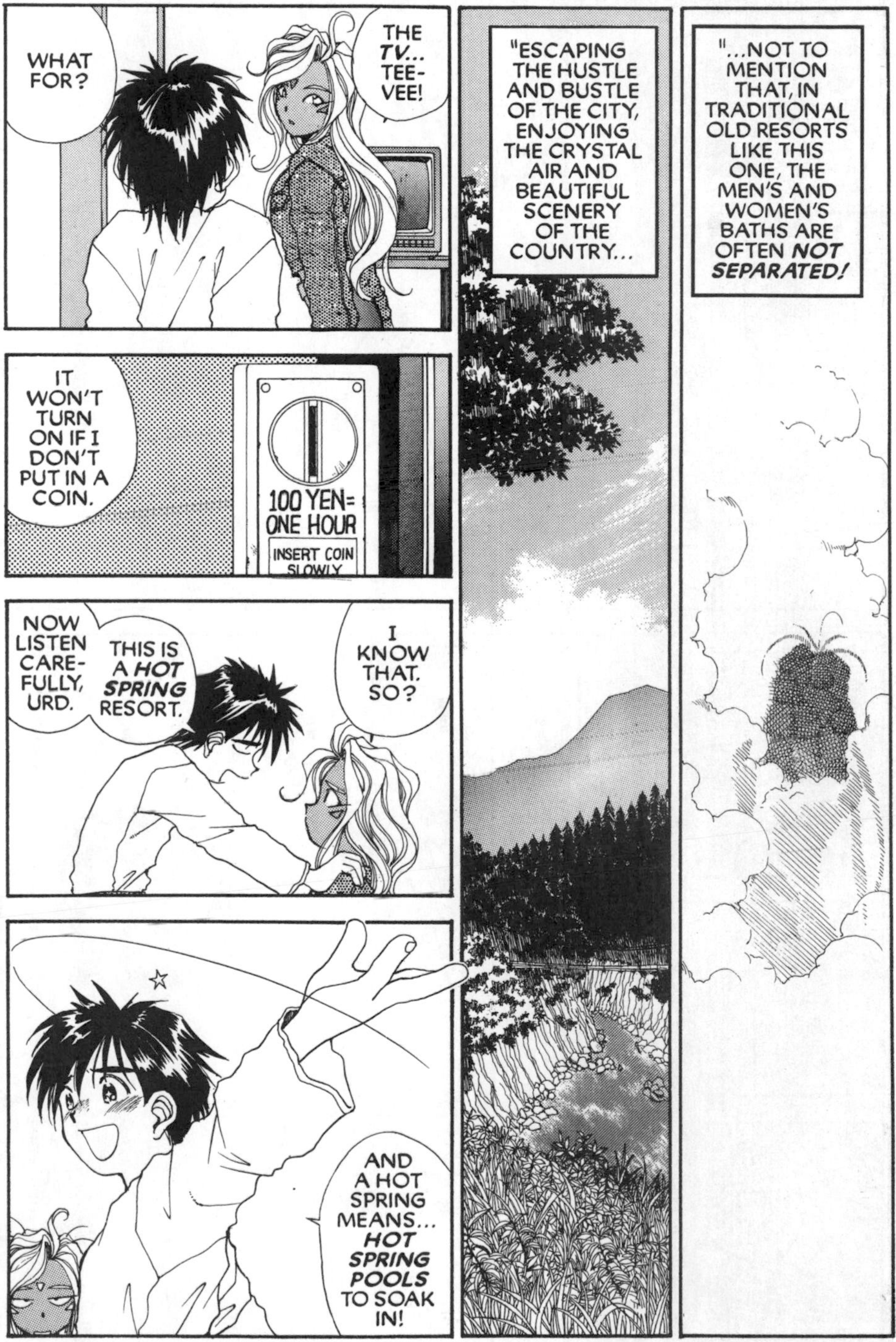
WHAT FOR?
THE *TV...* TEE-VEE!
IT WON'T TURN ON IF I DON'T PUT IN A COIN.
100 YEN= ONE HOUR
INSERT COIN SLOWLY
NOW LISTEN CARE-FULLY, URD.
THIS IS A ***HOT SPRING*** RESORT.
I KNOW THAT. SO?
AND A HOT SPRING MEANS... ***HOT SPRING POOLS*** TO SOAK IN!
"ESCAPING THE HUSTLE AND BUSTLE OF THE CITY, ENJOYING THE CRYSTAL AIR AND BEAUTIFUL SCENERY OF THE COUNTRY...
"...NOT TO MENTION THAT, IN TRADITIONAL OLD RESORTS LIKE THIS ONE, THE MEN'S AND WOMEN'S BATHS ARE OFTEN ***NOT SEPARATED!***

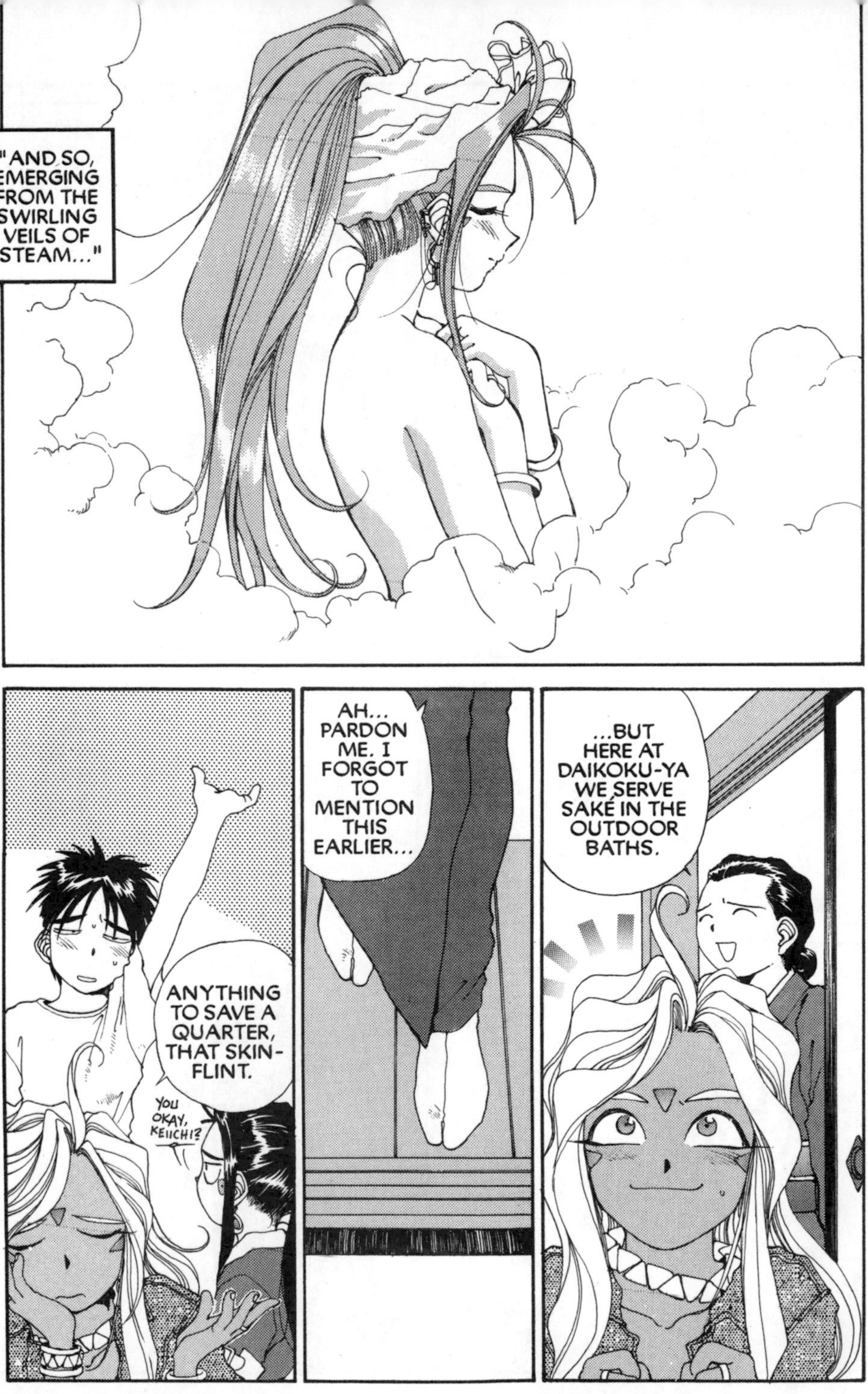
"AND SO, EMERGING FROM THE SWIRLING VEILS OF STEAM..."
ANYTHING TO SAVE A QUARTER, THAT SKIN-FLINT.
YOU OKAY, KEIICHI?
AH... PARDON ME. I FORGOT TO MENTION THIS EARLIER...
...BUT HERE AT DAIKOKU-YA WE SERVE SAKÉ IN THE OUTDOOR BATHS.

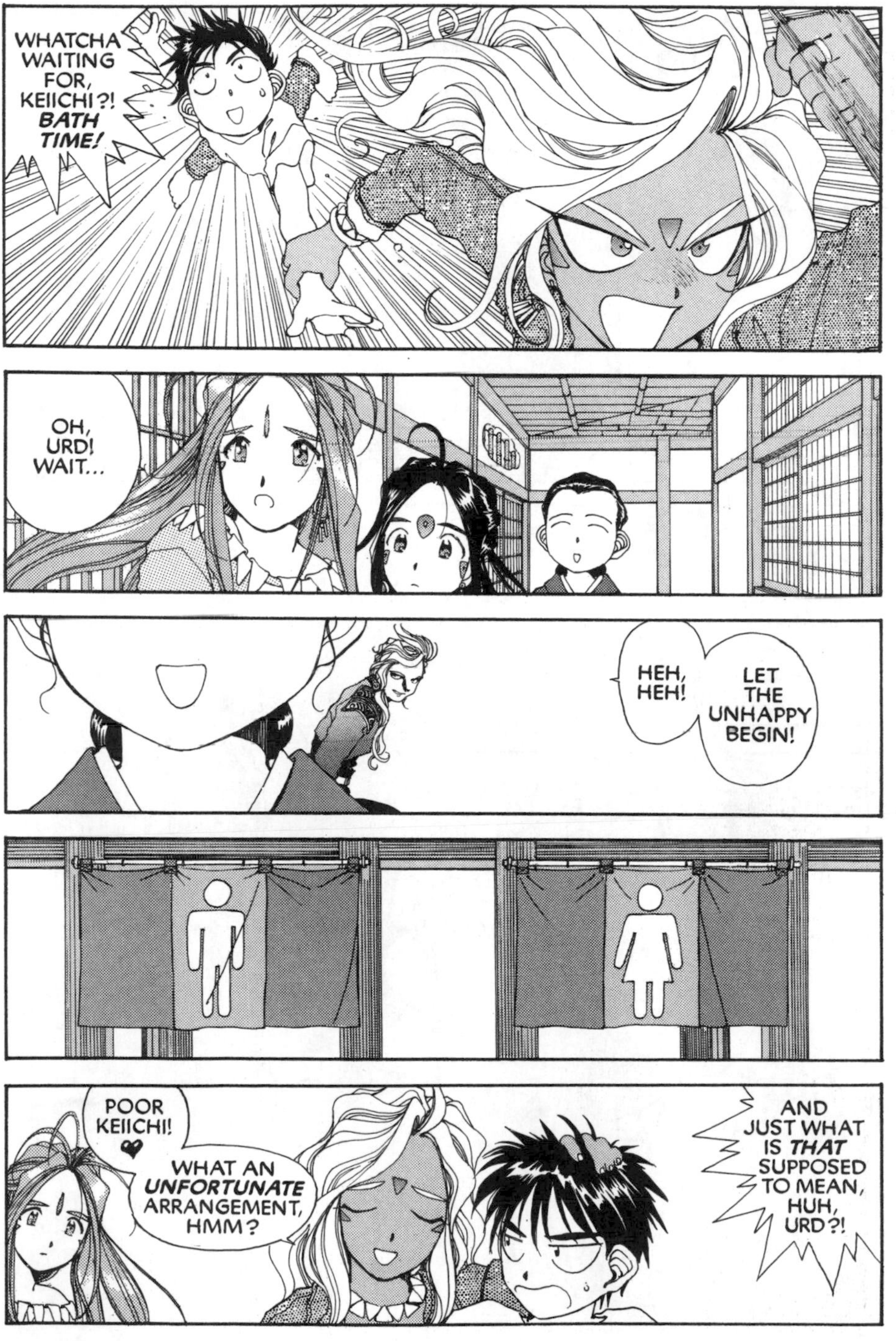
WHATCHA WAITING FOR, KEIICHI?! BATH TIME!
OH, URD! WAIT...
HEH, HEH!
LET THE UNHAPPY BEGIN!
POOR KEIICHI!
WHAT AN UNFORTUNATE ARRANGEMENT, HMM?
AND JUST WHAT IS THAT SUPPOSED TO MEAN, HUH, URD?!

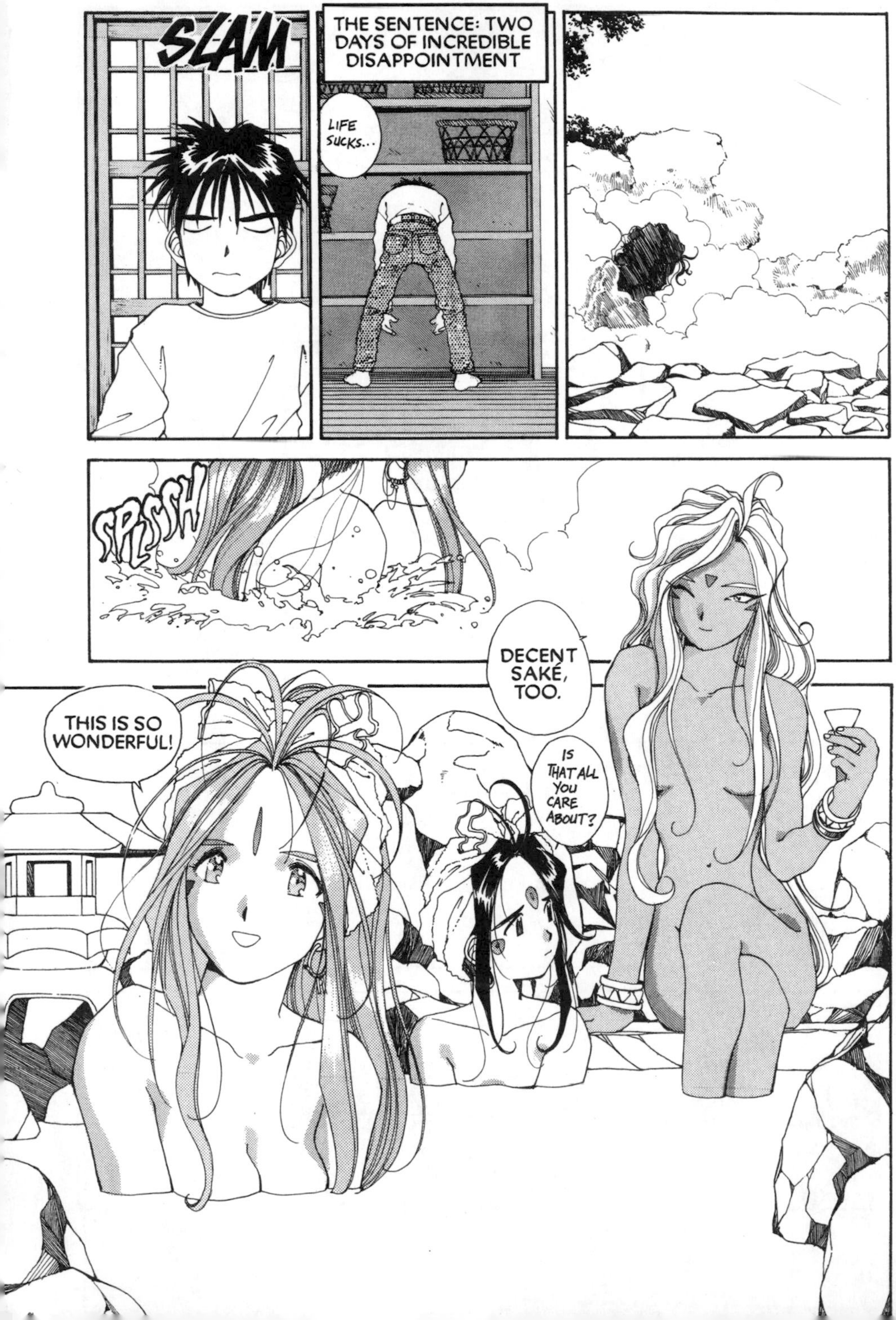
SLAM
THE SENTENCE: TWO DAYS OF INCREDIBLE DISAPPOINTMENT
LIFE SUCKS...
SPLISH
THIS IS SO WONDERFUL!
DECENT SAKÉ, TOO.
IS THAT ALL YOU CARE ABOUT?

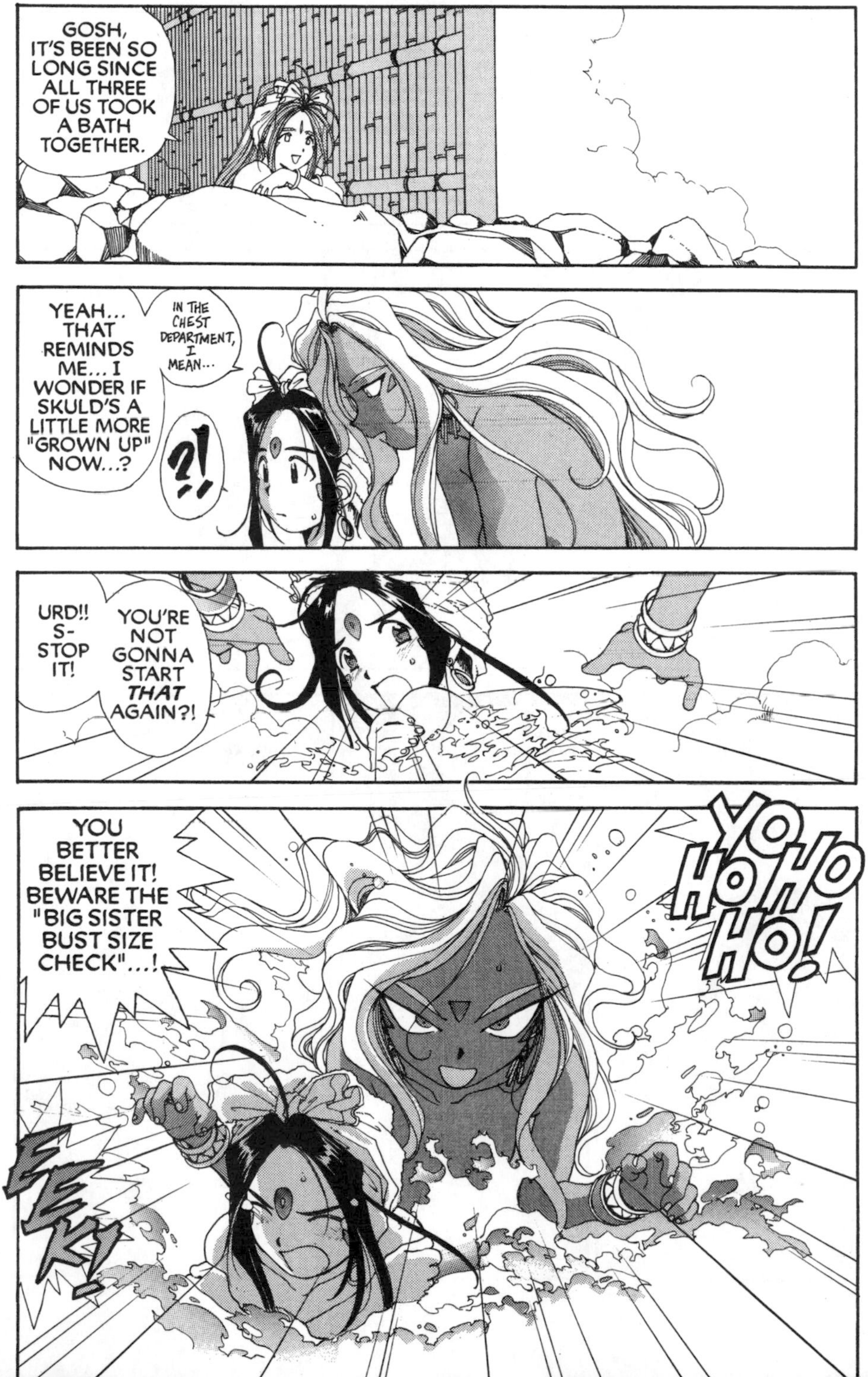
GOSH, IT'S BEEN SO LONG SINCE ALL THREE OF US TOOK A BATH TOGETHER.
YEAH... THAT REMINDS ME... I WONDER IF SKULD'S A LITTLE MORE "GROWN UP" NOW...?
IN THE CHEST DEPARTMENT, I MEAN...
?!
URD!! S-STOP IT!
YOU'RE NOT GONNA START *THAT* AGAIN?!
YOU BETTER BELIEVE IT! BEWARE THE "BIG SISTER BUST SIZE CHECK"...!
YO HO HO HO HO!
EEEK!

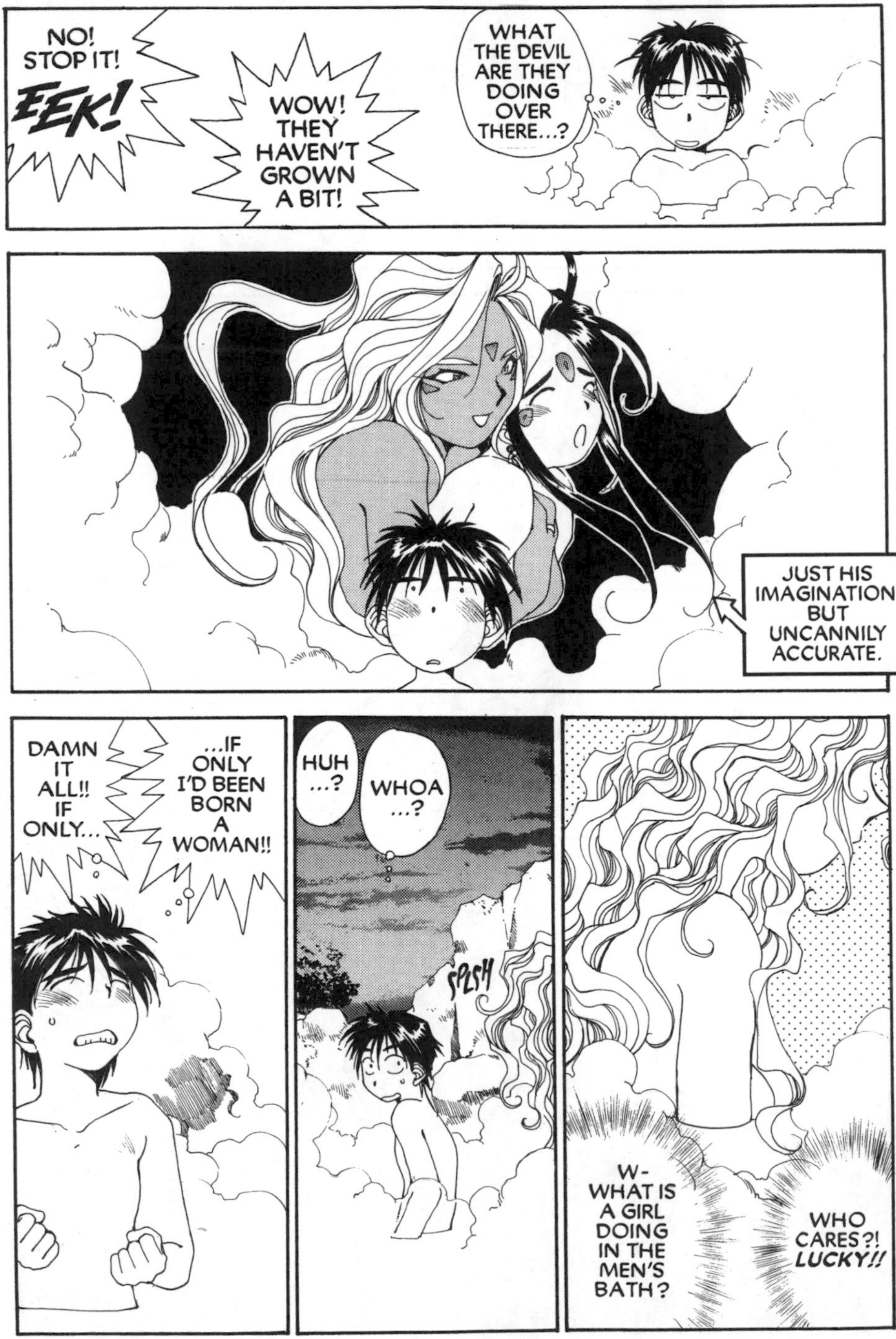
NO! STOP IT! EEK!
WOW! THEY HAVEN'T GROWN A BIT!
WHAT THE DEVIL ARE THEY DOING OVER THERE...?
JUST HIS IMAGINATION, BUT UNCANNILY ACCURATE.
DAMN IT ALL!! IF ONLY...
...IF ONLY I'D BEEN BORN A WOMAN!!
HUH ...?
WHOA ...?
SPLSH
W- WHAT IS A GIRL DOING IN THE MEN'S BATH?
WHO CARES?! LUCKY!!

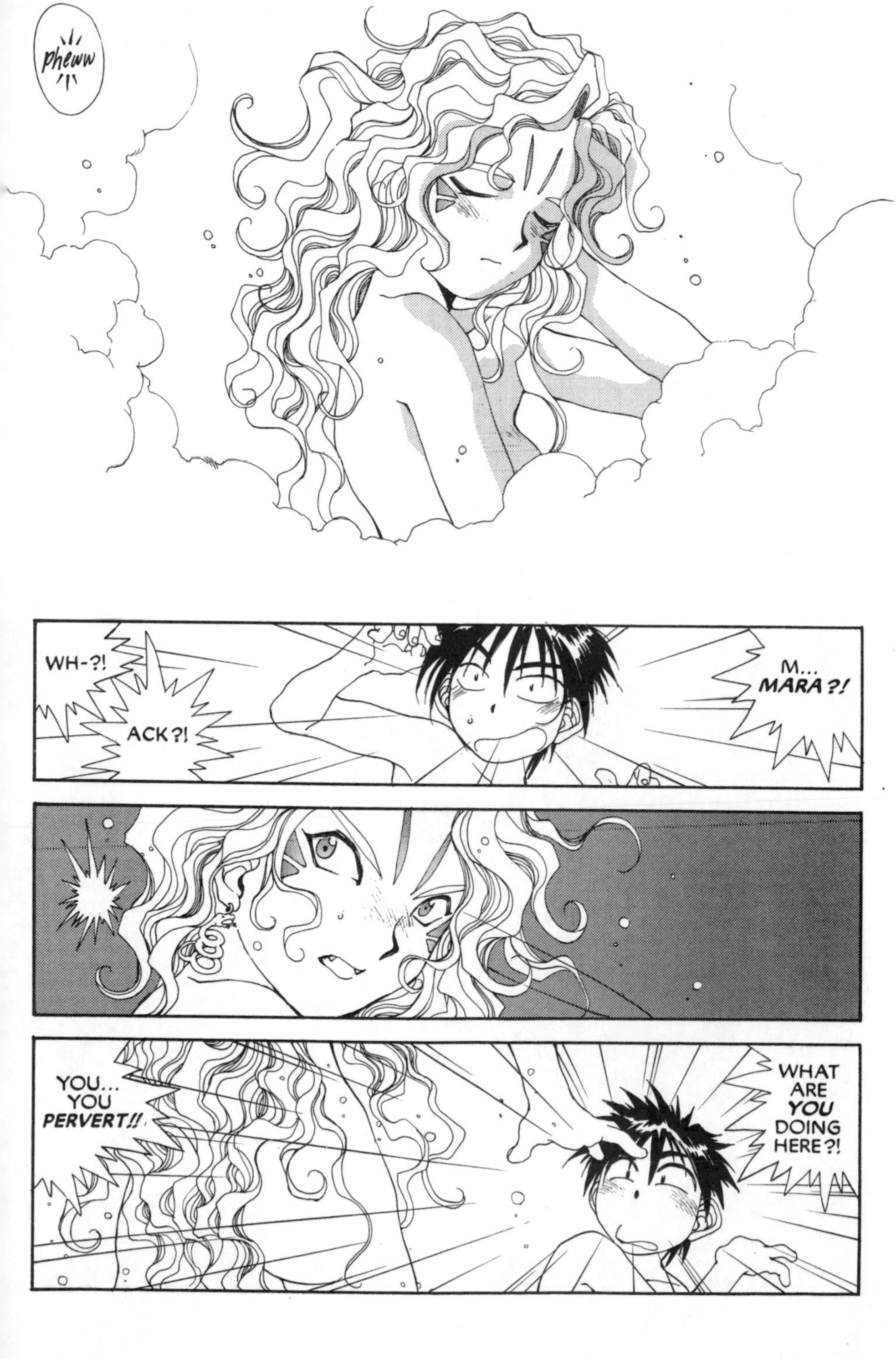
pheww
WH-?!
ACK?!
M... MARA?!
YOU... YOU PERVERT!!
WHAT ARE YOU DOING HERE?!

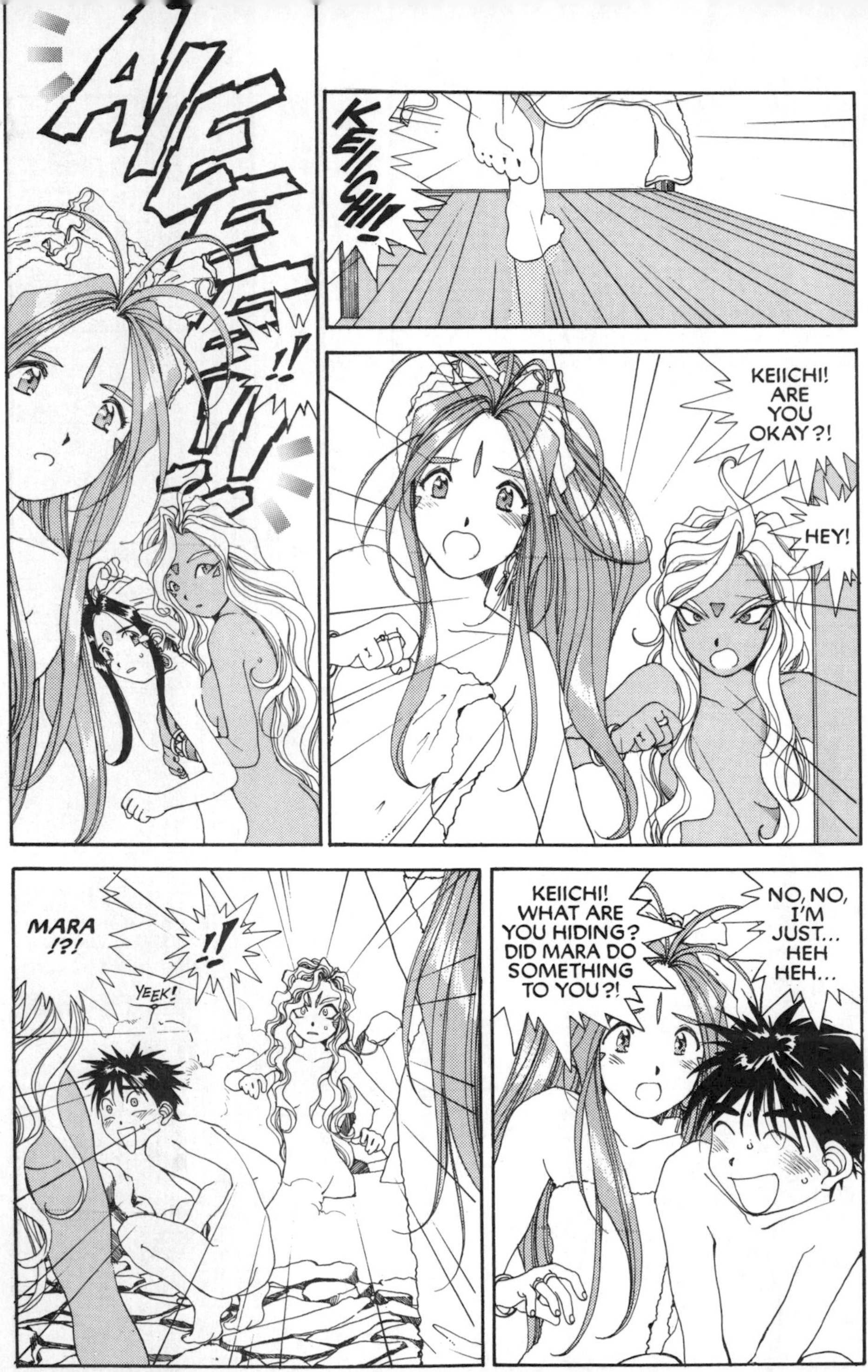
AIEEEEE!!
!!
KEIICHI!
KEIICHI! ARE YOU OKAY?!
HEY!
MARA !?!
YEEK!
!!
KEIICHI! WHAT ARE YOU HIDING? DID MARA DO SOMETHING TO YOU?!
NO, NO, I'M JUST... HEH HEH...

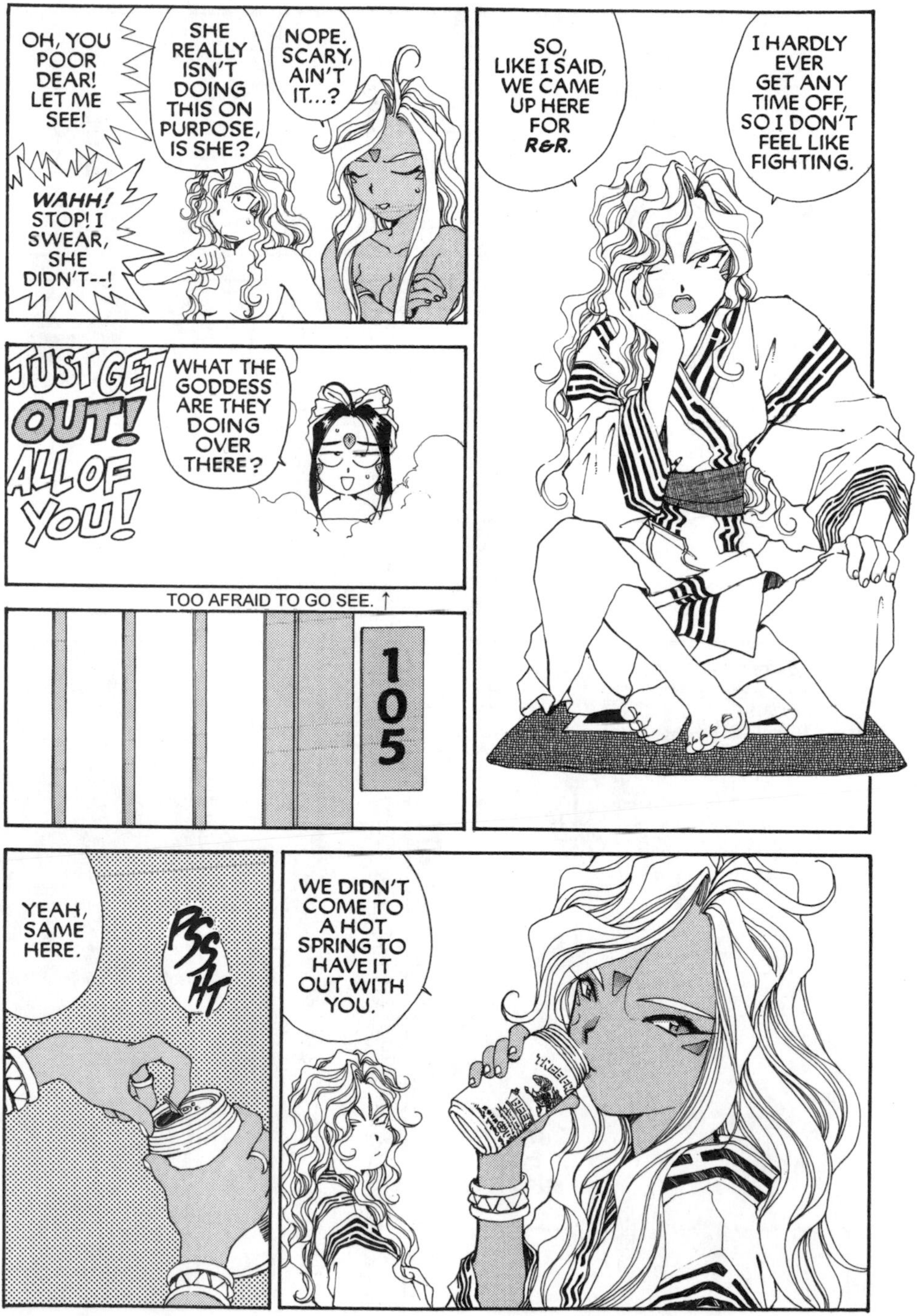
OH, YOU POOR DEAR! LET ME SEE!
SHE REALLY ISN'T DOING THIS ON PURPOSE, IS SHE?
NOPE. SCARY, AIN'T IT...?
WAHH! STOP! I SWEAR, SHE DIDN'T--!
JUST GET OUT! ALL OF YOU!
WHAT THE GODDESS ARE THEY DOING OVER THERE?
TOO AFRAID TO GO SEE. ↑
105
SO, LIKE I SAID, WE CAME UP HERE FOR R&R.
I HARDLY EVER GET ANY TIME OFF, SO I DON'T FEEL LIKE FIGHTING.
YEAH, SAME HERE.
PSSHT
WE DIDN'T COME TO A HOT SPRING TO HAVE IT OUT WITH YOU.

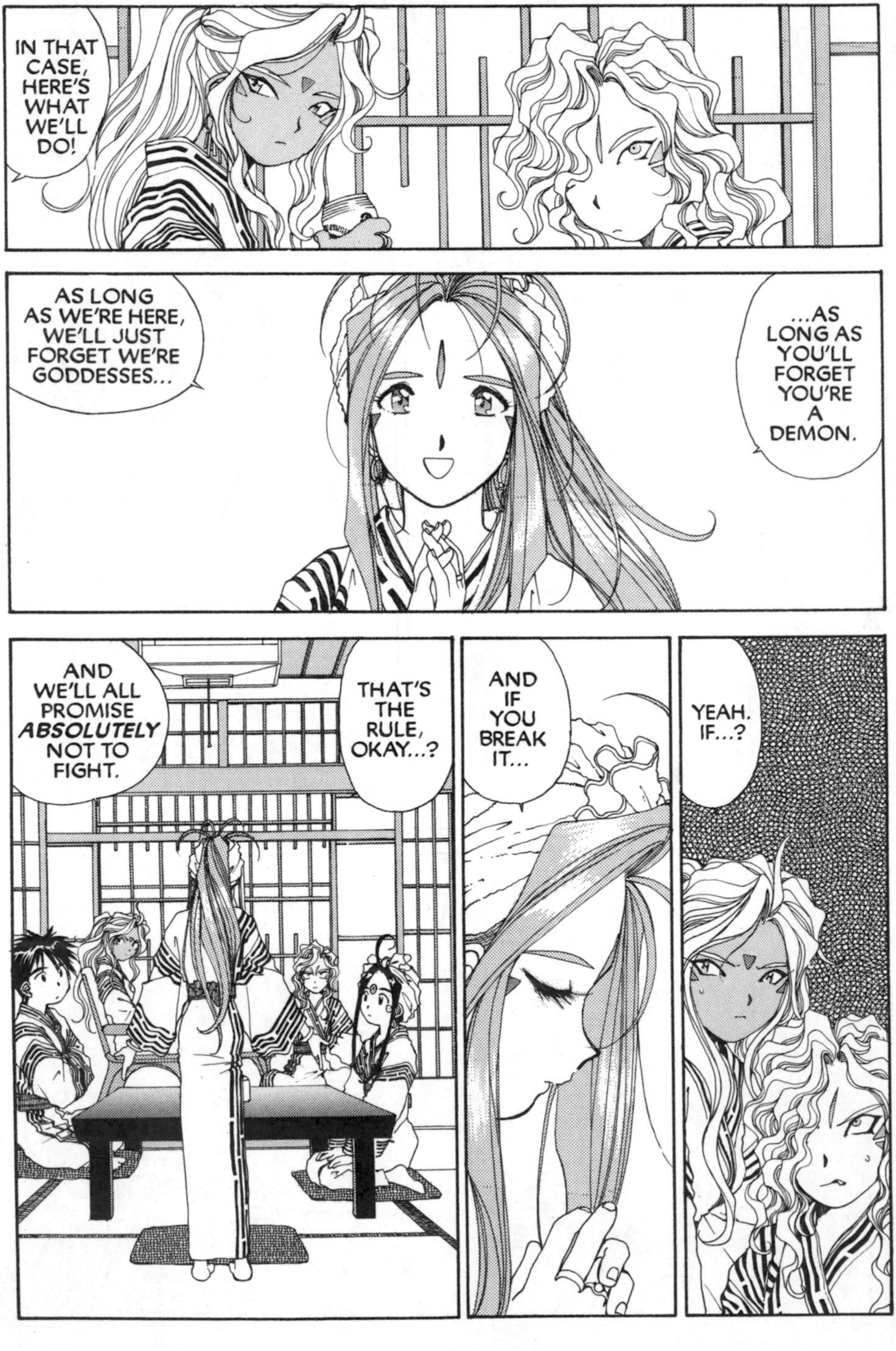
IN THAT CASE, HERE'S WHAT WE'LL DO!
AS LONG AS WE'RE HERE, WE'LL JUST FORGET WE'RE GODDESSES...
...AS LONG AS YOU'LL FORGET YOU'RE A DEMON.
AND WE'LL ALL PROMISE ***ABSOLUTELY*** NOT TO FIGHT.
THAT'S THE RULE, OKAY...?
AND IF YOU BREAK IT...
YEAH. IF...?

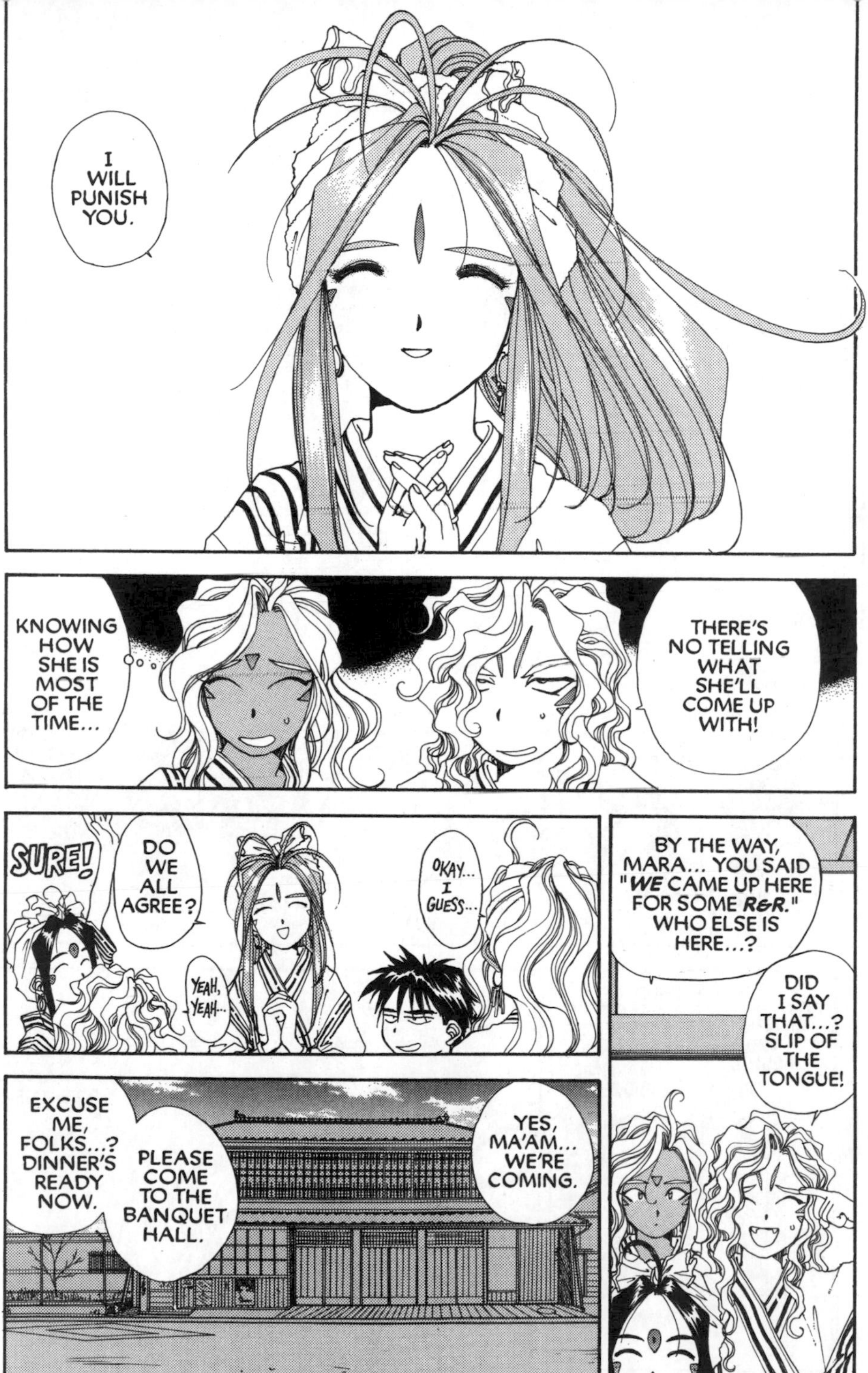
I WILL PUNISH YOU.
KNOWING HOW SHE IS MOST OF THE TIME...
THERE'S NO TELLING WHAT SHE'LL COME UP WITH!
SURE!
DO WE ALL AGREE?
YEAH, YEAH...
OKAY... I GUESS...
BY THE WAY, MARA... YOU SAID "WE CAME UP HERE FOR SOME R&R." WHO ELSE IS HERE...?
DID I SAY THAT...? SLIP OF THE TONGUE!
EXCUSE ME, FOLKS...? DINNER'S READY NOW.
PLEASE COME TO THE BANQUET HALL.
YES, MA'AM... WE'RE COMING.

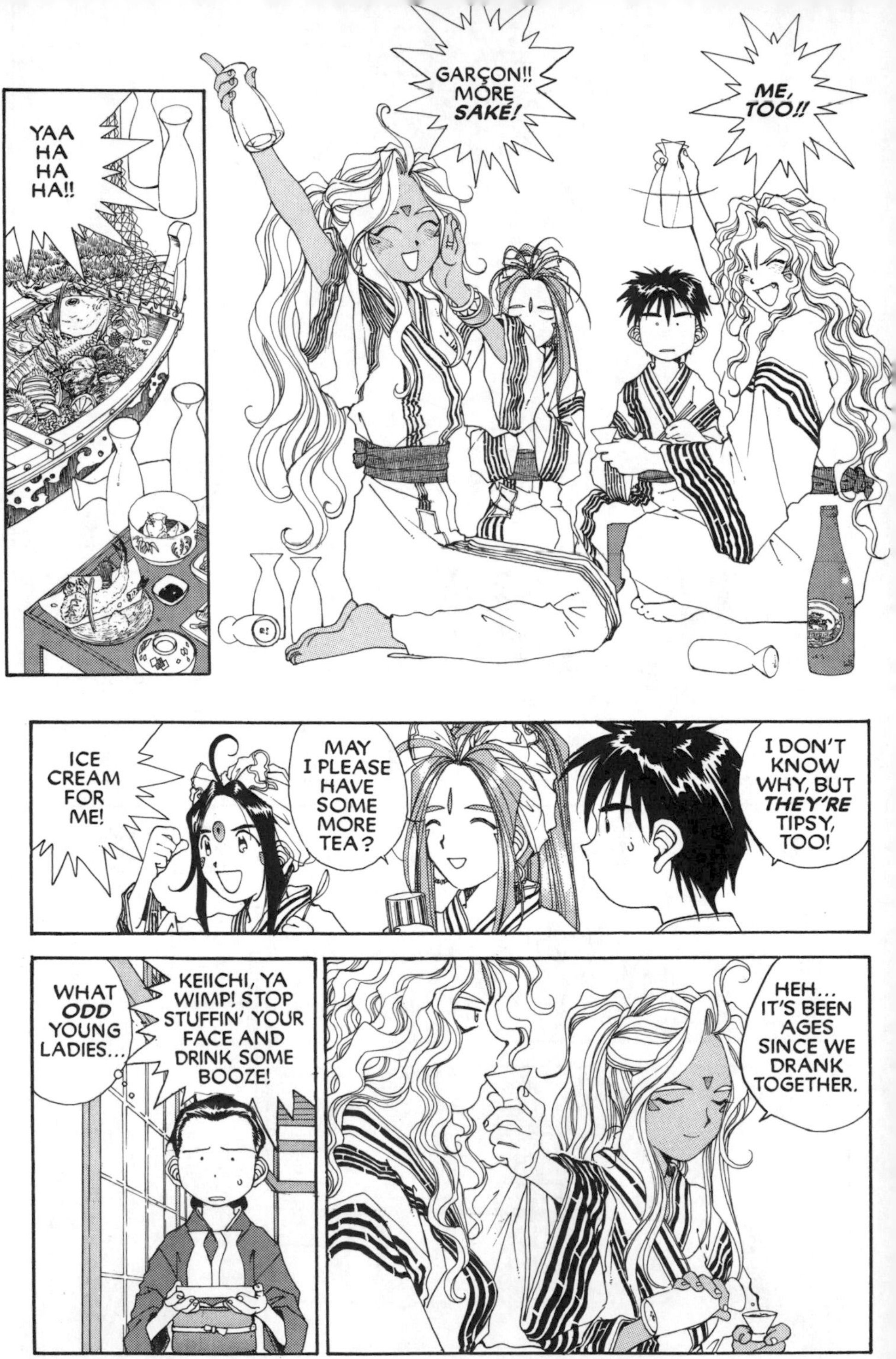
YAA HA HA HA!!
GARÇON!! MORE *SAKÉ!*
ME, TOO!!
ICE CREAM FOR ME!
MAY I PLEASE HAVE SOME MORE TEA?
I DON'T KNOW WHY, BUT *THEY'RE* TIPSY, TOO!
WHAT *ODD* YOUNG LADIES...
KEIICHI, YA WIMP! STOP STUFFIN' YOUR FACE AND DRINK SOME BOOZE!
HEH... IT'S BEEN AGES SINCE WE DRANK TOGETHER.

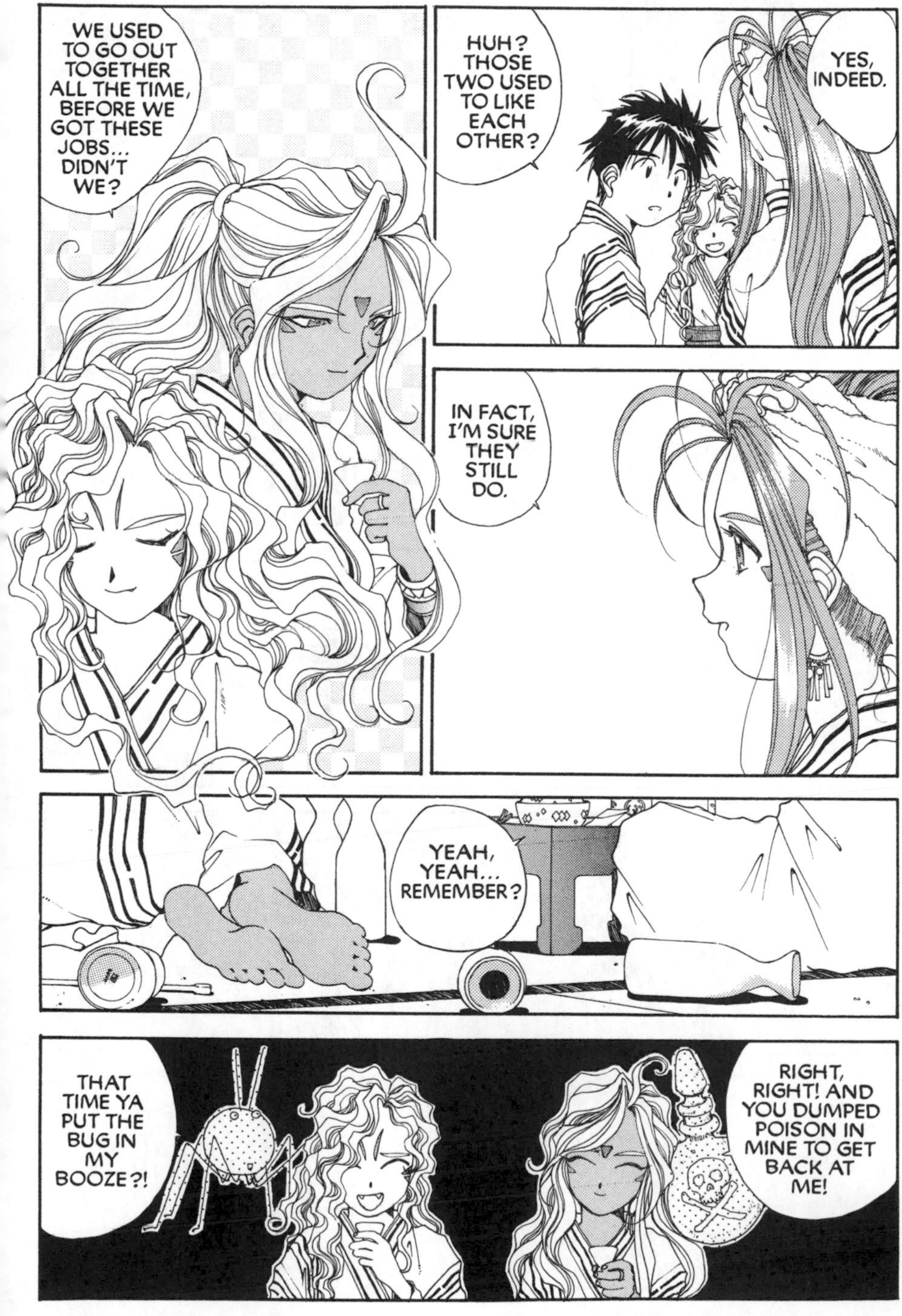
WE USED TO GO OUT TOGETHER ALL THE TIME, BEFORE WE GOT THESE JOBS... DIDN'T WE?
HUH? THOSE TWO USED TO LIKE EACH OTHER?
YES, INDEED.
IN FACT, I'M SURE THEY STILL DO.
YEAH, YEAH... REMEMBER?
THAT TIME YA PUT THE BUG IN MY BOOZE?!
RIGHT, RIGHT! AND YOU DUMPED POISON IN MINE TO GET BACK AT ME!

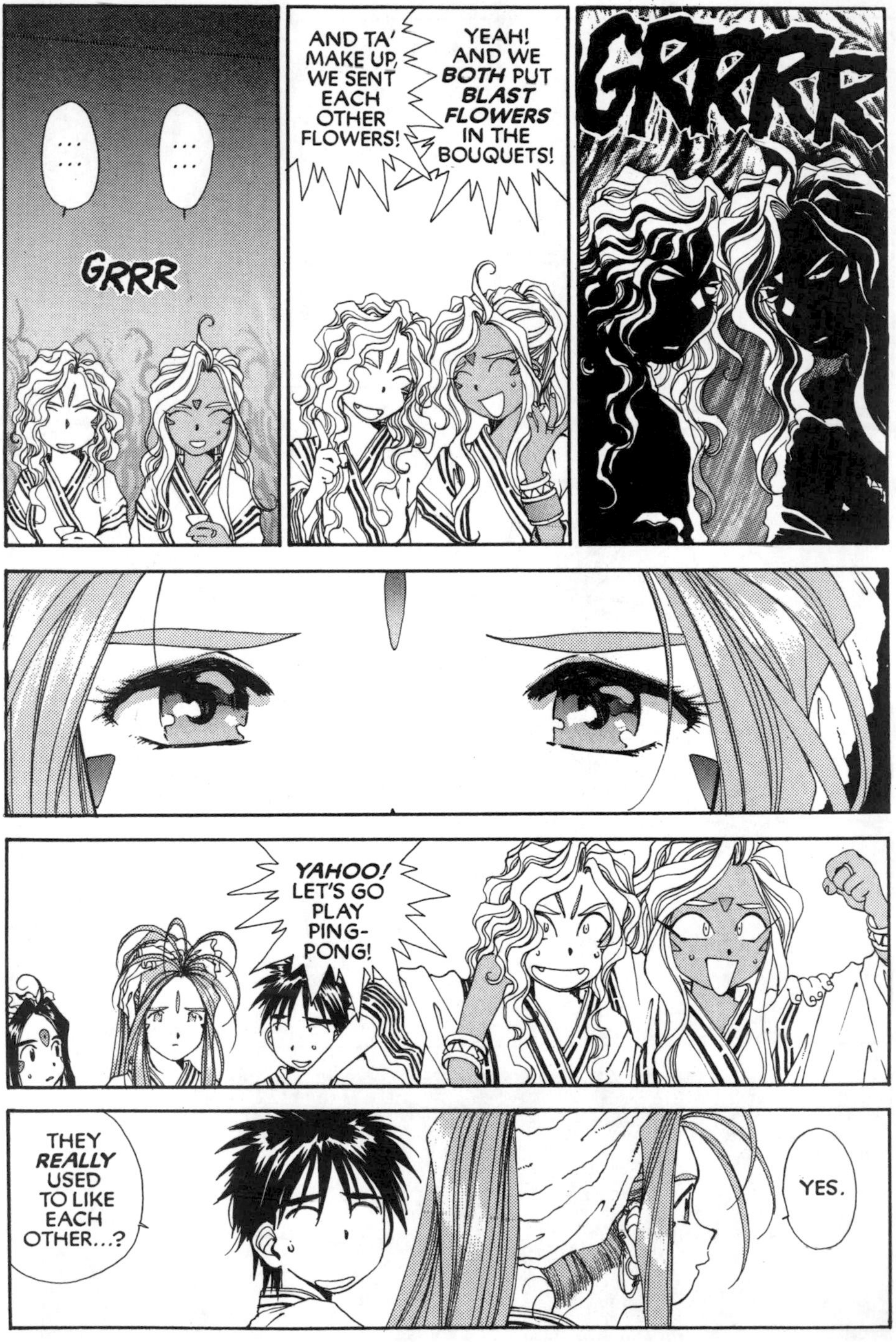

...
...
...
...
GRRR
AND TA' MAKE UP, WE SENT EACH OTHER FLOWERS!
YEAH! AND WE BOTH PUT BLAST FLOWERS IN THE BOUQUETS!
GRRRR
YAHOO! LET'S GO PLAY PING-PONG!
THEY REALLY USED TO LIKE EACH OTHER...?
YES.

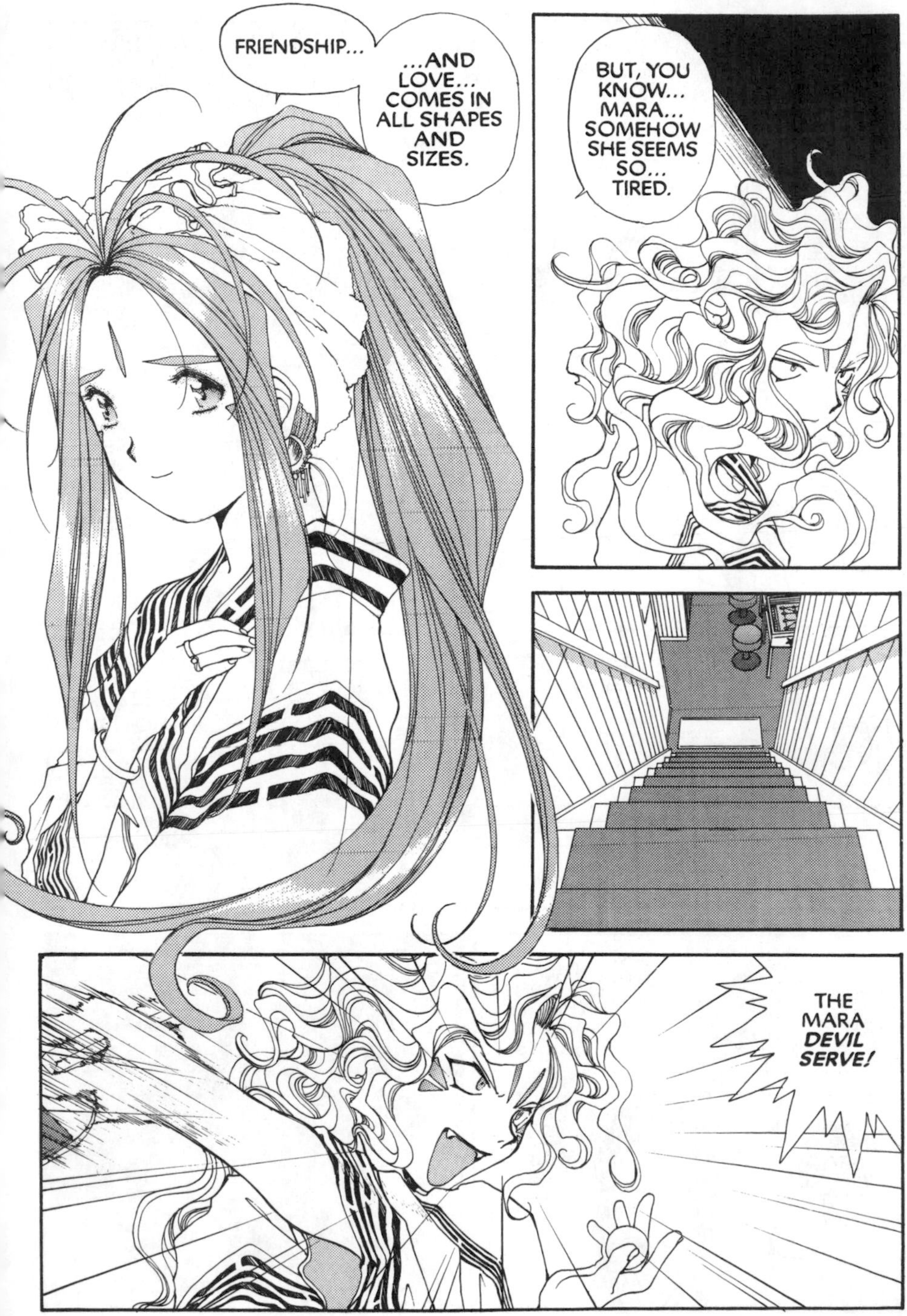
FRIENDSHIP...
...AND LOVE... COMES IN ALL SHAPES AND SIZES.
BUT, YOU KNOW... MARA... SOMEHOW SHE SEEMS SO... TIRED.
THE MARA *DEVIL SERVE!*

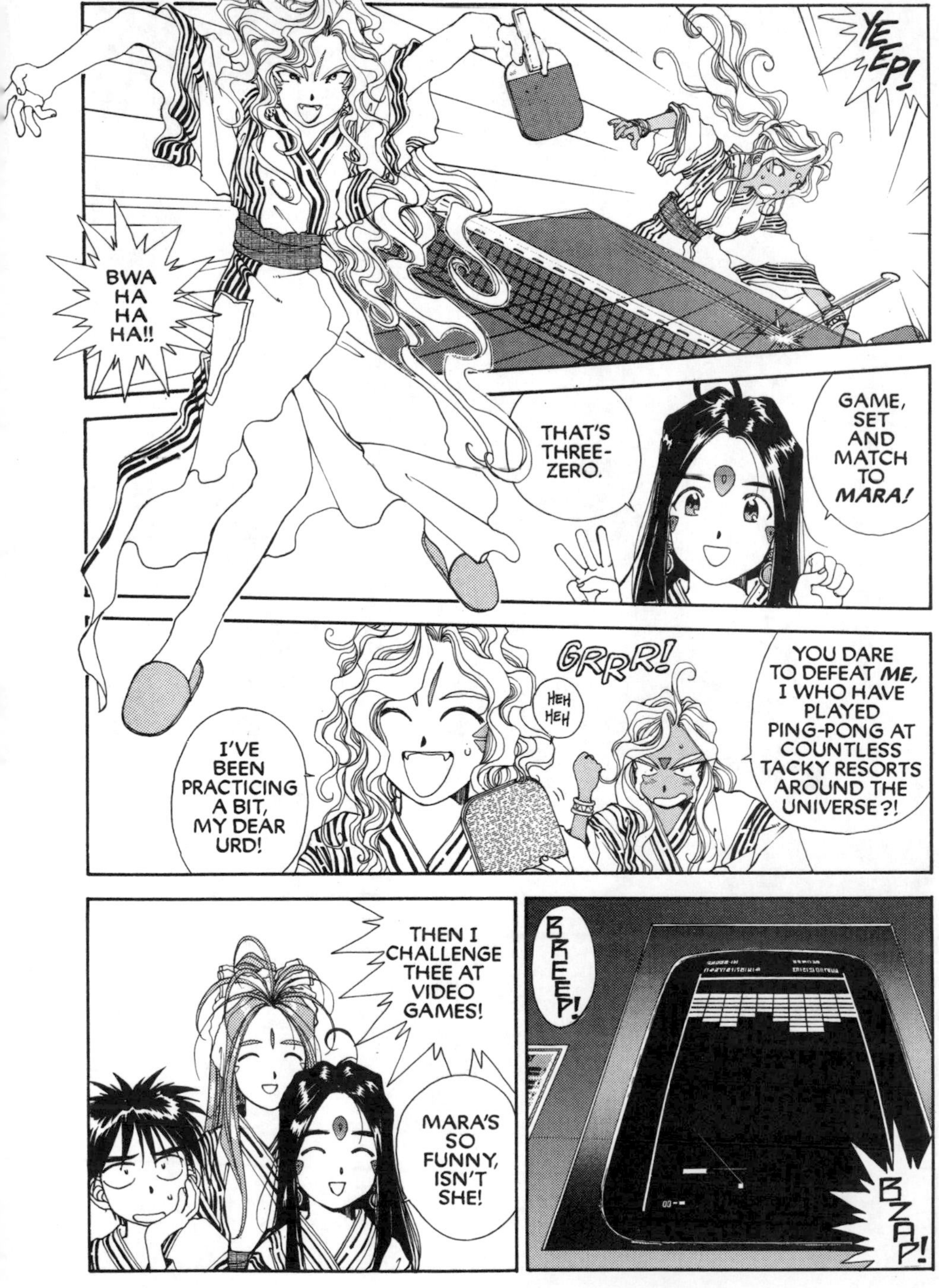
YEEP!
BWA HA HA HA!!
THAT'S THREE-ZERO.
GAME, SET AND MATCH TO *MARA!*
I'VE BEEN PRACTICING A BIT, MY DEAR URD!
HEH HEH
GRRR!
YOU DARE TO DEFEAT *ME,* I WHO HAVE PLAYED PING-PONG AT COUNTLESS TACKY RESORTS AROUND THE UNIVERSE?!
THEN I CHALLENGE THEE AT VIDEO GAMES!
MARA'S SO FUNNY, ISN'T SHE!
BREEP!
BZAP!

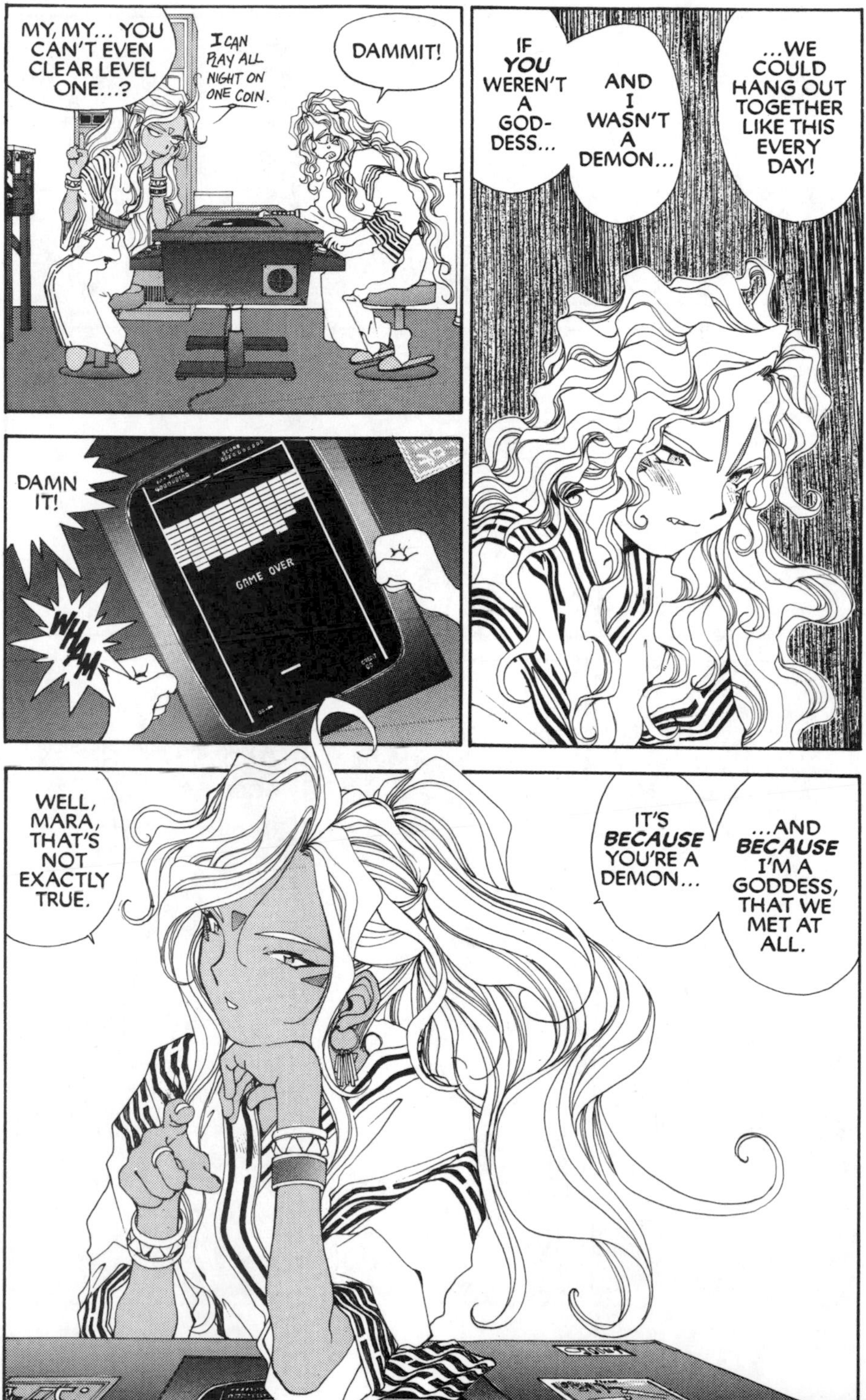
MY, MY... YOU CAN'T EVEN CLEAR LEVEL ONE...?
I CAN PLAY ALL NIGHT ON ONE COIN.
DAMMIT!
DAMN IT!
WHAM
GAME OVER
IF *YOU* WEREN'T A GOD-DESS...
AND I WASN'T A DEMON...
...WE COULD HANG OUT TOGETHER LIKE THIS EVERY DAY!
WELL, MARA, THAT'S NOT EXACTLY TRUE.
IT'S *BECAUSE* YOU'RE A DEMON...
...AND *BECAUSE* I'M A GODDESS, THAT WE MET AT ALL.

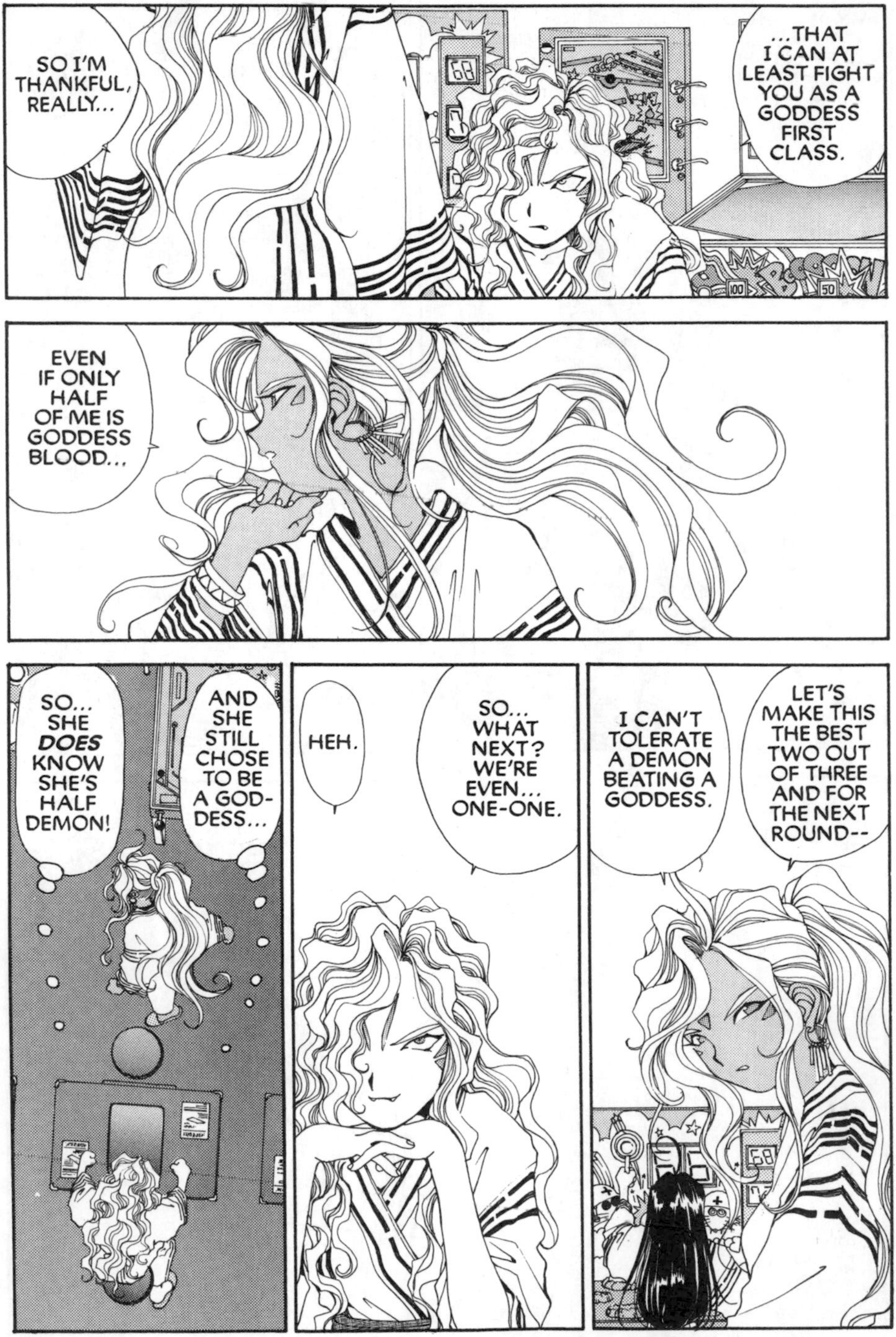
SO I'M THANKFUL, REALLY...
...THAT I CAN AT LEAST FIGHT YOU AS A GODDESS FIRST CLASS.
EVEN IF ONLY HALF OF ME IS GODDESS BLOOD...
SO... SHE *DOES* KNOW SHE'S HALF DEMON!
AND SHE STILL CHOSE TO BE A GOD-DESS...
HEH.
SO... WHAT NEXT? WE'RE EVEN... ONE-ONE.
I CAN'T TOLERATE A DEMON BEATING A GODDESS.
LET'S MAKE THIS THE BEST TWO OUT OF THREE AND FOR THE NEXT ROUND--

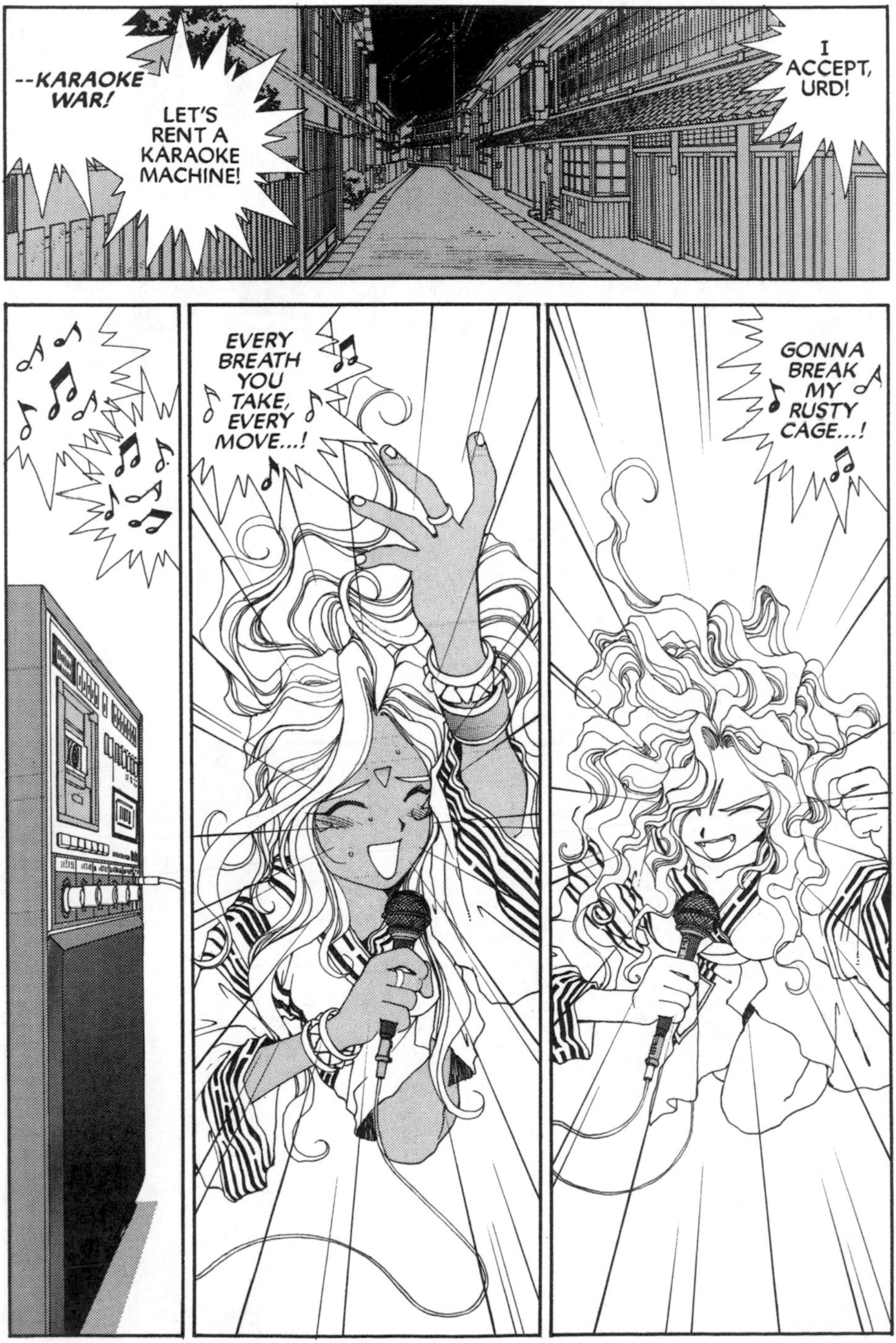
--KARAOKE WAR!
LET'S RENT A KARAOKE MACHINE!
I ACCEPT, URD!
EVERY BREATH YOU TAKE, EVERY MOVE...!
GONNA BREAK MY RUSTY CAGE...!

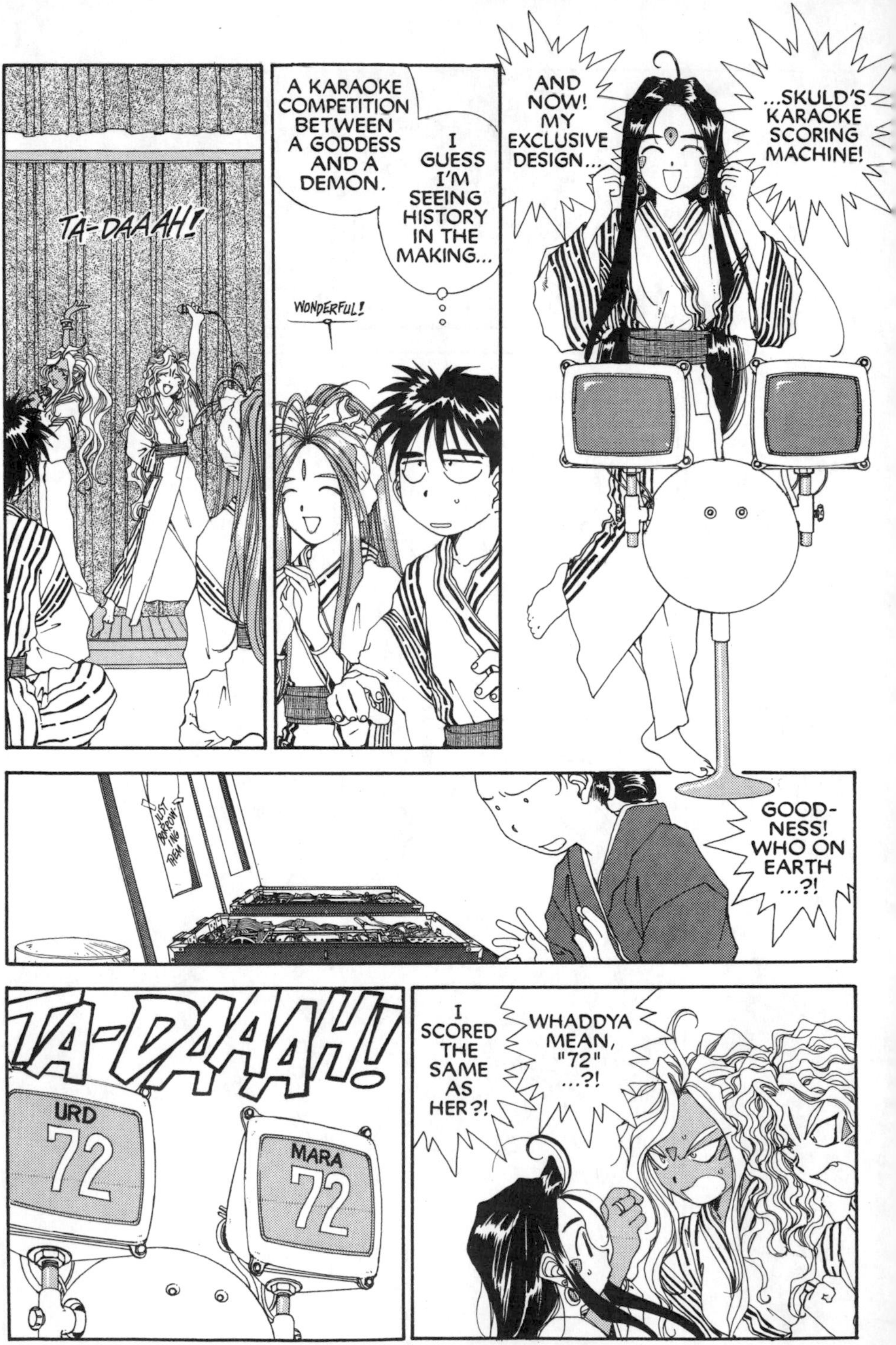
TA-DAAAH!
A KARAOKE COMPETITION BETWEEN A GODDESS AND A DEMON.
I GUESS I'M SEEING HISTORY IN THE MAKING...
WONDERFUL!
AND NOW! MY EXCLUSIVE DESIGN...
...SKULD'S KARAOKE SCORING MACHINE!
JUST BORROWING THEM
GOODNESS! WHO ON EARTH ...?!
TA-DAAAH!
URD
72
MARA
72
I SCORED THE SAME AS HER?!
WHADDYA MEAN, "72" ...?!

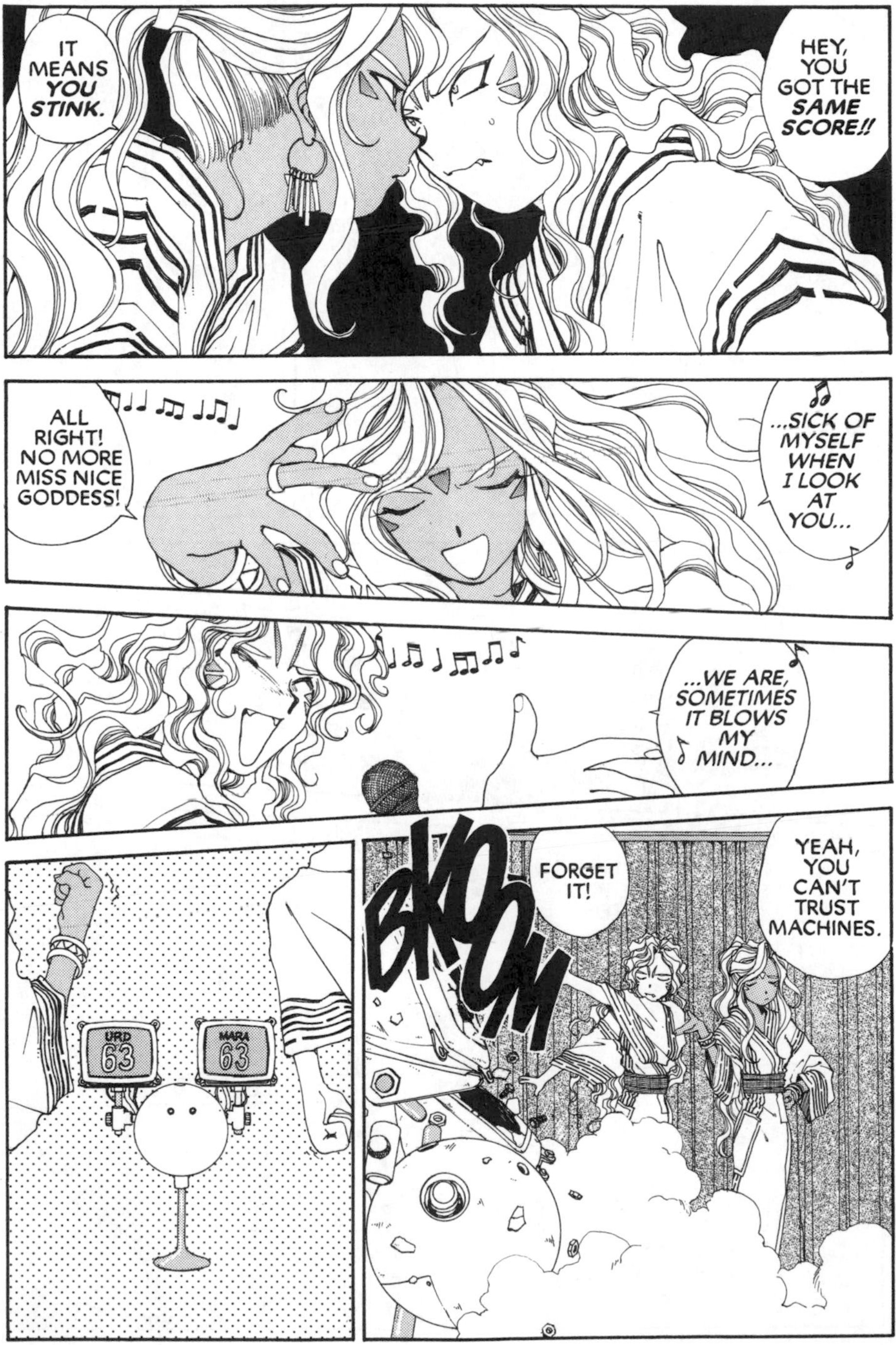

IT MEANS *YOU* STINK.
HEY, YOU GOT THE *SAME SCORE!!*
ALL RIGHT! NO MORE MISS NICE GODDESS!
...SICK OF MYSELF WHEN I LOOK AT YOU...
...WE ARE, SOMETIMES IT BLOWS MY MIND...
URD
63
MARA
63
BKOOM
FORGET IT!
YEAH, YOU CAN'T TRUST MACHINES.

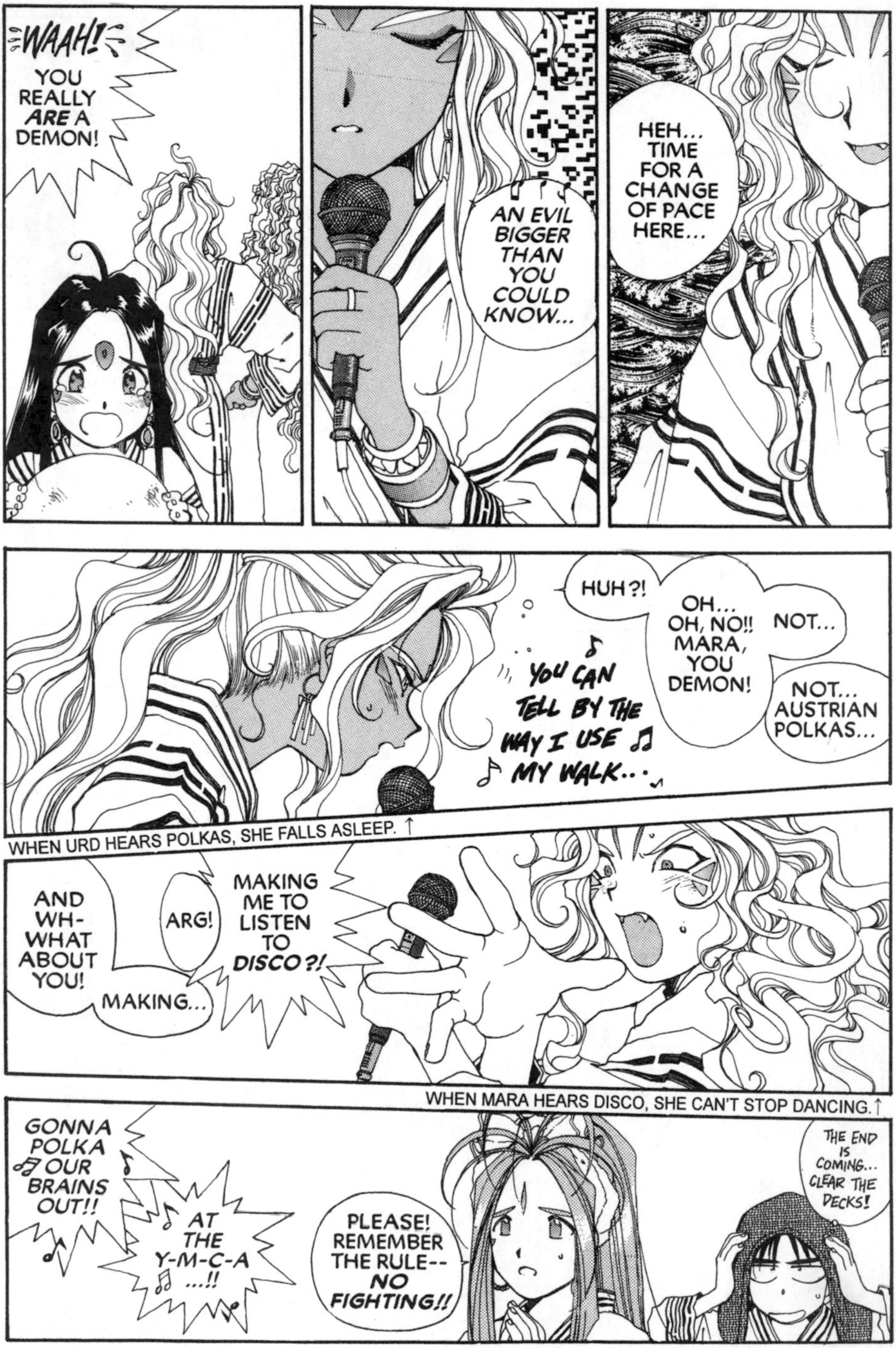
WAAH!
YOU REALLY ARE A DEMON!
AN EVIL BIGGER THAN YOU COULD KNOW...
HEH... TIME FOR A CHANGE OF PACE HERE...
YOU CAN TELL BY THE WAY I USE MY WALK...
HUH?!
OH... OH, NO!! MARA, YOU DEMON!
NOT...
NOT... AUSTRIAN POLKAS...
WHEN URD HEARS POLKAS, SHE FALLS ASLEEP. ↑
AND WH-WHAT ABOUT YOU!
MAKING...
ARG!
MAKING ME TO LISTEN TO DISCO?!
WHEN MARA HEARS DISCO, SHE CAN'T STOP DANCING. ↑
GONNA POLKA OUR BRAINS OUT!!
AT THE Y-M-C-A ...!!
PLEASE! REMEMBER THE RULE-- NO FIGHTING!!
THE END IS COMING... CLEAR THE DECKS!

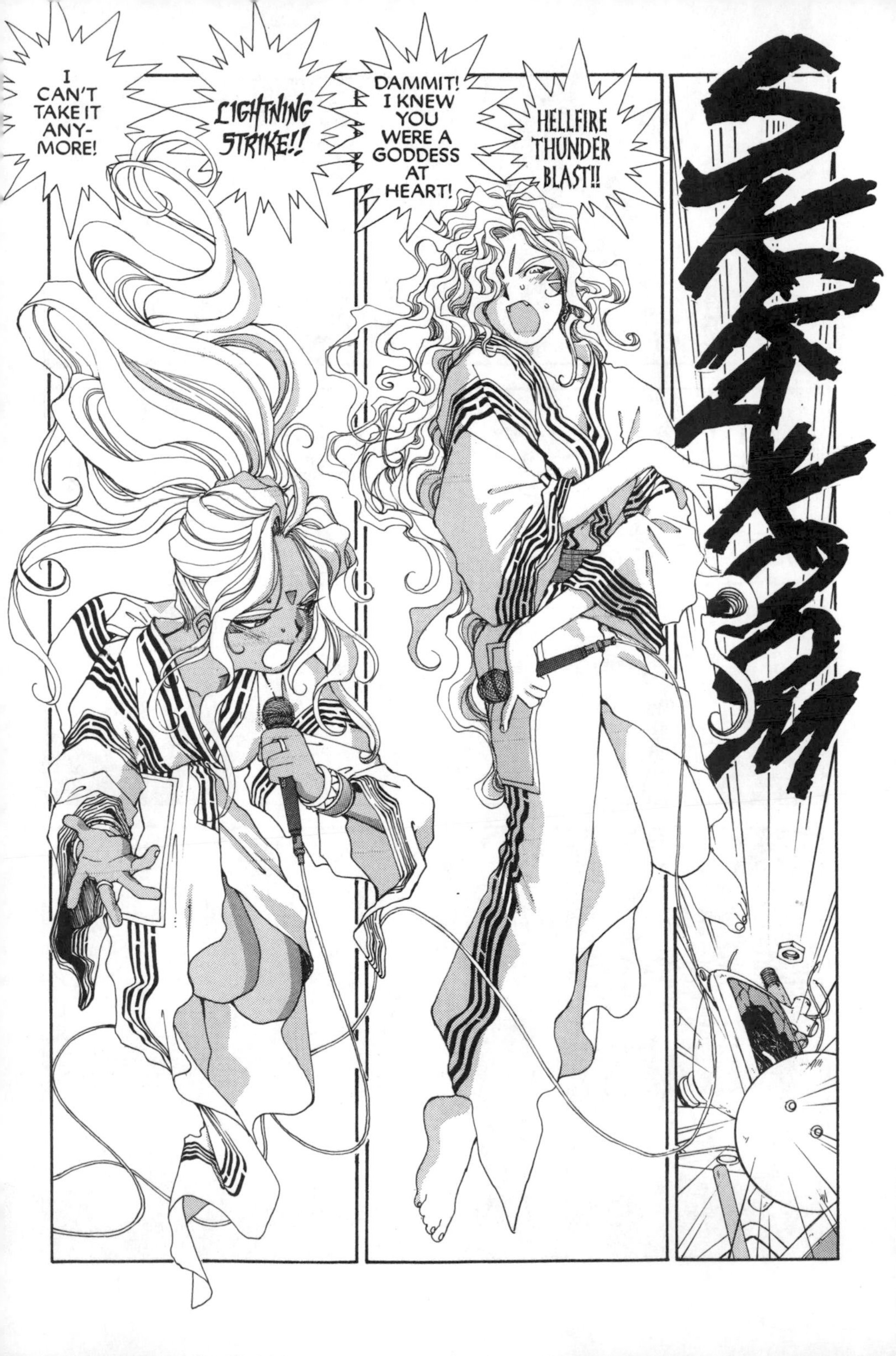
I CAN'T TAKE IT ANY-MORE!
LIGHTNING STRIKE!!
DAMMIT! I KNEW YOU WERE A GODDESS AT HEART!
HELLFIRE THUNDER BLAST!!

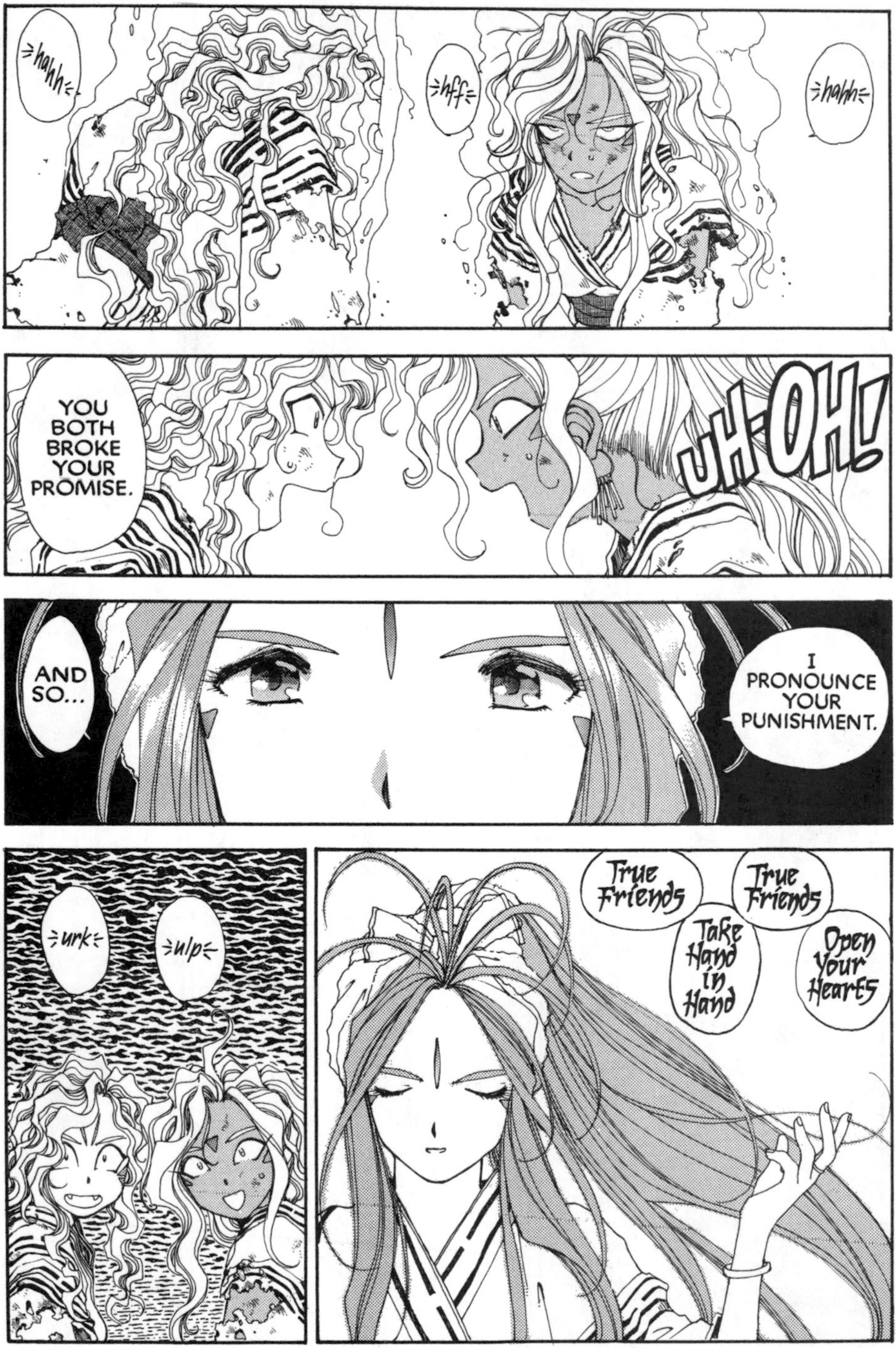

hahh
hff
hahh
YOU BOTH BROKE YOUR PROMISE.
UH-OH!
AND SO...
I PRONOUNCE YOUR PUNISHMENT.
urk
ulp
True Friends
Take Hand in Hand
True Friends
Open Your Hearts

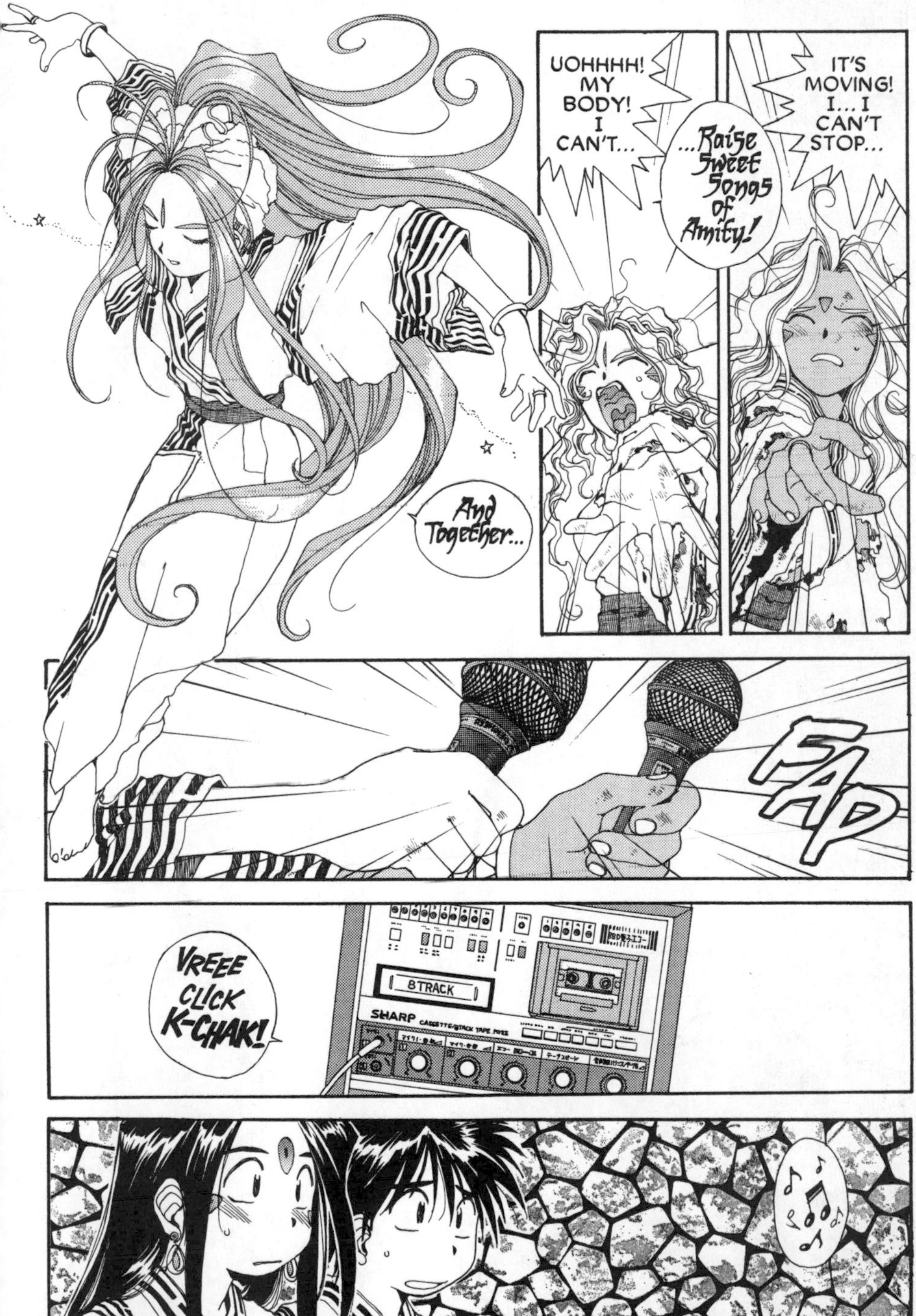
And Together...
UOHHHH! MY BODY! I CAN'T...
...Raise Sweet Songs of Amity!
IT'S MOVING! I... I CAN'T STOP...
FAP
VREEE CLICK K-CHAK!
8TRACK
SHARP

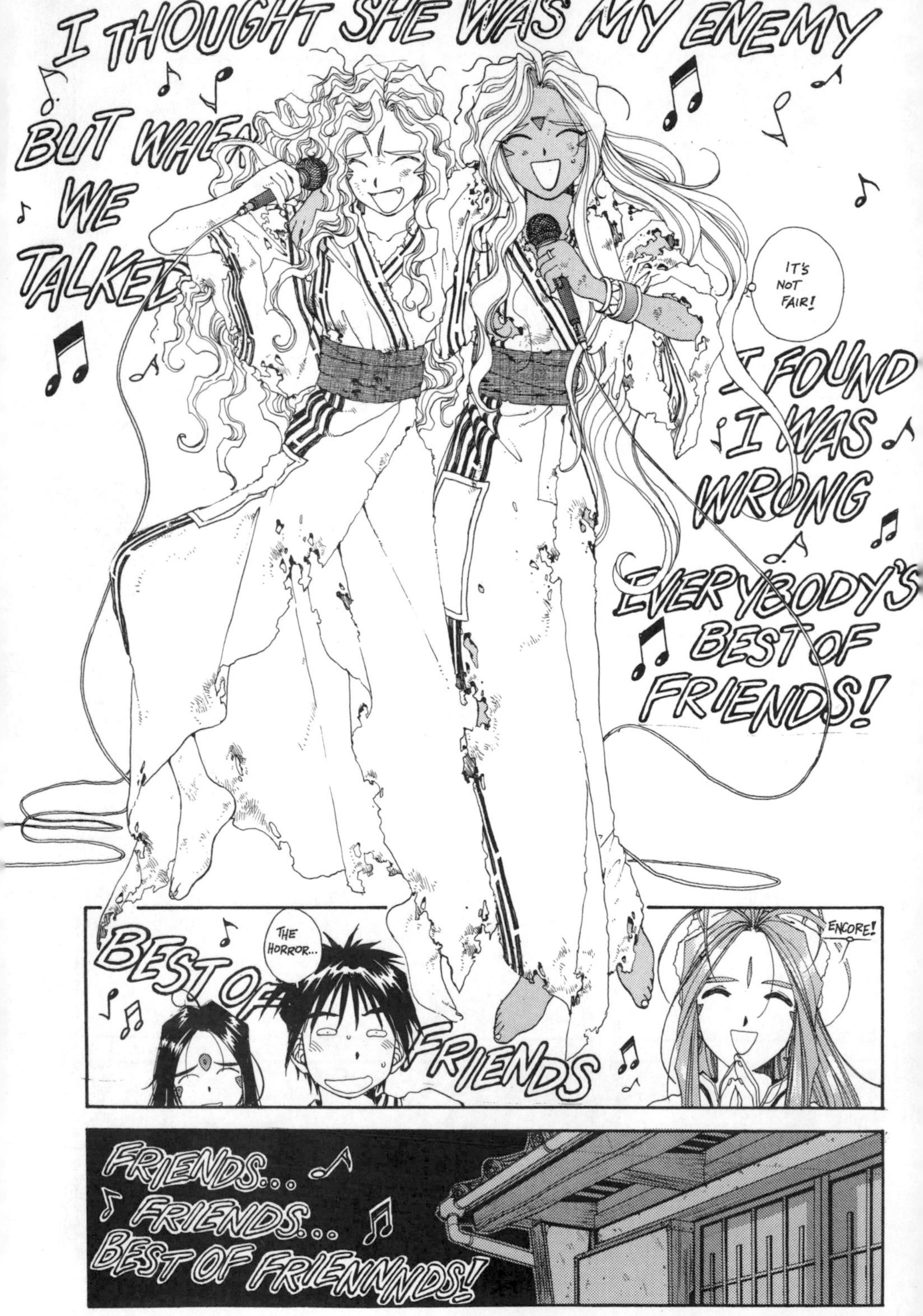
I THOUGHT SHE WAS MY ENEMY
BUT WHEN WE TALKED
IT'S NOT FAIR!
I FOUND I WAS WRONG
EVERYBODY'S BEST OF FRIENDS!
BEST OF FRIENDS
THE HORROR...
ENCORE!
FRIENDS... FRIENDS... BEST OF FRIENNNDS!

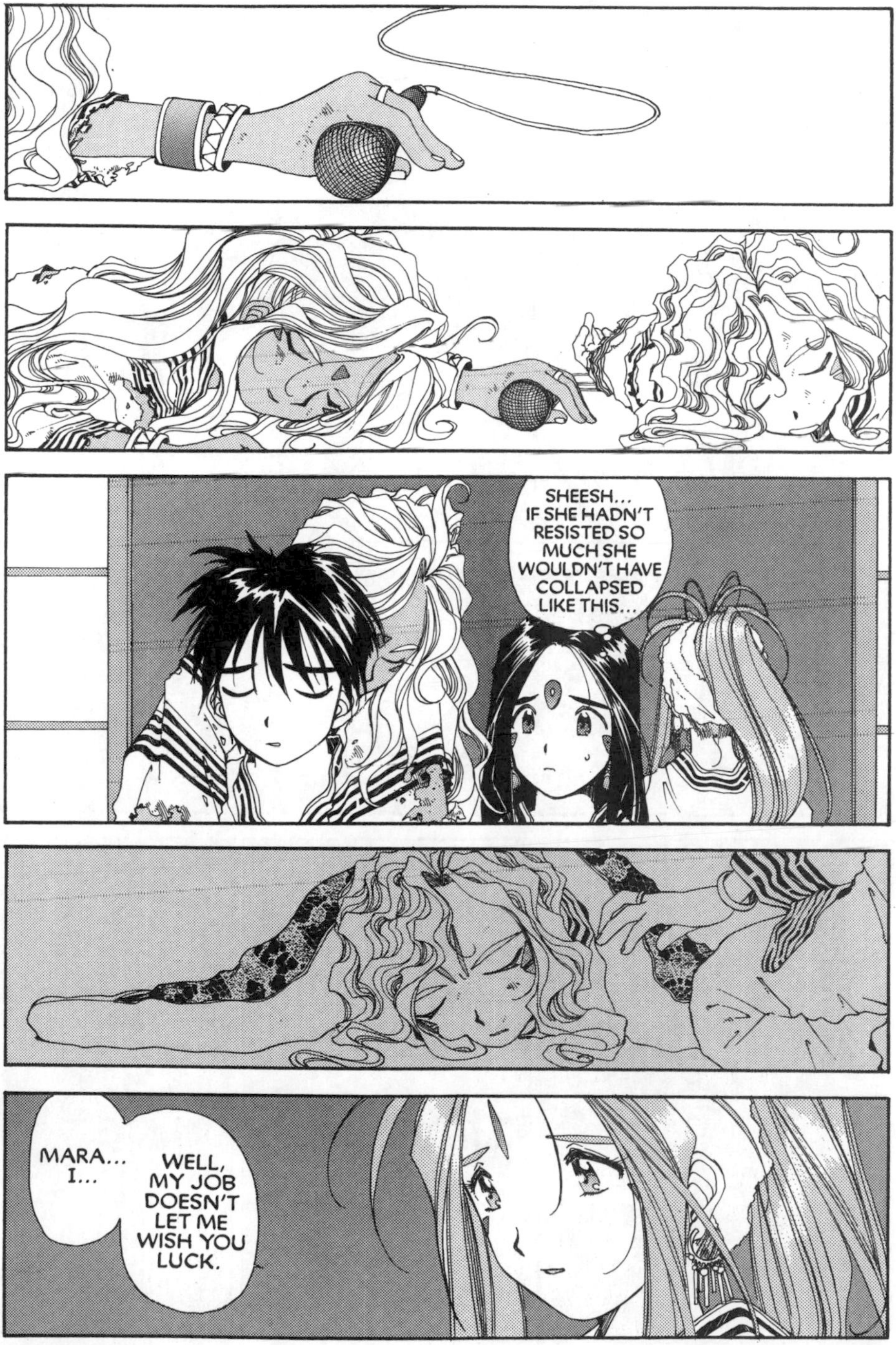
SHEESH... IF SHE HADN'T RESISTED SO MUCH SHE WOULDN'T HAVE COLLAPSED LIKE THIS...
MARA... I...
WELL, MY JOB DOESN'T LET ME WISH YOU LUCK.

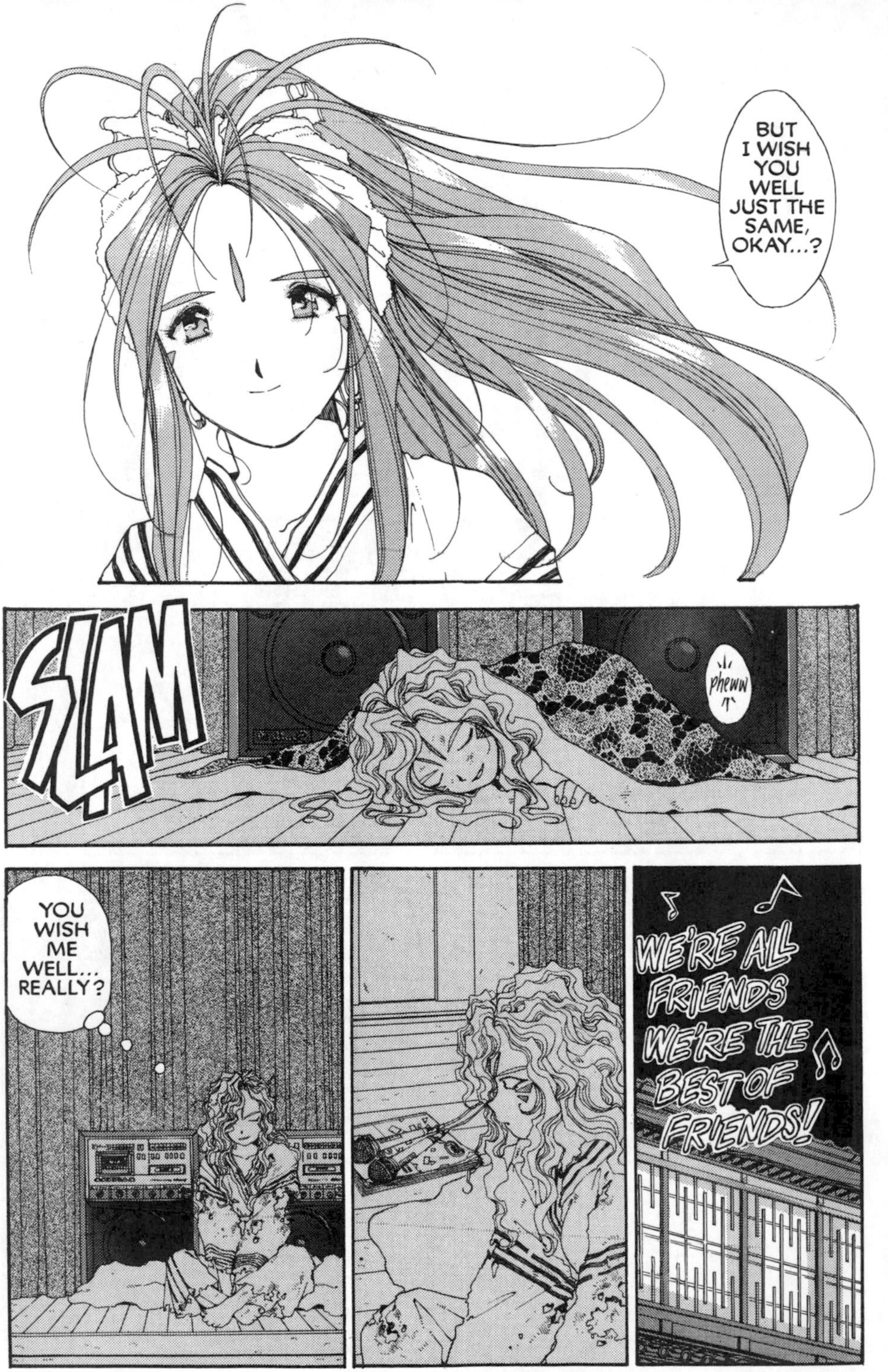
BUT I WISH YOU WELL JUST THE SAME, OKAY...?
SLAM
pheww
YOU WISH ME WELL... REALLY?
WE'RE ALL FRIENDS WE'RE THE BEST OF FRIENDS!

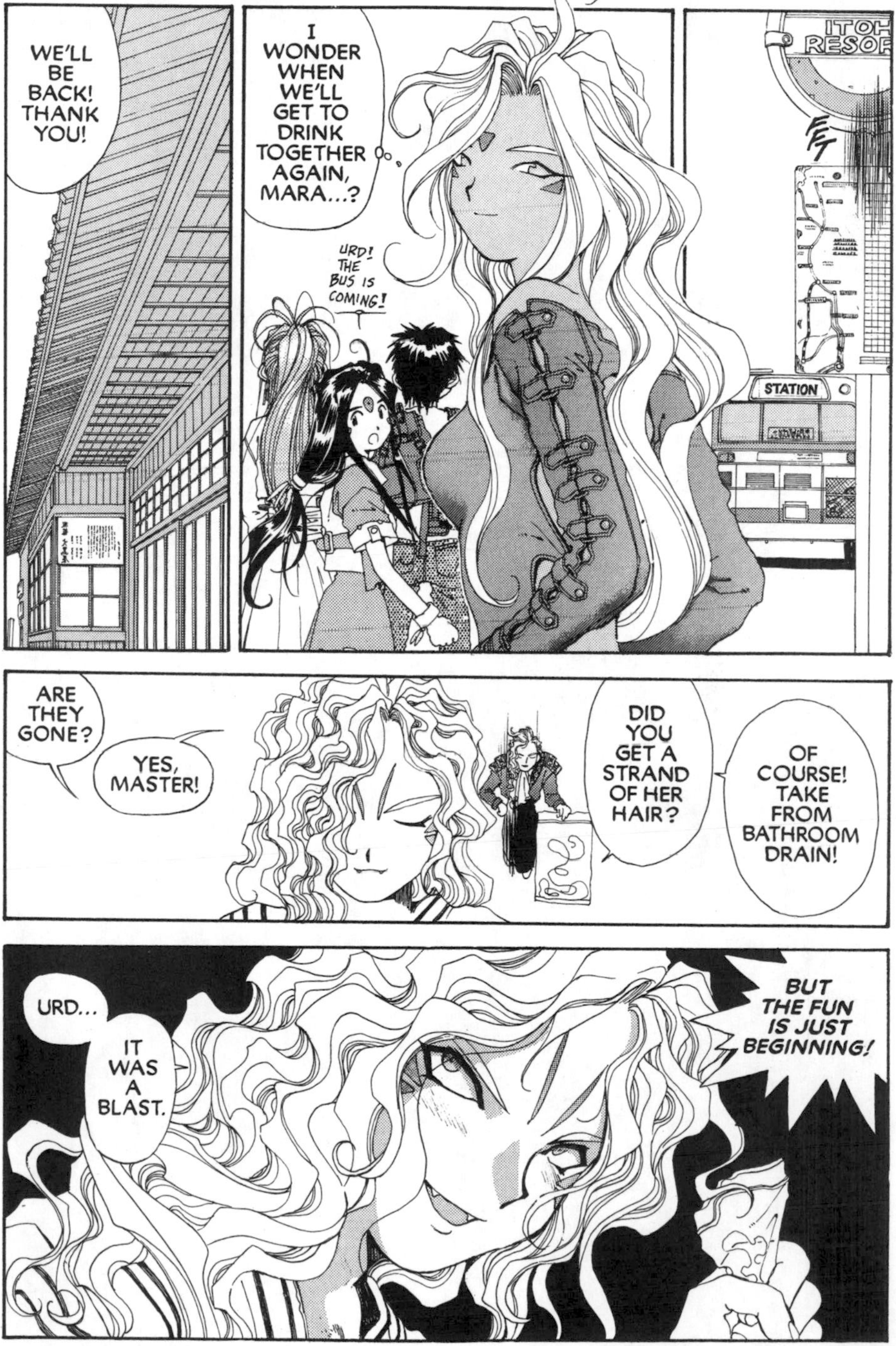
WE'LL BE BACK! THANK YOU!
I WONDER WHEN WE'LL GET TO DRINK TOGETHER AGAIN, MARA...?
URD! THE BUS IS COMING!
ITOH RESOR
FFT
STATION
ARE THEY GONE?
YES, MASTER!
DID YOU GET A STRAND OF HER HAIR?
OF COURSE! TAKE FROM BATHROOM DRAIN!
URD...
IT WAS A BLAST.
BUT THE FUN IS JUST BEGINNING!

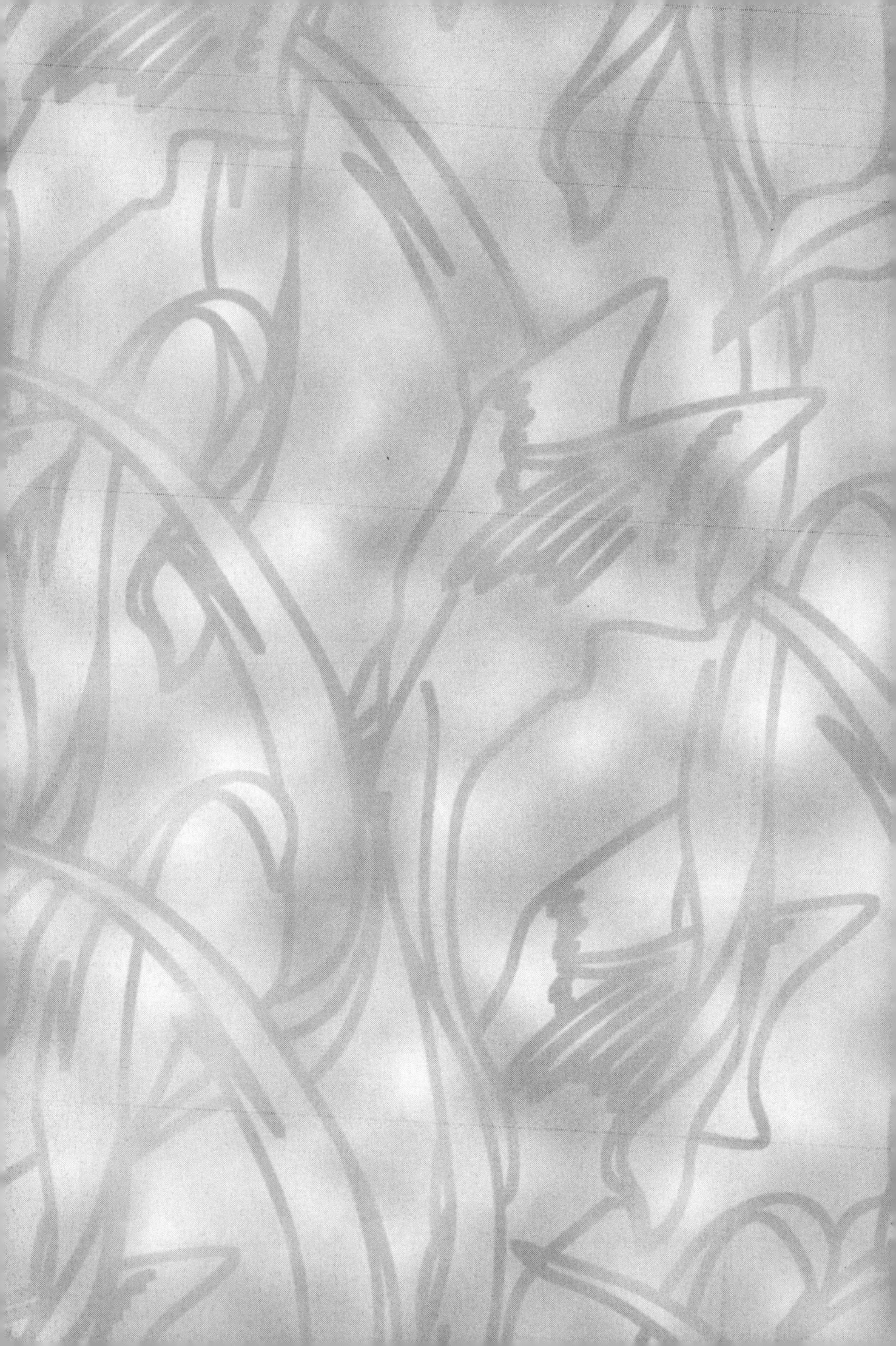

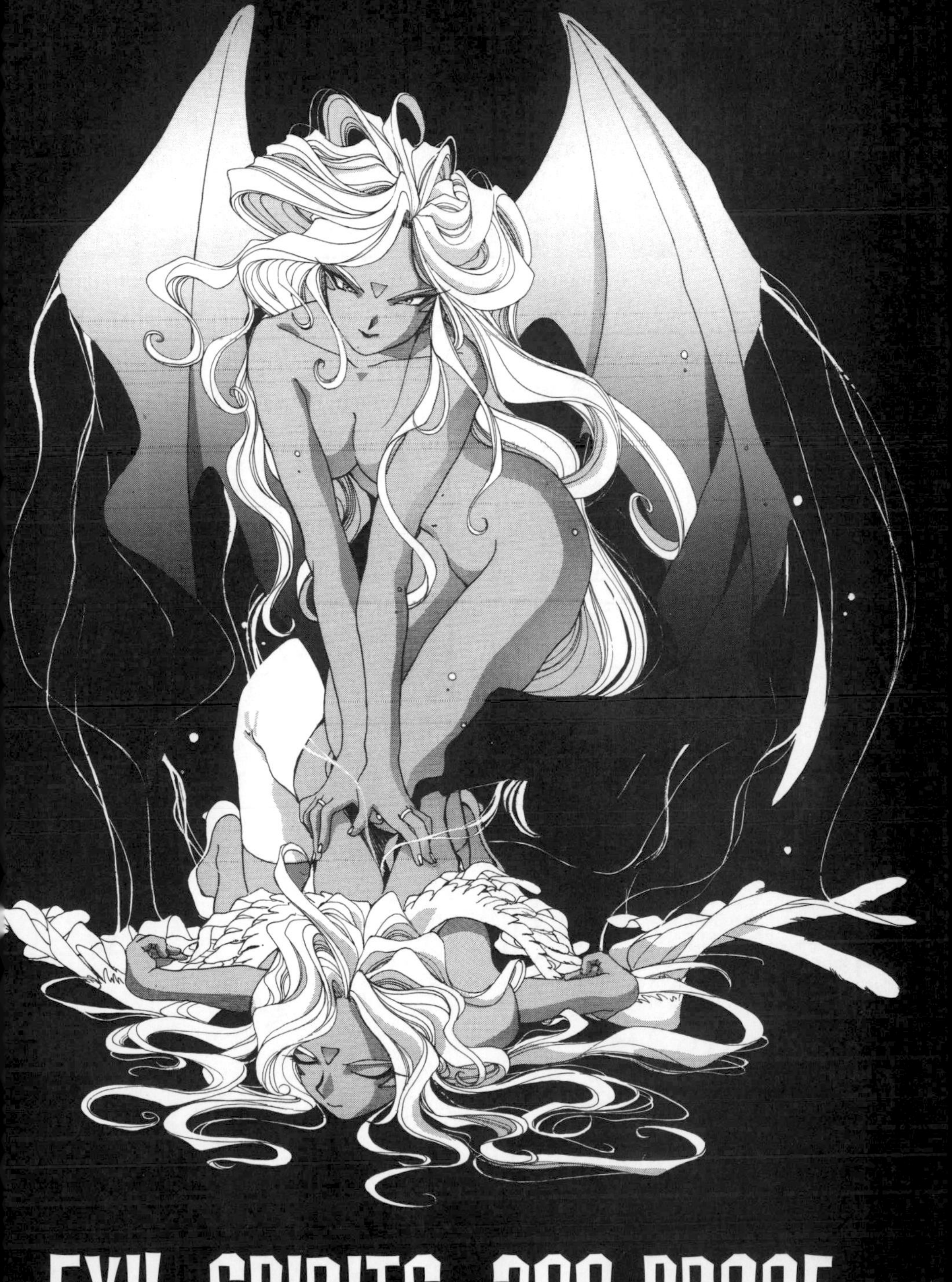

EVIL SPIRITS: 200 PROOF

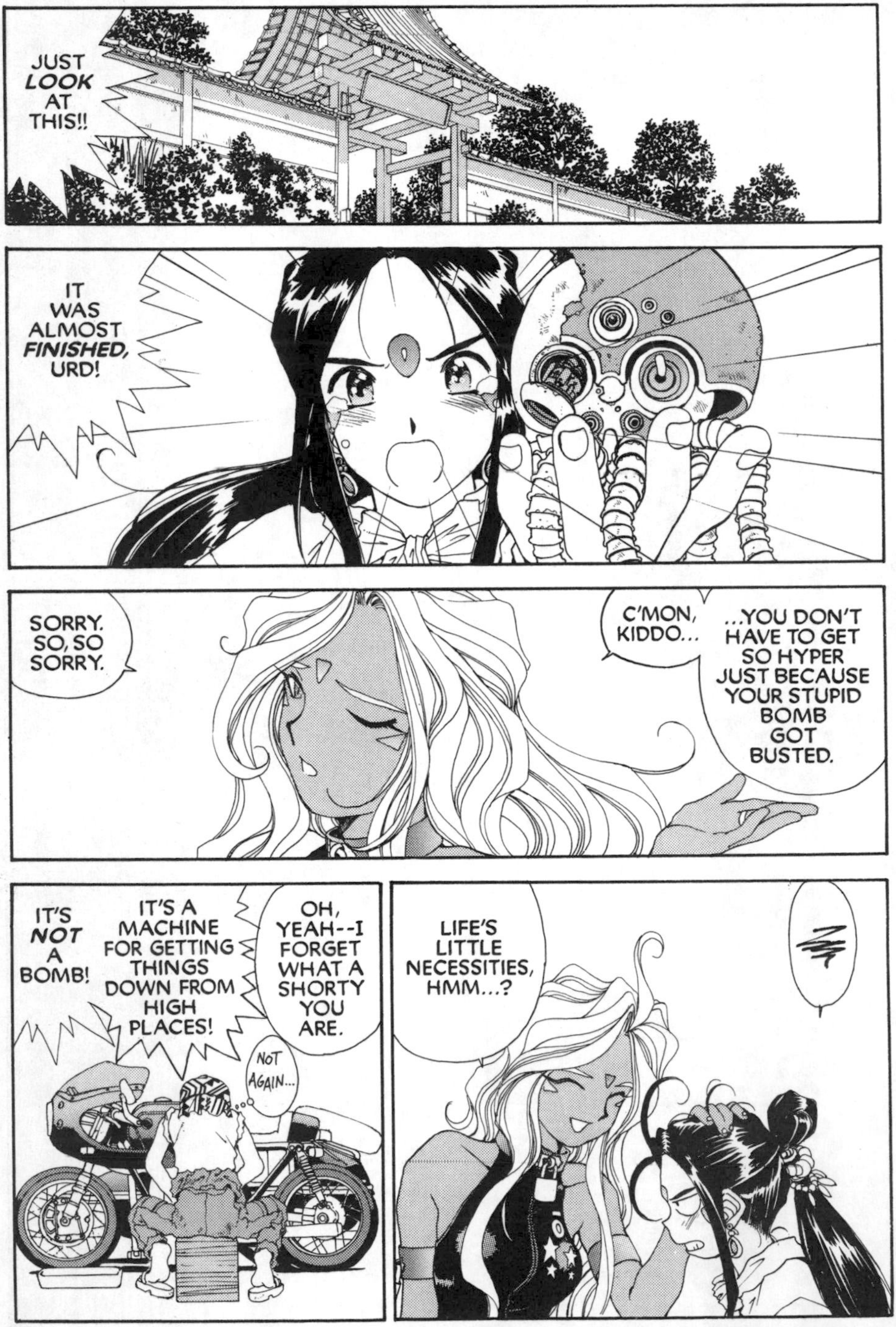
JUST LOOK AT THIS!!
IT WAS ALMOST FINISHED, URD!
C'MON, KIDDO...
...YOU DON'T HAVE TO GET SO HYPER JUST BECAUSE YOUR STUPID BOMB GOT BUSTED.
SORRY. SO, SO SORRY.
LIFE'S LITTLE NECESSITIES, HMM...?
OH, YEAH--I FORGET WHAT A SHORTY YOU ARE.
IT'S A MACHINE FOR GETTING THINGS DOWN FROM HIGH PLACES!
IT'S NOT A BOMB!
NOT AGAIN...

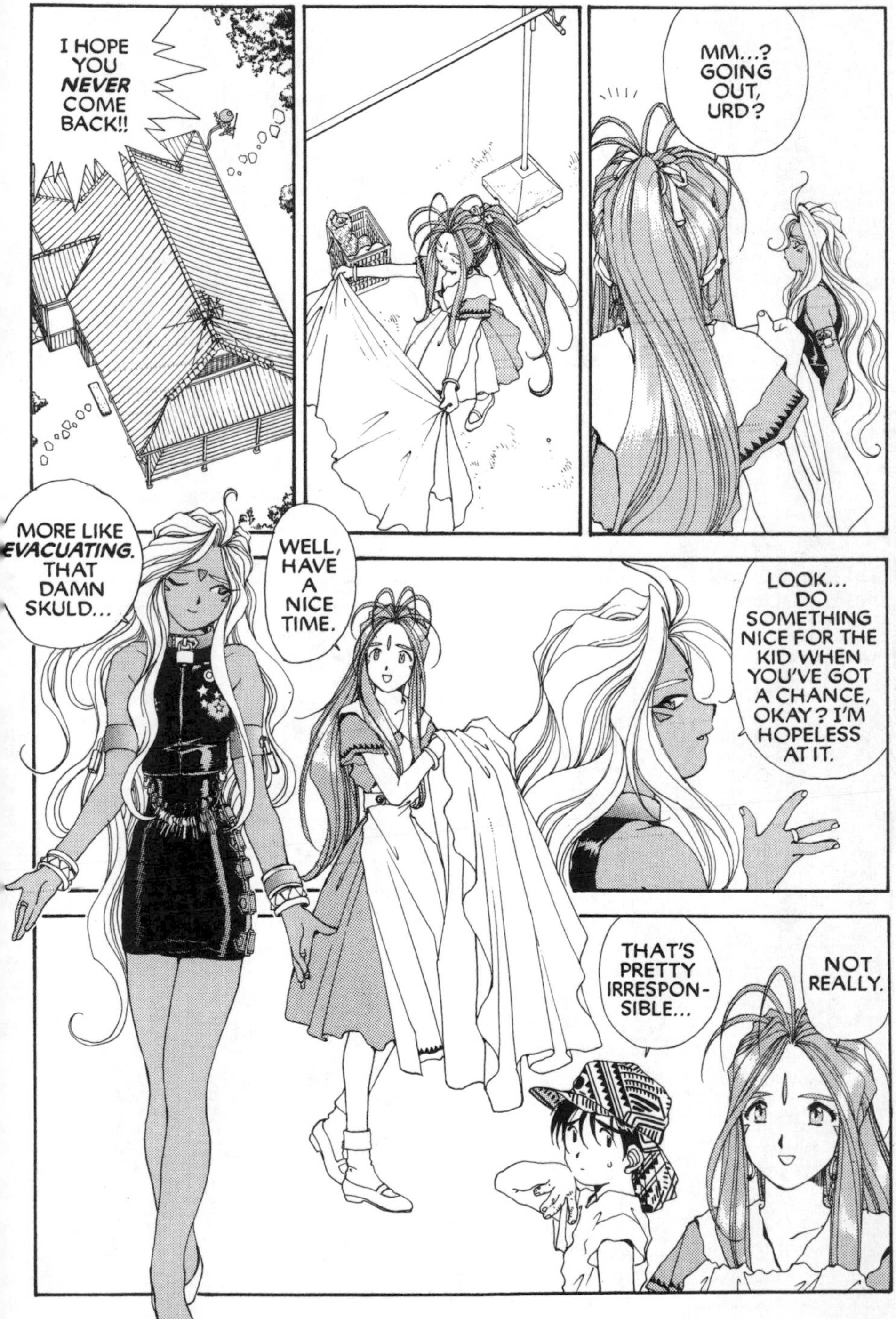

I HOPE YOU ***NEVER*** COME BACK!!
MM...? GOING OUT, URD?
MORE LIKE ***EVACUATING.*** THAT DAMN SKULD...
WELL, HAVE A NICE TIME.
LOOK... DO SOMETHING NICE FOR THE KID WHEN YOU'VE GOT A CHANCE, OKAY? I'M HOPELESS AT IT.
THAT'S PRETTY IRRESPON-SIBLE...
NOT REALLY.

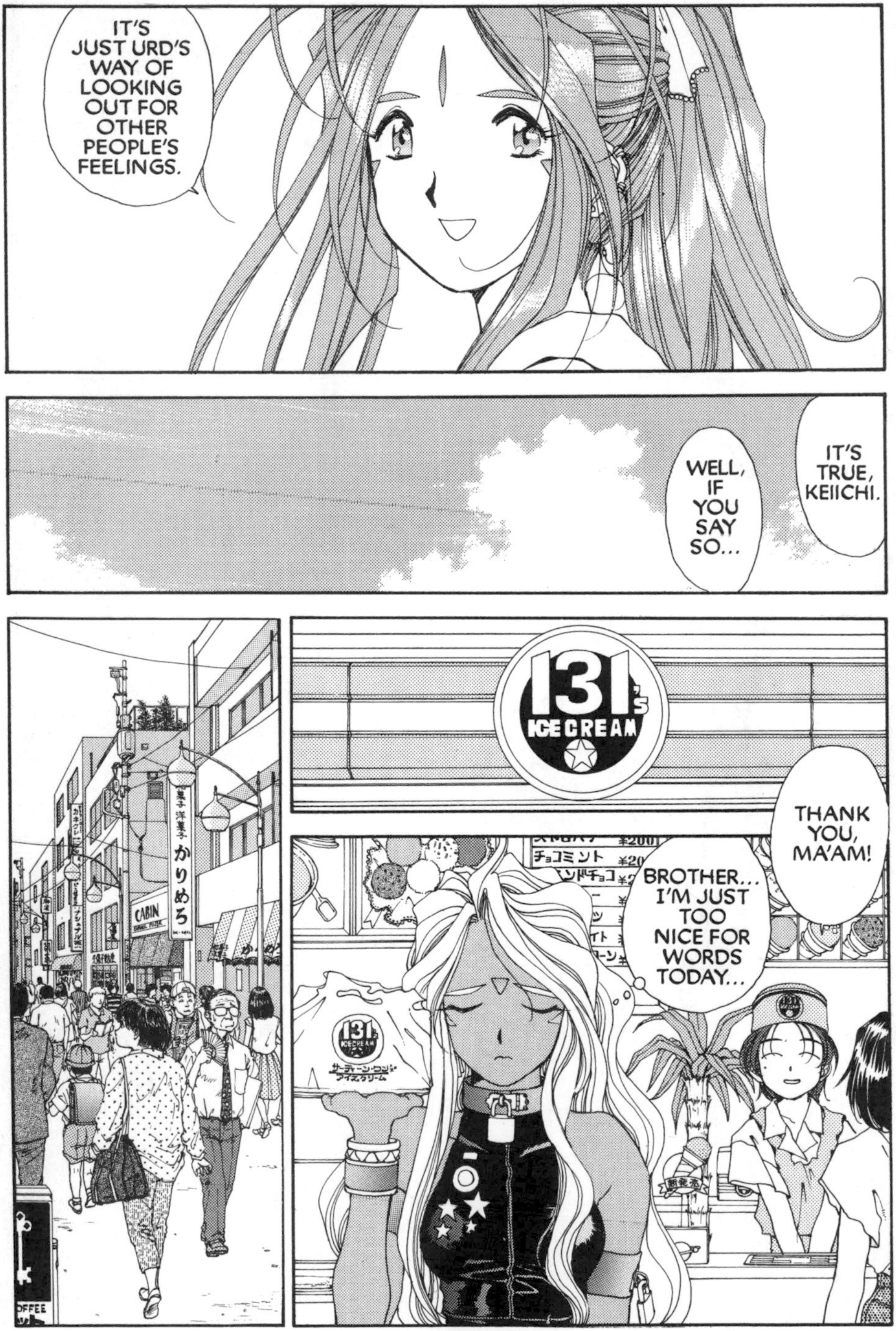
IT'S JUST URD'S WAY OF LOOKING OUT FOR OTHER PEOPLE'S FEELINGS.
IT'S TRUE, KEIICHI.
WELL, IF YOU SAY SO...
菓子洋菓子
かりめろ
CABIN
131's
ICE CREAM
チョコミント
THANK YOU, MA'AM!
BROTHER... I'M JUST TOO NICE FOR WORDS TODAY...

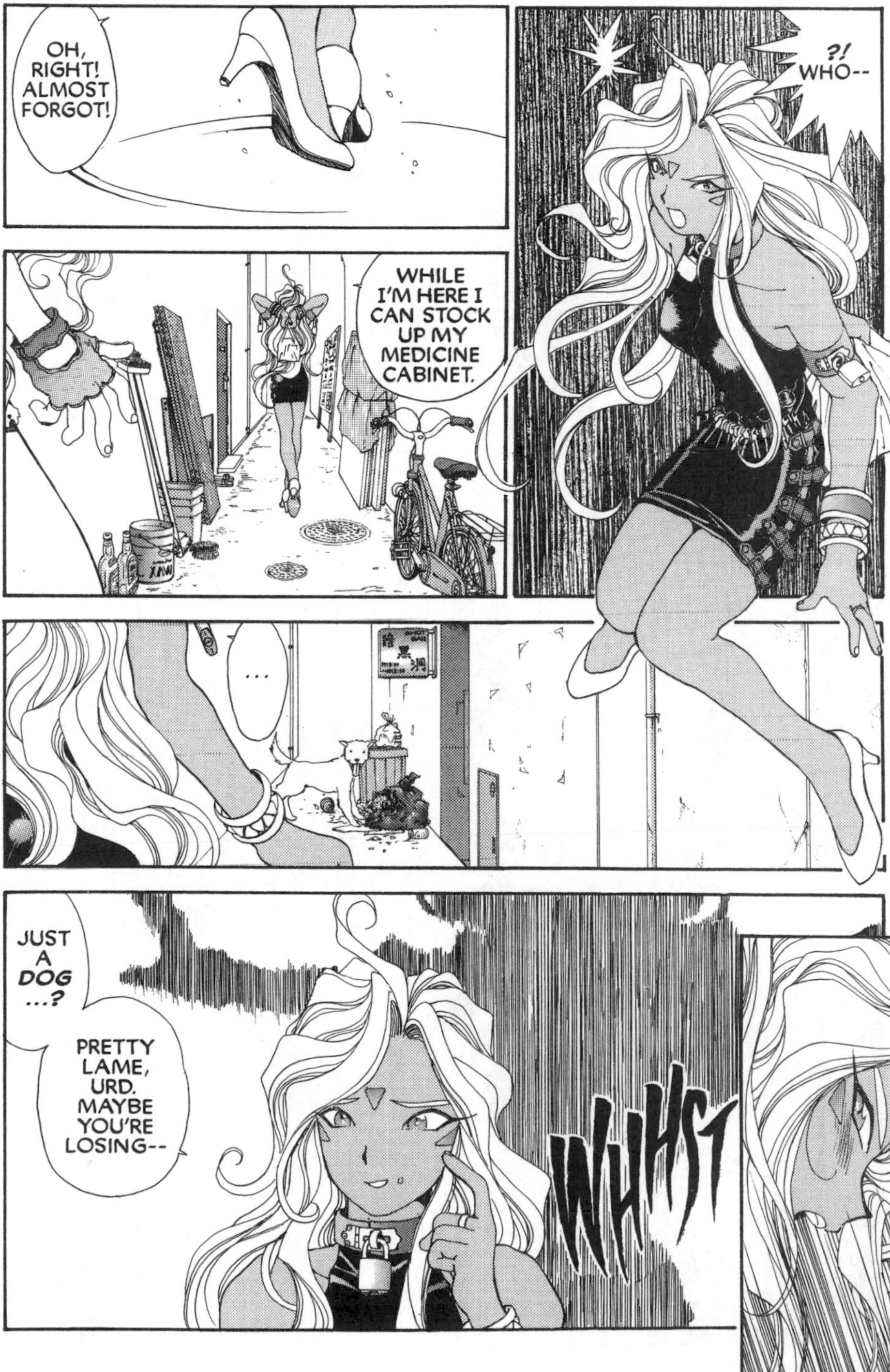
OH, RIGHT! ALMOST FORGOT!
?! WHO--
WHILE I'M HERE I CAN STOCK UP MY MEDICINE CABINET.
...
JUST A DOG ...?
PRETTY LAME, URD. MAYBE YOU'RE LOSING--
WHHST

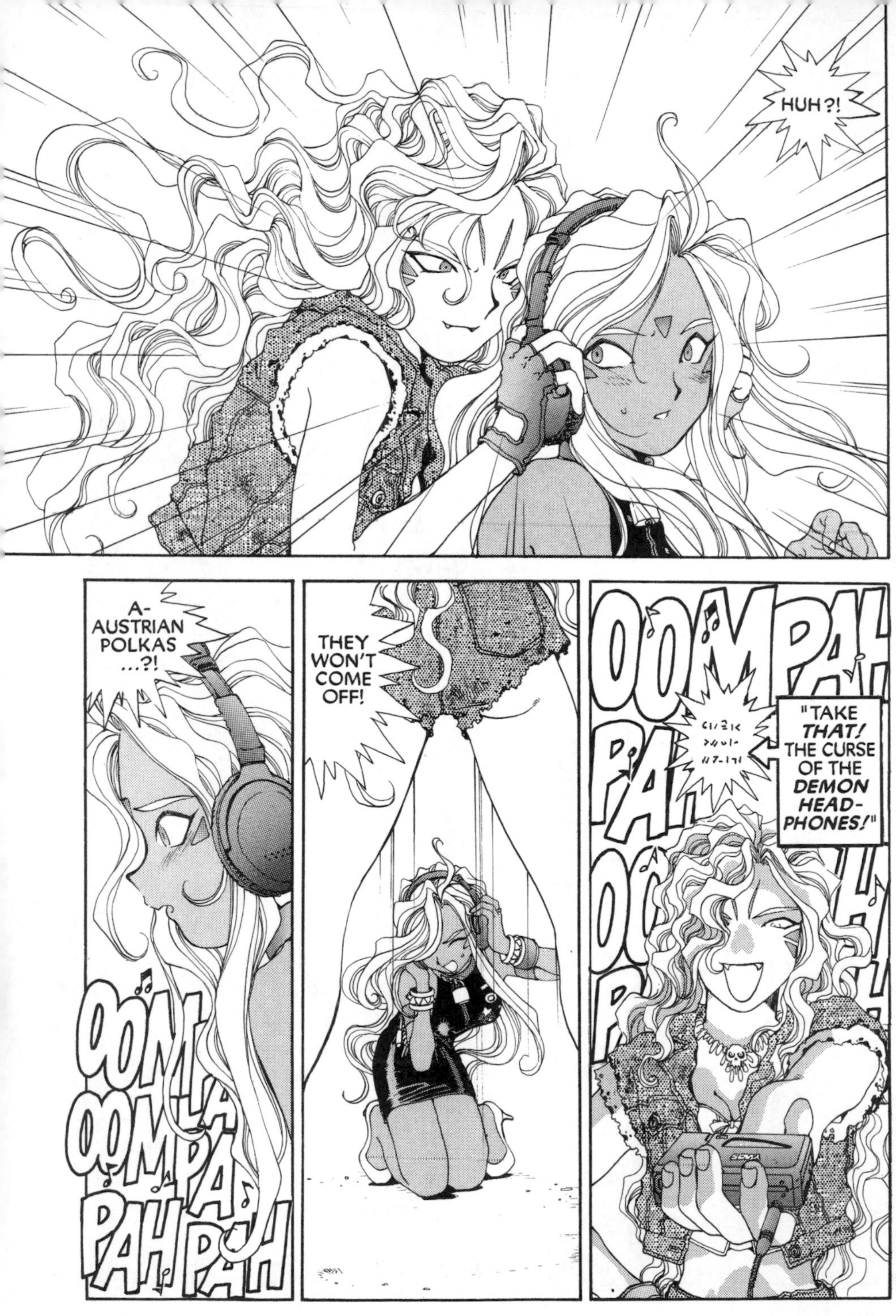
HUH?!
A- AUSTRIAN POLKAS ...?!
OOMPA OOMPA PAH PAH
THEY WON'T COME OFF!
OOMPAH PAH OOMPAH PAH
"TAKE THAT! THE CURSE OF THE DEMON HEAD-PHONES!"

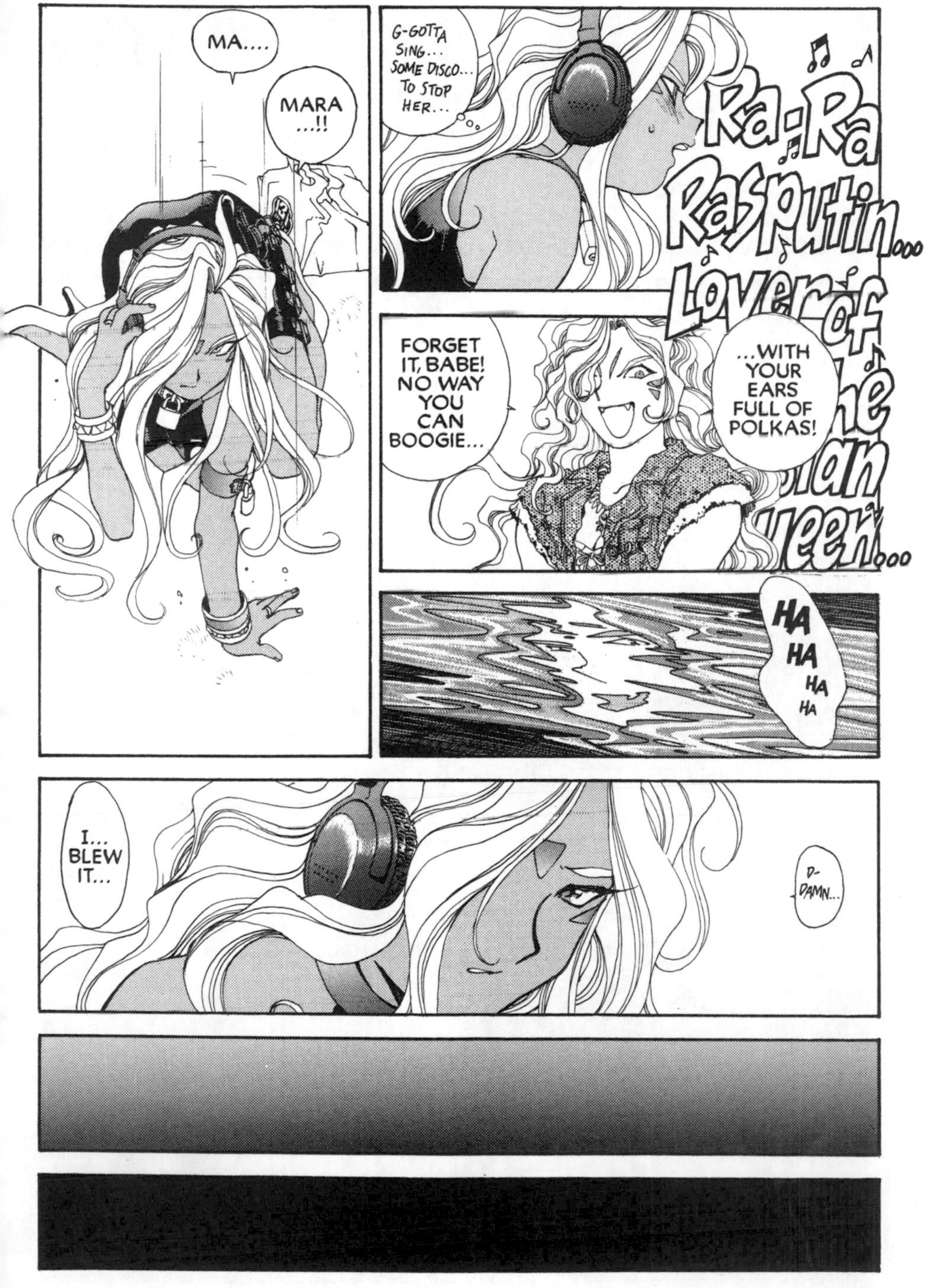

MA....
MARA ...!!
G-GOTTA SING... SOME DISCO... TO STOP HER...
Ra-Ra Rasputin... Lover of
FORGET IT, BABE! NO WAY YOU CAN BOOGIE...
...WITH YOUR EARS FULL OF POLKAS!
HA HA HA HA
I... BLEW IT...
D-DAMN...

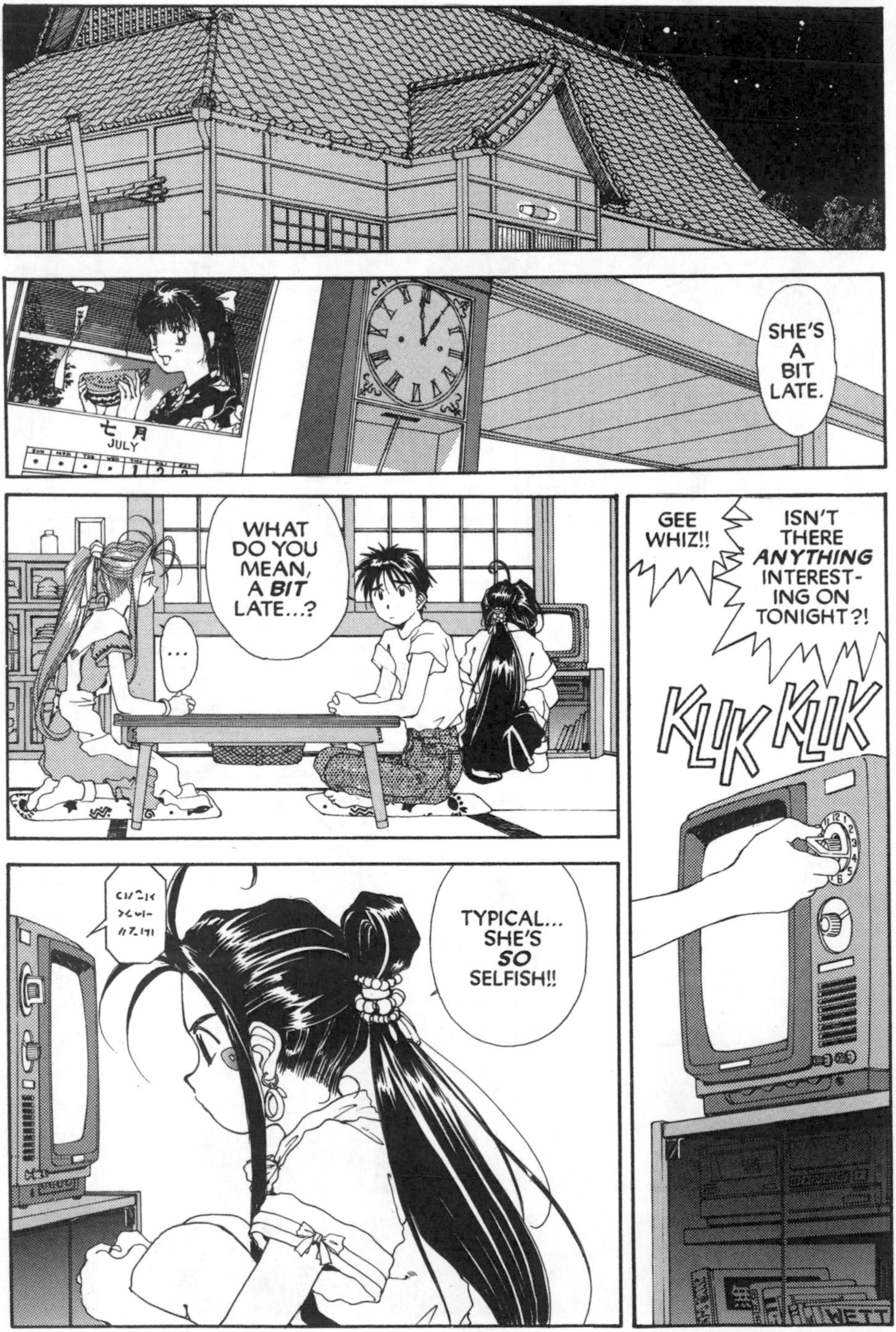
七月
JULY
SHE'S A BIT LATE.
. . .
WHAT DO YOU MEAN, A *BIT* LATE...?
TYPICAL... SHE'S *SO* SELFISH!!
GEE WHIZ!!
ISN'T THERE *ANYTHING* INTEREST-ING ON TONIGHT?!
KLIK KLIK

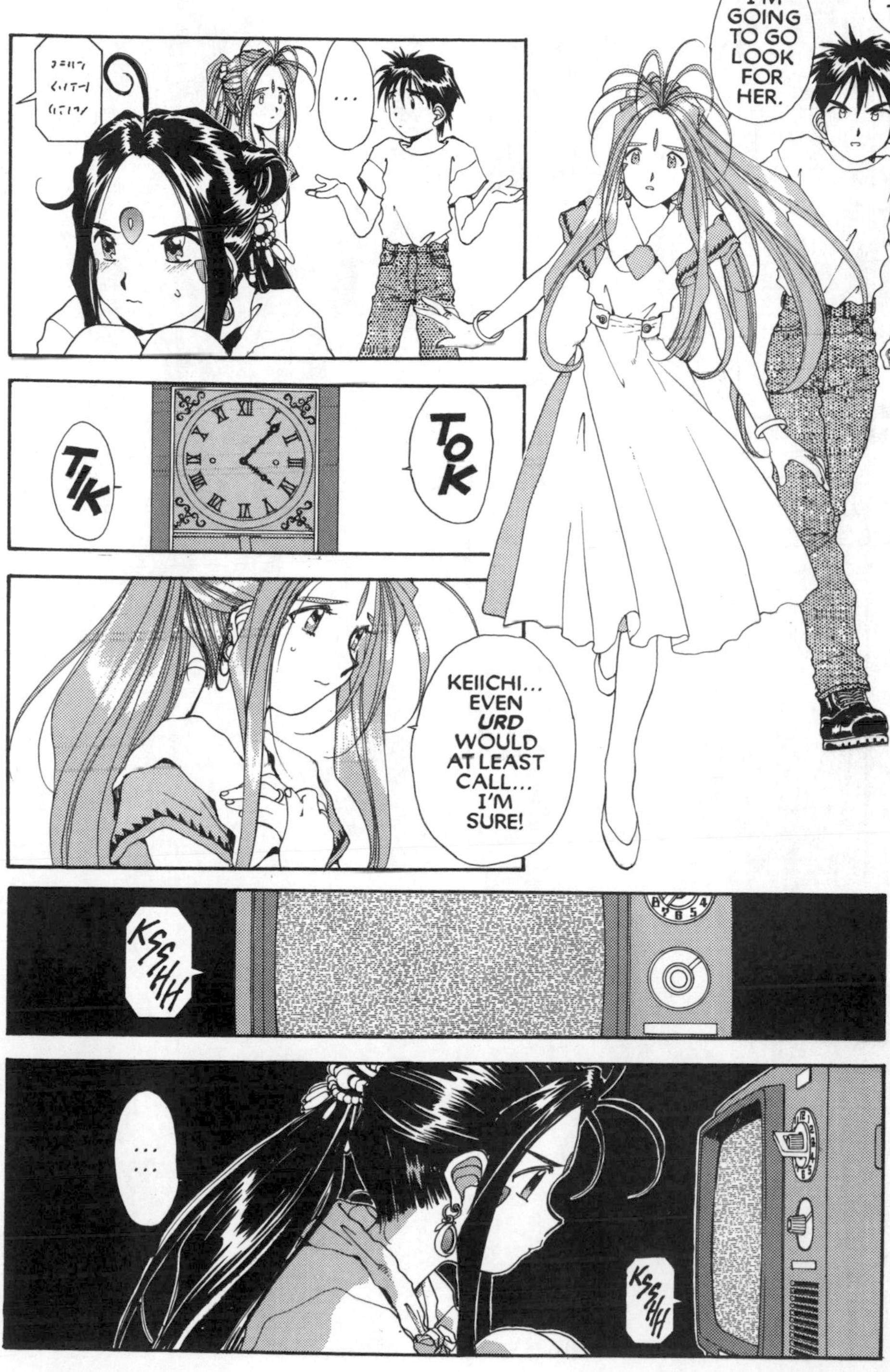
. . .
TIK
TOK
KEIICHI... EVEN URD WOULD AT LEAST CALL... I'M SURE!
I'M GOING TO GO LOOK FOR HER.
ME, TOO!
KSSHH
. . .
. . .
KSSHH

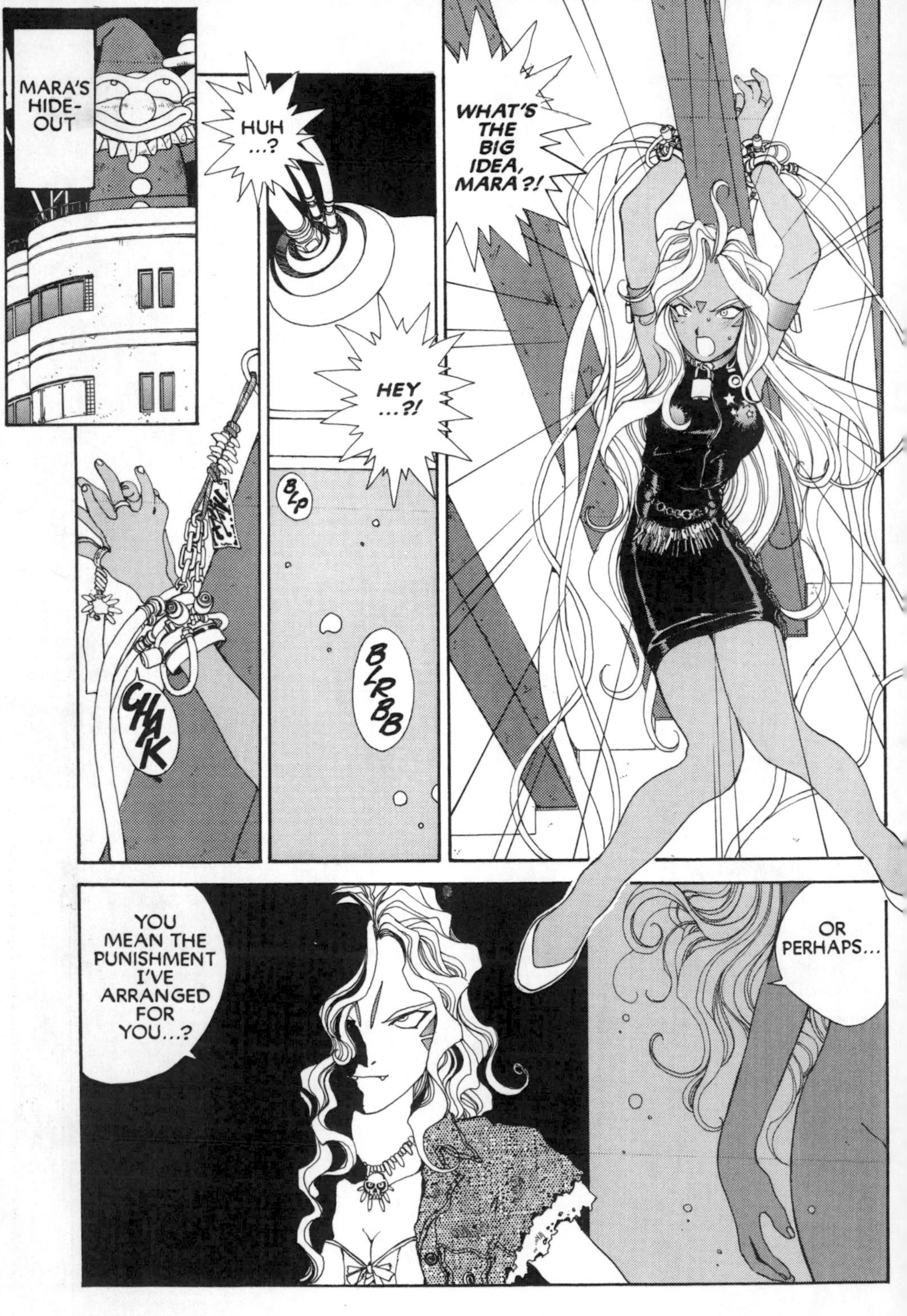
MARA'S HIDE-OUT
CHAK
HUH ...?
HEY ...?!
BLP
BLRBB
WHAT'S THE BIG IDEA, MARA?!
YOU MEAN THE PUNISHMENT I'VE ARRANGED FOR YOU...?
OR PERHAPS...

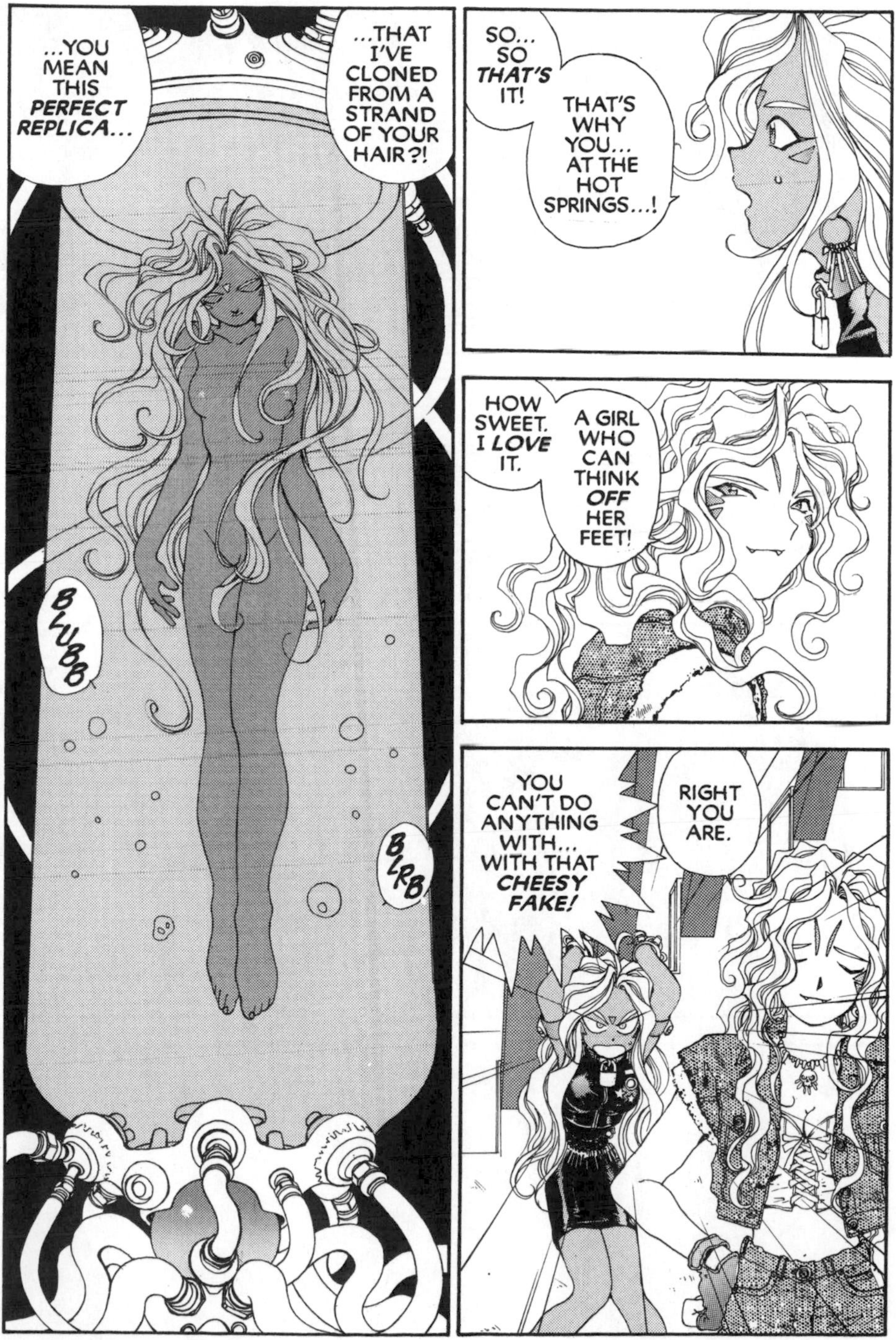
...YOU MEAN THIS PERFECT REPLICA...
...THAT I'VE CLONED FROM A STRAND OF YOUR HAIR?!
BLUBB
BLRB
SO... SO THAT'S IT!
THAT'S WHY YOU... AT THE HOT SPRINGS...!
HOW SWEET. I LOVE IT.
A GIRL WHO CAN THINK OFF HER FEET!
YOU CAN'T DO ANYTHING WITH... WITH THAT CHEESY FAKE!
RIGHT YOU ARE.

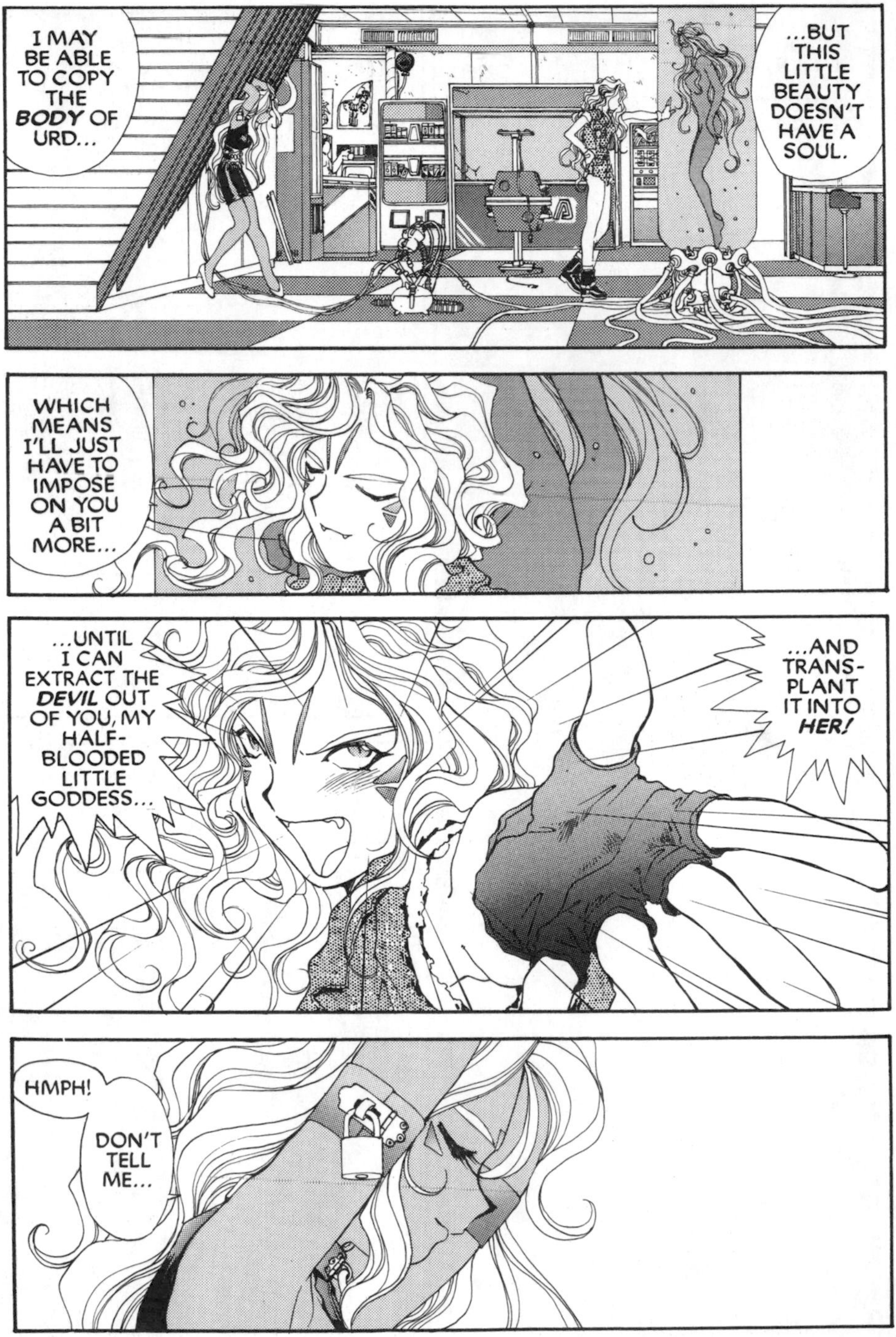
I MAY BE ABLE TO COPY THE BODY OF URD...
...BUT THIS LITTLE BEAUTY DOESN'T HAVE A SOUL.
WHICH MEANS I'LL JUST HAVE TO IMPOSE ON YOU A BIT MORE...
...UNTIL I CAN EXTRACT THE DEVIL OUT OF YOU, MY HALF-BLOODED LITTLE GODDESS...
...AND TRANS-PLANT IT INTO HER!
HMPH!
DON'T TELL ME...

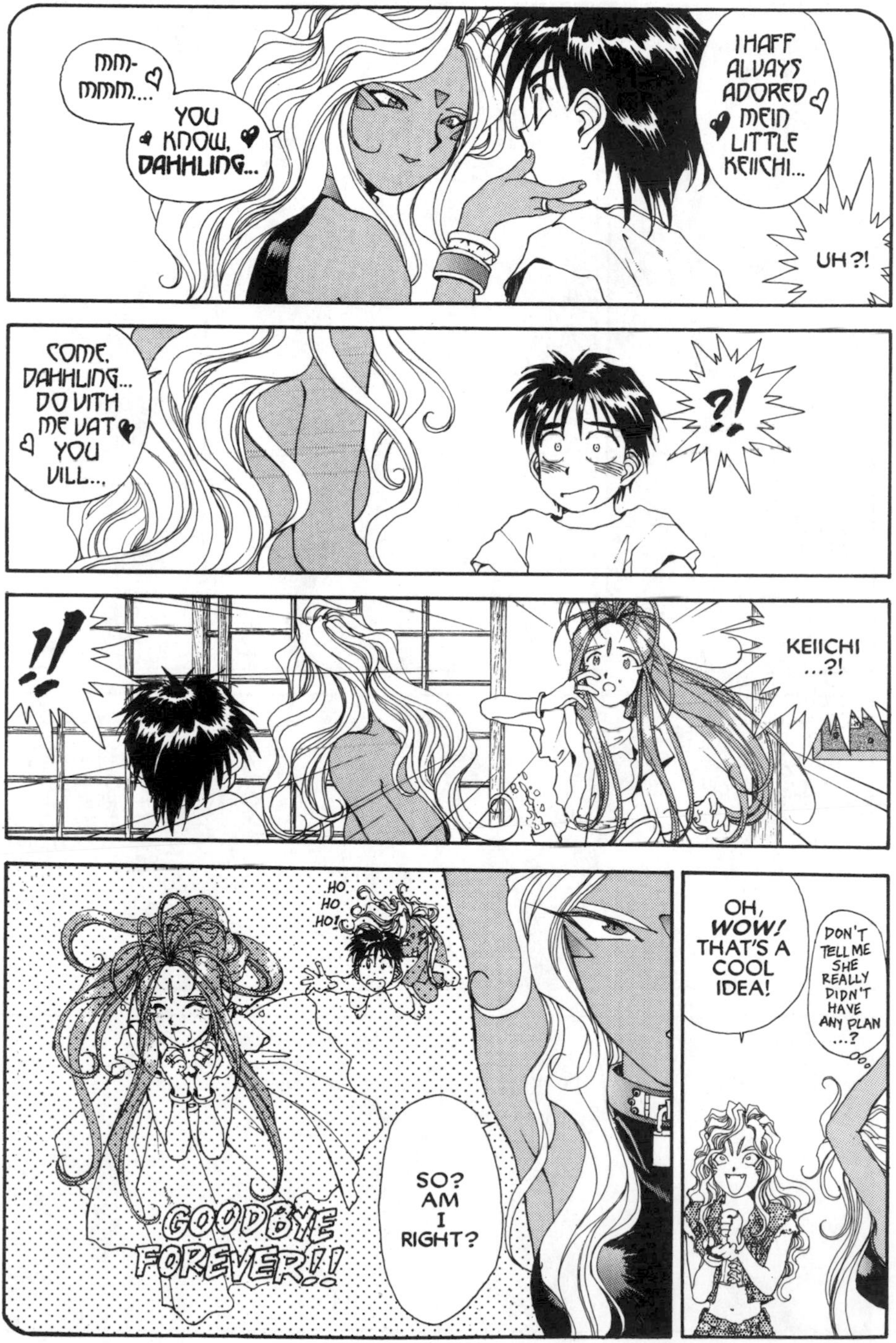
I HAFF ALVAYS ADORED MEIN LITTLE KEIICHI...
MM-MMM....
YOU KNOW, DAHHLING...
UH?!
?!
COME, DAHHLING... DO VITH ME VAT YOU VILL...,
KEIICHI ...?!
!!
DON'T TELL ME SHE REALLY DIDN'T HAVE ANY PLAN ...?
OH, WOW! THAT'S A COOL IDEA!
SO? AM I RIGHT?
HO HO HO!
GOODBYE FOREVER!!

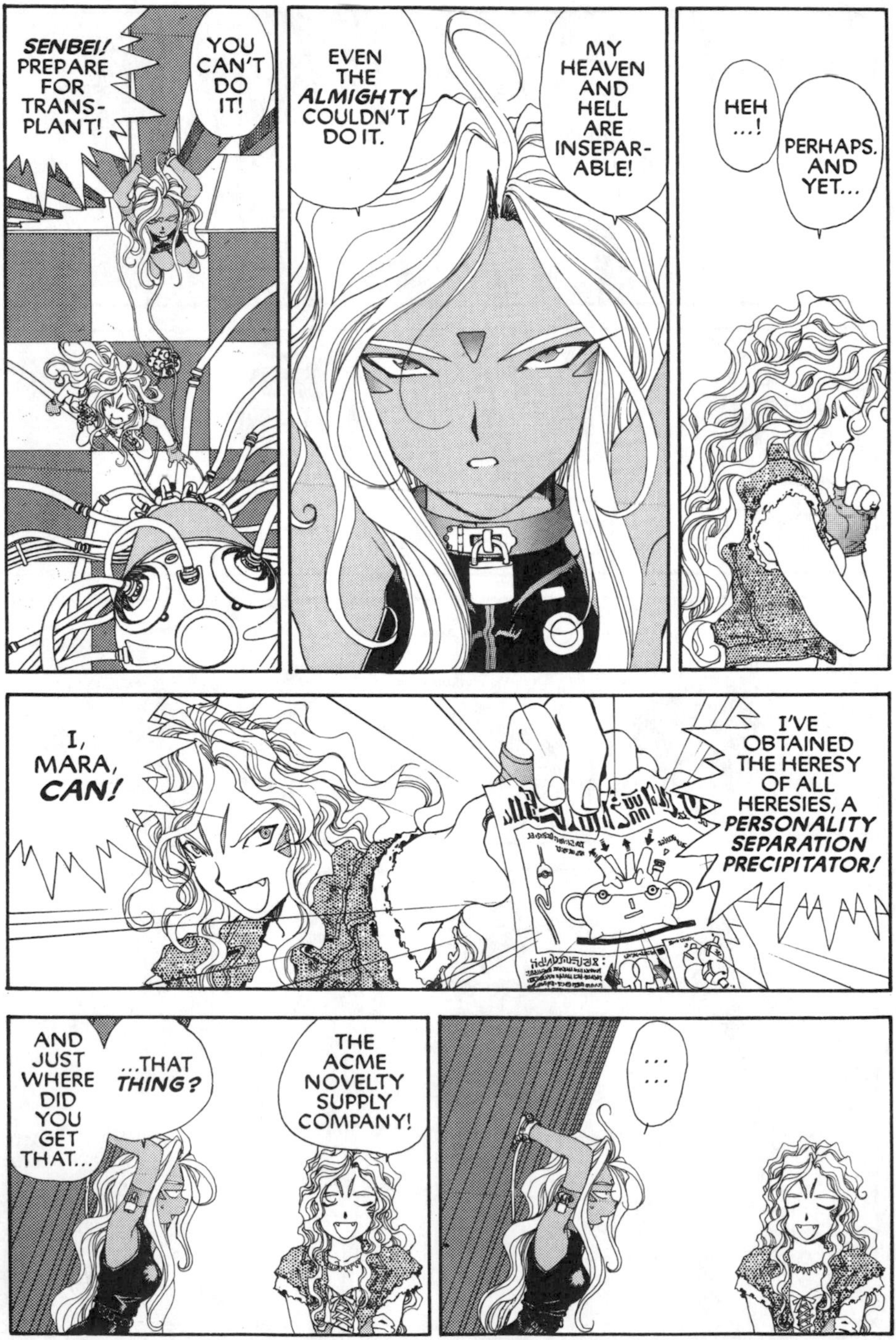
SENBEI! PREPARE FOR TRANS-PLANT!
YOU CAN'T DO IT!
EVEN THE ALMIGHTY COULDN'T DO IT.
MY HEAVEN AND HELL ARE INSEPAR-ABLE!
HEH ...!
PERHAPS. AND YET...
I, MARA, CAN!
I'VE OBTAINED THE HERESY OF ALL HERESIES, A PERSONALITY SEPARATION PRECIPITATOR!
AND JUST WHERE DID YOU GET THAT...
...THAT THING?
THE ACME NOVELTY SUPPLY COMPANY!
... ...

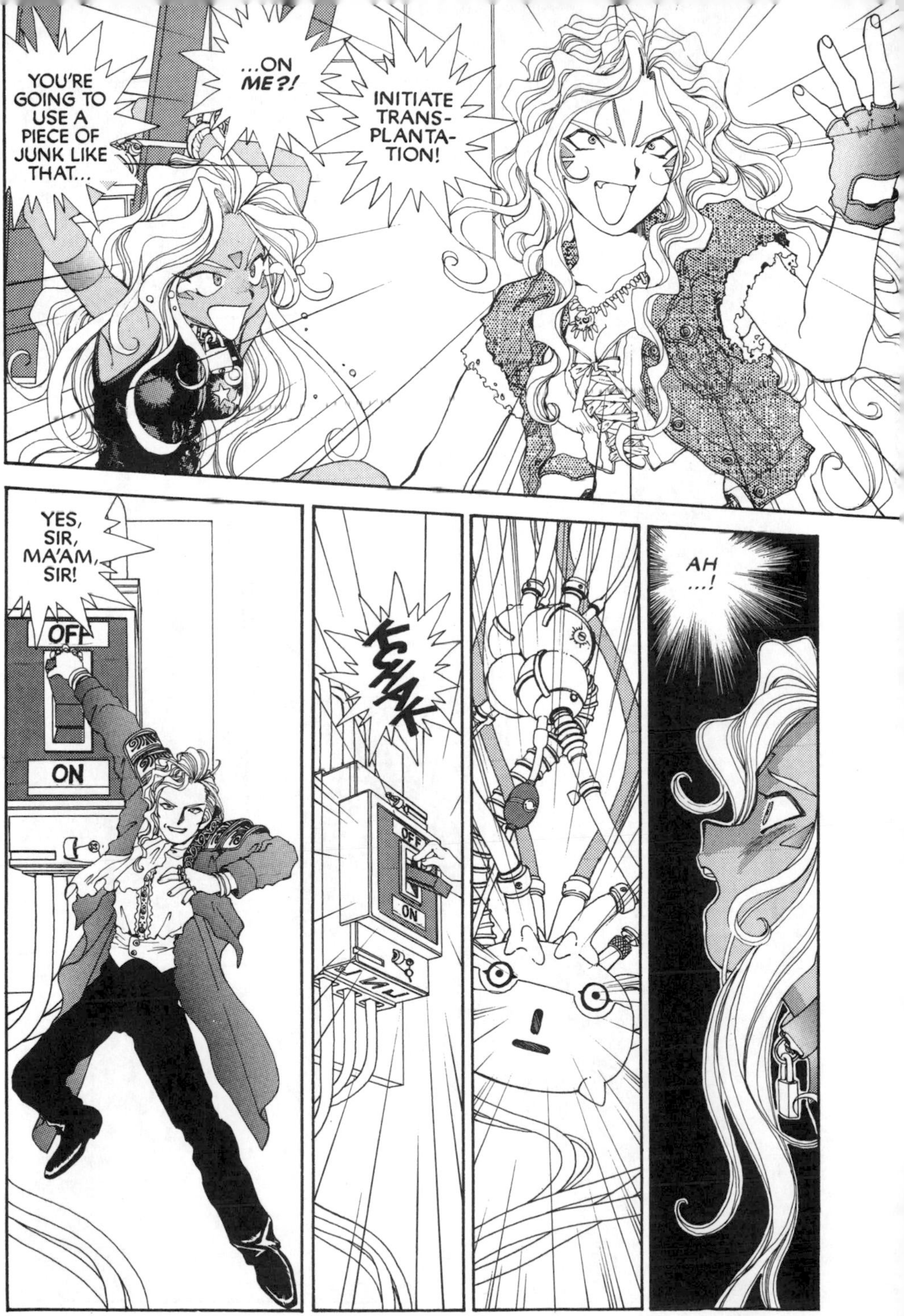
YOU'RE GOING TO USE A PIECE OF JUNK LIKE THAT...
...ON *ME?!*
INITIATE TRANS-PLANTA-TION!
YES, SIR, MA'AM, SIR!
OFF
ON
KCHAK
OFF
ON
AH ...!

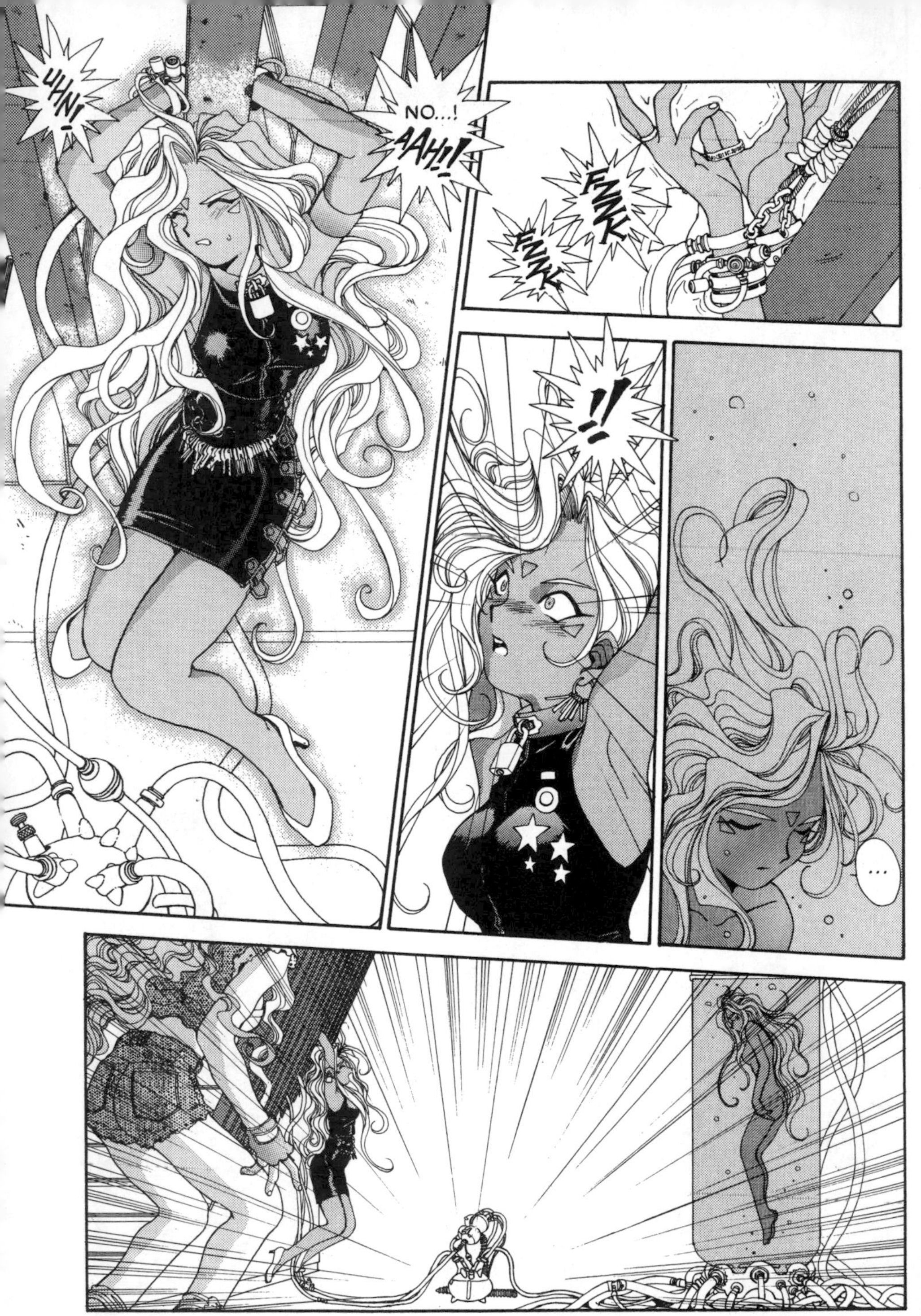

UHN!
NO...!
AAH!!
FZZZK
FZZZK
!!
...

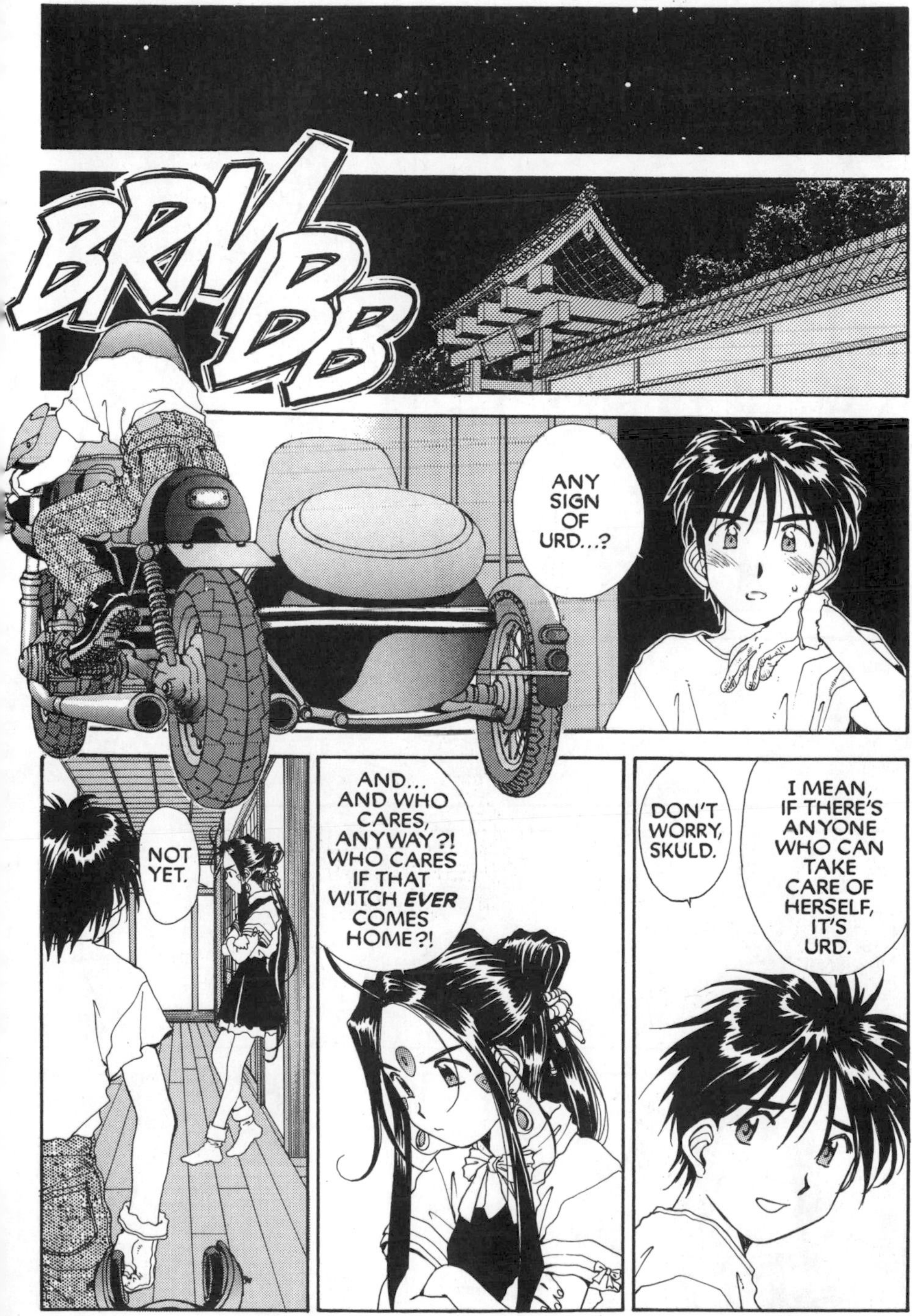
BRMBB
ANY SIGN OF URD...?
NOT YET.
AND... AND WHO CARES, ANYWAY?! WHO CARES IF THAT WITCH *EVER* COMES HOME?!
DON'T WORRY, SKULD.
I MEAN, IF THERE'S ANYONE WHO CAN TAKE CARE OF HERSELF, IT'S URD.

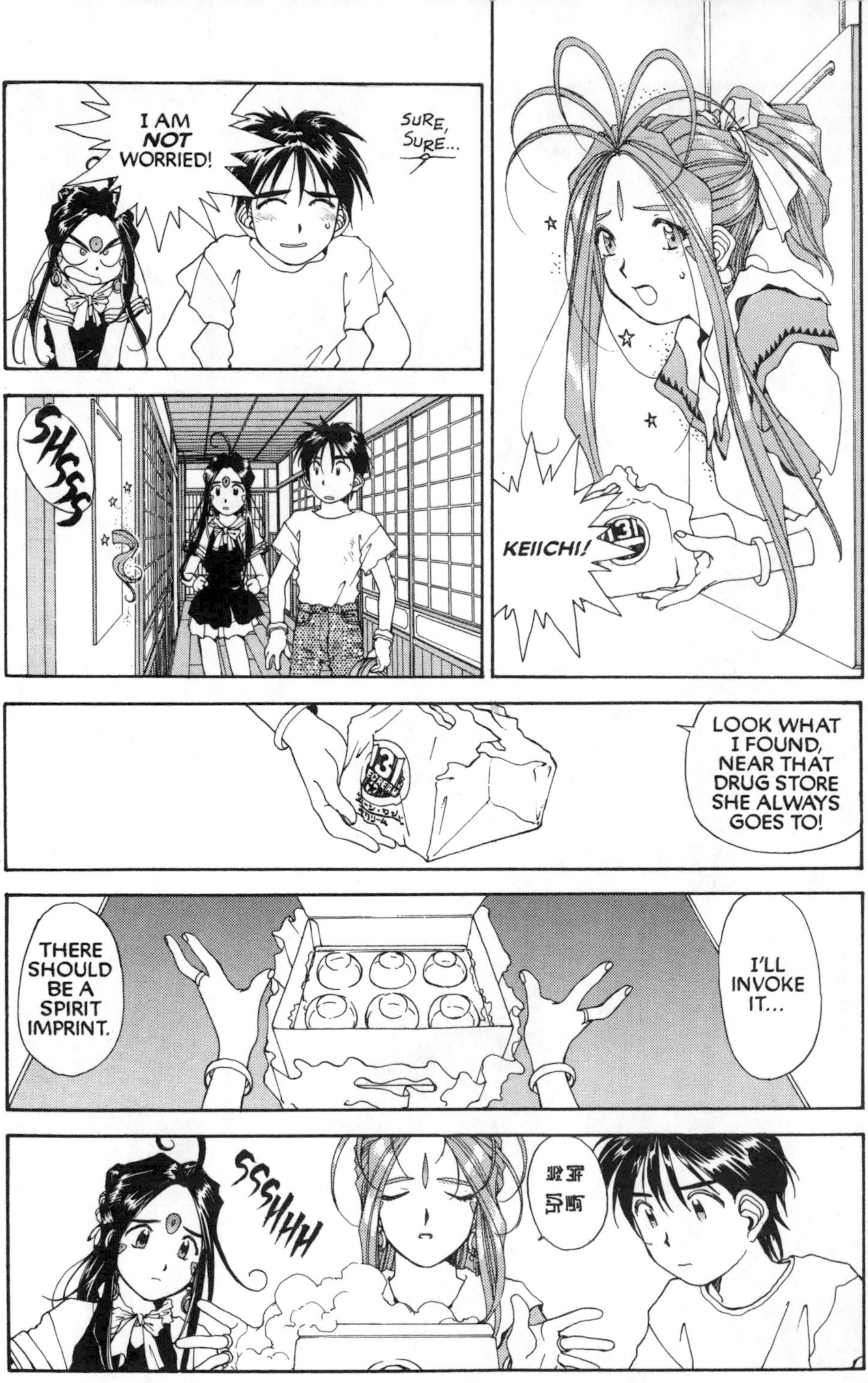
I AM NOT WORRIED!
SURE, SURE...
SHSSS
KEIICHI!
LOOK WHAT I FOUND, NEAR THAT DRUG STORE SHE ALWAYS GOES TO!
THERE SHOULD BE A SPIRIT IMPRINT.
I'LL INVOKE IT...
SSSHHH

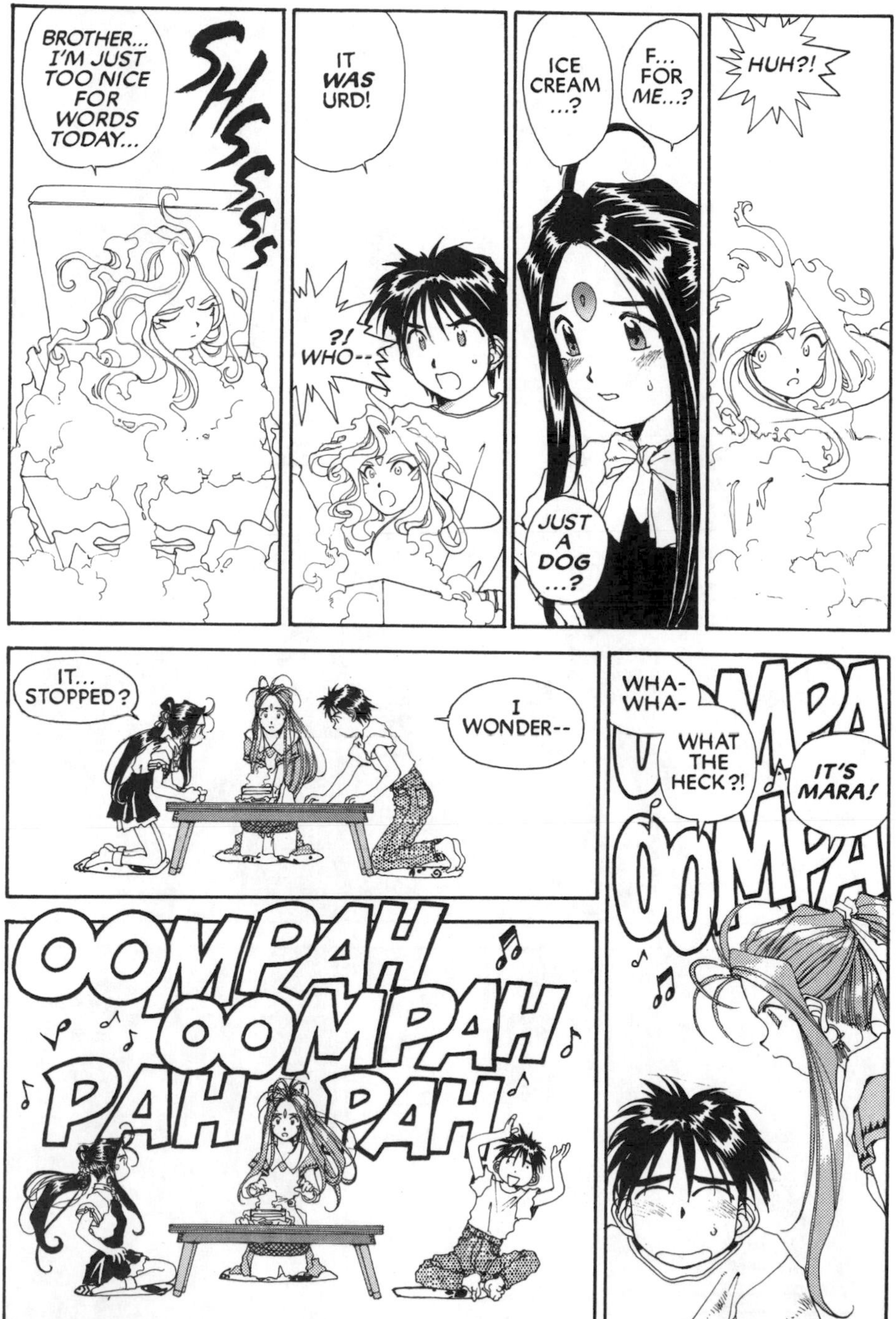
BROTHER... I'M JUST TOO NICE FOR WORDS TODAY...
SHSSSSS
IT WAS URD!
?! WHO--
ICE CREAM ...?
F... FOR ME...?
JUST A DOG ...?
HUH?!
IT... STOPPED?
I WONDER--
OOMPAH OOMPAH PAH PAH
WHA-WHA-
WHAT THE HECK?!
IT'S MARA!
OOMPA OOMPA

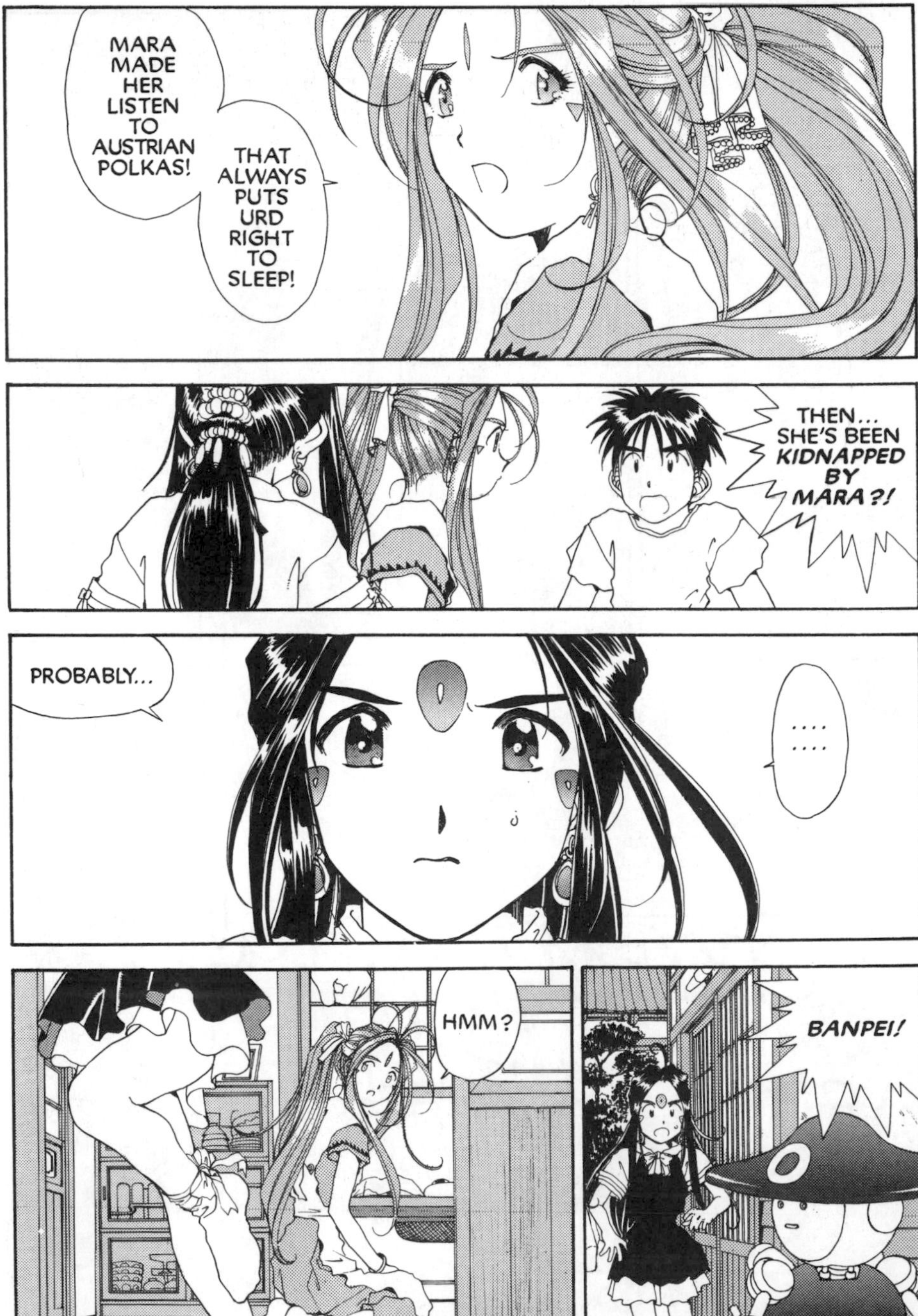
MARA MADE HER LISTEN TO AUSTRIAN POLKAS!
THAT ALWAYS PUTS URD RIGHT TO SLEEP!
THEN... SHE'S BEEN *KIDNAPPED* BY MARA?!
PROBABLY...
....
HMM?
BANPEI!

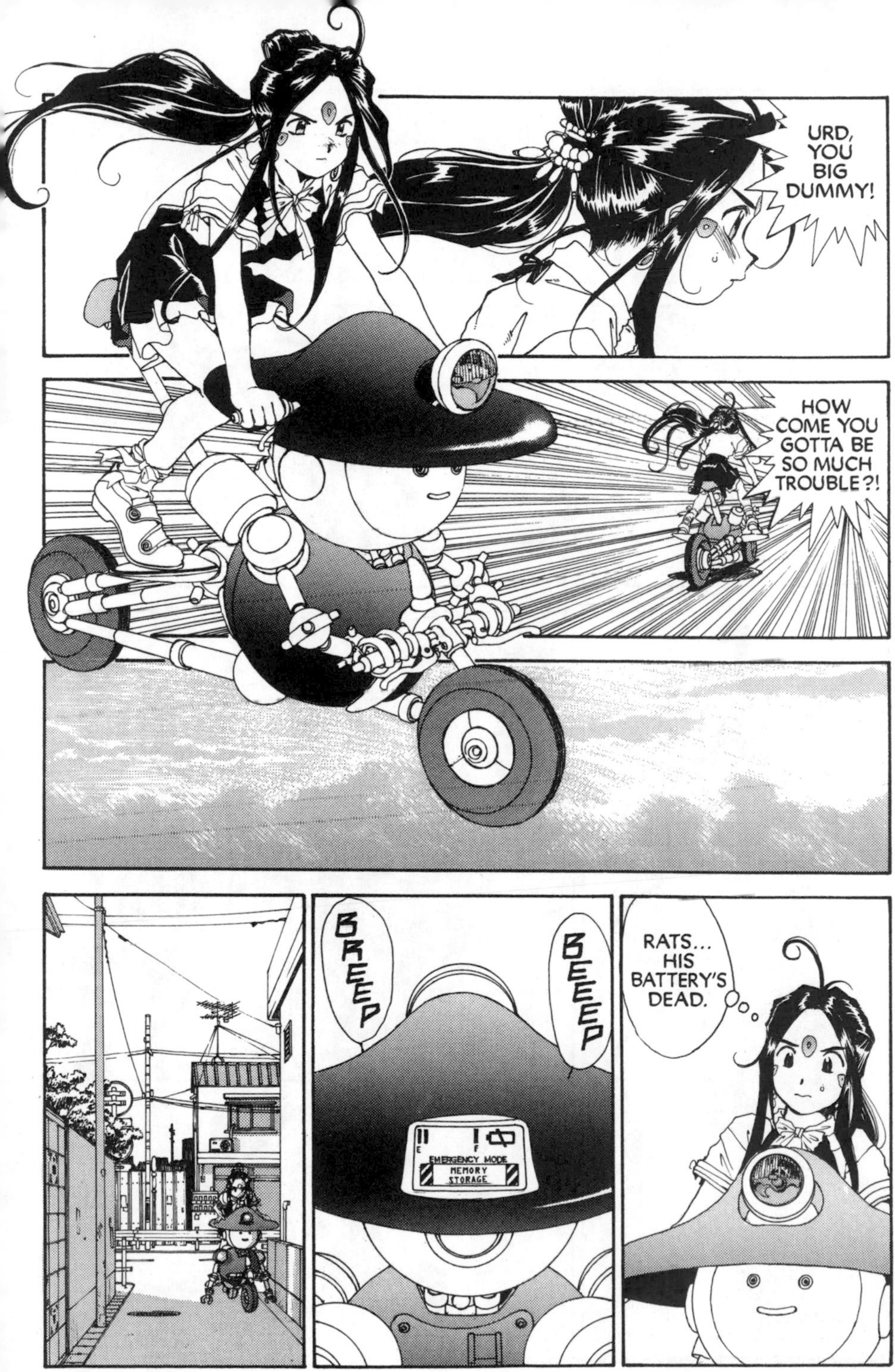
URD, YOU BIG DUMMY!
HOW COME YOU GOTTA BE SO MUCH TROUBLE?!
BREEP
BEEEP
EMERGENCY MODE
MEMORY STORAGE
RATS... HIS BATTERY'S DEAD.

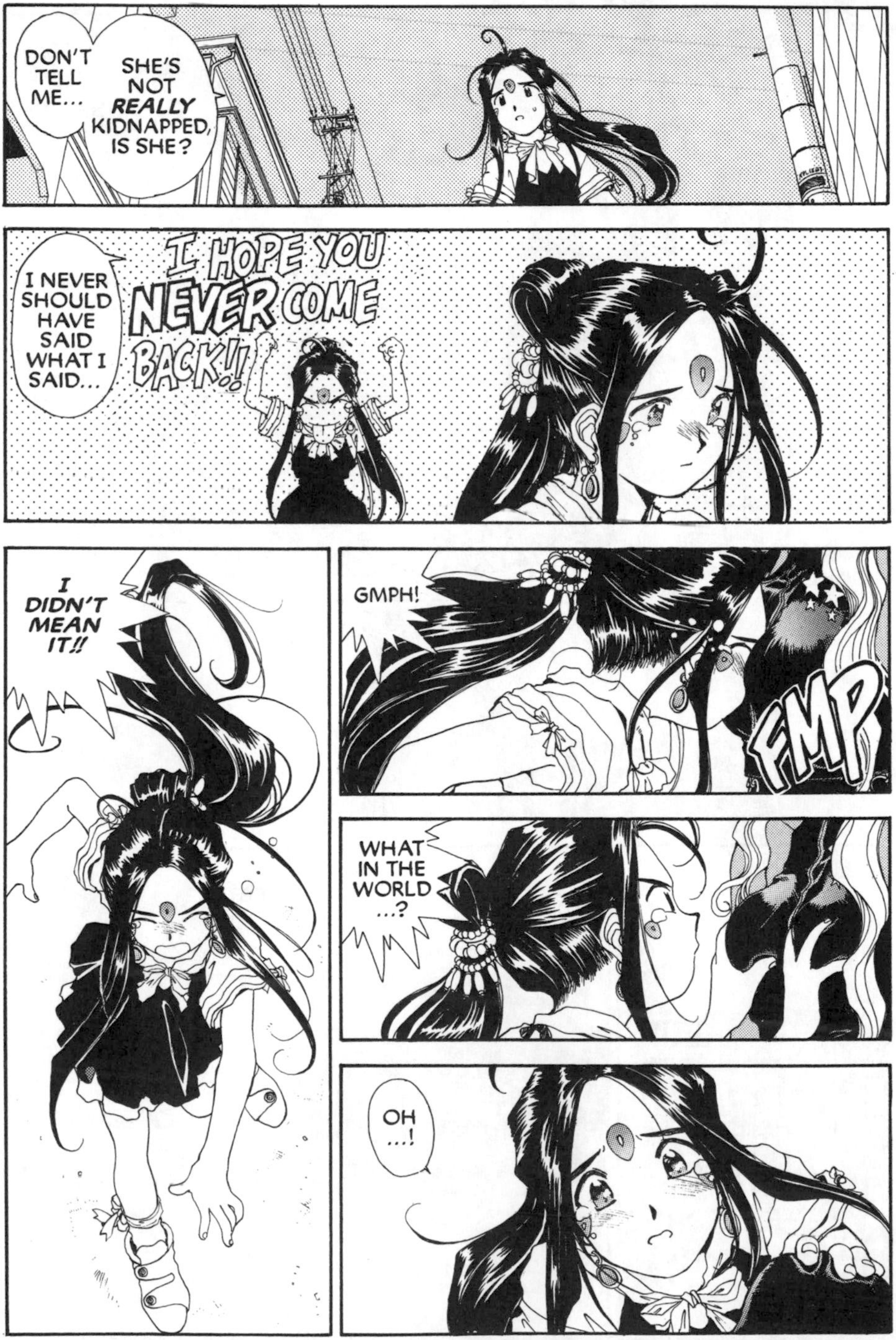
DON'T TELL ME...
SHE'S NOT REALLY KIDNAPPED, IS SHE?
I NEVER SHOULD HAVE SAID WHAT I SAID...
I HOPE YOU NEVER COME BACK!!
I DIDN'T MEAN IT!!
GMPH!
FMP
WHAT IN THE WORLD ...?
OH ...!

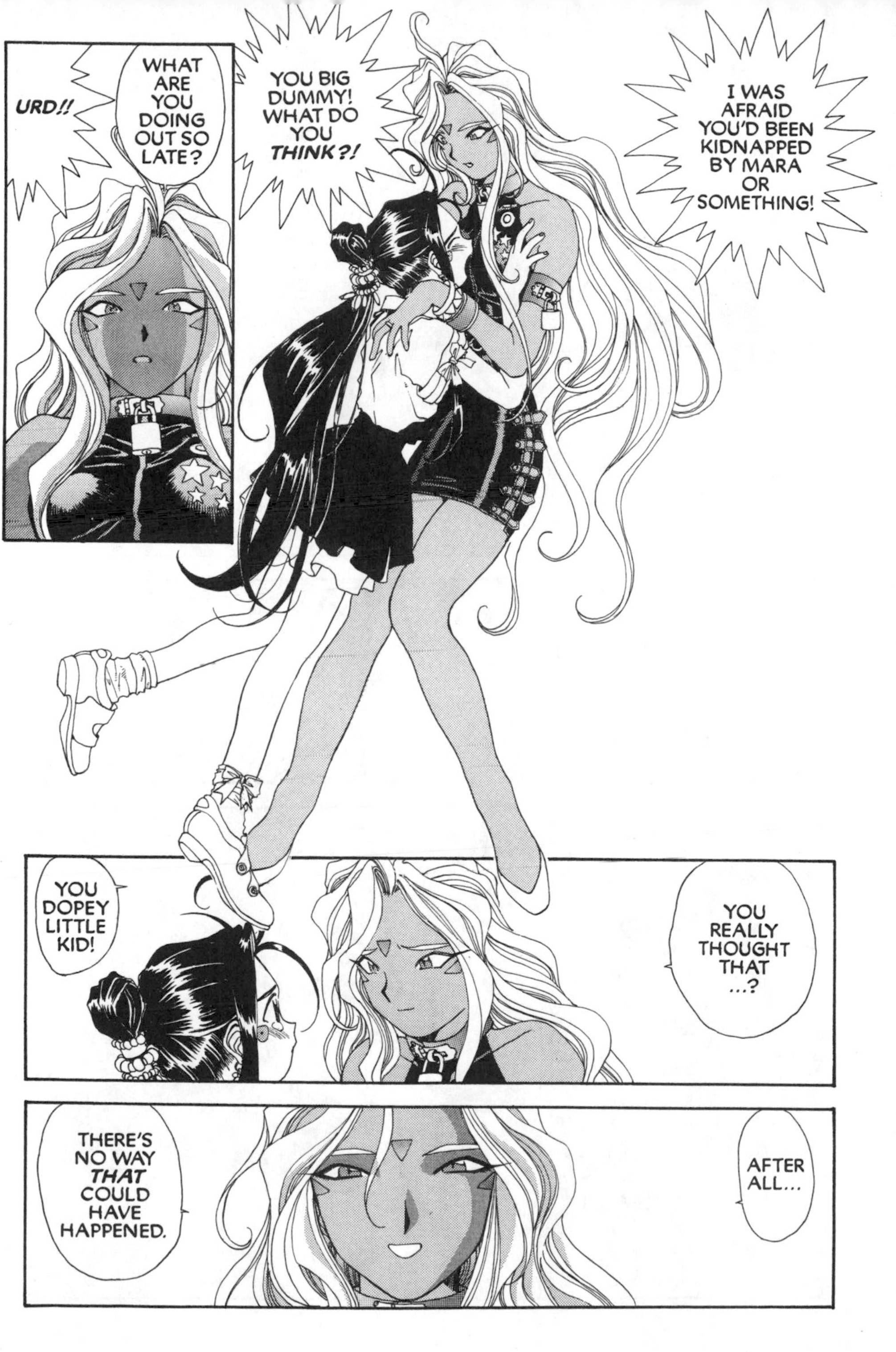
URD!!
WHAT ARE YOU DOING OUT SO LATE?
YOU BIG DUMMY! WHAT DO YOU *THINK?!*
I WAS AFRAID YOU'D BEEN KIDNAPPED BY MARA OR SOMETHING!
YOU DOPEY LITTLE KID!
YOU REALLY THOUGHT THAT ...?
THERE'S NO WAY *THAT* COULD HAVE HAPPENED.
AFTER ALL...

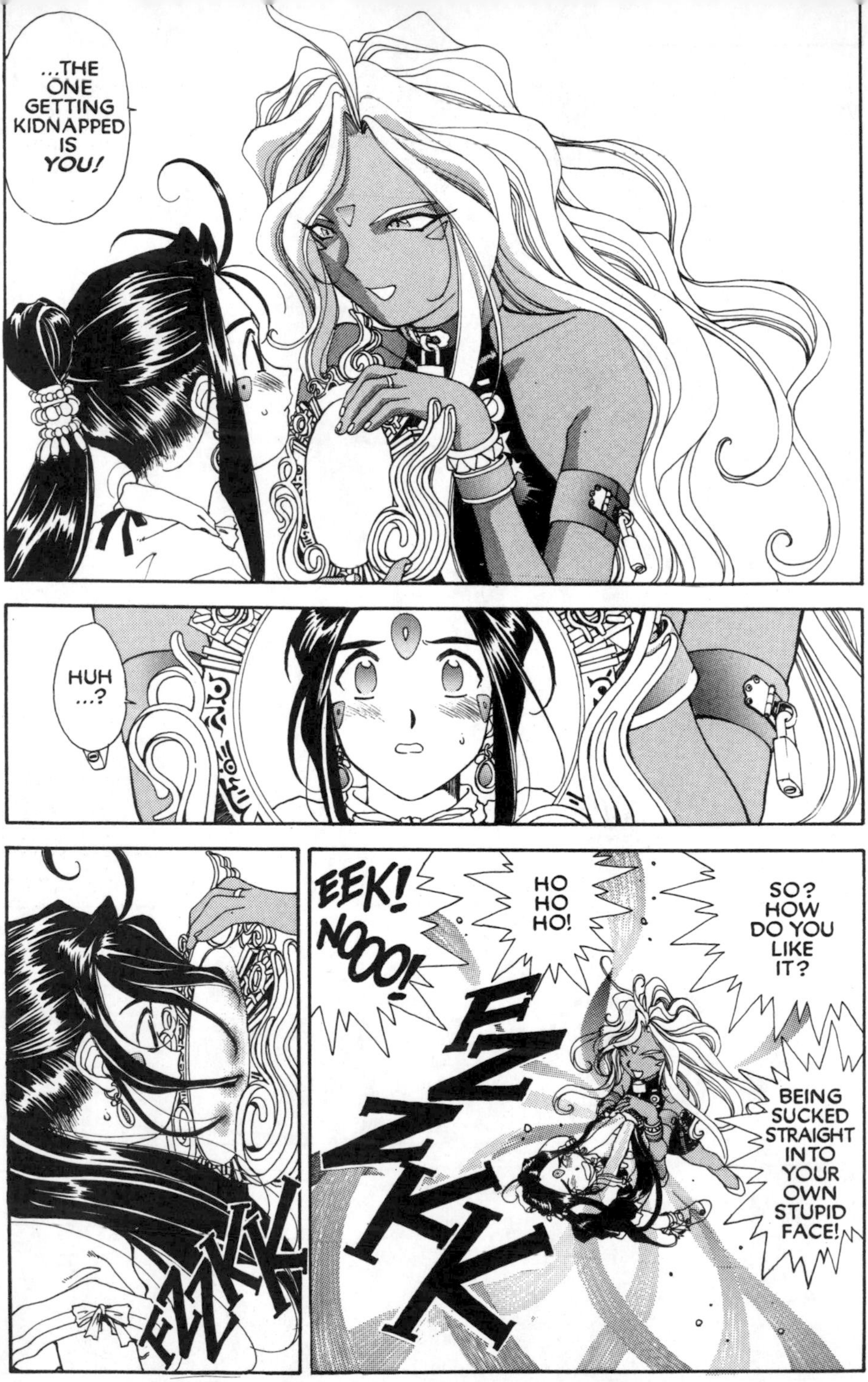
...THE ONE GETTING KIDNAPPED IS YOU!
HUH ...?
FZZKK
EEK! NOOO!
HO HO HO!
SO? HOW DO YOU LIKE IT?
BEING SUCKED STRAIGHT INTO YOUR OWN STUPID FACE!
FZZKK

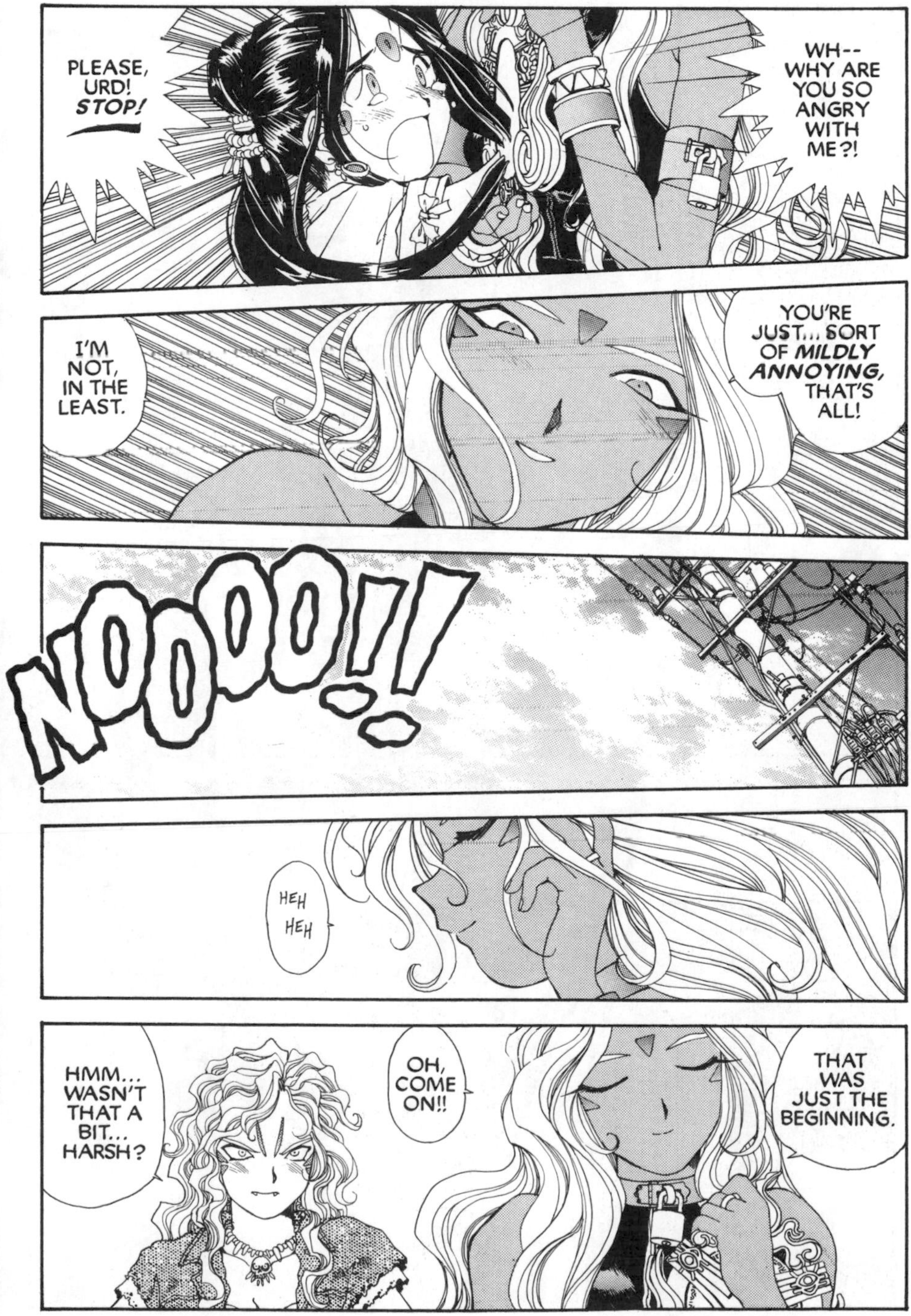
PLEASE, URD! STOP!
WH-- WHY ARE YOU SO ANGRY WITH ME?!
I'M NOT, IN THE LEAST.
YOU'RE JUST... SORT OF MILDLY ANNOYING, THAT'S ALL!
NOOOO!!
HEH HEH
HMM... WASN'T THAT A BIT... HARSH?
OH, COME ON!!
THAT WAS JUST THE BEGINNING.

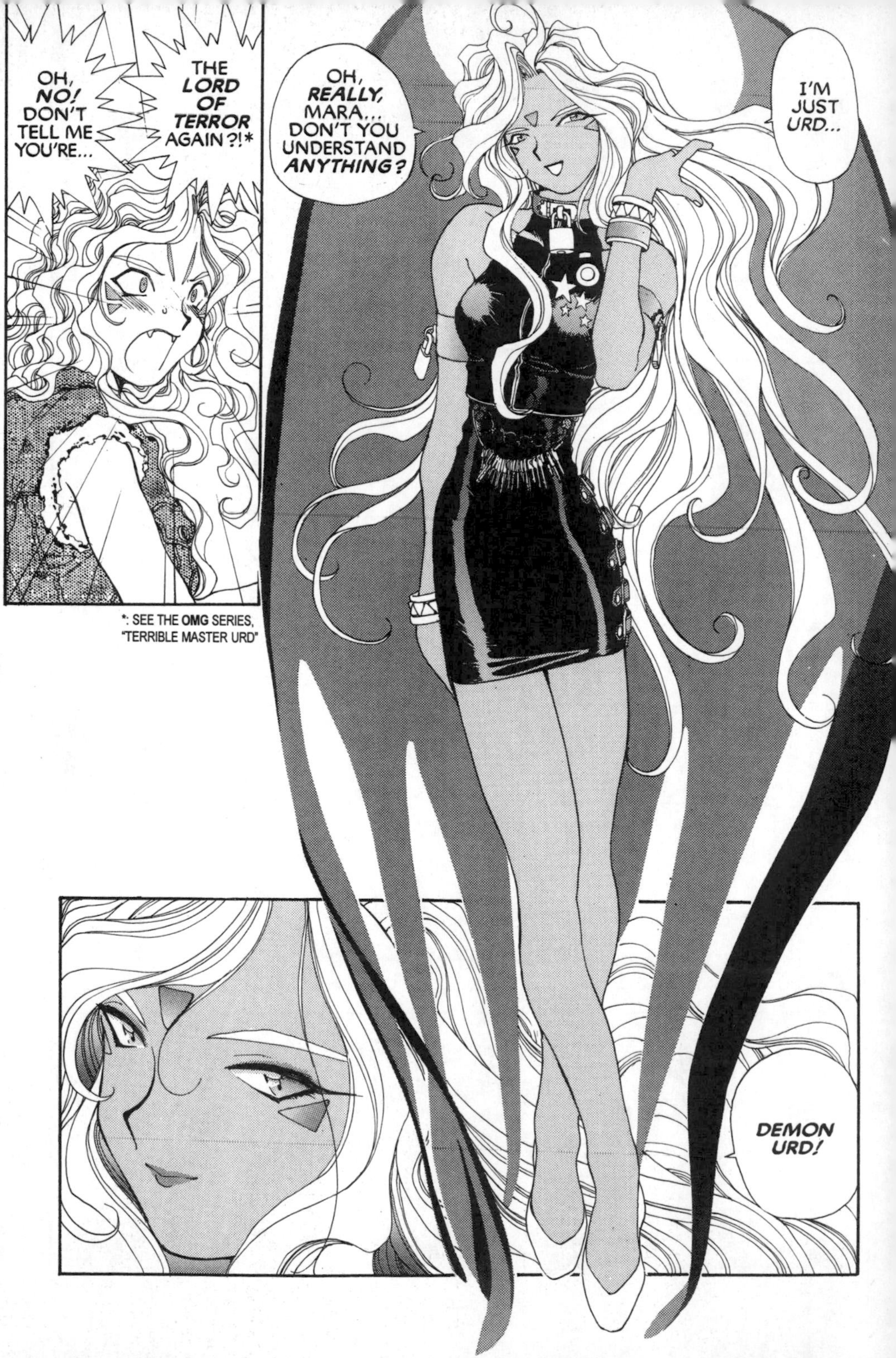
OH, NO! DON'T TELL ME YOU'RE...
THE LORD OF TERROR AGAIN?!*
OH, REALLY, MARA... DON'T YOU UNDERSTAND ANYTHING?
I'M JUST URD...
DEMON URD!

*: SEE THE OMG SERIES, "TERRIBLE MASTER URD"

SKULD STRIKES BACK!

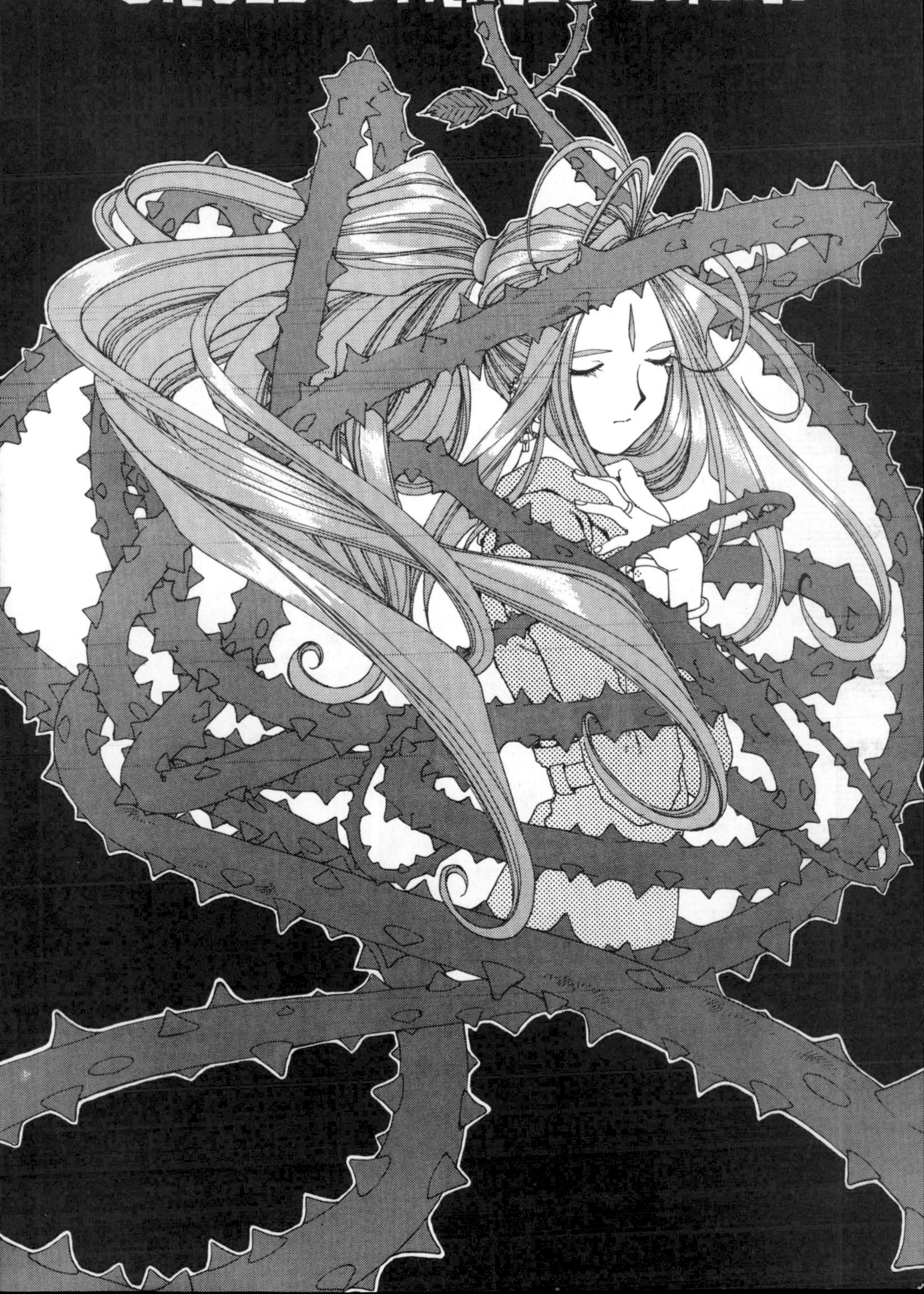

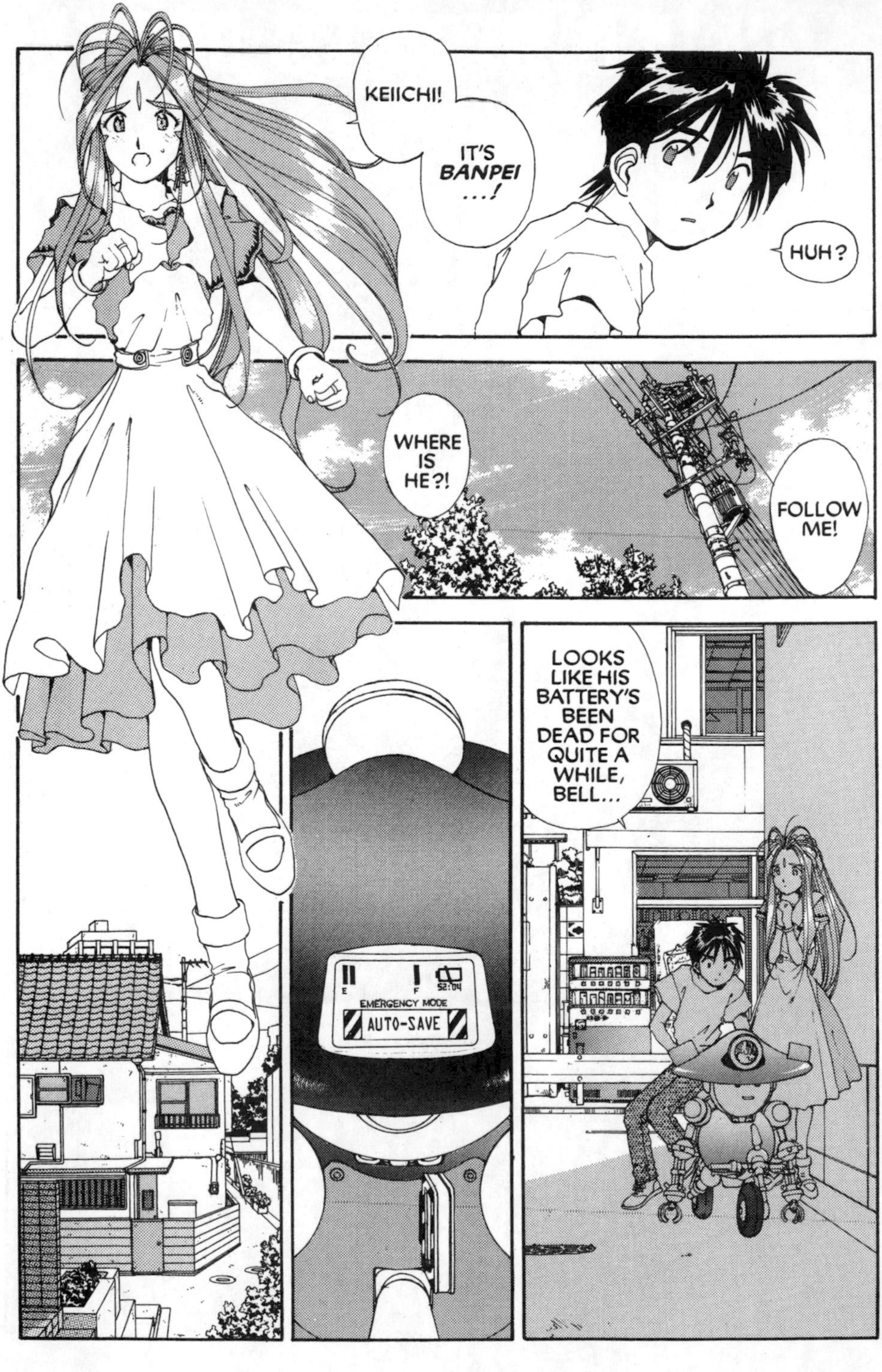
KEIICHI!
IT'S BANPEI ...!
HUH?
WHERE IS HE?!
FOLLOW ME!
EMERGENCY MODE
AUTO-SAVE
LOOKS LIKE HIS BATTERY'S BEEN DEAD FOR QUITE A WHILE, BELL...

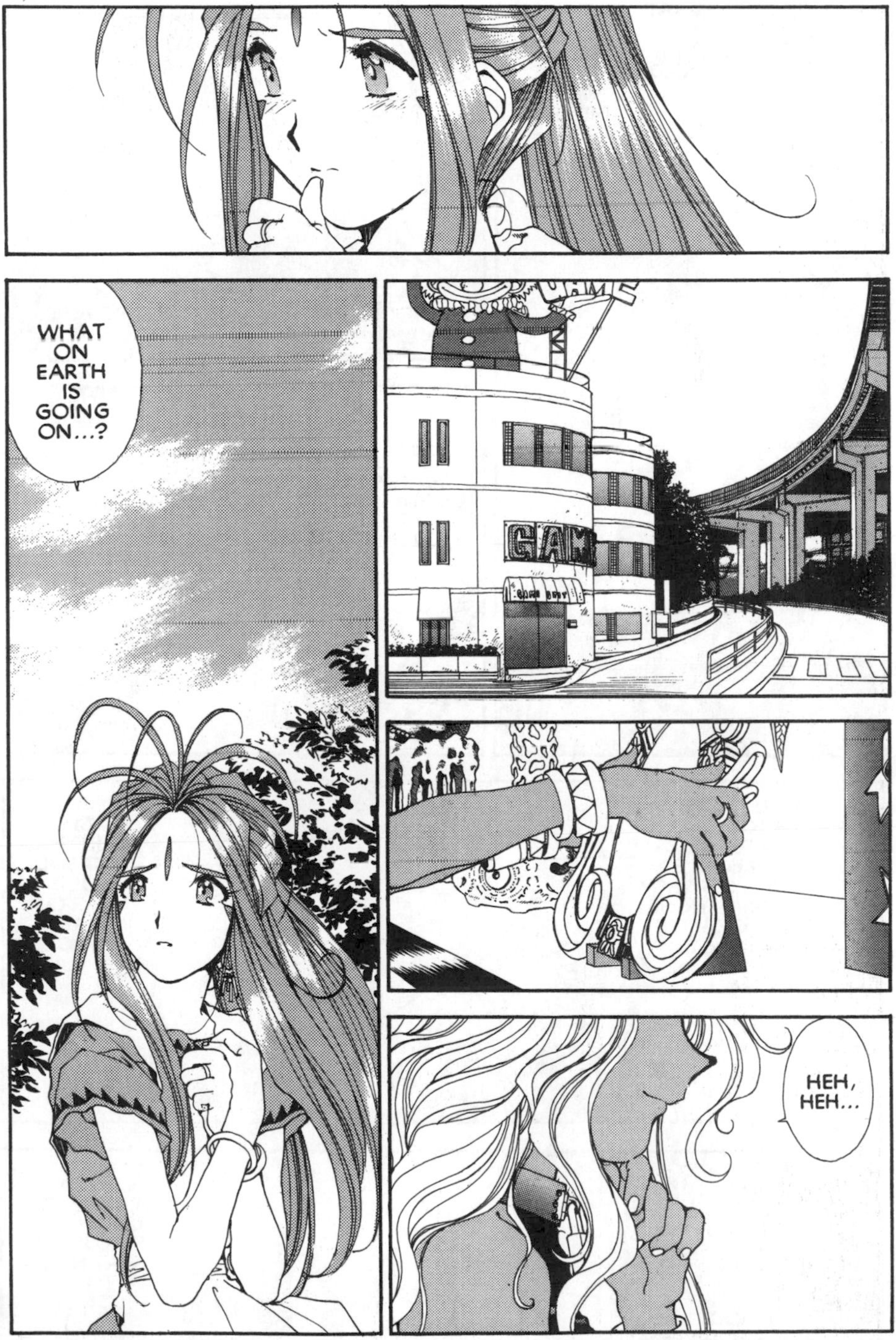
WHAT ON EARTH IS GOING ON...?
HEH, HEH...

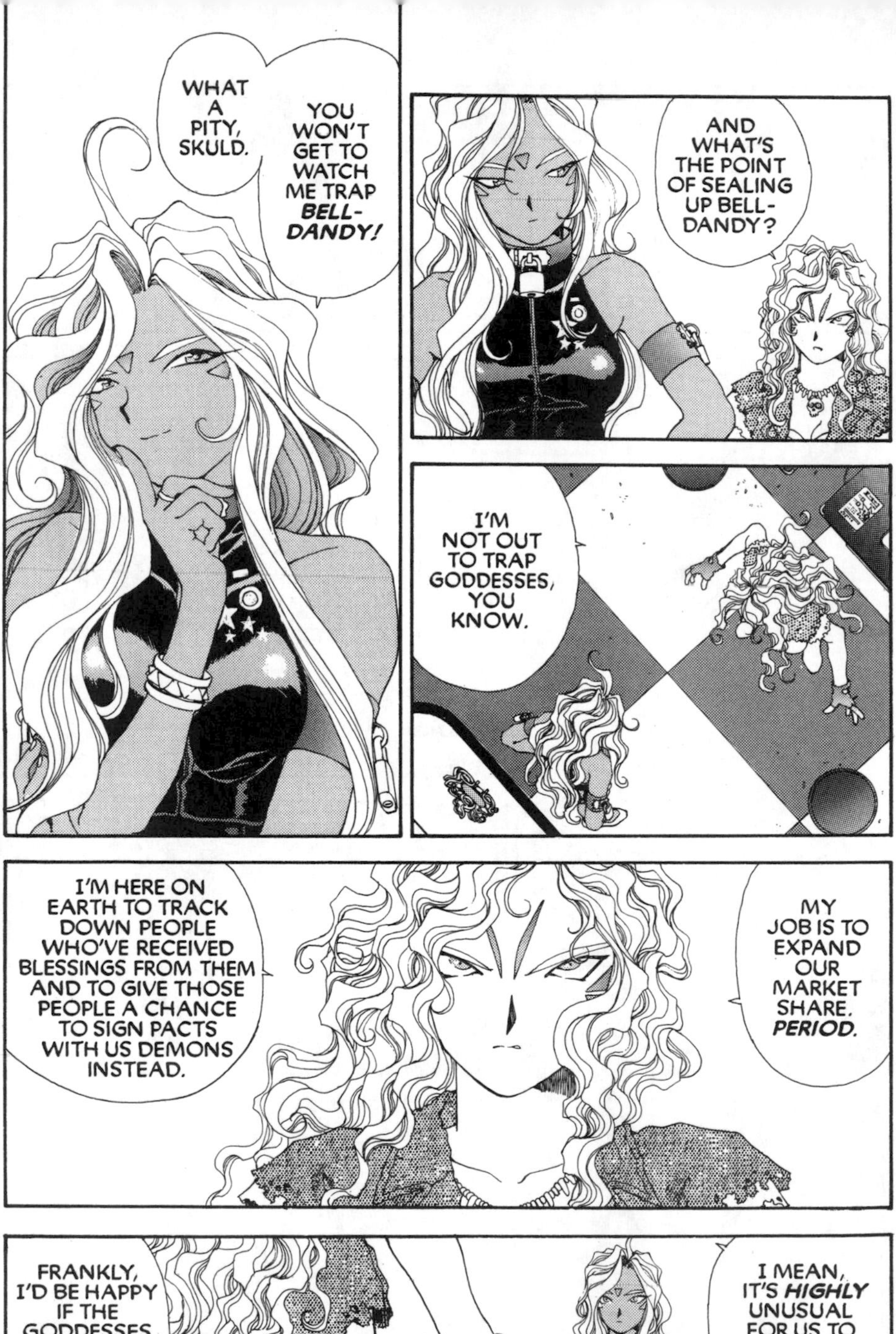
WHAT A PITY, SKULD.
YOU WON'T GET TO WATCH ME TRAP ***BELL-DANDY!***
AND WHAT'S THE POINT OF SEALING UP BELL-DANDY?
I'M NOT OUT TO TRAP GODDESSES, YOU KNOW.
I'M HERE ON EARTH TO TRACK DOWN PEOPLE WHO'VE RECEIVED BLESSINGS FROM THEM AND TO GIVE THOSE PEOPLE A CHANCE TO SIGN PACTS WITH US DEMONS INSTEAD.
MY JOB IS TO EXPAND OUR MARKET SHARE. ***PERIOD.***
FRANKLY, I'D BE HAPPY IF THE GODDESSES PACKED UP AND WENT HOME.
I MEAN, IT'S ***HIGHLY*** UNUSUAL FOR US TO STAY HERE THIS LONG!

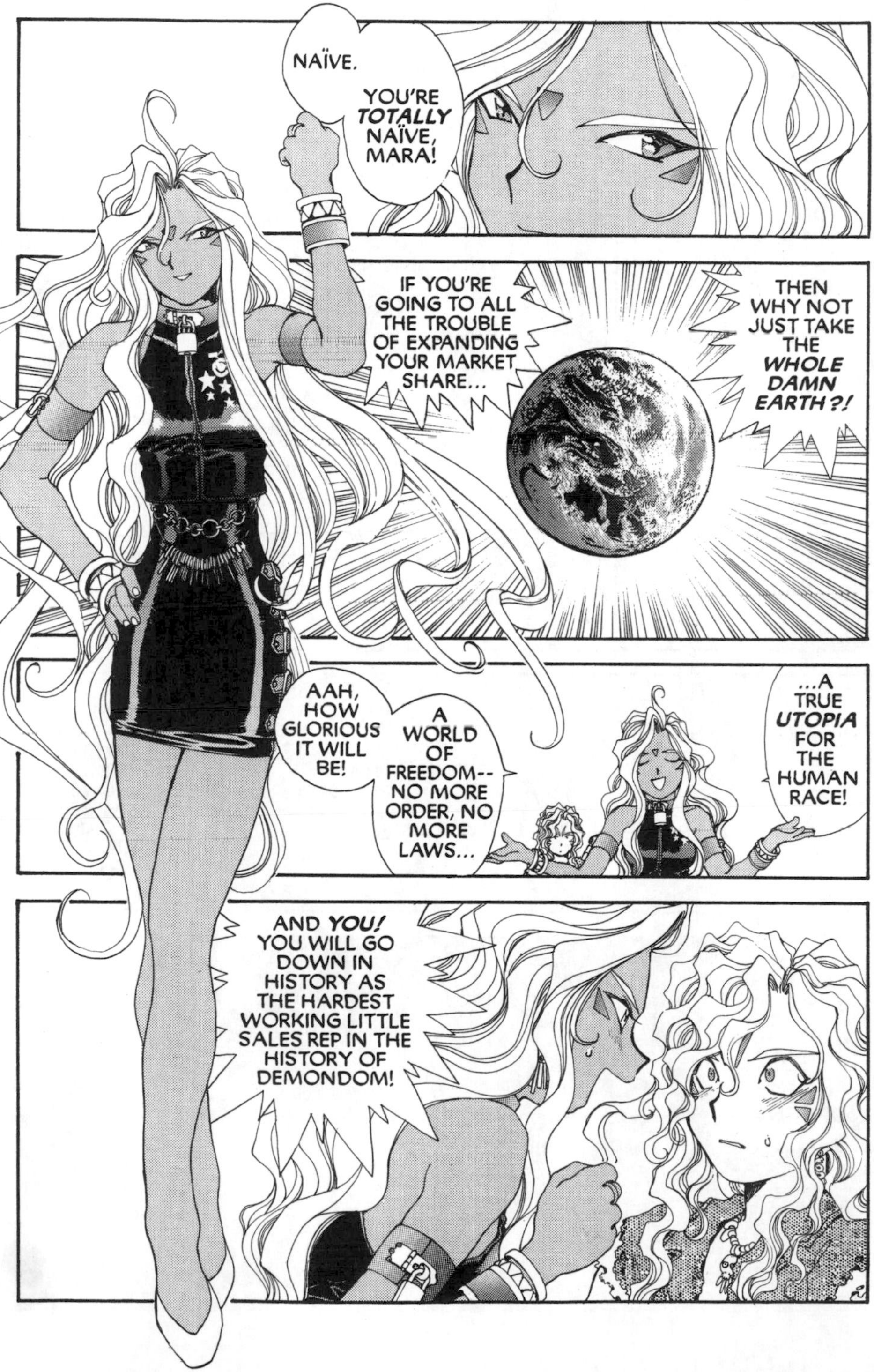
NAÏVE.
YOU'RE *TOTALLY* NAÏVE, MARA!
IF YOU'RE GOING TO ALL THE TROUBLE OF EXPANDING YOUR MARKET SHARE...
THEN WHY NOT JUST TAKE THE *WHOLE DAMN EARTH?!*
AAH, HOW GLORIOUS IT WILL BE!
A WORLD OF FREEDOM-- NO MORE ORDER, NO MORE LAWS...
...A TRUE *UTOPIA* FOR THE HUMAN RACE!
AND *YOU!* YOU WILL GO DOWN IN HISTORY AS THE HARDEST WORKING LITTLE SALES REP IN THE HISTORY OF DEMONDOM!

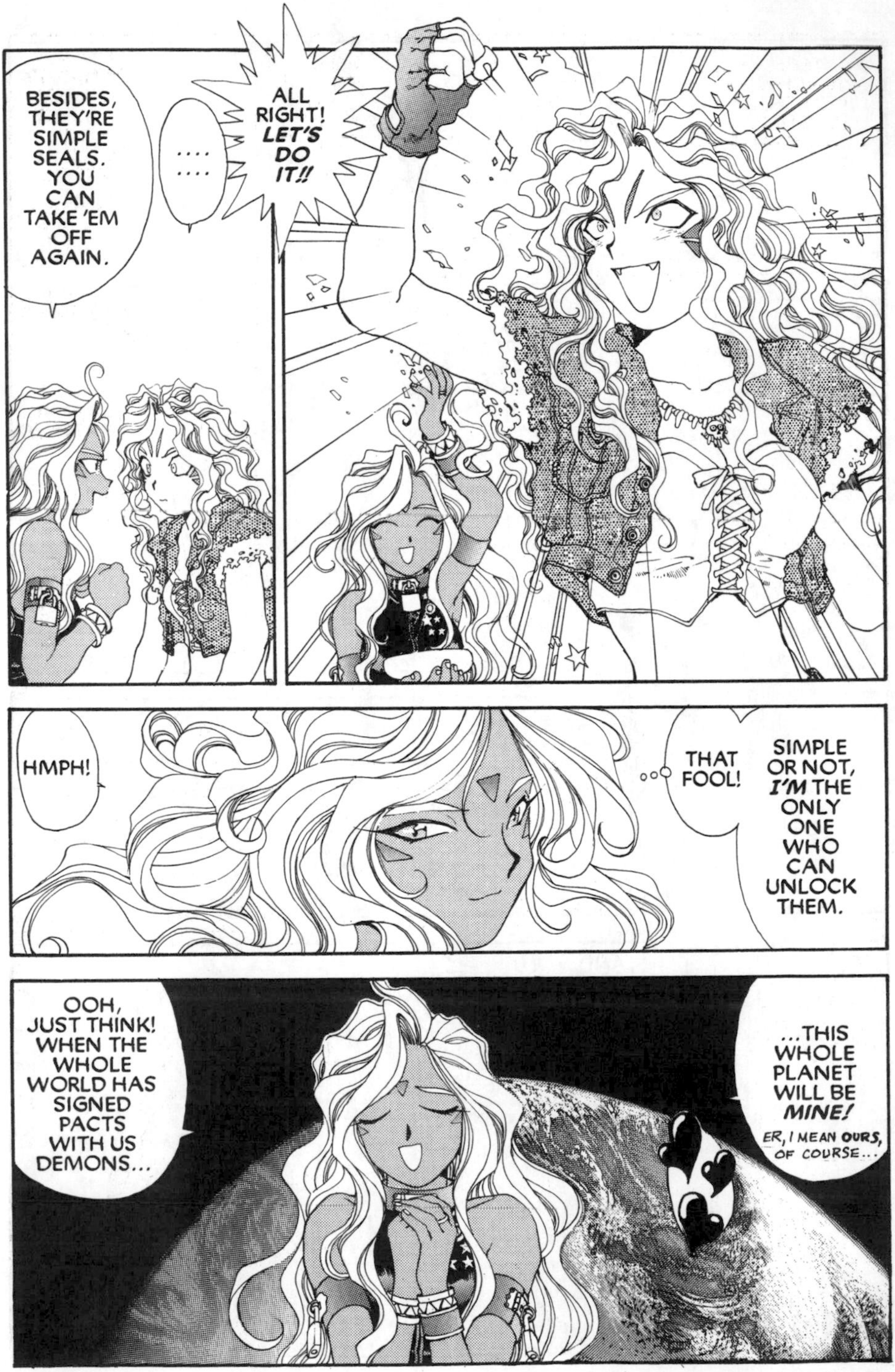
BESIDES, THEY'RE SIMPLE SEALS. YOU CAN TAKE 'EM OFF AGAIN.
....
ALL RIGHT! LET'S DO IT!!
HMPH!
THAT FOOL!
SIMPLE OR NOT, I'M THE ONLY ONE WHO CAN UNLOCK THEM.
OOH, JUST THINK! WHEN THE WHOLE WORLD HAS SIGNED PACTS WITH US DEMONS...
...THIS WHOLE PLANET WILL BE MINE!
ER, I MEAN OURS, OF COURSE...

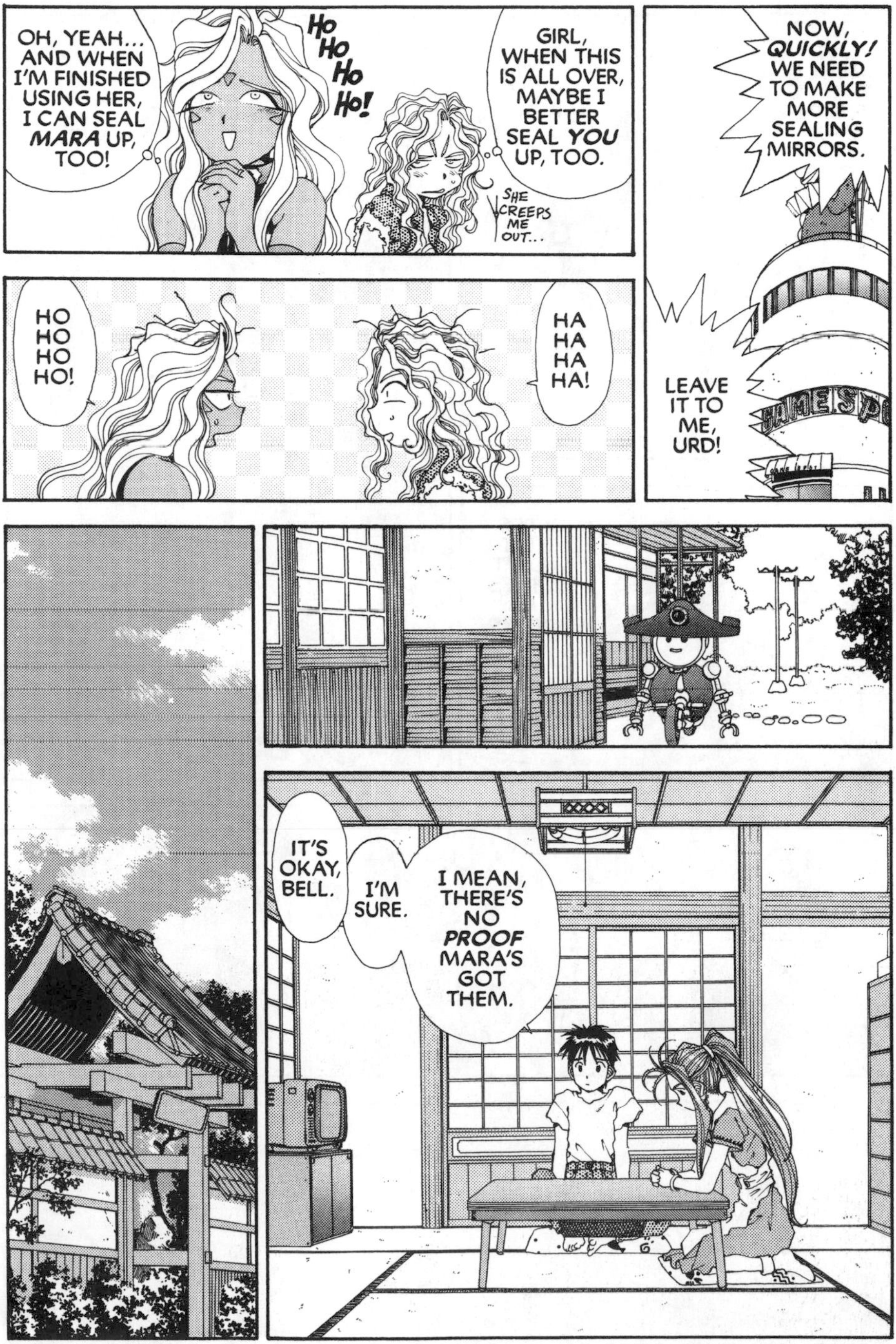
OH, YEAH... AND WHEN I'M FINISHED USING HER, I CAN SEAL MARA UP, TOO!
HO HO HO HO!
GIRL, WHEN THIS IS ALL OVER, MAYBE I BETTER SEAL YOU UP, TOO.
SHE CREEPS ME OUT...
HO HO HO HO!
HA HA HA HA!
NOW, QUICKLY! WE NEED TO MAKE MORE SEALING MIRRORS.
LEAVE IT TO ME, URD!
IT'S OKAY, BELL.
I'M SURE.
I MEAN, THERE'S NO PROOF MARA'S GOT THEM.

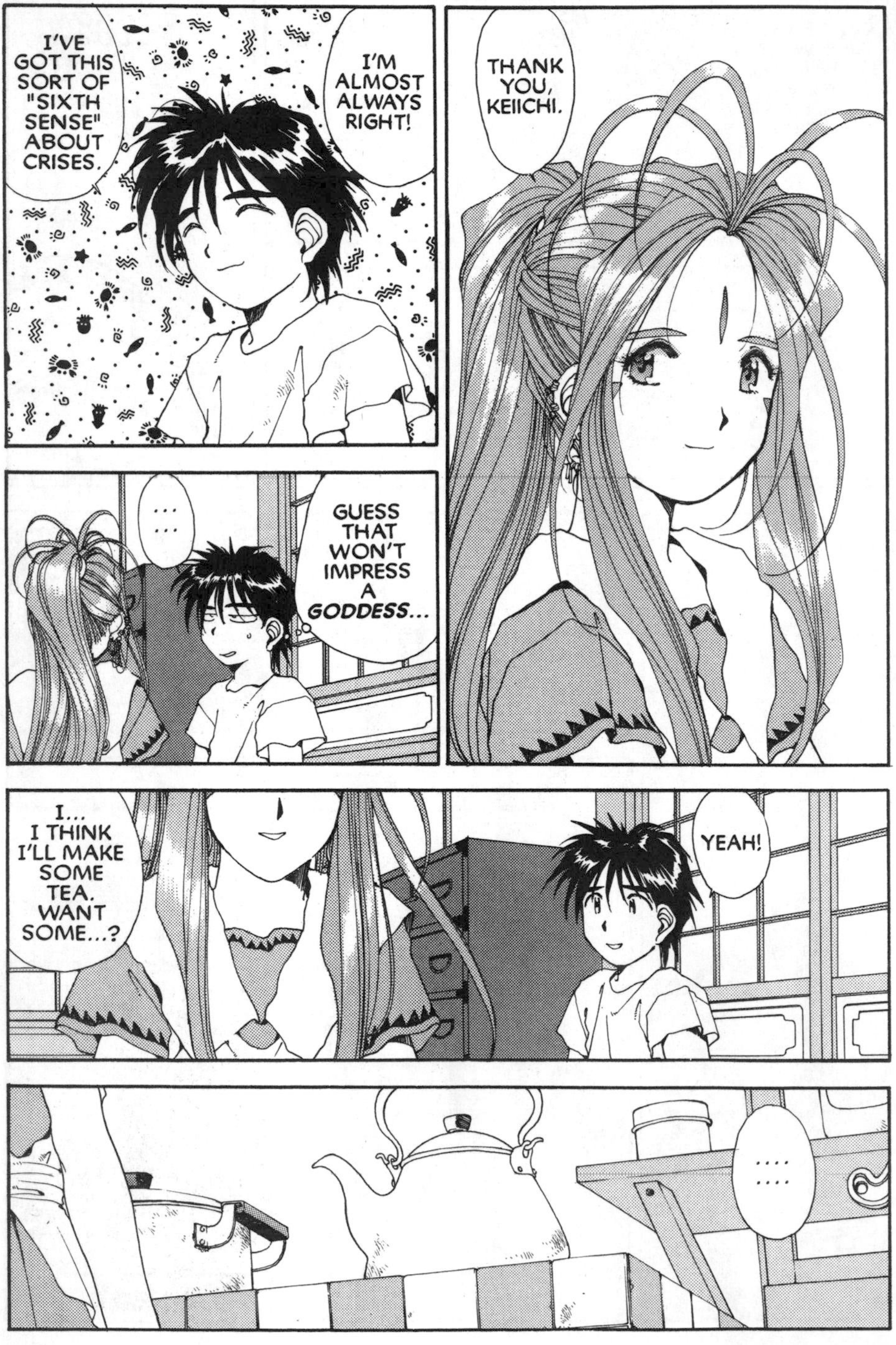
I'VE GOT THIS SORT OF "SIXTH SENSE" ABOUT CRISES.
I'M ALMOST ALWAYS RIGHT!
....
GUESS THAT WON'T IMPRESS A *GODDESS*...
THANK YOU, KEIICHI.
I... I THINK I'LL MAKE SOME TEA. WANT SOME...?
YEAH!
....

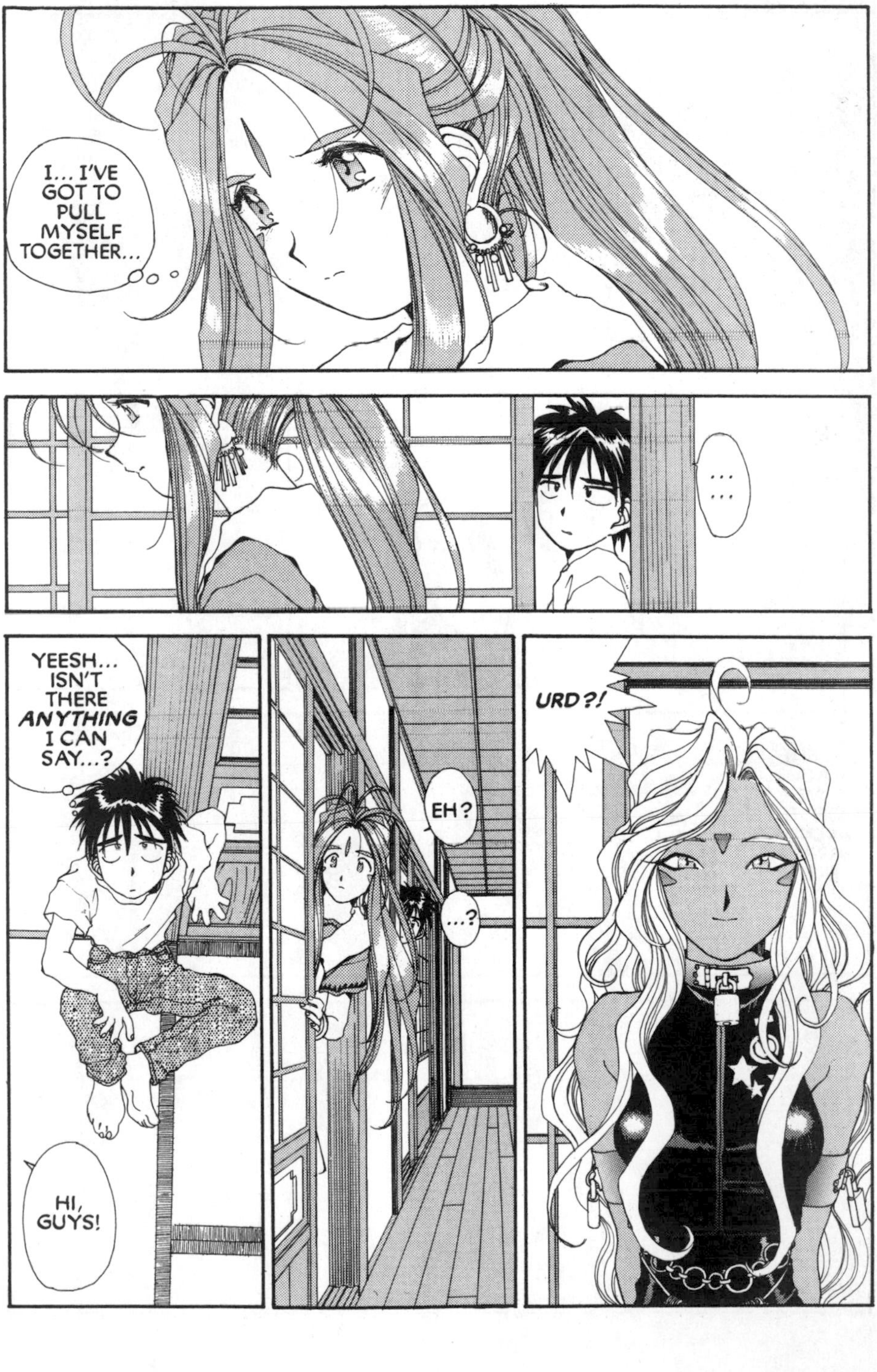
I... I'VE GOT TO PULL MYSELF TOGETHER...
... ...
YEESH... ISN'T THERE *ANYTHING* I CAN SAY...?
HI, GUYS!
EH?
...?
URD?!

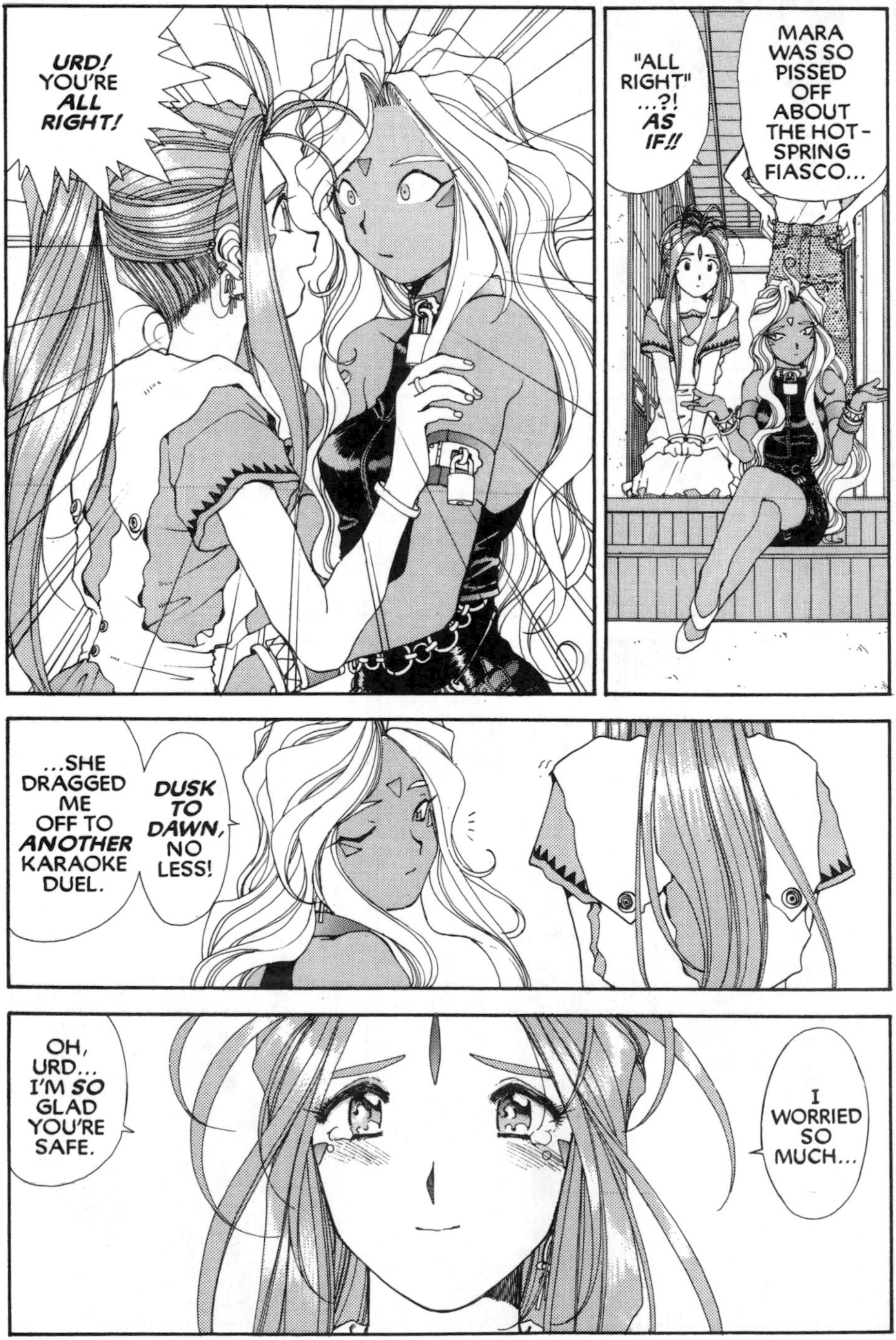

URD! YOU'RE ALL RIGHT!
"ALL RIGHT" ...?! AS IF!!
MARA WAS SO PISSED OFF ABOUT THE HOT-SPRING FIASCO...
...SHE DRAGGED ME OFF TO ANOTHER KARAOKE DUEL.
DUSK TO DAWN, NO LESS!
OH, URD... I'M SO GLAD YOU'RE SAFE.
I WORRIED SO MUCH...

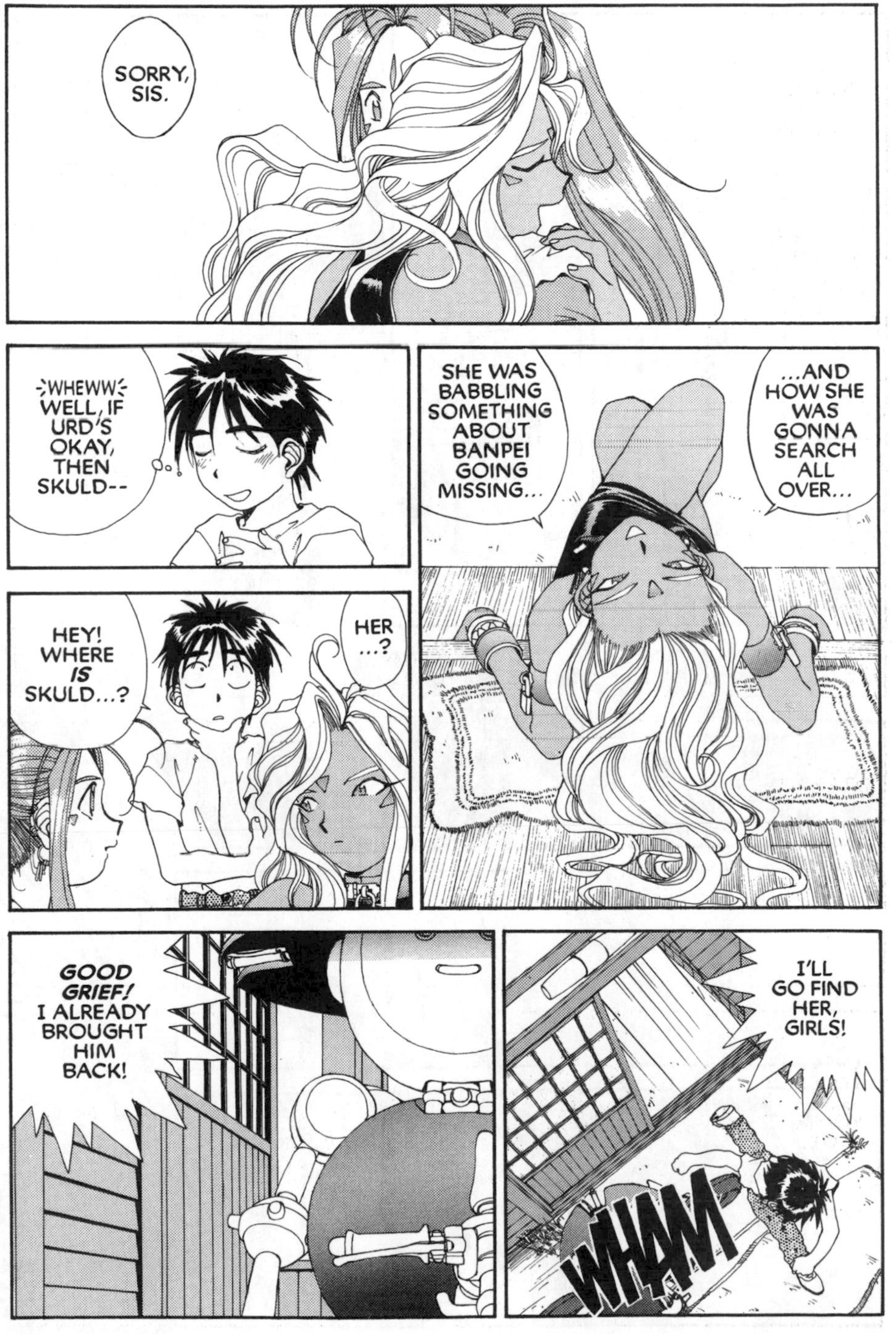
SORRY, SIS.
WHEWW WELL, IF URD'S OKAY, THEN SKULD--
SHE WAS BABBLING SOMETHING ABOUT BANPEI GOING MISSING...
...AND HOW SHE WAS GONNA SEARCH ALL OVER...
HEY! WHERE *IS* SKULD...?
HER ...?
GOOD GRIEF! I ALREADY BROUGHT HIM BACK!
I'LL GO FIND HER, GIRLS!
WHAM

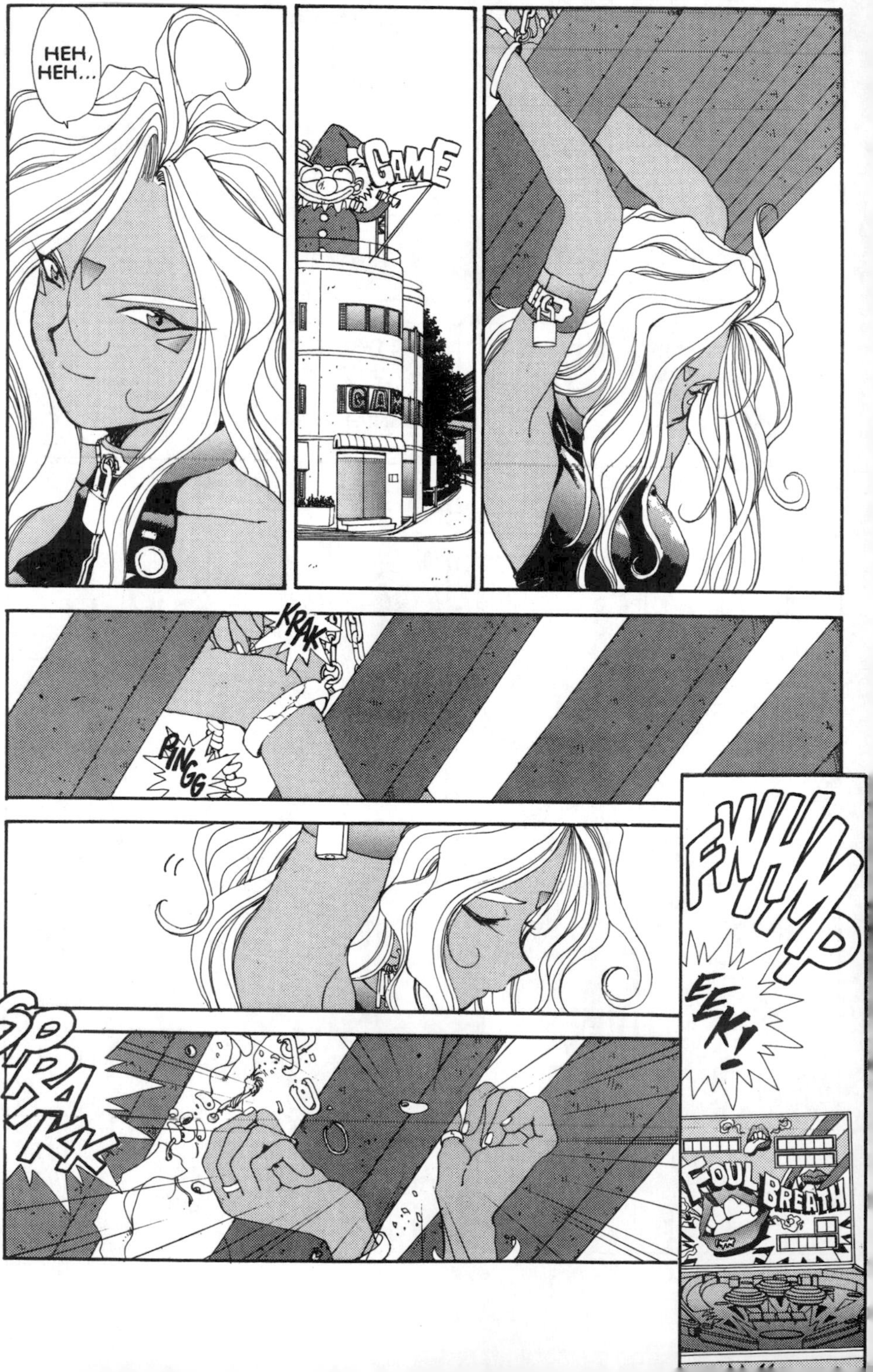
HEH,
HEH...
GAME
GAM
KRAK
PINGG
FWHMP
EEK!
SPRAKK
FOUL BREATH

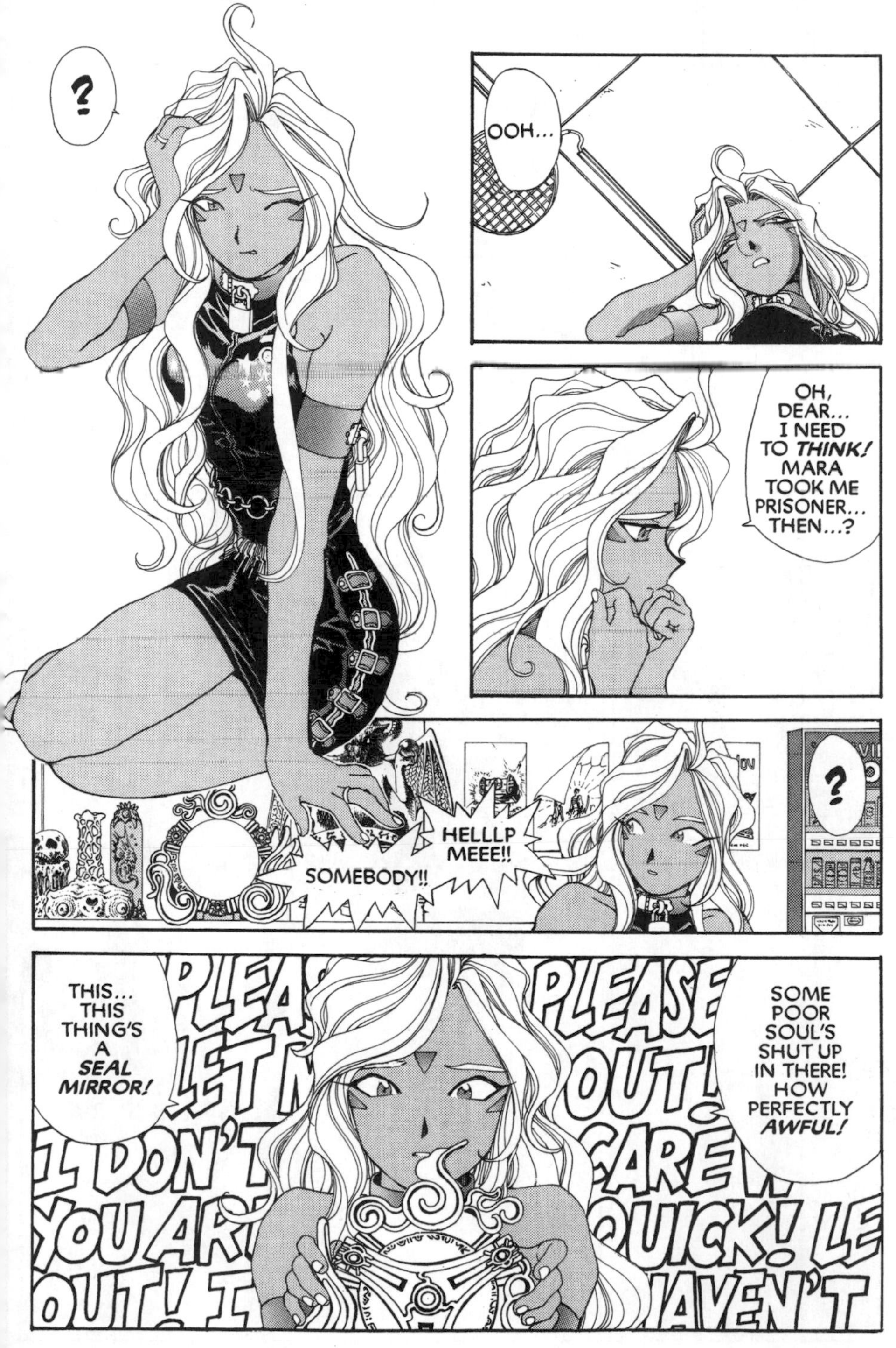
?
OOH...
OH, DEAR... I NEED TO *THINK!* MARA TOOK ME PRISONER... THEN...?
HELLLP MEEE!!
SOMEBODY!!
?
THIS... THIS THING'S A *SEAL MIRROR!*
PLEASE
SOME POOR SOUL'S SHUT UP IN THERE! HOW PERFECTLY *AWFUL!*
QUICK!

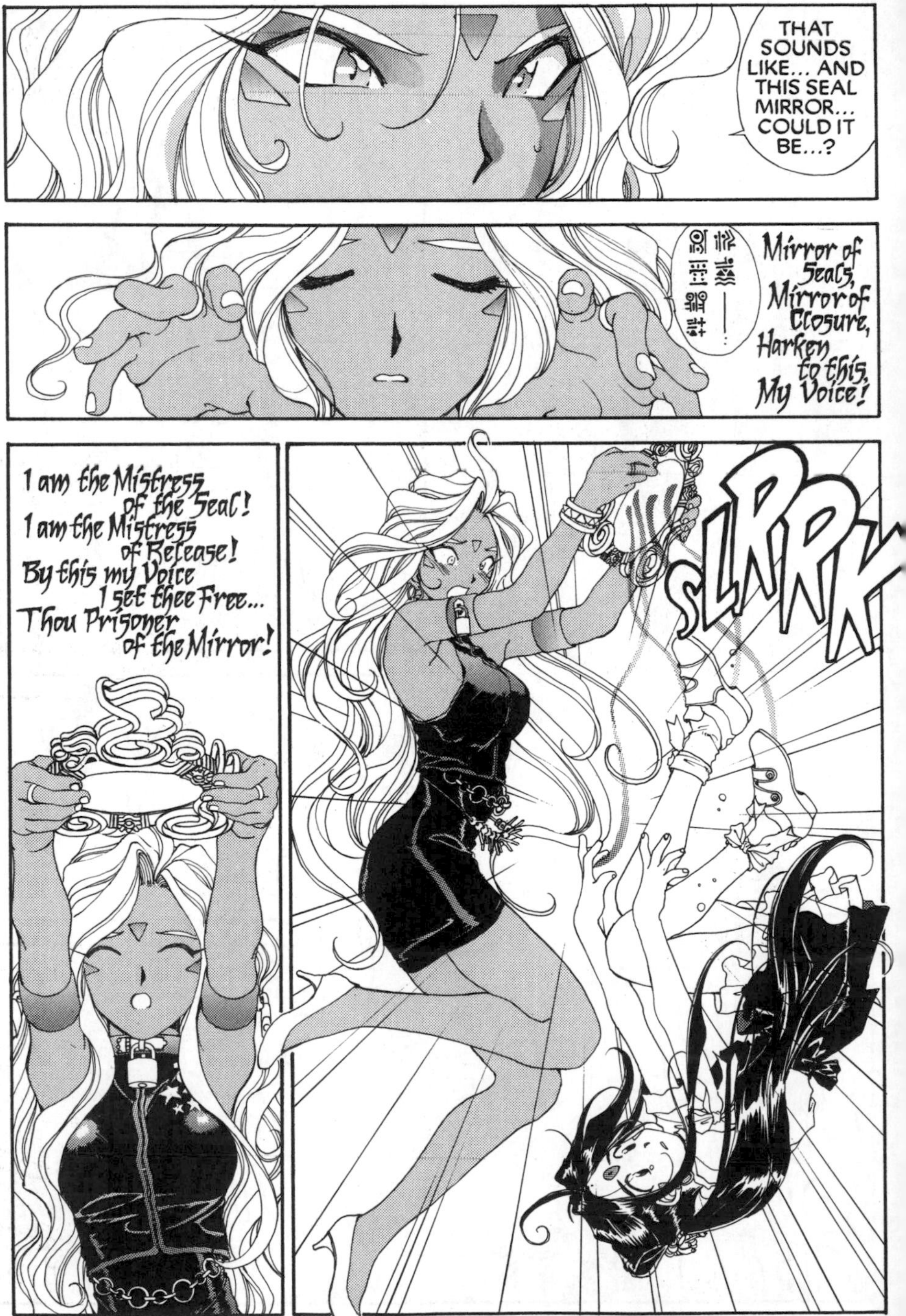
THAT SOUNDS LIKE... AND THIS SEAL MIRROR... COULD IT BE...?
Mirror of Seals, Mirror of Closure, Harken to this, My Voice!
I am the Mistress of the Seal! I am the Mistress of Release! By this my Voice I set thee Free... Thou Prisoner of the Mirror!
SLRRK

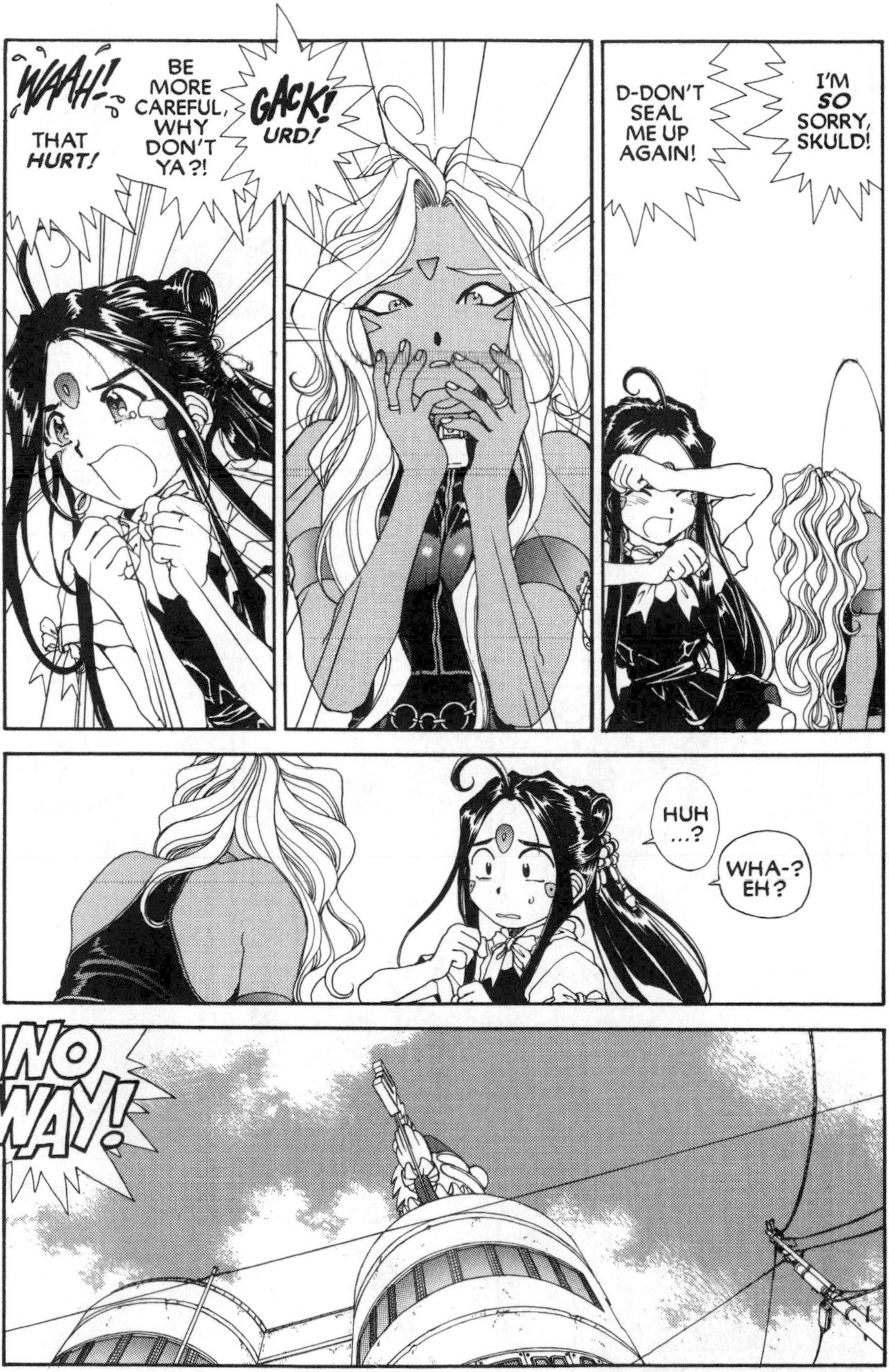
WAAH!
THAT HURT!
BE MORE CAREFUL, WHY DON'T YA?!
GACK! URD!
D-DON'T SEAL ME UP AGAIN!
I'M SO SORRY, SKULD!
HUH ...?
WHA-? EH?
NO WAY!

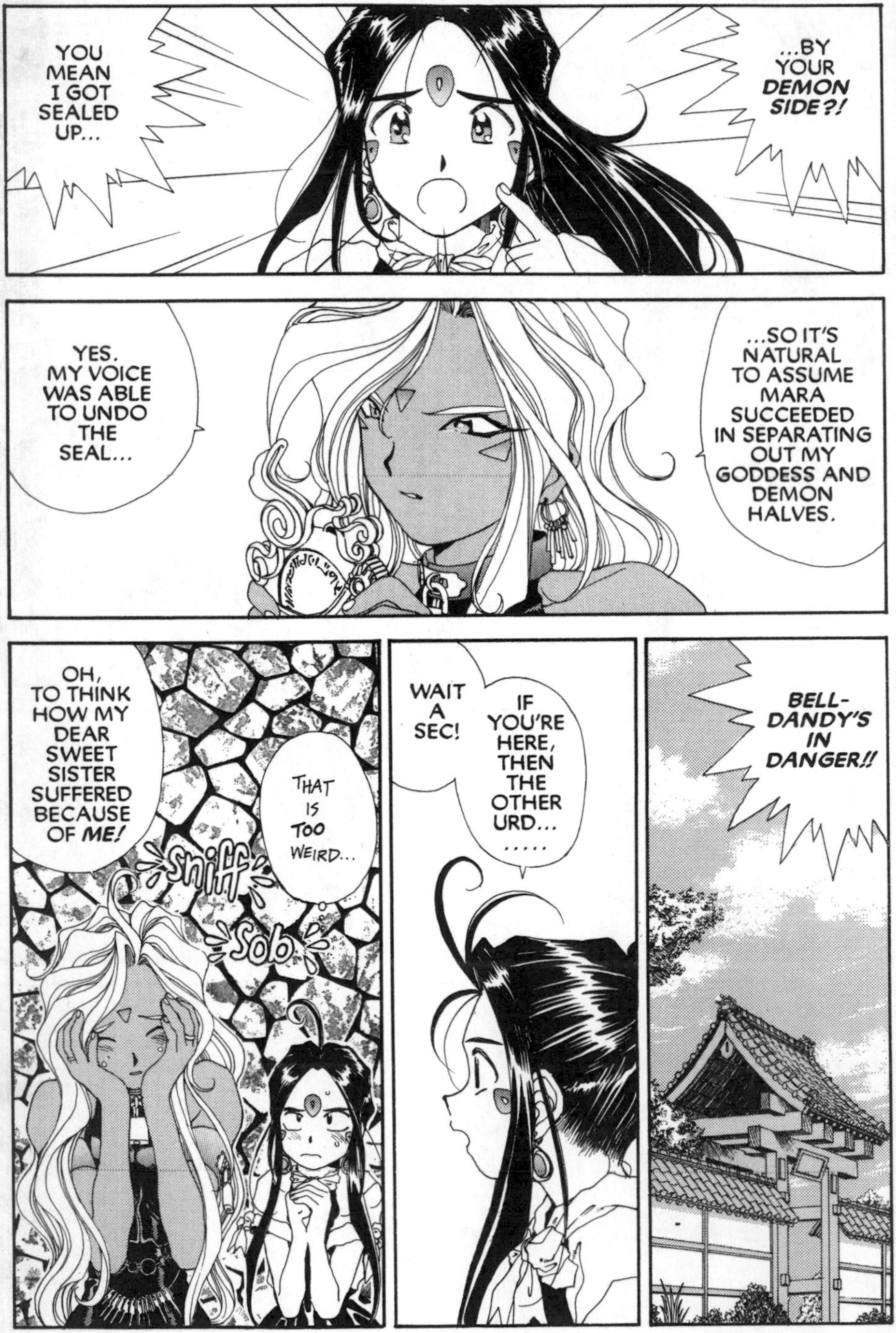
YOU MEAN I GOT SEALED UP...
...BY YOUR ***DEMON SIDE?!***
YES. MY VOICE WAS ABLE TO UNDO THE SEAL...
...SO IT'S NATURAL TO ASSUME MARA SUCCEEDED IN SEPARATING OUT MY GODDESS AND DEMON HALVES.
OH, TO THINK HOW MY DEAR SWEET SISTER SUFFERED BECAUSE OF ***ME!***
THAT IS **TOO** WEIRD...
sniff
sob
WAIT A SEC!
IF YOU'RE HERE, THEN THE OTHER URD...
.....
BELL-DANDY'S IN DANGER!!

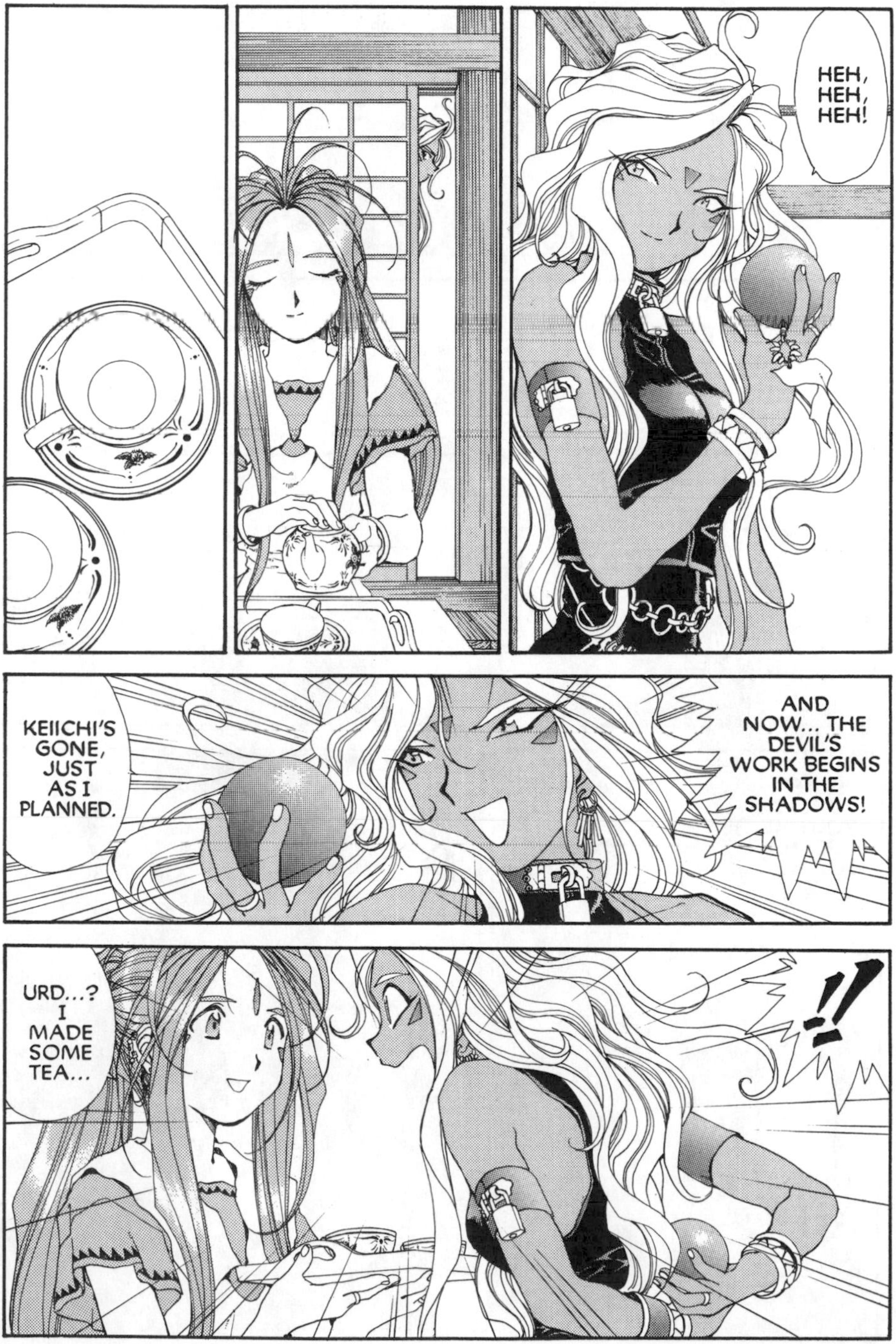
HEH, HEH, HEH!
KEIICHI'S GONE, JUST AS I PLANNED.
AND NOW... THE DEVIL'S WORK BEGINS IN THE SHADOWS!
URD...? I MADE SOME TEA...
!!

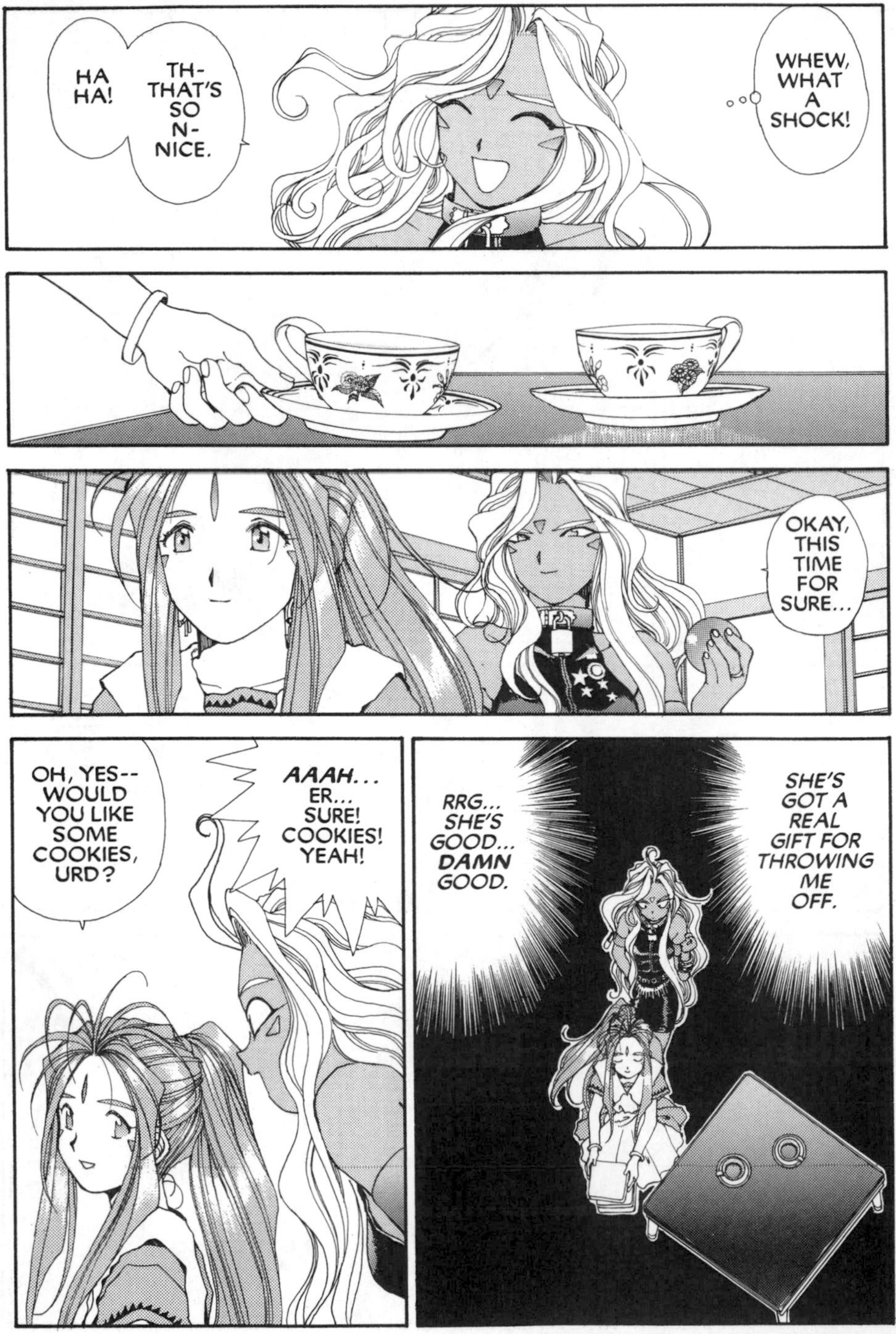
TH-THAT'S SO N-NICE.
HA HA!
WHEW, WHAT A SHOCK!
OKAY, THIS TIME FOR SURE...
OH, YES--WOULD YOU LIKE SOME COOKIES, URD?
AAAH... ER... SURE! COOKIES! YEAH!
RRG... SHE'S GOOD... DAMN GOOD.
SHE'S GOT A REAL GIFT FOR THROWING ME OFF.

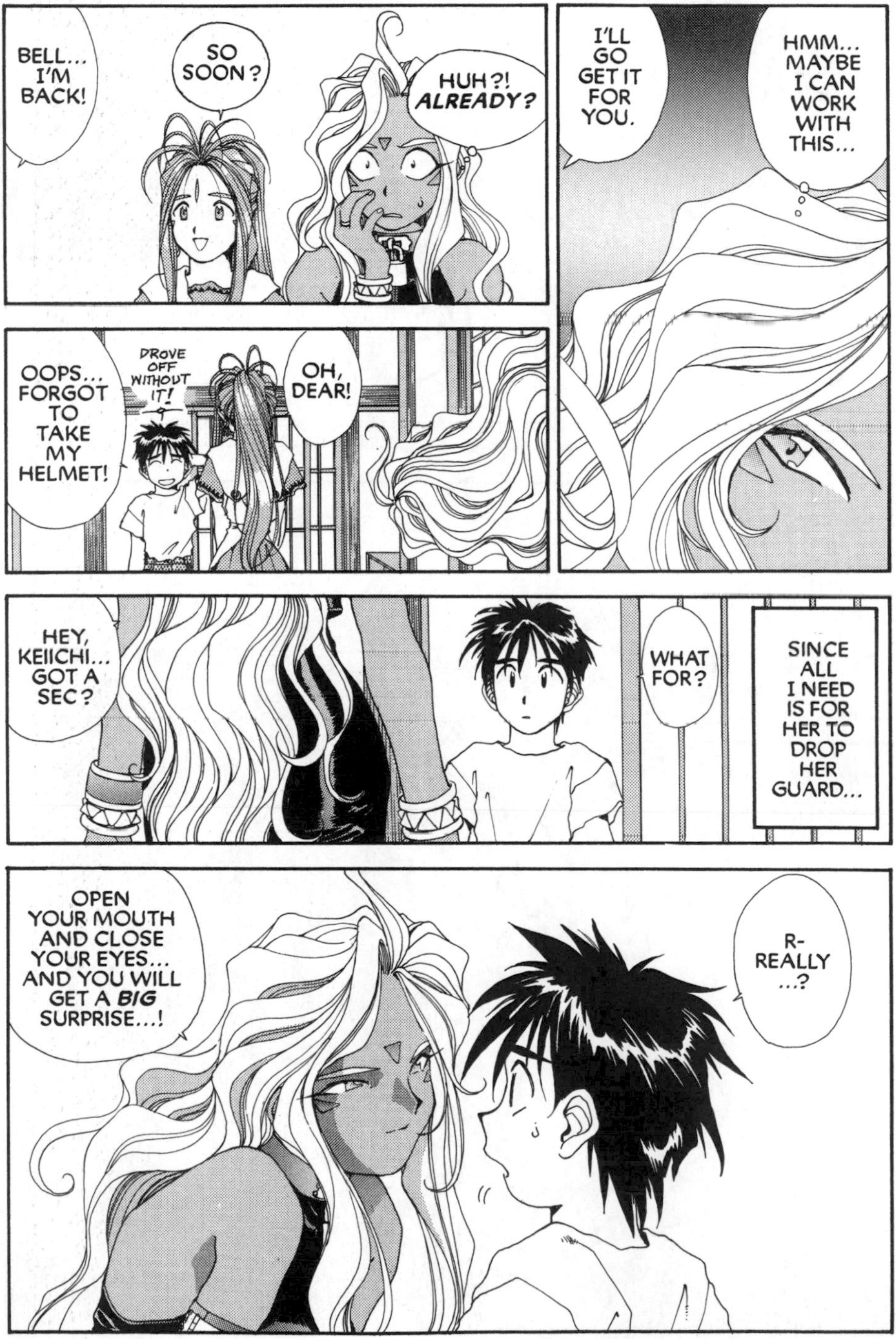

BELL... I'M BACK!
SO SOON?
HUH?! *ALREADY?*
OOPS... FORGOT TO TAKE MY HELMET!
DROVE OFF WITHOUT IT!
OH, DEAR!
I'LL GO GET IT FOR YOU.
HMM... MAYBE I CAN WORK WITH THIS...
HEY, KEIICHI... GOT A SEC?
WHAT FOR?
SINCE ALL I NEED IS FOR HER TO DROP HER GUARD...
OPEN YOUR MOUTH AND CLOSE YOUR EYES... AND YOU WILL GET A *BIG* SURPRISE...!
R- REALLY ...?

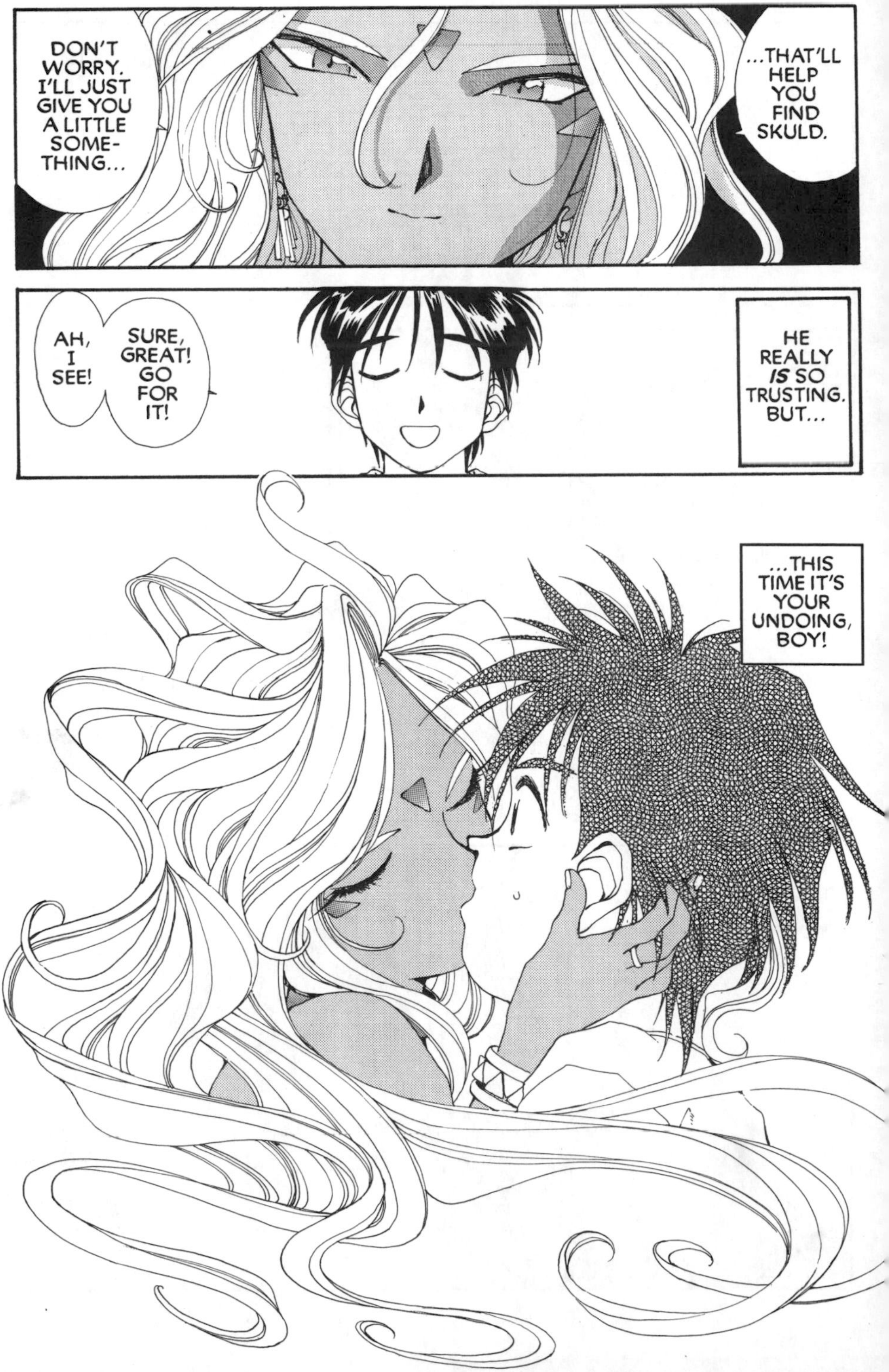
DON'T WORRY. I'LL JUST GIVE YOU A LITTLE SOME-THING...
...THAT'LL HELP YOU FIND SKULD.
AH, I SEE!
SURE, GREAT! GO FOR IT!
HE REALLY *IS* SO TRUSTING. BUT...
...THIS TIME IT'S YOUR UNDOING, BOY!

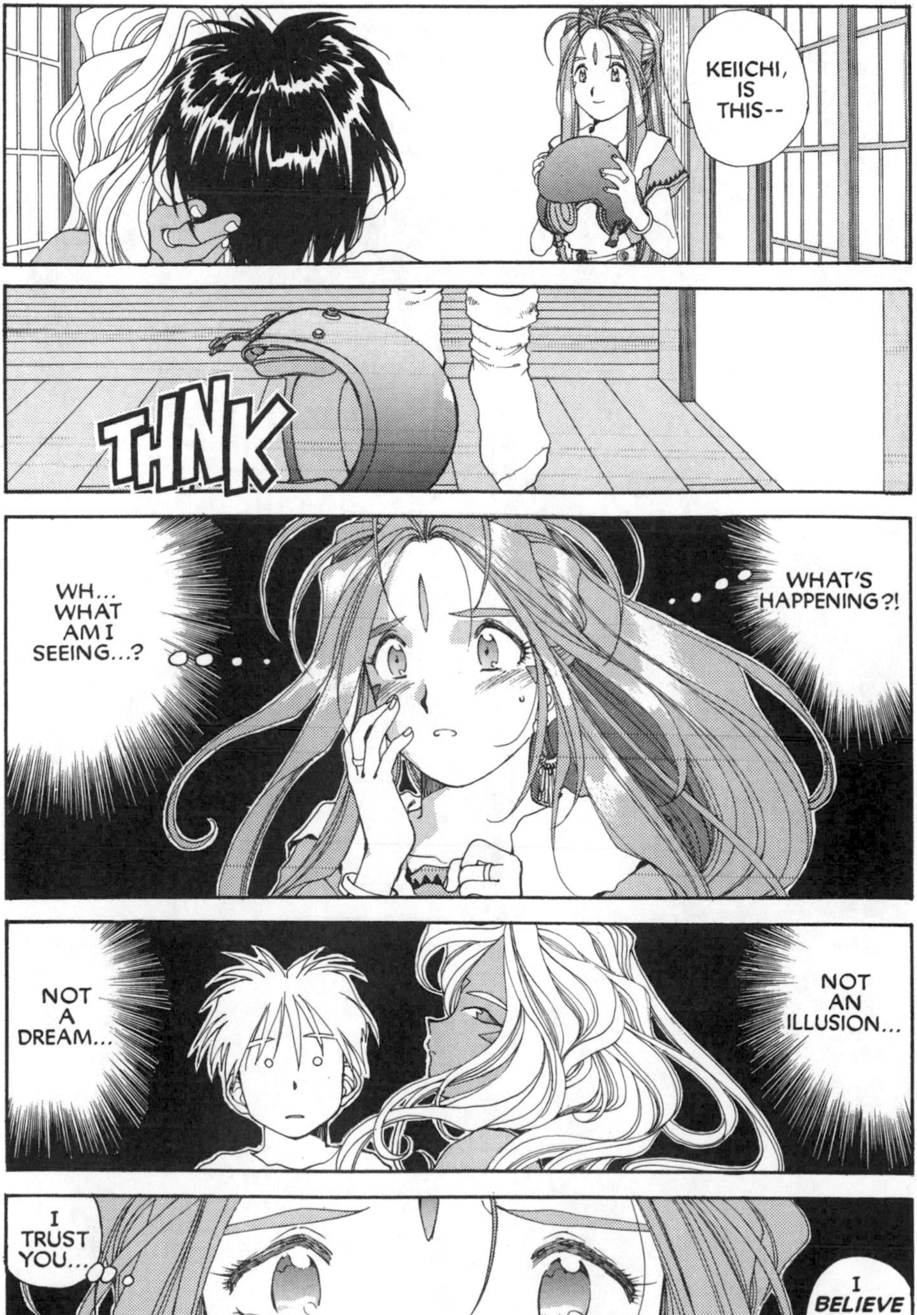
KEIICHI, IS THIS--
THNK
WH... WHAT AM I SEEING...?
WHAT'S HAPPENING?!
NOT A DREAM...
NOT AN ILLUSION...
I TRUST YOU...
I *BELIEVE* YOU, KEIICHI!

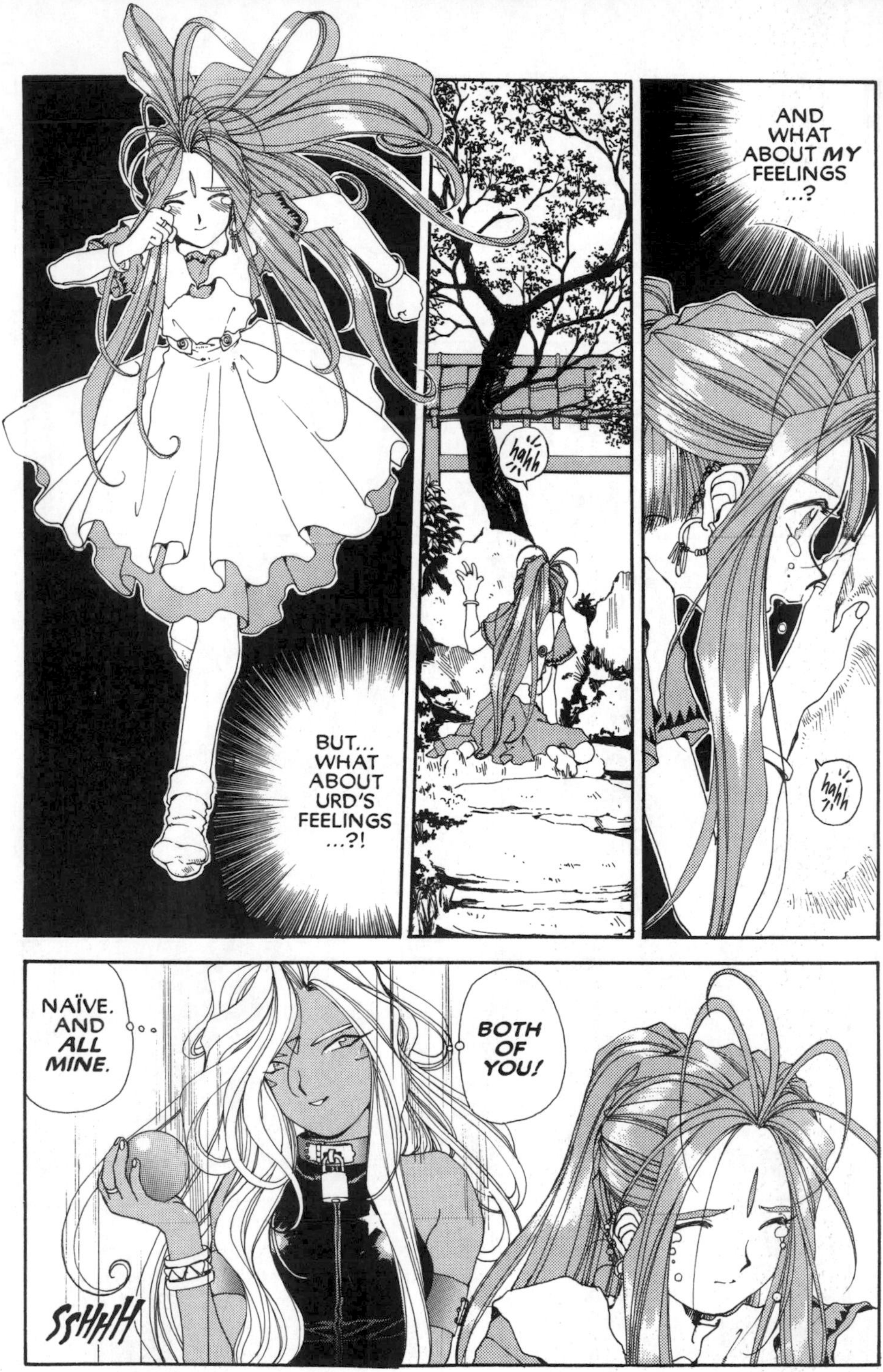
BUT... WHAT ABOUT URD'S FEELINGS ...?!
hahh
AND WHAT ABOUT MY FEELINGS ...?
hahh
NAÏVE. AND ALL MINE.
BOTH OF YOU!
SSHHH

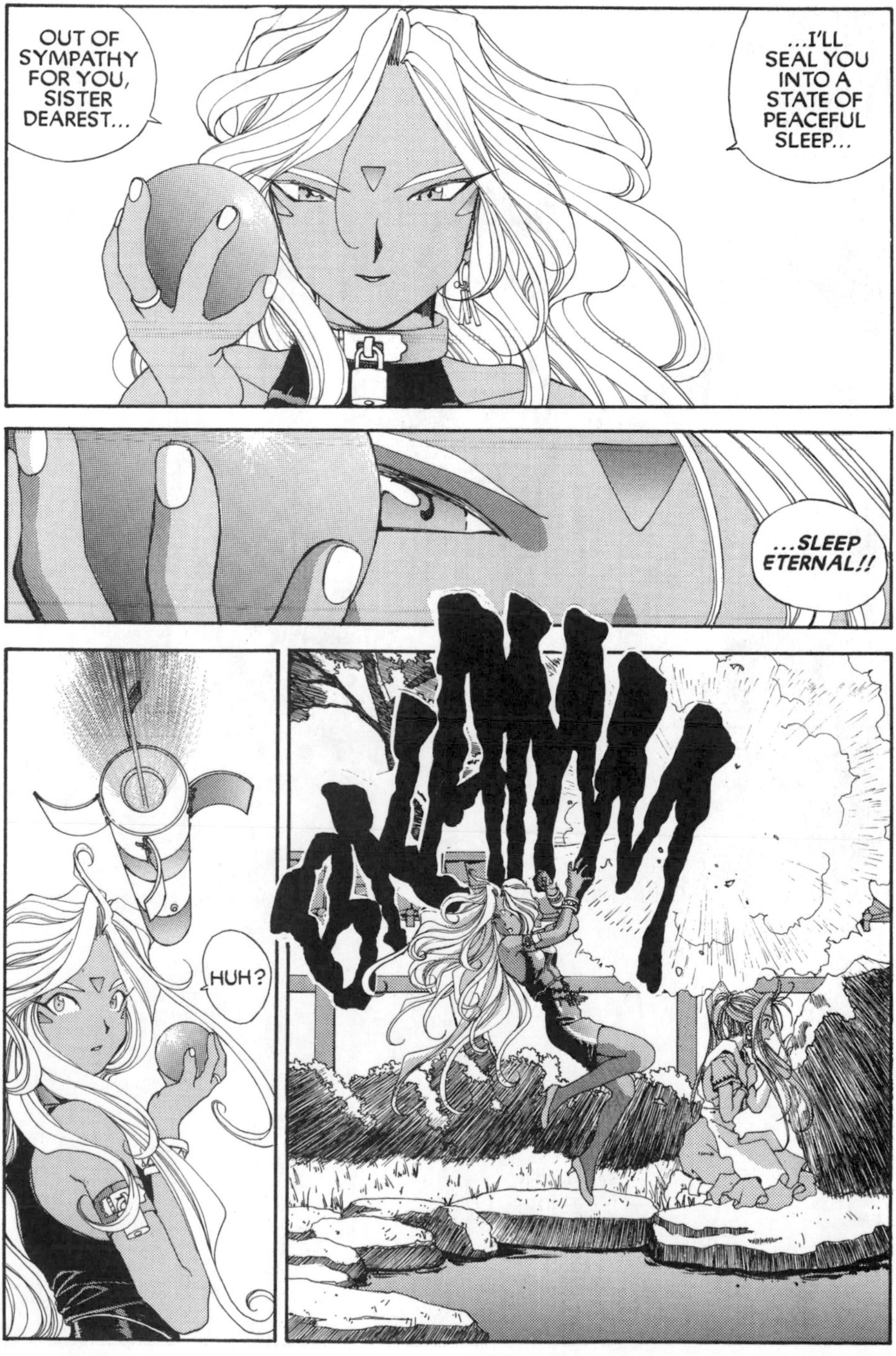
OUT OF SYMPATHY FOR YOU, SISTER DEAREST...
...I'LL SEAL YOU INTO A STATE OF PEACEFUL SLEEP...
...SLEEP ETERNAL!!
HUH?

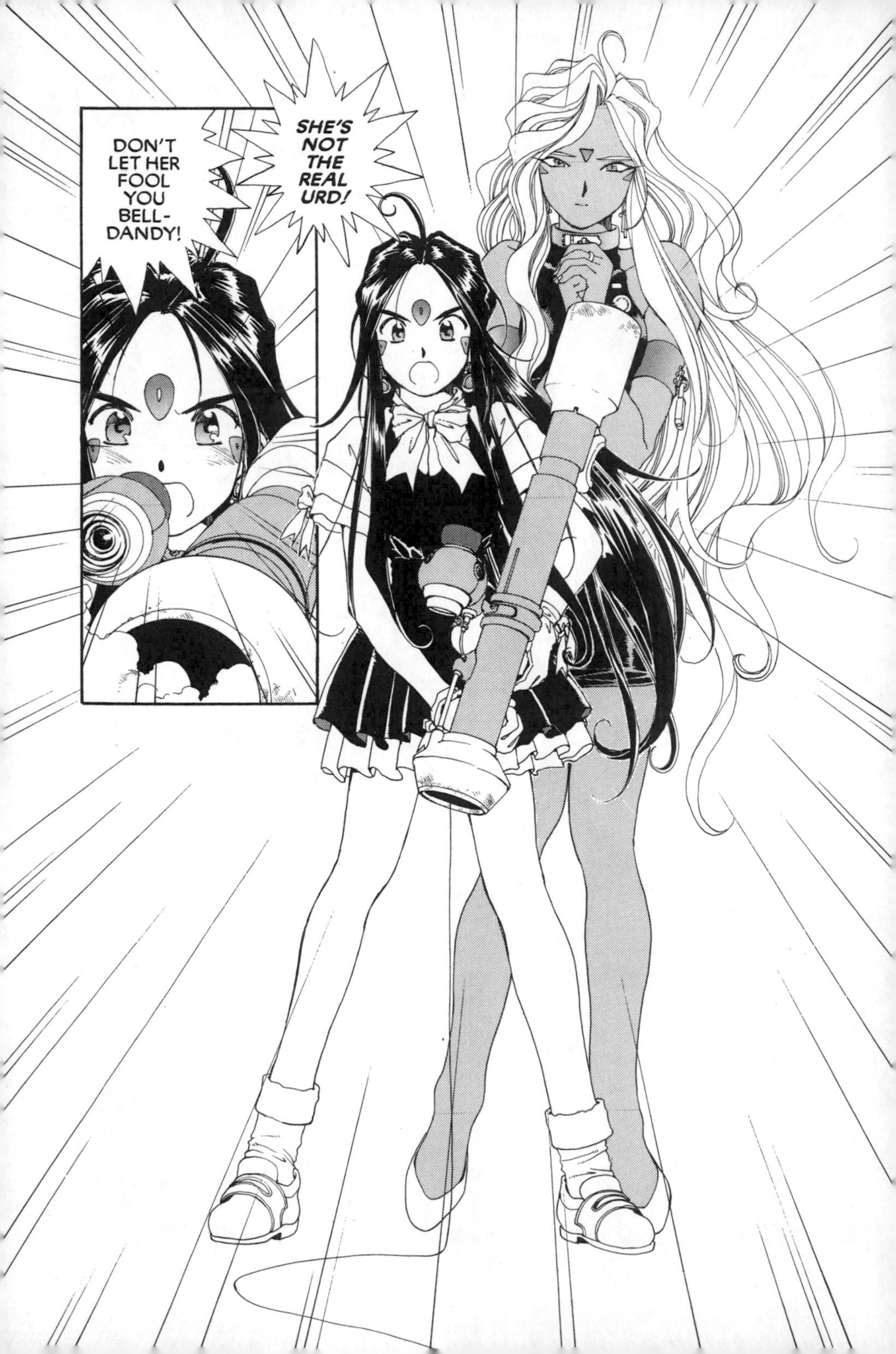
DON'T LET HER FOOL YOU BELL-DANDY!
SHE'S NOT THE REAL URD!

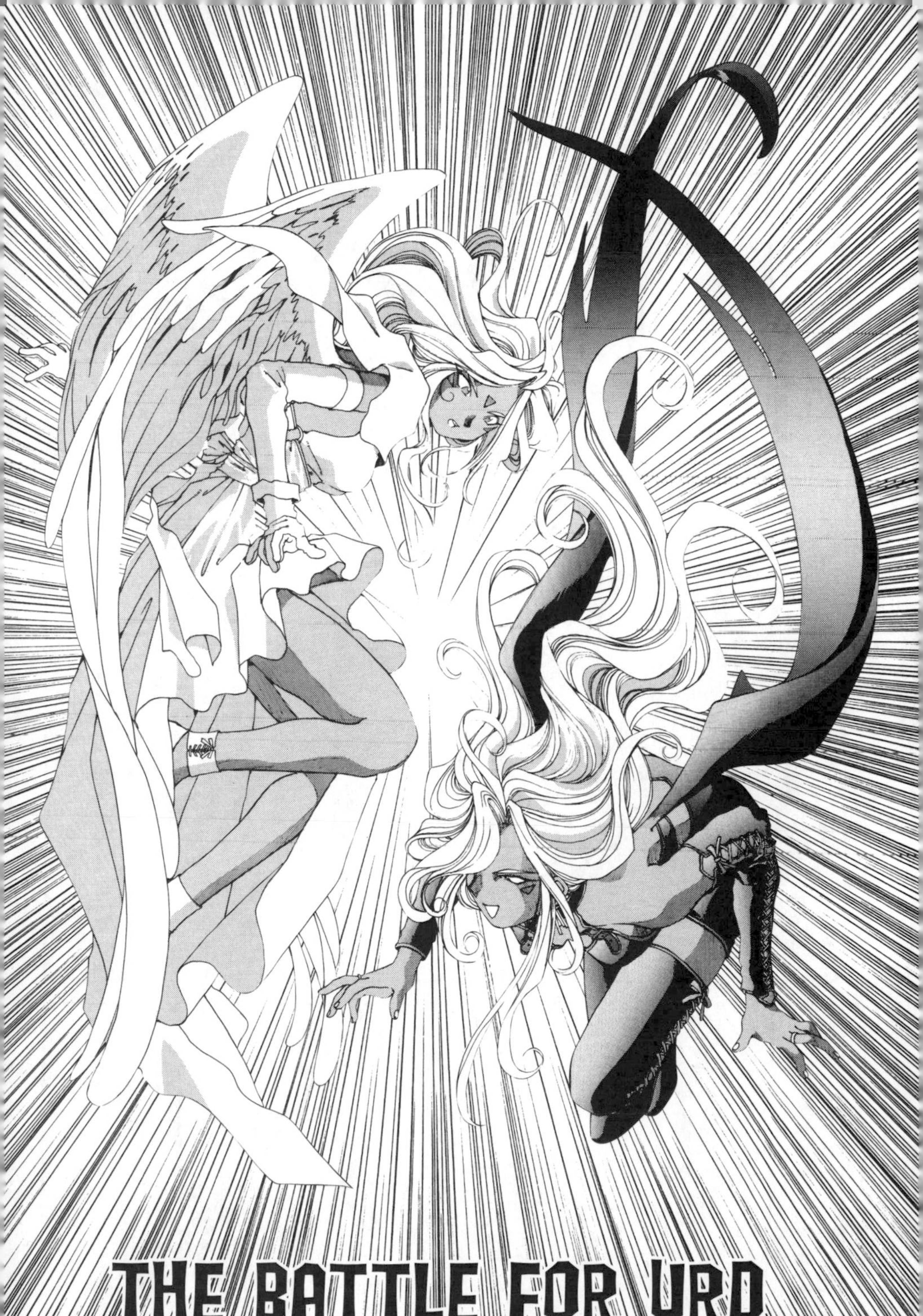

THE BATTLE FOR URD

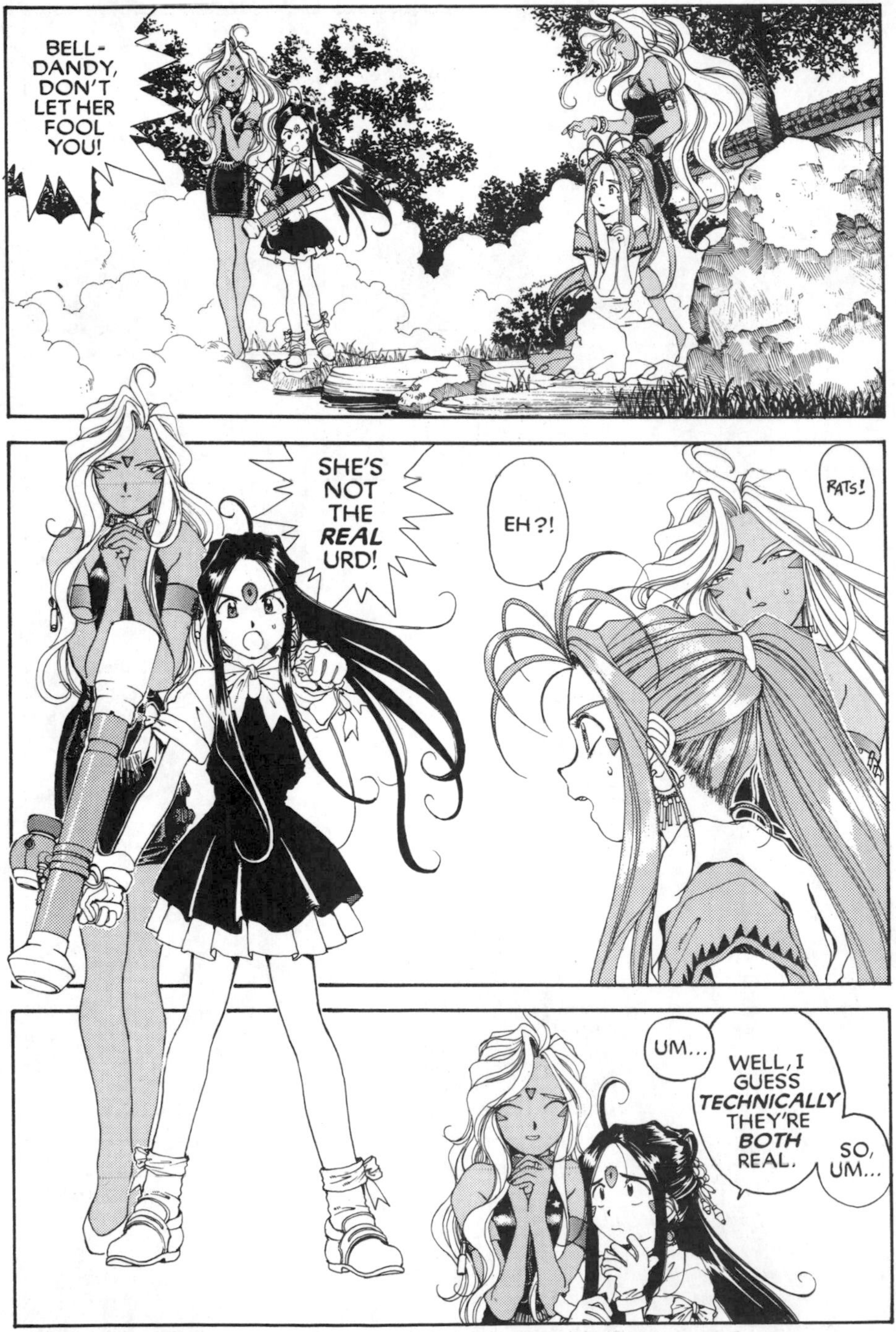
BELL-DANDY, DON'T LET HER FOOL YOU!
SHE'S NOT THE REAL URD!
EH?!
RATS!
UM...
WELL, I GUESS TECHNICALLY THEY'RE BOTH REAL.
SO, UM...

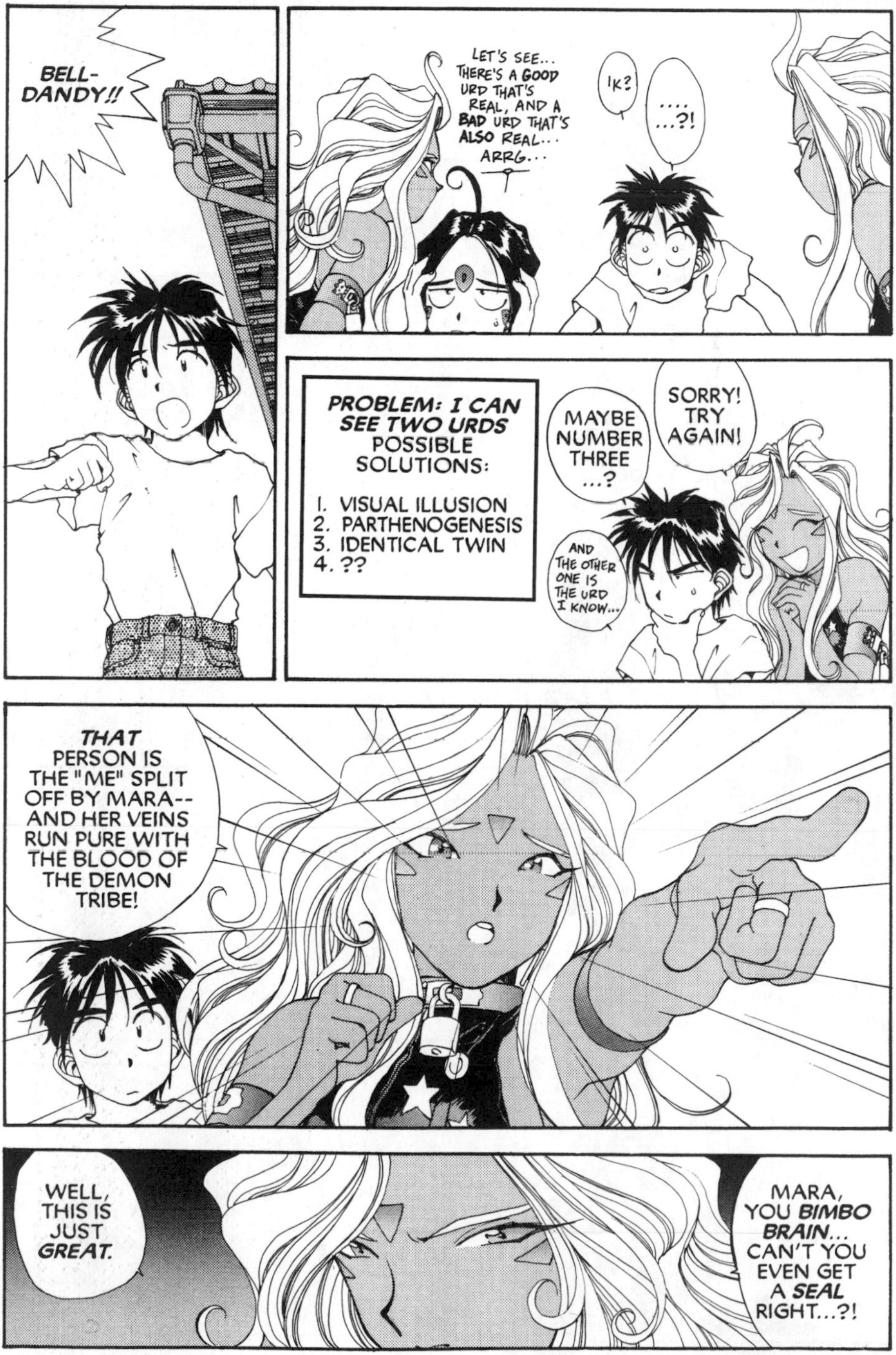
BELL-DANDY!!
LET'S SEE... THERE'S A GOOD URD THAT'S REAL, AND A BAD URD THAT'S ALSO REAL... ARRG...
IK?
....?!
PROBLEM: I CAN SEE TWO URDS POSSIBLE SOLUTIONS:
1. VISUAL ILLUSION
2. PARTHENOGENESIS
3. IDENTICAL TWIN
4. ??
MAYBE NUMBER THREE ...?
SORRY! TRY AGAIN!
AND THE OTHER ONE IS THE URD I KNOW...
THAT PERSON IS THE "ME" SPLIT OFF BY MARA-- AND HER VEINS RUN PURE WITH THE BLOOD OF THE DEMON TRIBE!
WELL, THIS IS JUST GREAT.
MARA, YOU BIMBO BRAIN... CAN'T YOU EVEN GET A SEAL RIGHT...?!

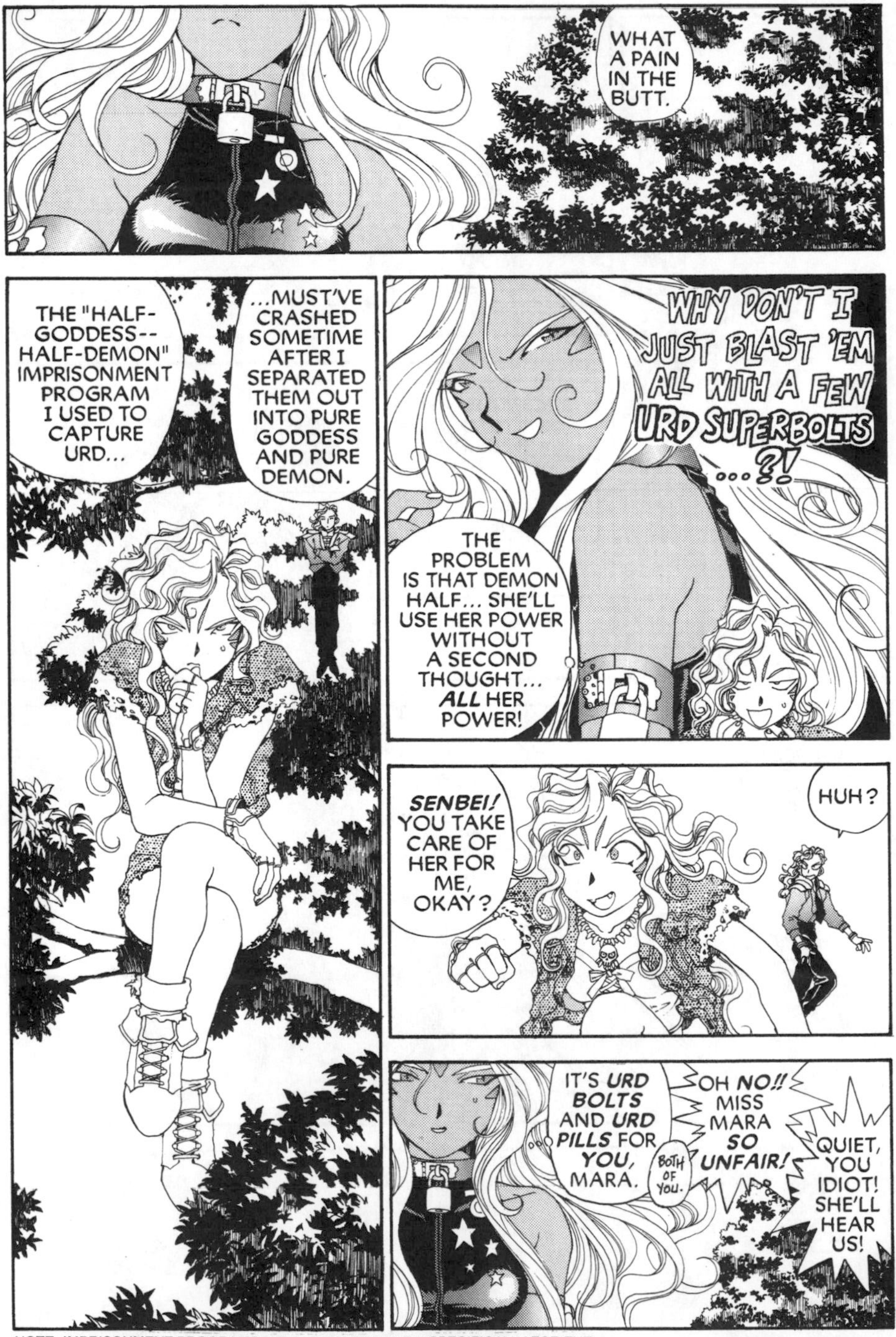
WHAT A PAIN IN THE BUTT.
THE "HALF-GODDESS--HALF-DEMON" IMPRISONMENT PROGRAM I USED TO CAPTURE URD...
...MUST'VE CRASHED SOMETIME AFTER I SEPARATED THEM OUT INTO PURE GODDESS AND PURE DEMON.
WHY DON'T I JUST BLAST 'EM ALL WITH A FEW URD SUPERBOLTS ...?!
THE PROBLEM IS THAT DEMON HALF... SHE'LL USE HER POWER WITHOUT A SECOND THOUGHT... ALL HER POWER!
SENBEI! YOU TAKE CARE OF HER FOR ME, OKAY?
HUH?
IT'S URD BOLTS AND URD PILLS FOR YOU, MARA.
BOTH OF YOU.
OH NO!! MISS MARA SO UNFAIR!
QUIET, YOU IDIOT! SHE'LL HEAR US!

NOTE: IMPRISONMENT PROGRAMS HAVE TO BE DESIGNED SPECIFICALLY FOR THE CHARACTERISTICS OF THE TARGET SUBJECT. IN THIS CASE, SINCE URD'S CHARACTERISTICS CHANGED (SHE BECAME PURE GODDESS) IT COULD NO LONGER CONFINE HER.

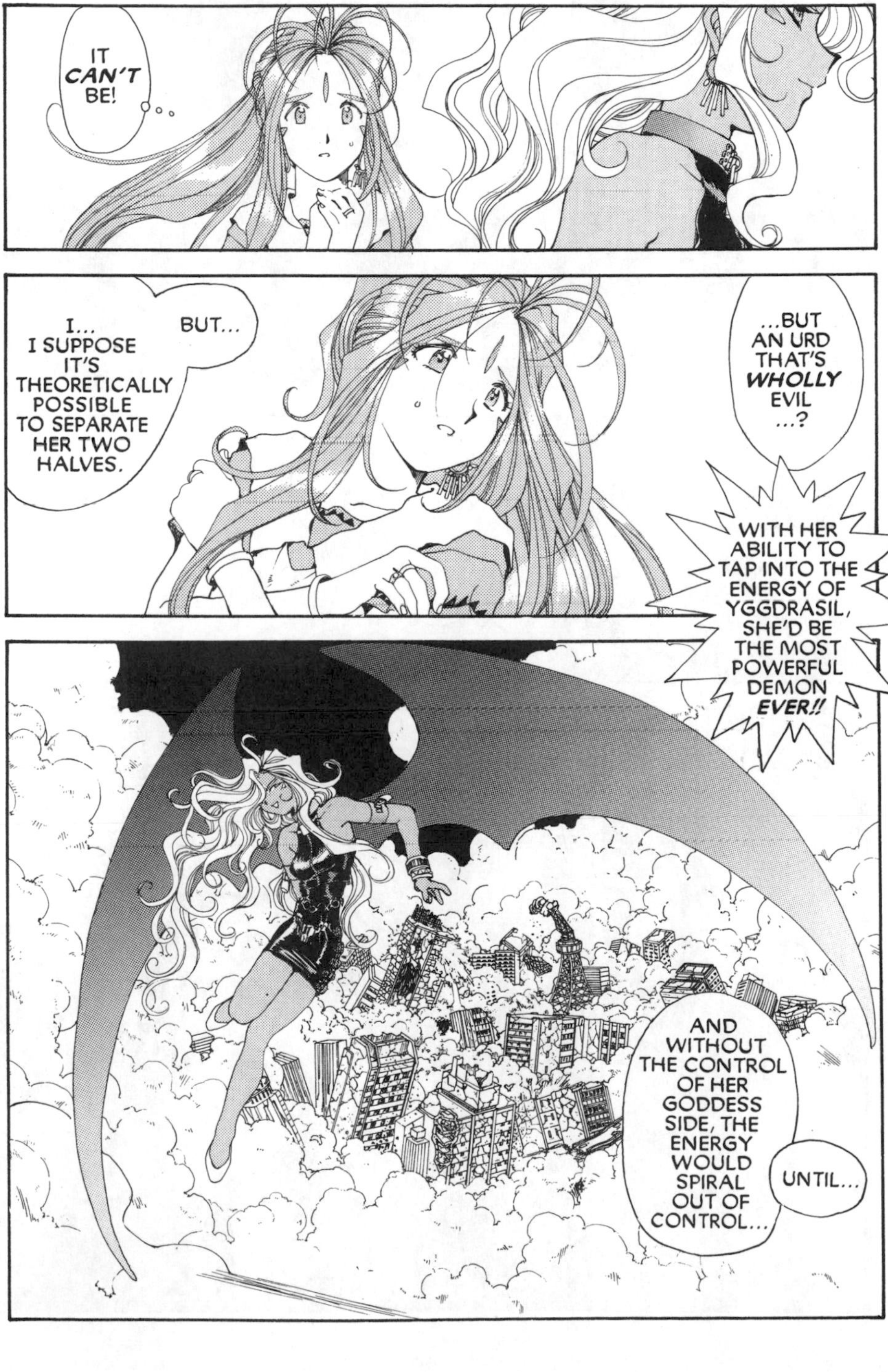
IT *CAN'T* BE!
I... I SUPPOSE IT'S THEORETICALLY POSSIBLE TO SEPARATE HER TWO HALVES.
BUT...
...BUT AN URD THAT'S *WHOLLY* EVIL ...?
WITH HER ABILITY TO TAP INTO THE ENERGY OF YGGDRASIL, SHE'D BE THE MOST POWERFUL DEMON *EVER!!*
AND WITHOUT THE CONTROL OF HER GODDESS SIDE, THE ENERGY WOULD SPIRAL OUT OF CONTROL...
UNTIL...

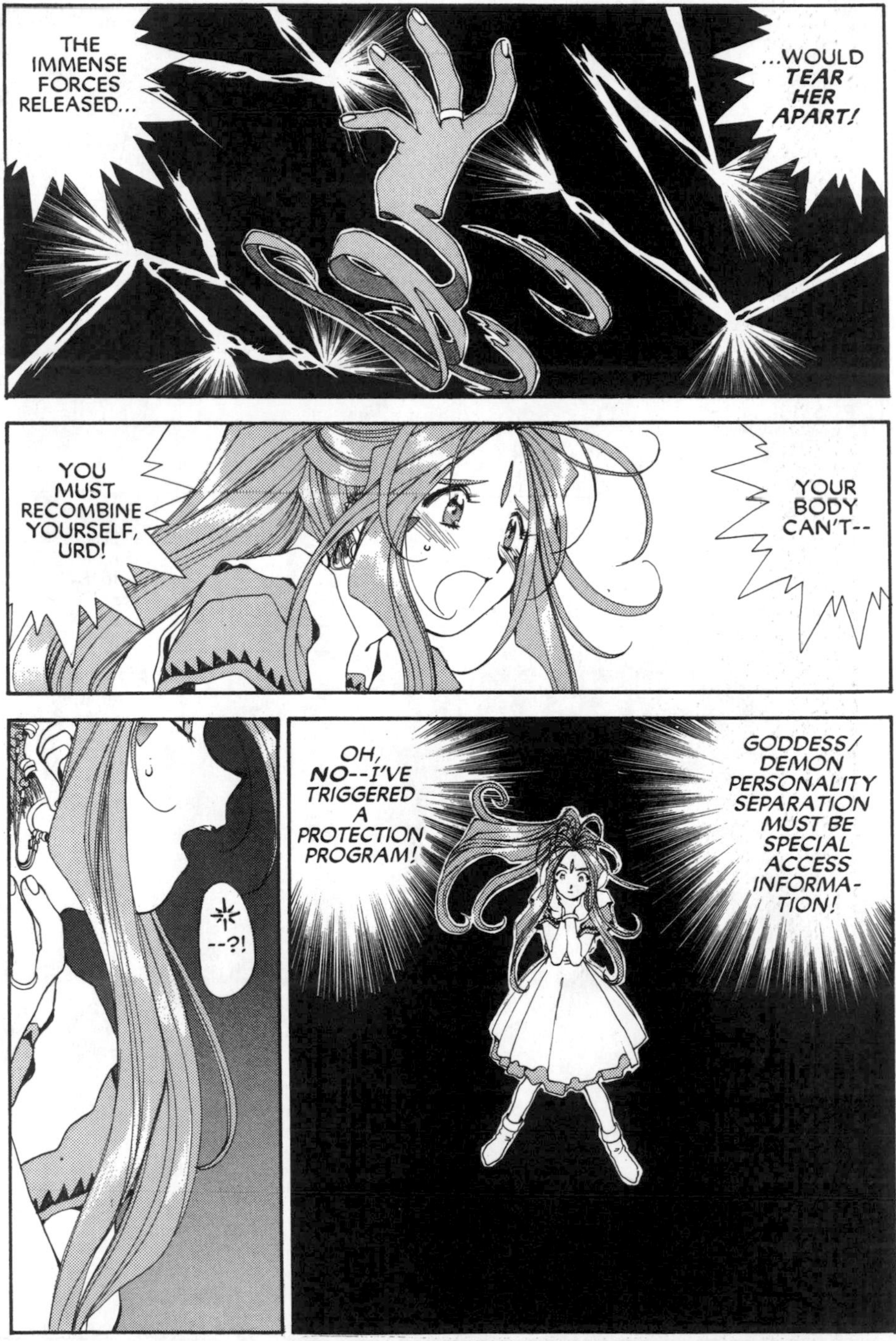
THE IMMENSE FORCES RELEASED...
...WOULD *TEAR HER APART!*
YOU MUST RECOMBINE YOURSELF, URD!
YOUR BODY CAN'T--
--?!
OH, *NO*--I'VE TRIGGERED A PROTECTION PROGRAM!
GODDESS/DEMON PERSONALITY SEPARATION MUST BE SPECIAL ACCESS INFORMATION!

NOTE: SPECIAL ACCESS INFORMATION IS TAGGED WITH A SOFTWARE LOCK CALLED A PROTECTION PROGRAM THAT PREVENTS A GODDESS FROM SPEAKING ABOUT IT OR OTHERWISE TRANSFERRING THE INFORMATION.

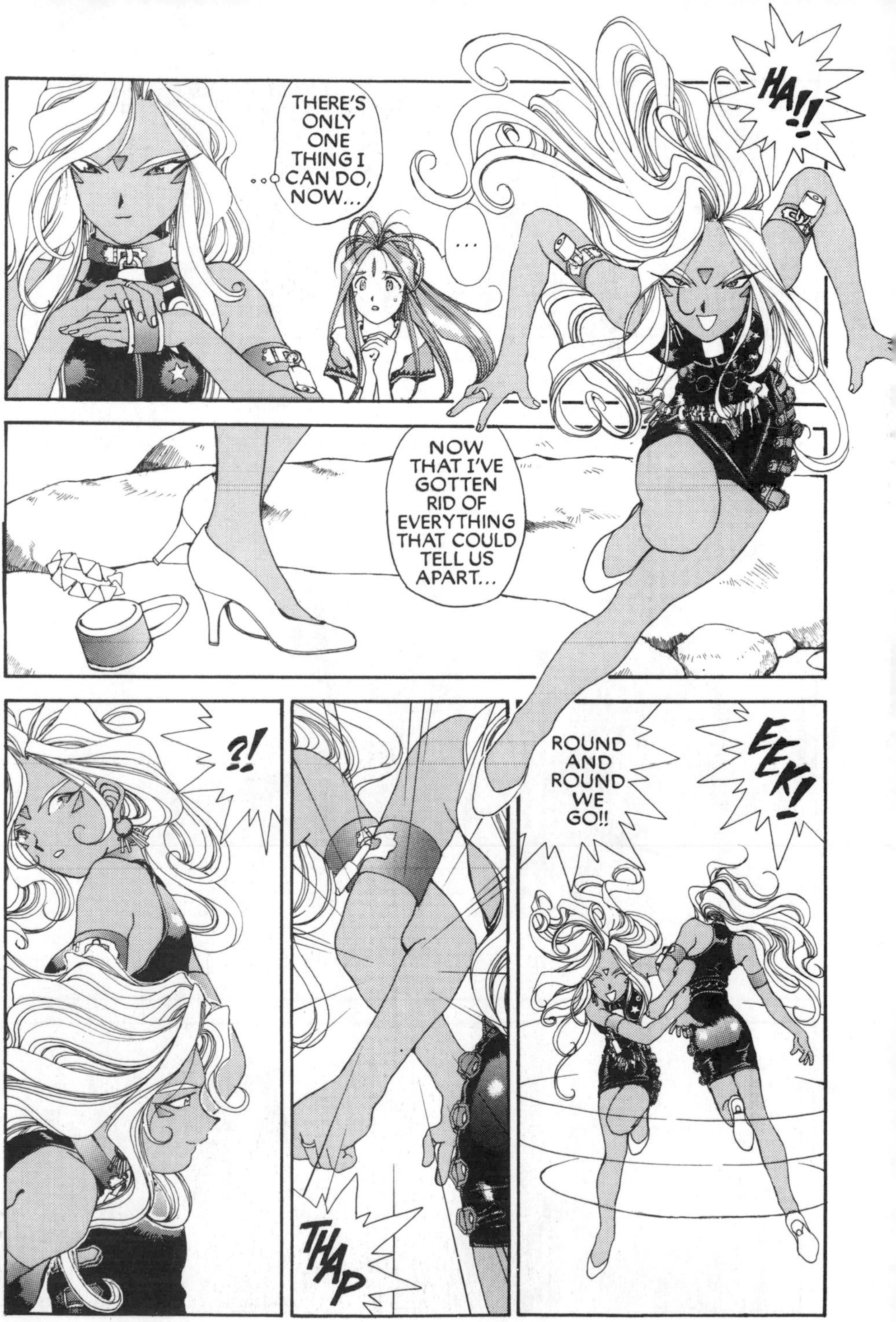
THERE'S ONLY ONE THING I CAN DO, NOW...
...
HA!!
NOW THAT I'VE GOTTEN RID OF EVERYTHING THAT COULD TELL US APART...
?!
THAP
ROUND AND ROUND WE GO!!
EEEK!

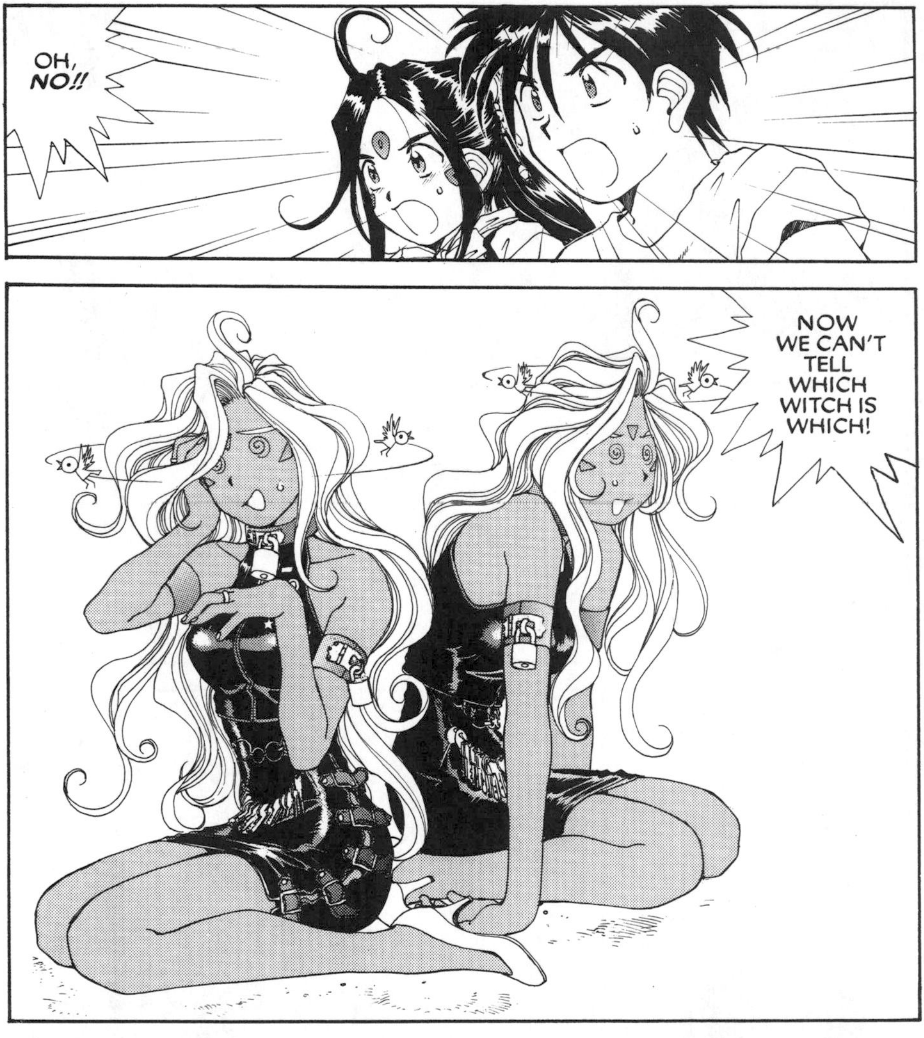
OH, NO!!
NOW WE CAN'T TELL WHICH WITCH IS WHICH!
DON'T LET HER TRICK YOU!
I AM THE GODDESS URD!
SO YOU SAY, BUT...

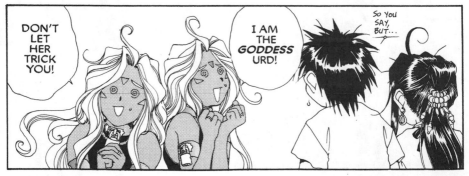

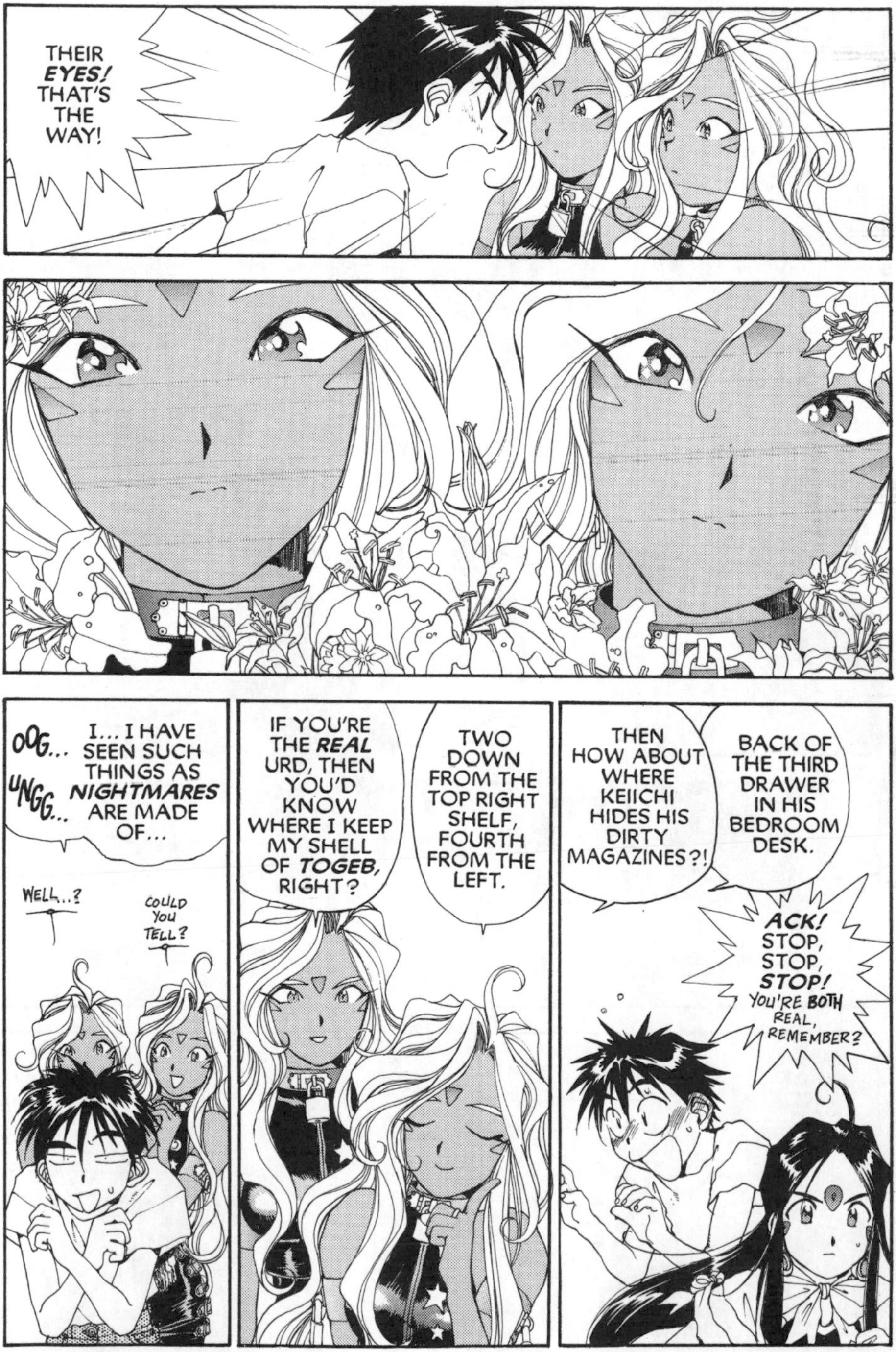
THEIR EYES! THAT'S THE WAY!
OOG... UNGG...
I... I HAVE SEEN SUCH THINGS AS NIGHTMARES ARE MADE OF...
WELL...?
COULD YOU TELL?
IF YOU'RE THE REAL URD, THEN YOU'D KNOW WHERE I KEEP MY SHELL OF TOGEB, RIGHT?
TWO DOWN FROM THE TOP RIGHT SHELF, FOURTH FROM THE LEFT.
THEN HOW ABOUT WHERE KEIICHI HIDES HIS DIRTY MAGAZINES?!
BACK OF THE THIRD DRAWER IN HIS BEDROOM DESK.
ACK! STOP, STOP, STOP! YOU'RE BOTH REAL, REMEMBER?

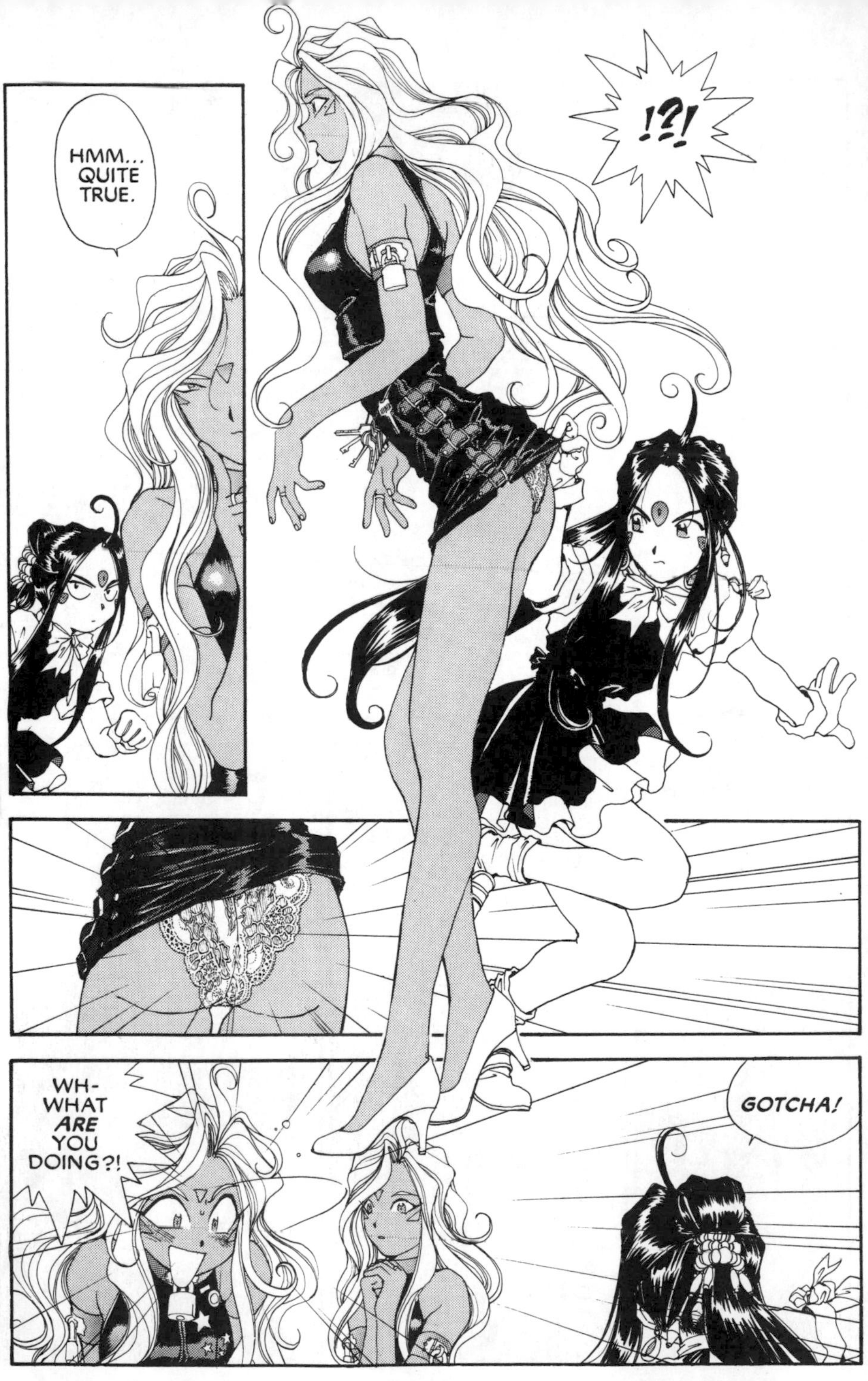
HMM... QUITE TRUE.
!?!
WH- WHAT *ARE* YOU DOING?!
GOTCHA!

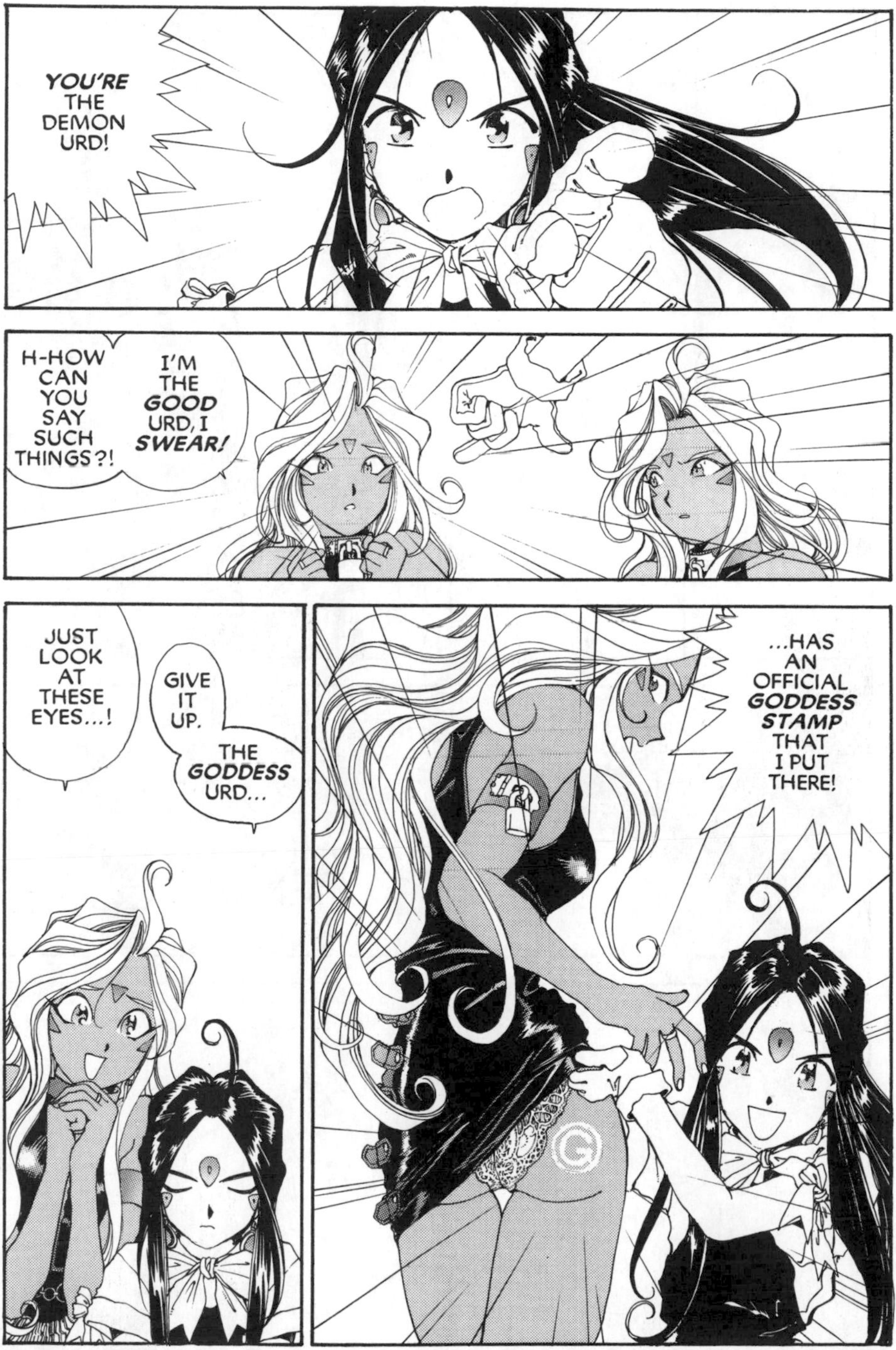
YOU'RE THE DEMON URD!
H-HOW CAN YOU SAY SUCH THINGS?!
I'M THE GOOD URD, I SWEAR!
JUST LOOK AT THESE EYES...!
GIVE IT UP.
THE GODDESS URD...
...HAS AN OFFICIAL GODDESS STAMP THAT I PUT THERE!

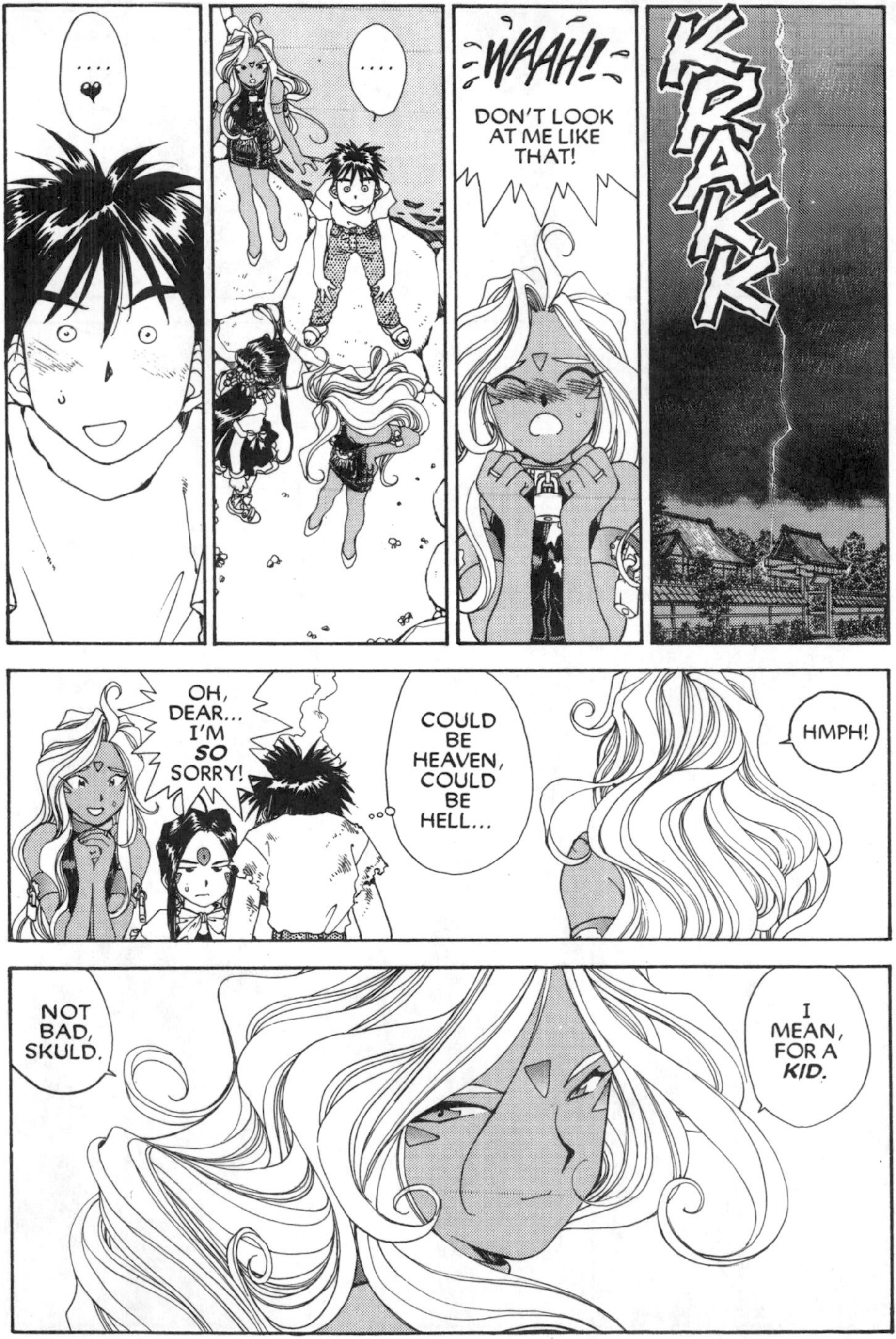
....
....
WAAH!
DON'T LOOK AT ME LIKE THAT!
KRAKK
OH, DEAR... I'M *SO* SORRY!
COULD BE HEAVEN, COULD BE HELL...
HMPH!
NOT BAD, SKULD.
I MEAN, FOR A *KID*.

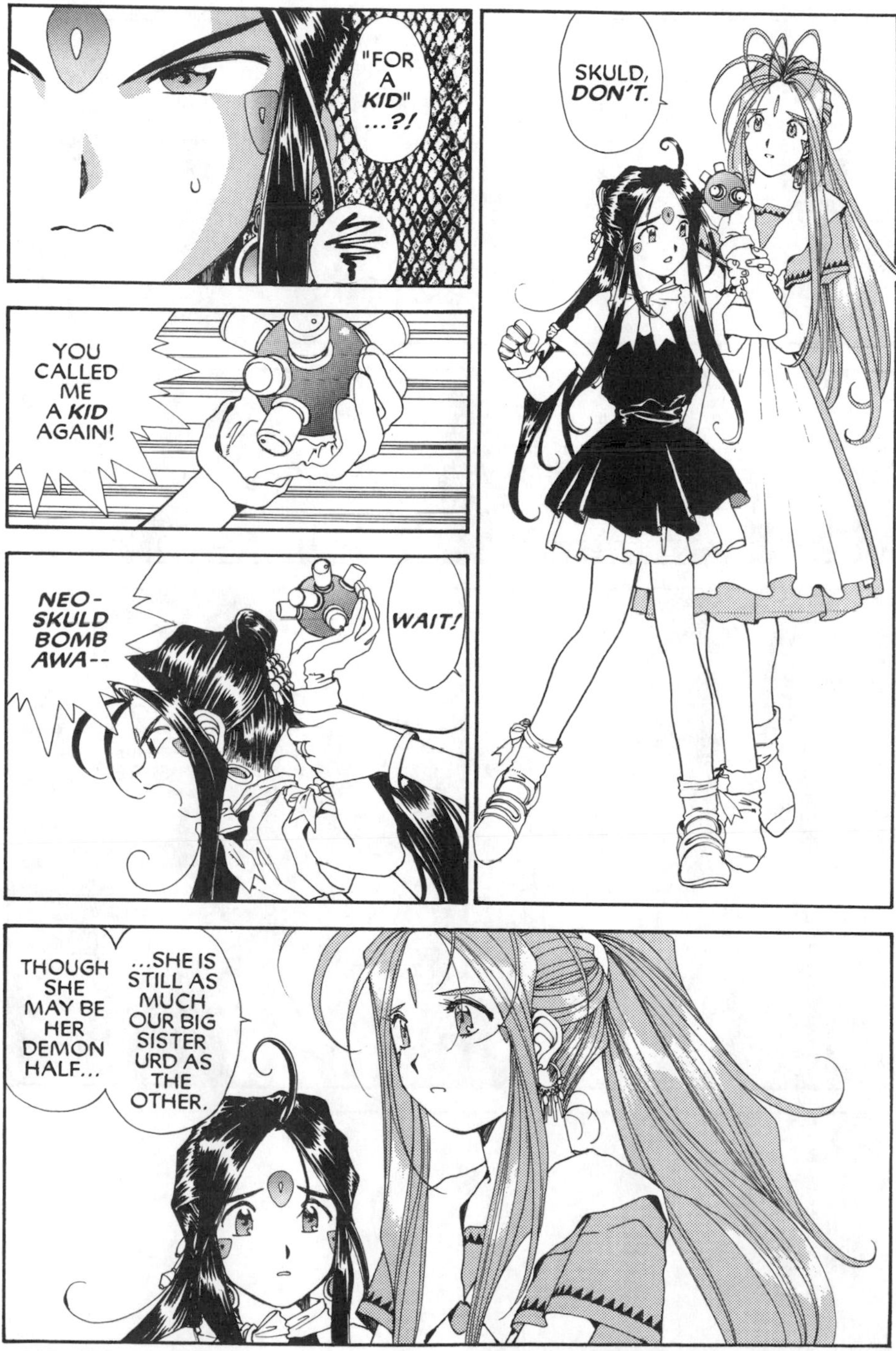
"FOR A KID" ...?!
YOU CALLED ME A KID AGAIN!
NEO-SKULD BOMB AWA--
WAIT!
SKULD, DON'T.
THOUGH SHE MAY BE HER DEMON HALF...
...SHE IS STILL AS MUCH OUR BIG SISTER URD AS THE OTHER.

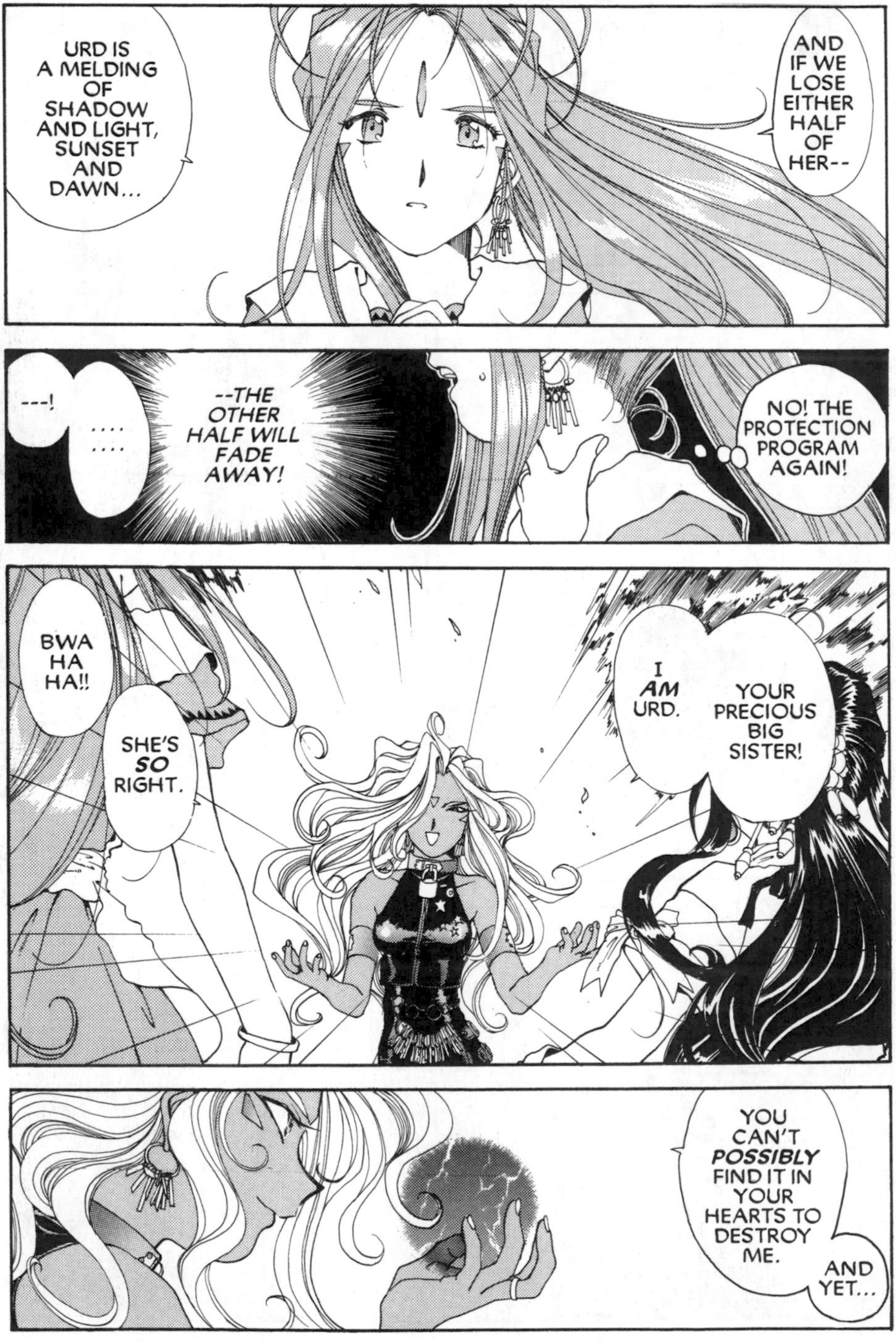
URD IS A MELDING OF SHADOW AND LIGHT, SUNSET AND DAWN...
AND IF WE LOSE EITHER HALF OF HER--
---!
....
....
--THE OTHER HALF WILL FADE AWAY!
NO! THE PROTECTION PROGRAM AGAIN!
BWA HA HA!!
SHE'S *SO* RIGHT.
I *AM* URD.
YOUR PRECIOUS BIG SISTER!
YOU CAN'T ***POSSIBLY*** FIND IT IN YOUR HEARTS TO DESTROY ME.
AND YET...

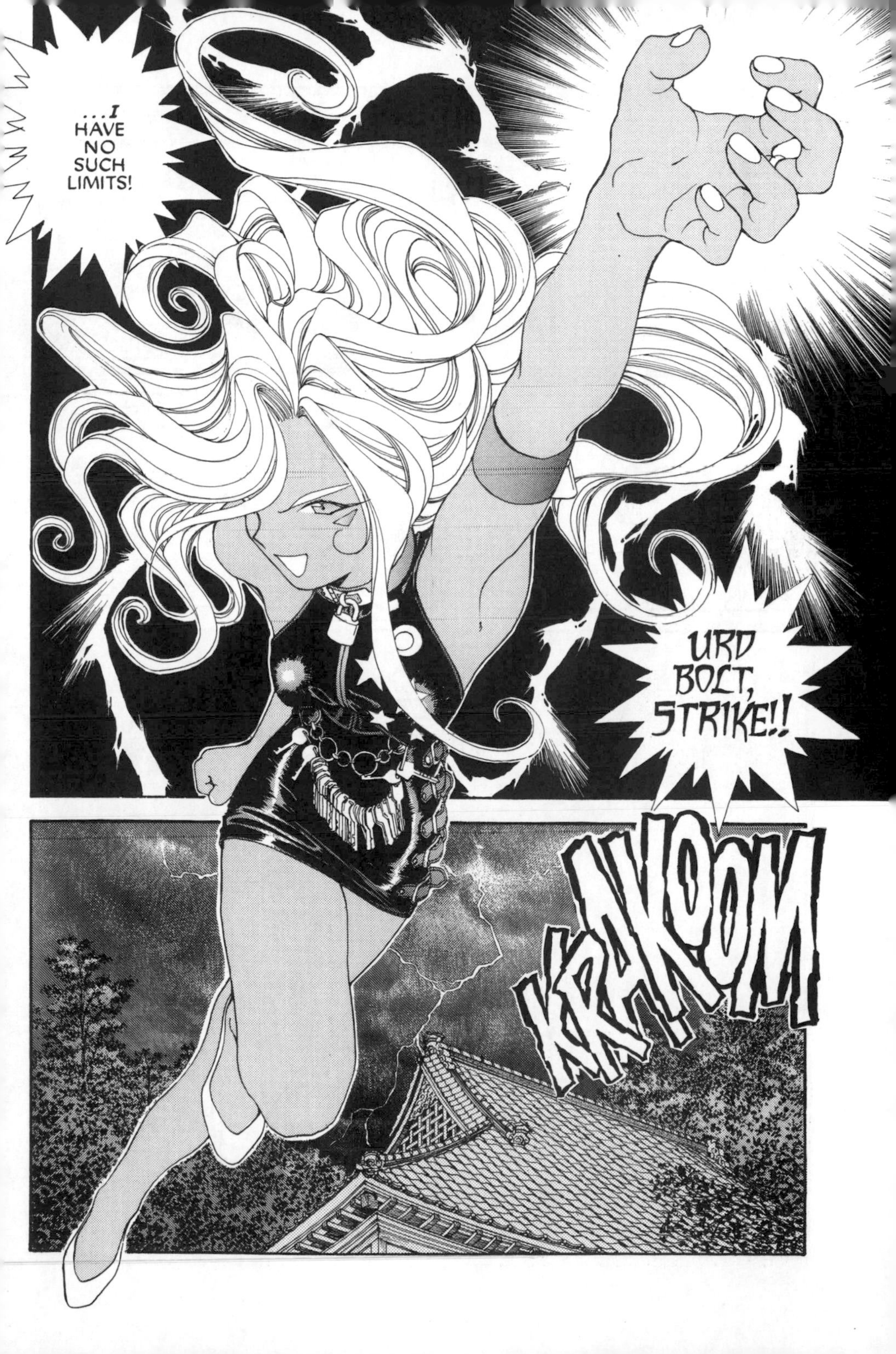
...I HAVE NO SUCH LIMITS!
URD BOLT, STRIKE!!
KRAKOOM

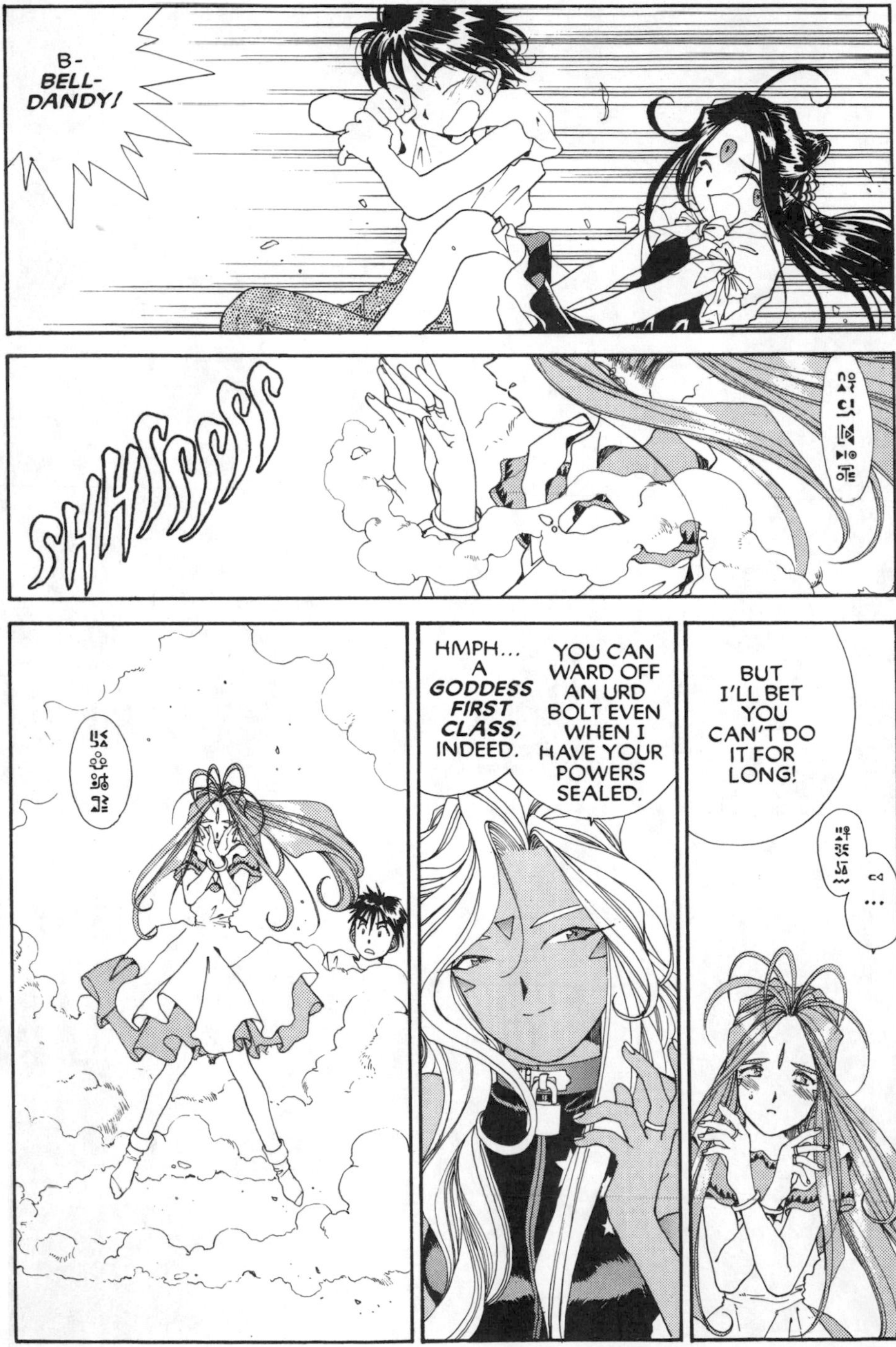
B-
BELL-
DANDY!
SHHSSSSS
HMPH... A GODDESS FIRST CLASS, INDEED.
YOU CAN WARD OFF AN URD BOLT EVEN WHEN I HAVE YOUR POWERS SEALED.
BUT I'LL BET YOU CAN'T DO IT FOR LONG!
...

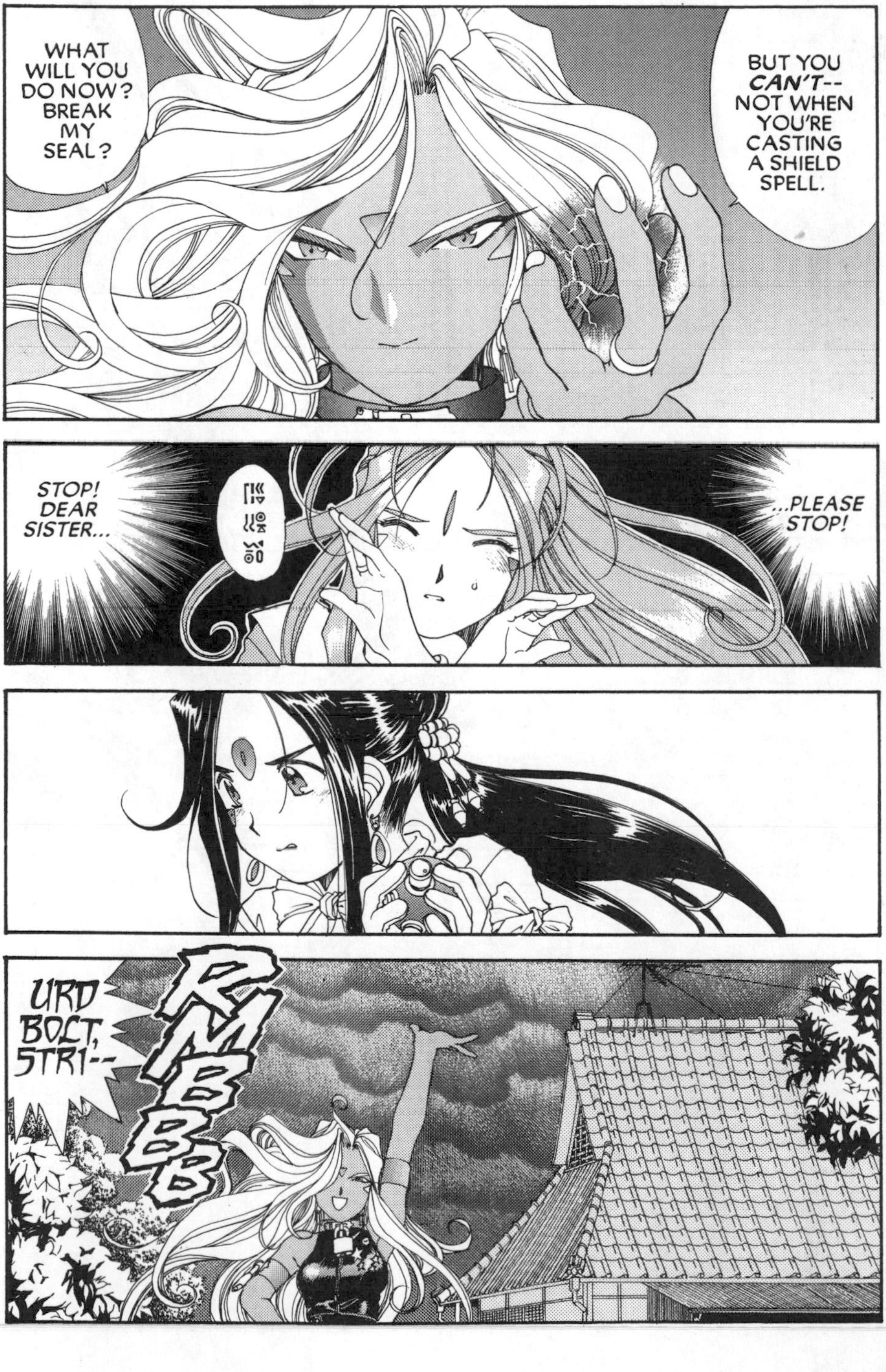

WHAT WILL YOU DO NOW? BREAK MY SEAL?
BUT YOU *CAN'T*-- NOT WHEN YOU'RE CASTING A SHIELD SPELL.
STOP! DEAR SISTER...
...PLEASE STOP!
URD BOLT, STRI--
RMBBBB

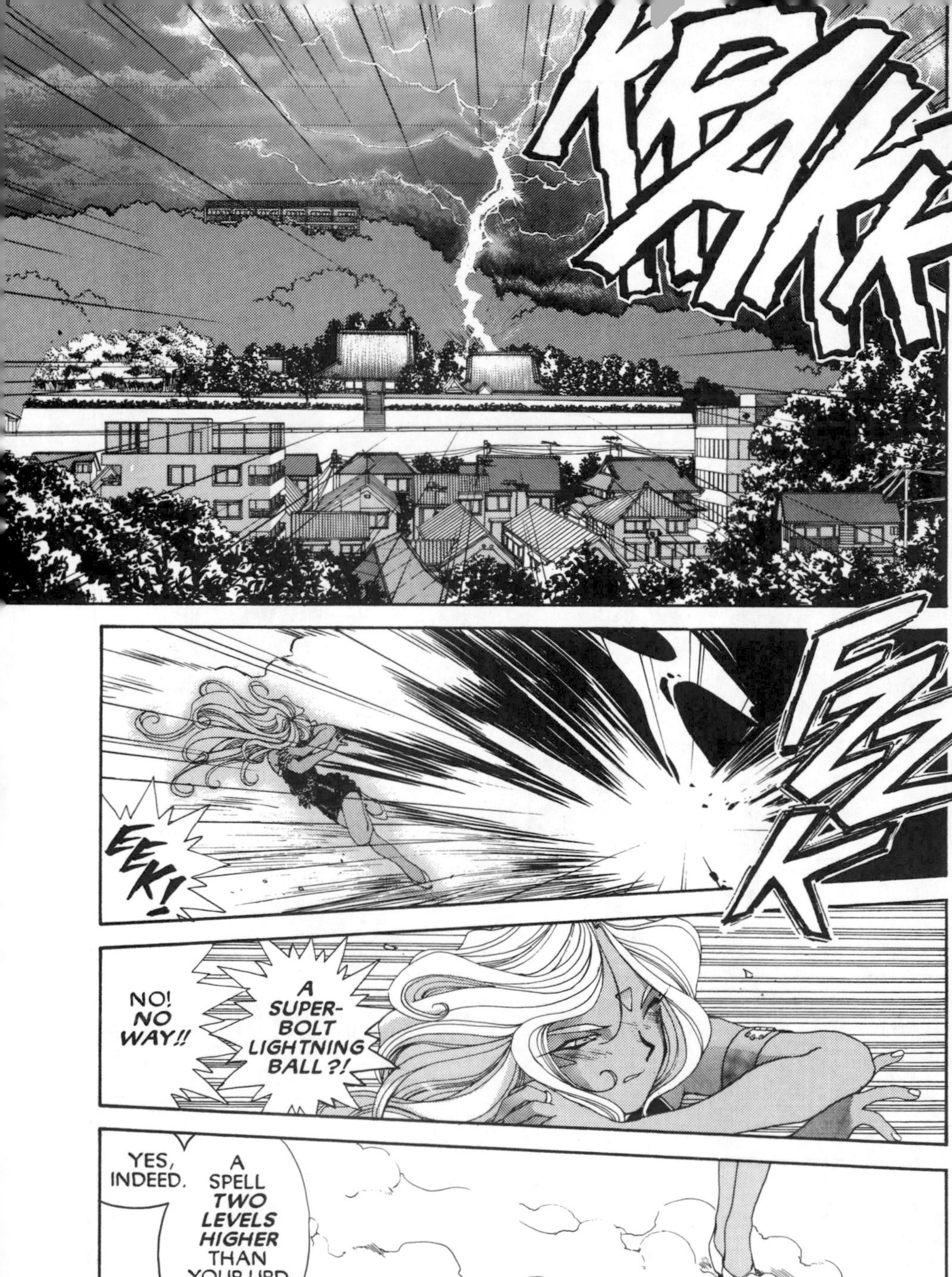
EEK!
NO! NO WAY!!
A SUPER-BOLT LIGHTNING BALL?!
YES, INDEED.
A SPELL TWO LEVELS HIGHER THAN YOUR URD BOLT.

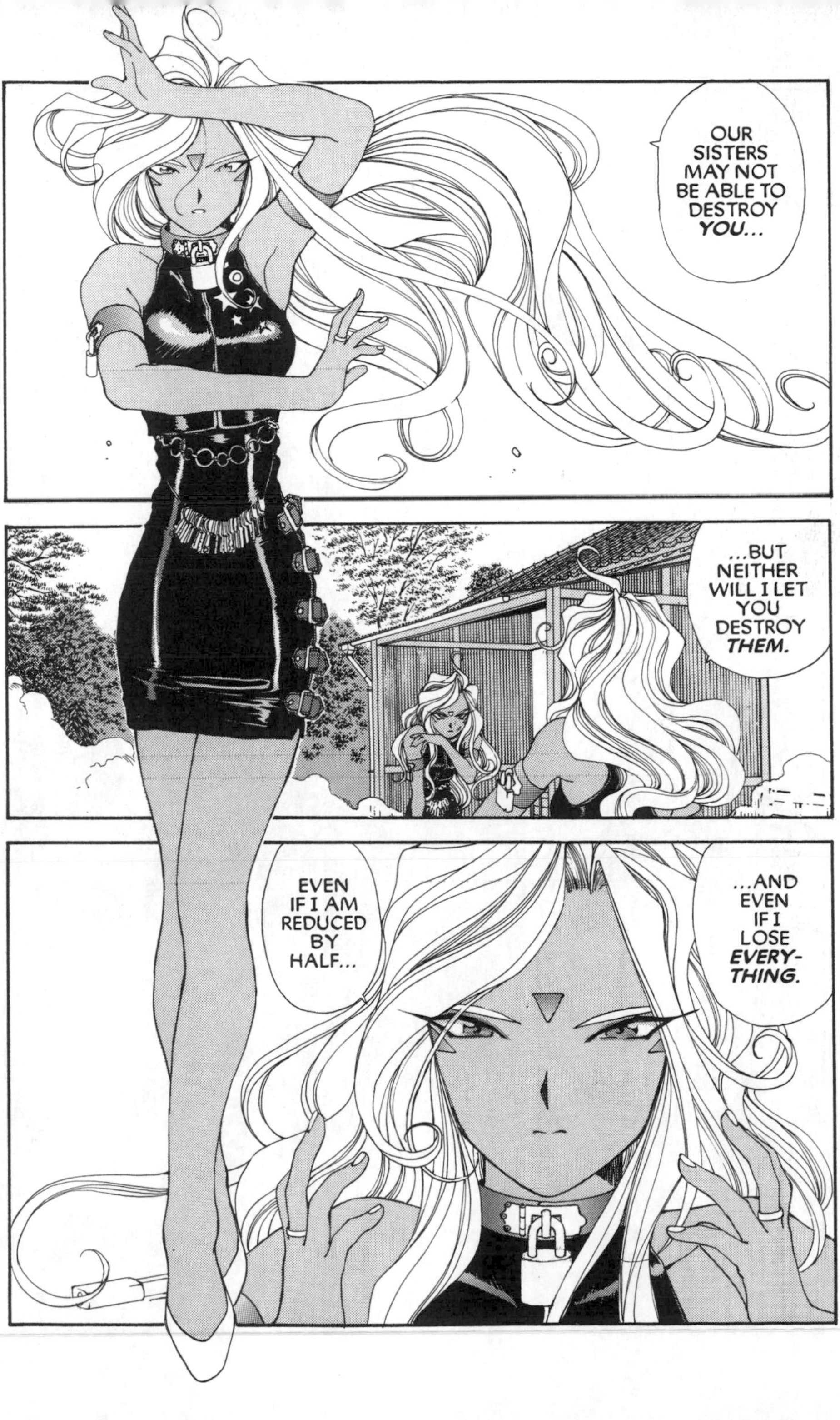
OUR SISTERS MAY NOT BE ABLE TO DESTROY *YOU...*
...BUT NEITHER WILL I LET YOU DESTROY *THEM.*
EVEN IF I AM REDUCED BY HALF...
...AND EVEN IF I LOSE *EVERY-THING.*

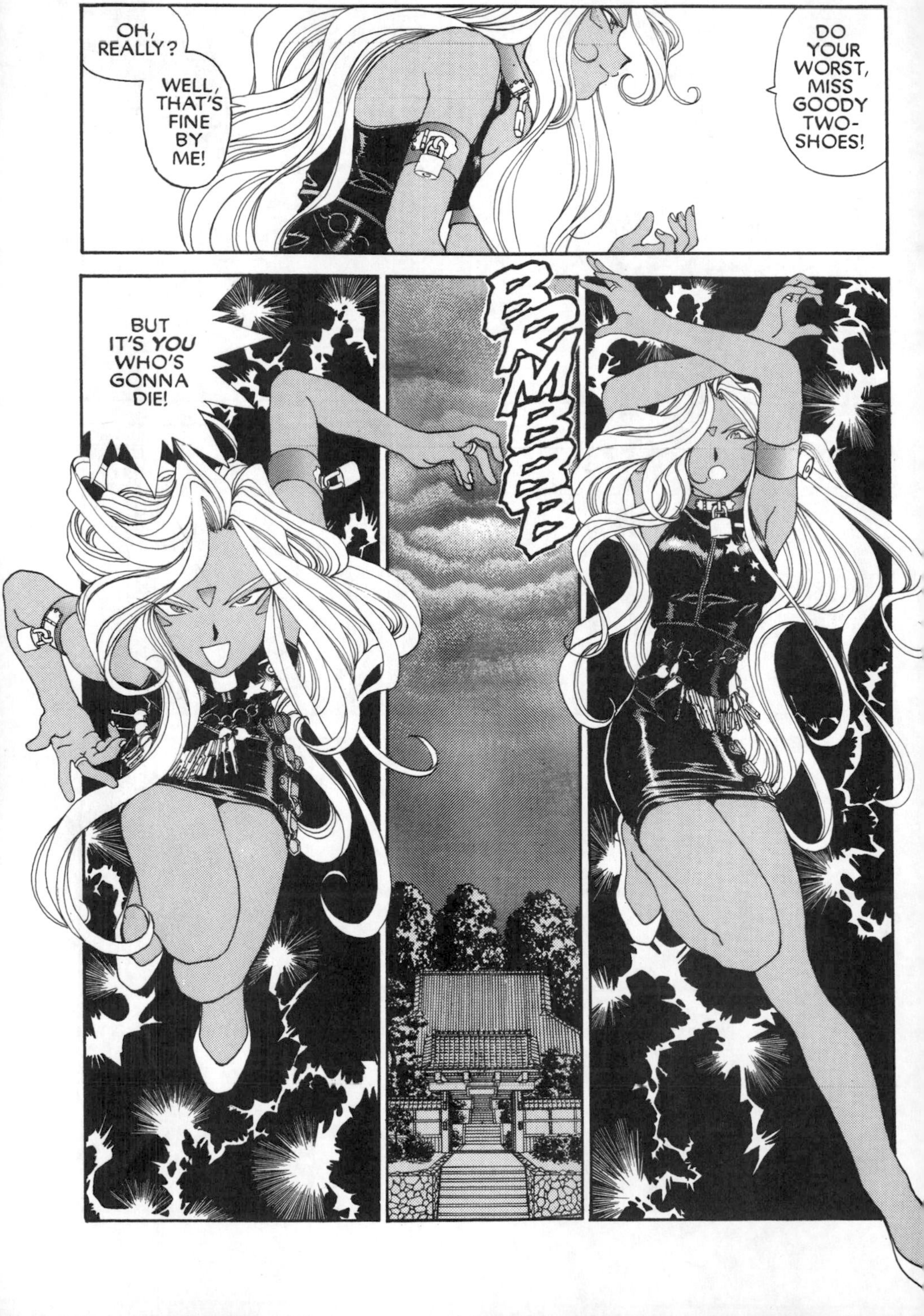
OH, REALLY?
WELL, THAT'S FINE BY ME!
DO YOUR WORST, MISS GOODY TWO-SHOES!
BUT IT'S *YOU* WHO'S GONNA DIE!
BRMBBB

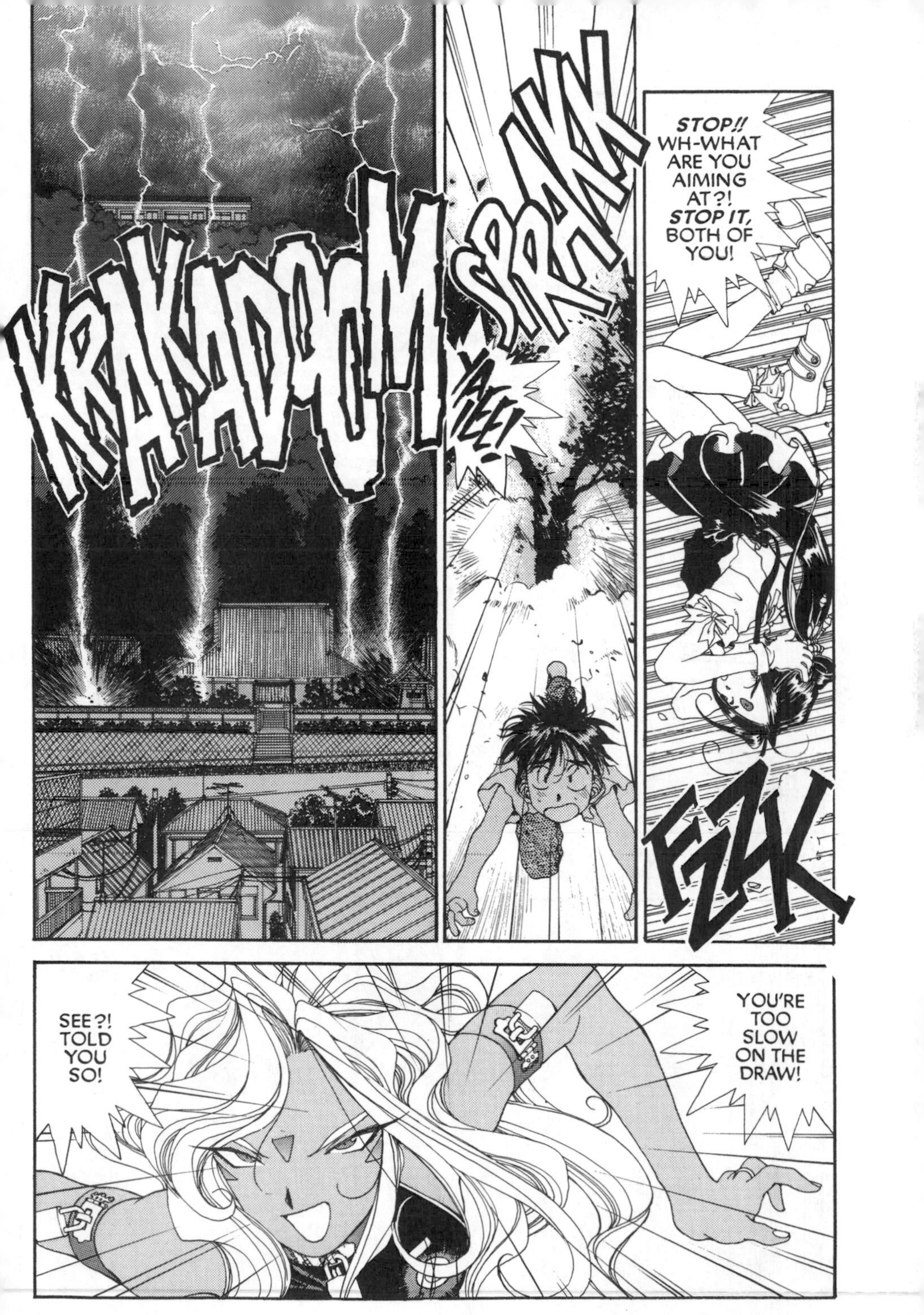
KRAKADOOM
SPRAKK
YAEEE!
STOP!! WH-WHAT ARE YOU AIMING AT?! STOP IT, BOTH OF YOU!
FZZK
SEE?! TOLD YOU SO!
YOU'RE TOO SLOW ON THE DRAW!

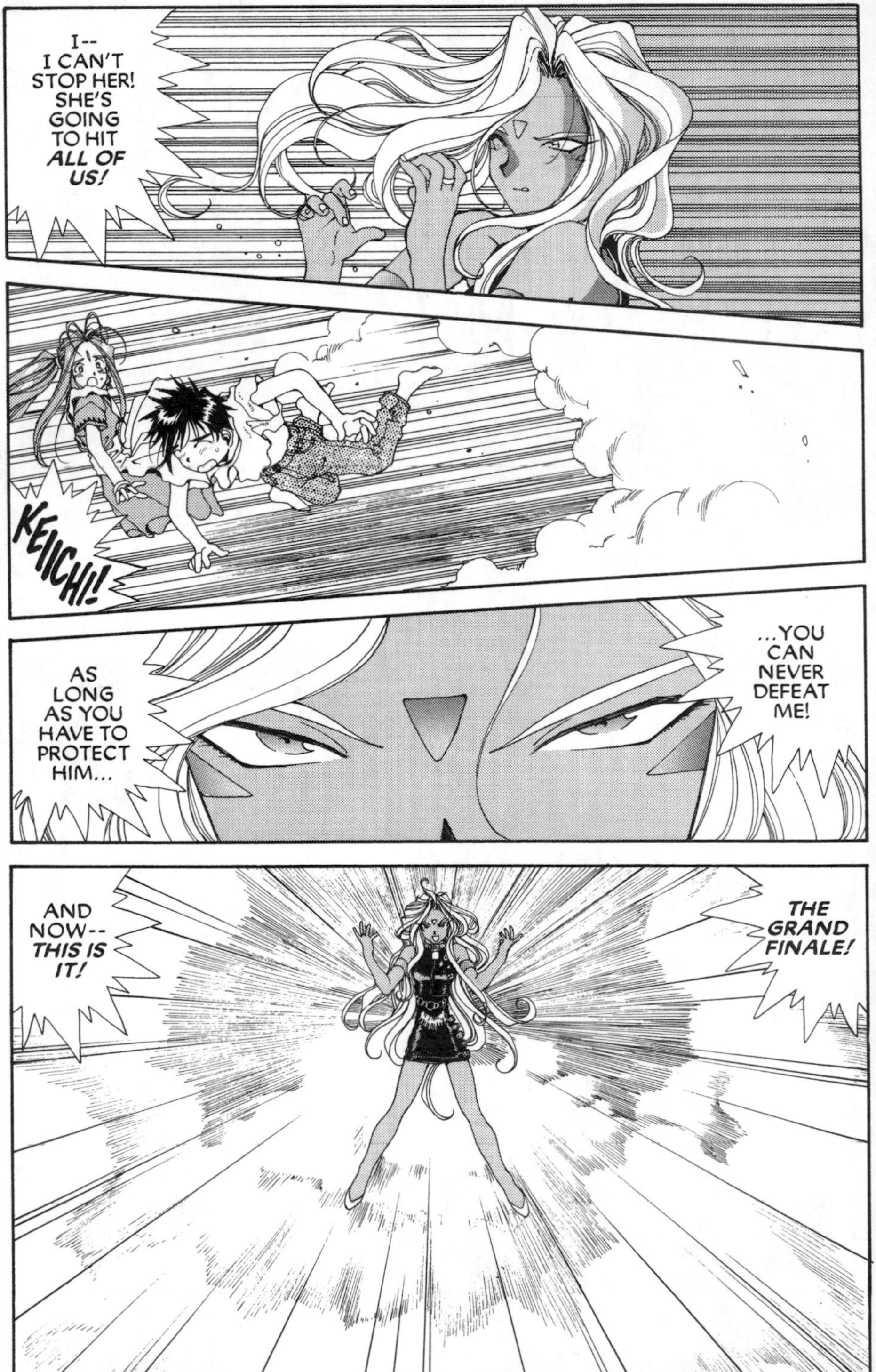
I-- I CAN'T STOP HER! SHE'S GOING TO HIT *ALL OF US!*
KEIICHI!
AS LONG AS YOU HAVE TO PROTECT HIM...
...YOU CAN NEVER DEFEAT ME!
AND NOW-- *THIS IS IT!*
THE GRAND FINALE!

OH, MAN! THIS IS GONNA BE *BAD!*

'BYE-'BYE, KIDDIES!

FIZZLE

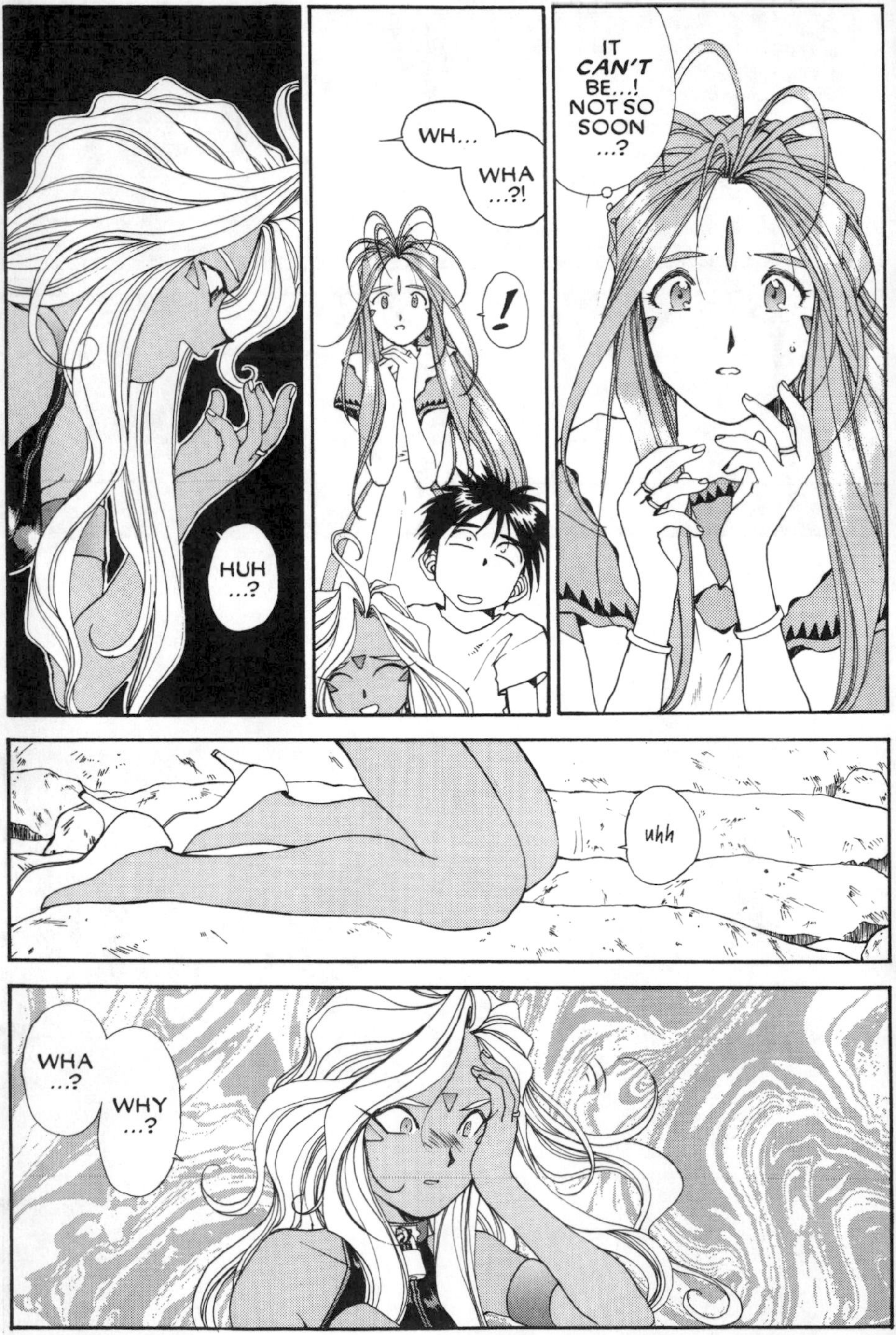
HUH ...?
WH...
WHA ...?!
!
IT CAN'T BE...! NOT SO SOON ...?
uhh
WHA ...?
WHY ...?

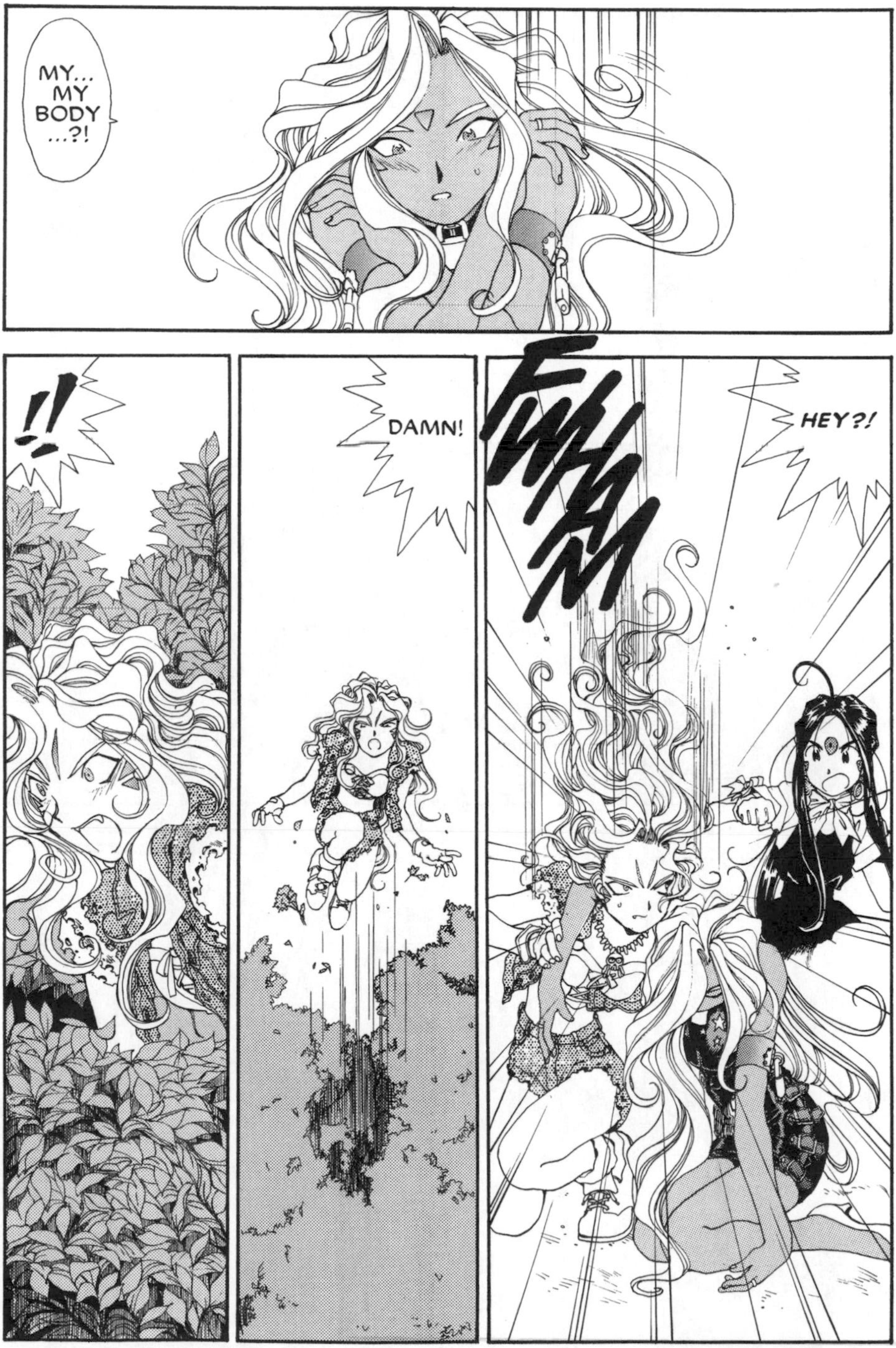
MY... MY BODY ...?!
!!
DAMN!
HEY?!

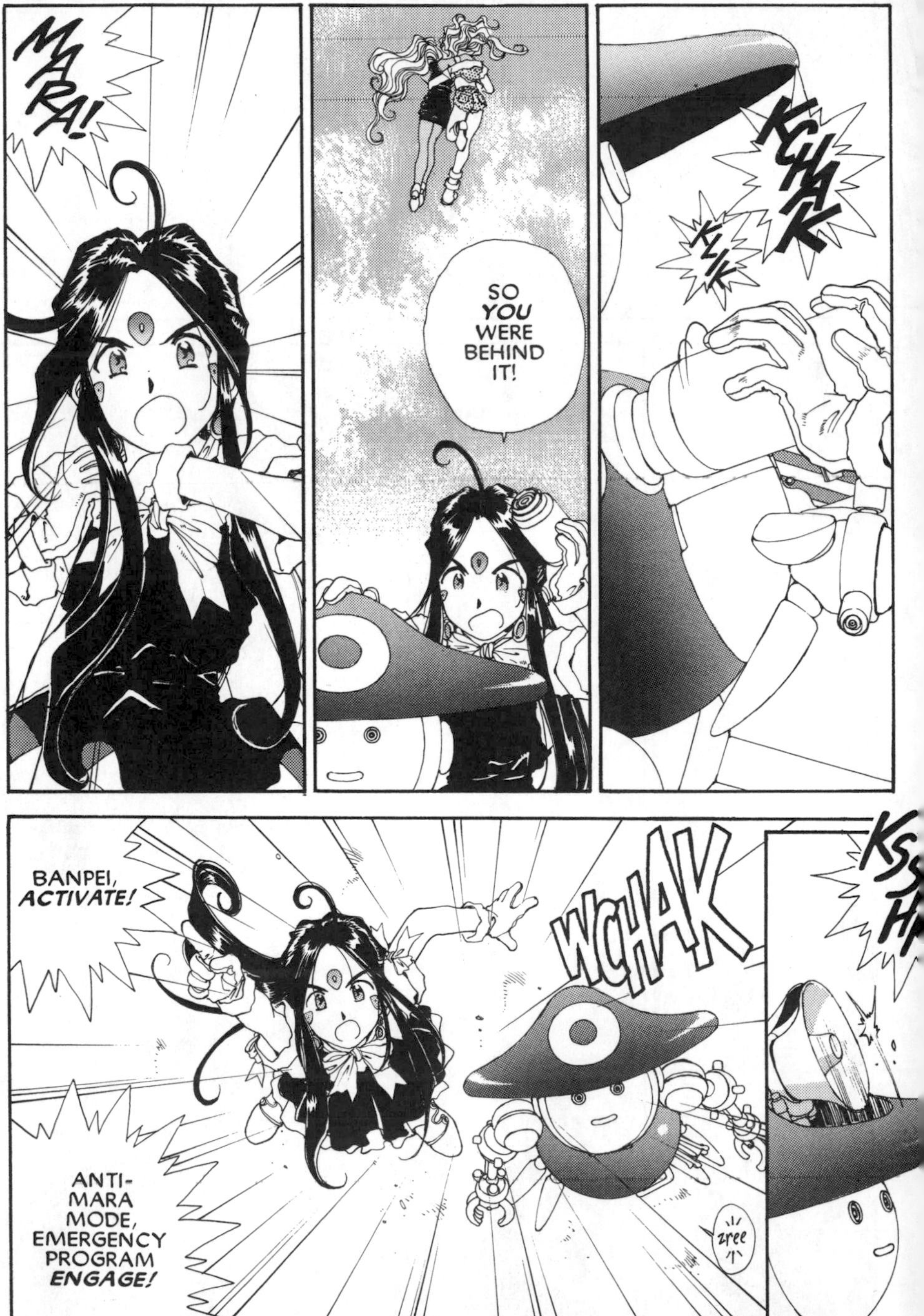
MARA!
SO YOU WERE BEHIND IT!
KCHAK
KLIK
BANPEI, ACTIVATE!
WCHAK
ANTI-MARA MODE, EMERGENCY PROGRAM ENGAGE!
zree

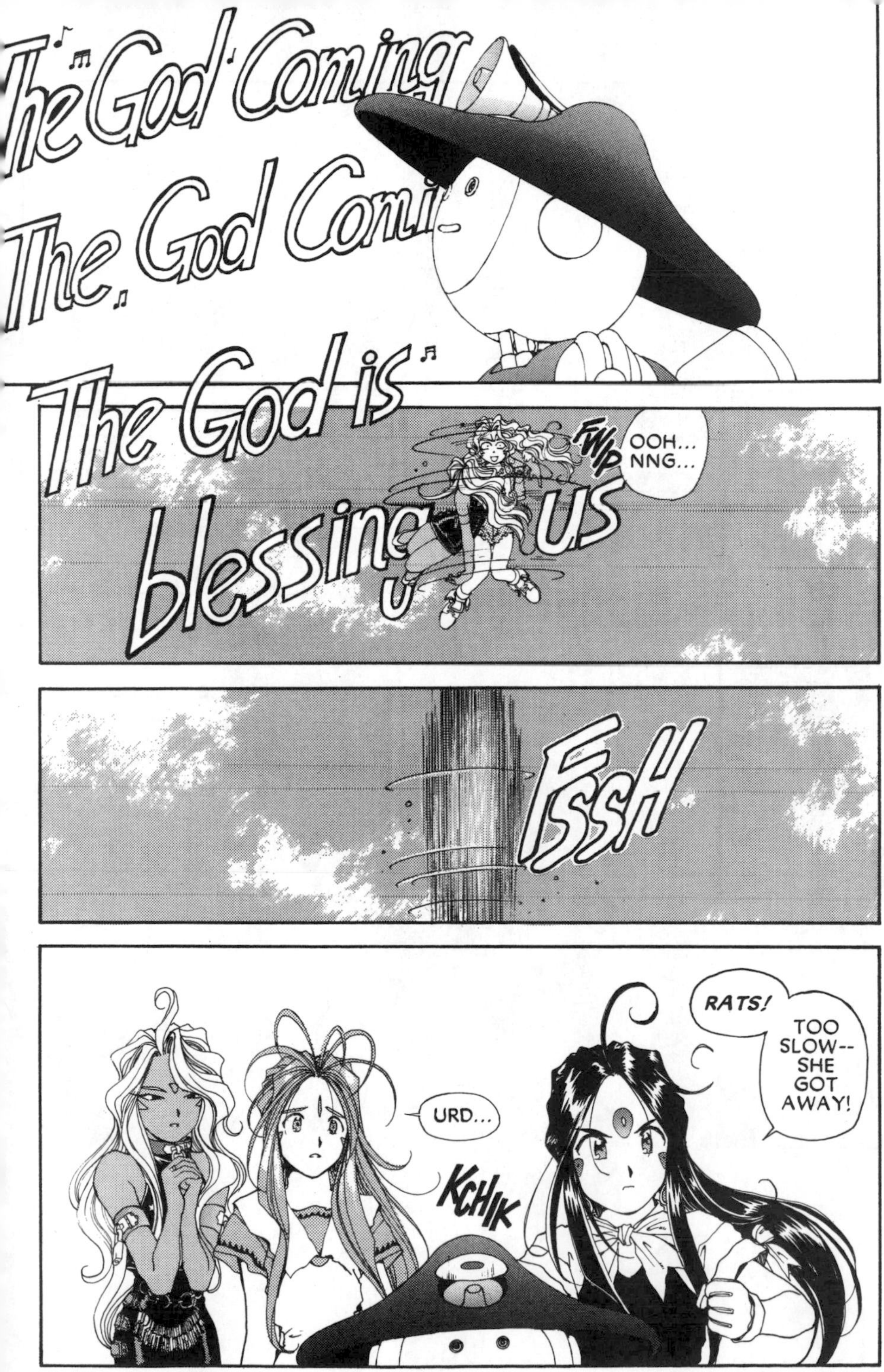
The God Coming
The God Comi
The God is
blessing us
FWIP
OOH... NNG...
FSSH
RATS! TOO SLOW--SHE GOT AWAY!
URD...
KCHIK

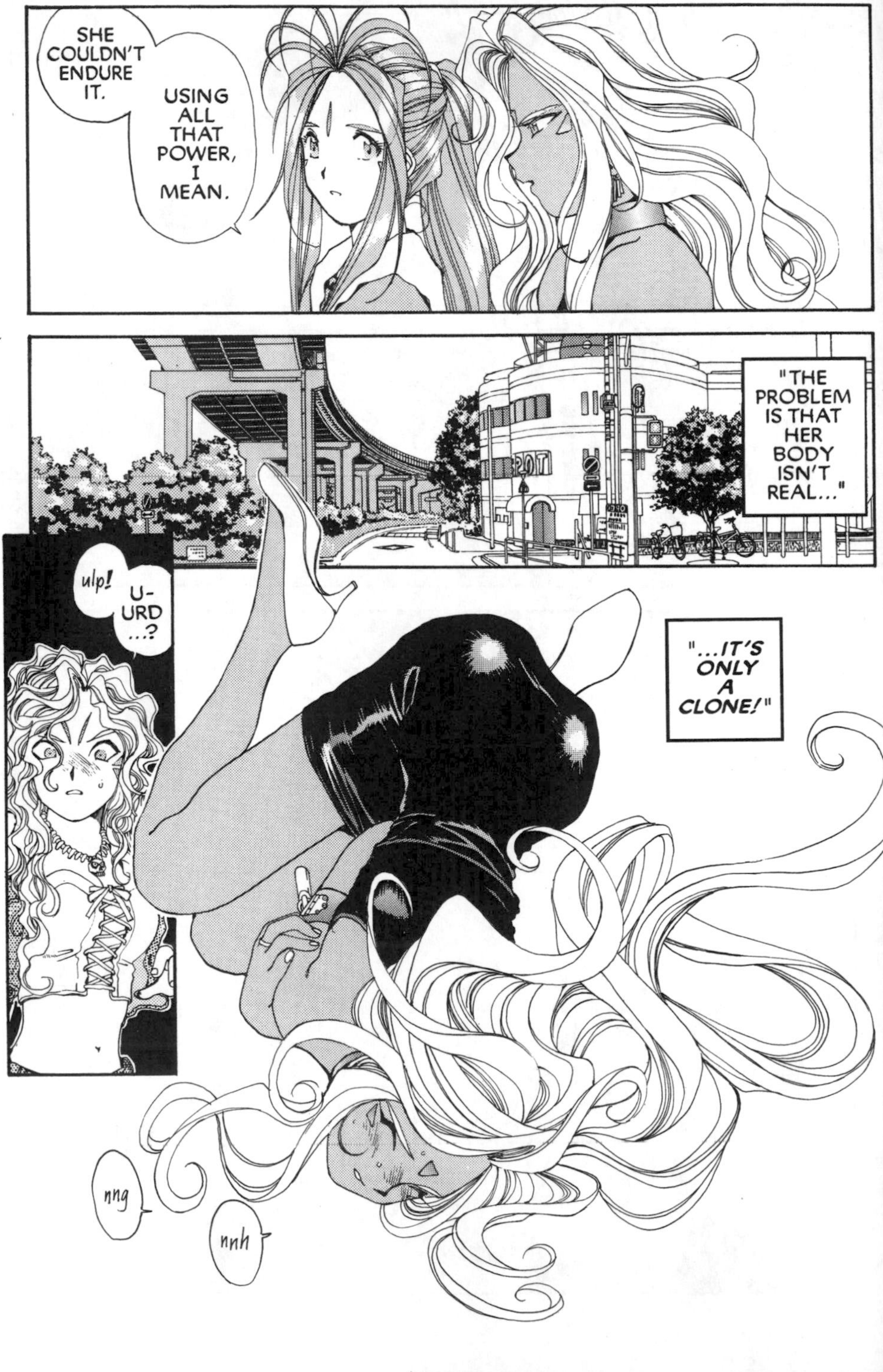
SHE COULDN'T ENDURE IT.
USING ALL THAT POWER, I MEAN.
"THE PROBLEM IS THAT HER BODY ISN'T REAL..."
ulp!
U-URD ...?
"...IT'S ONLY A CLONE!"
nng
nnh

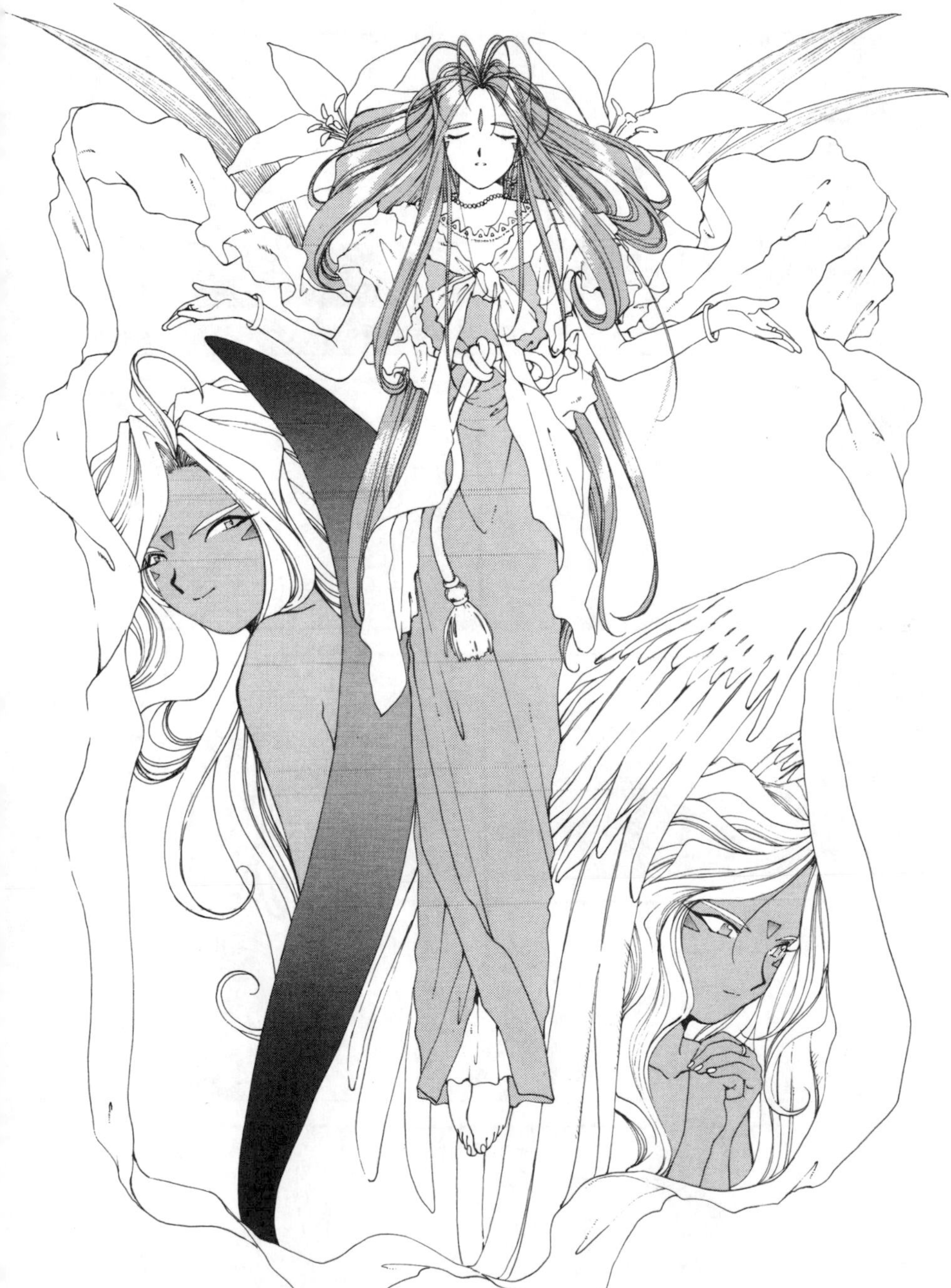

SHADOW & LIGHT

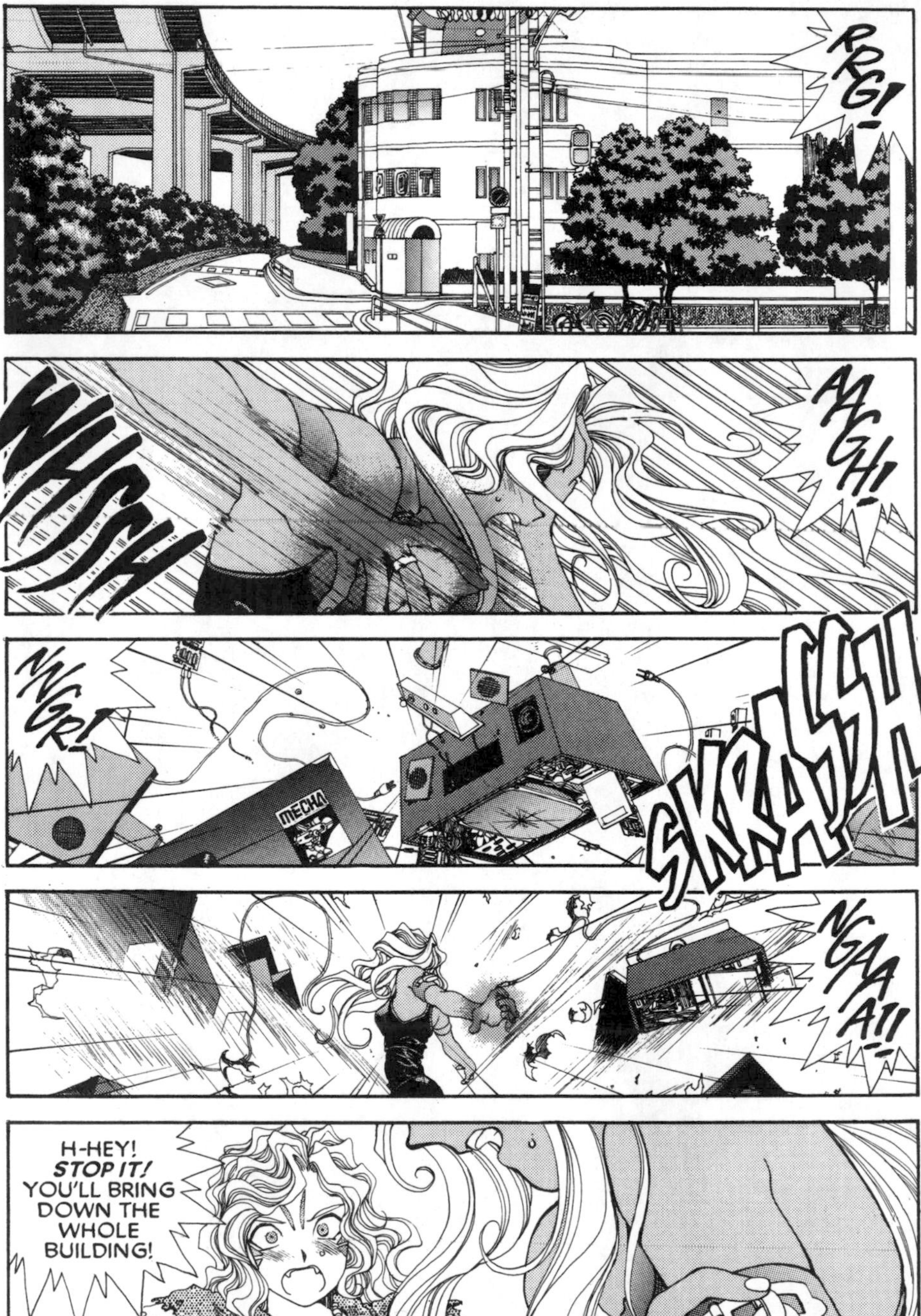
RRG!
WHSSH
AAGH!
NNGR!
SKRASSH
NGAAA!!
H-HEY! STOP IT! YOU'LL BRING DOWN THE WHOLE BUILDING!

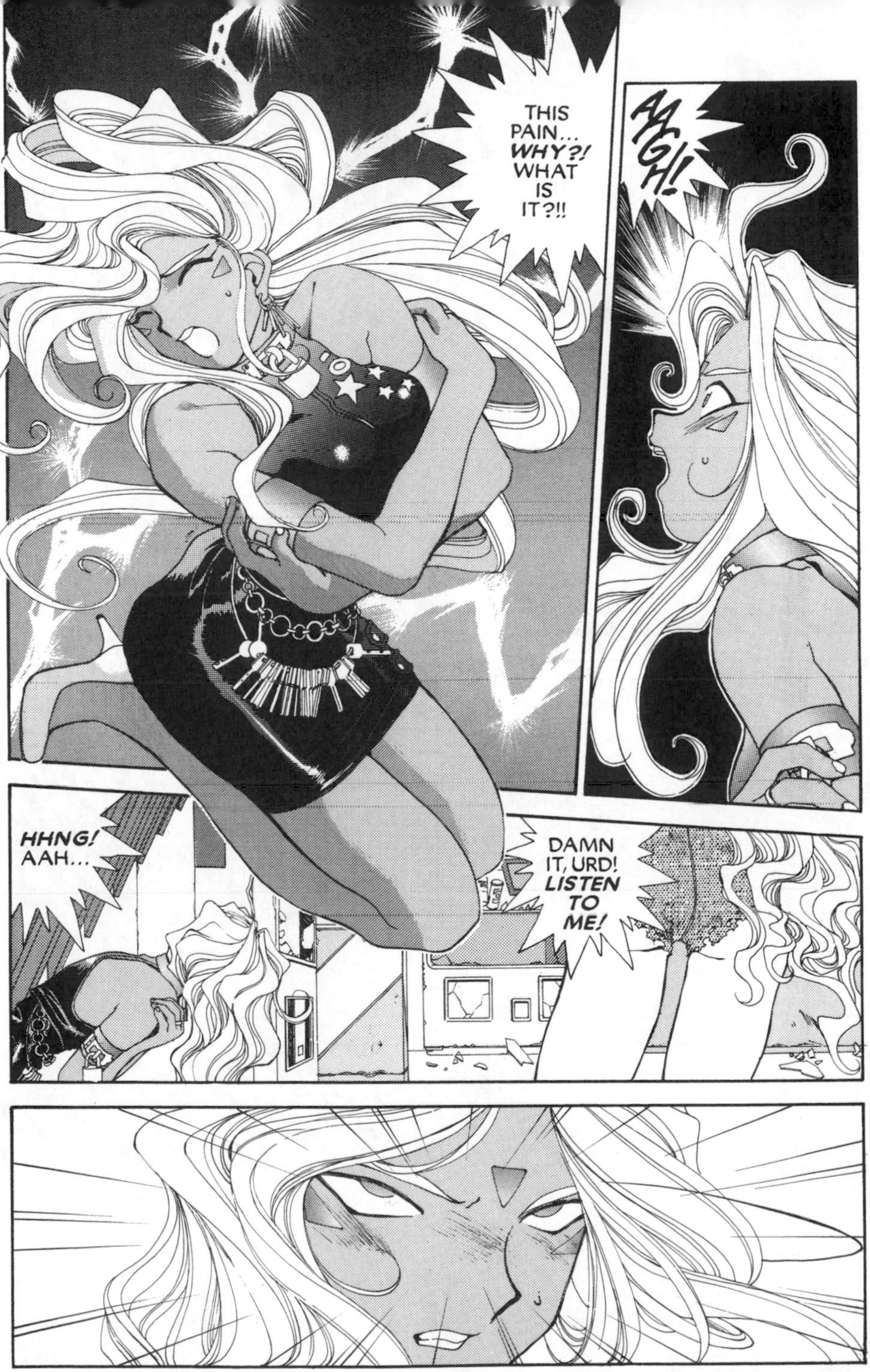
THIS PAIN... WHY?! WHAT IS IT?!!
AAAGH!
HHNG! AAH...
DAMN IT, URD! LISTEN TO ME!

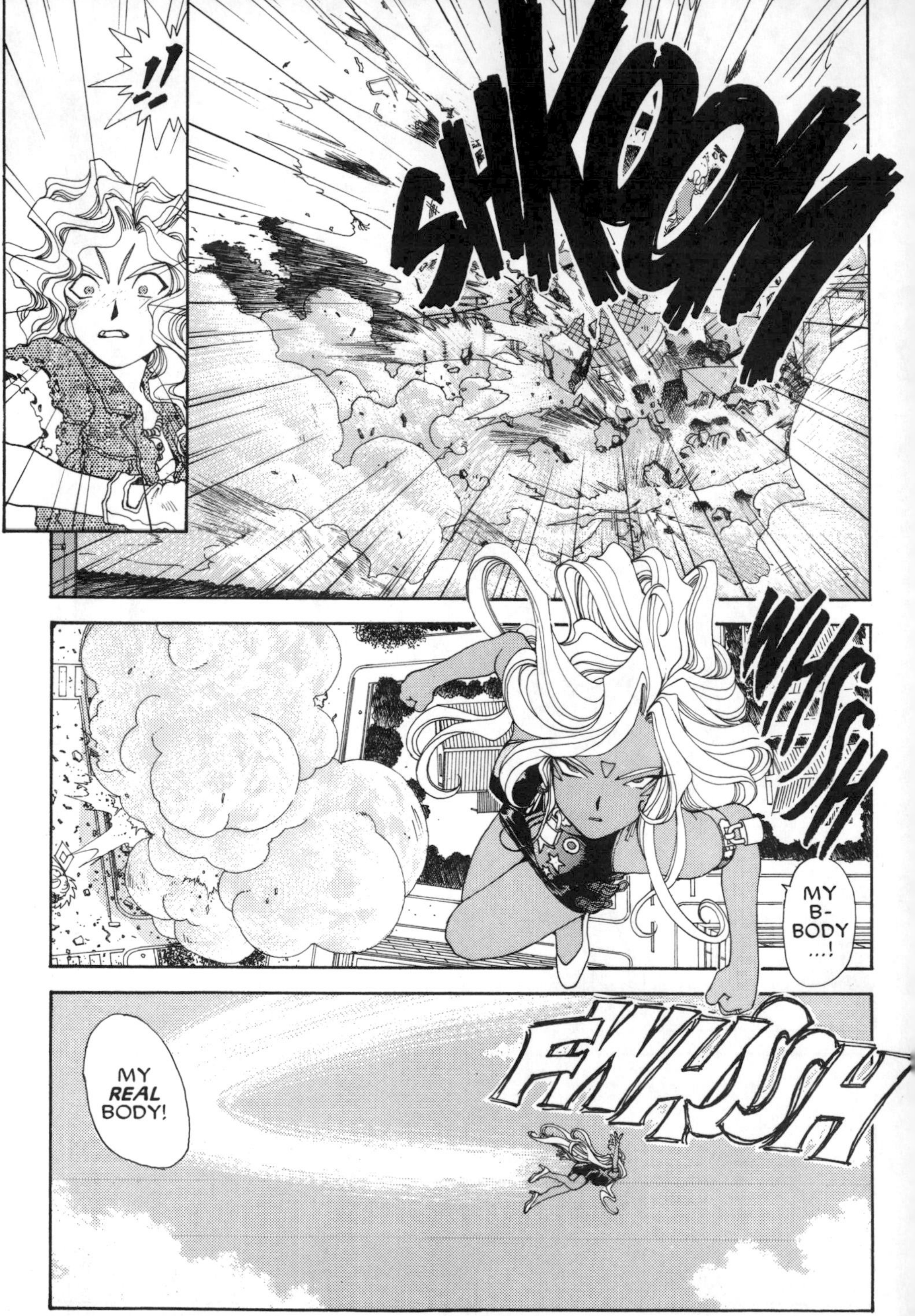
!!
SHKOOM
WHSSH
MY B-BODY ...!
MY REAL BODY!
FWOOSH

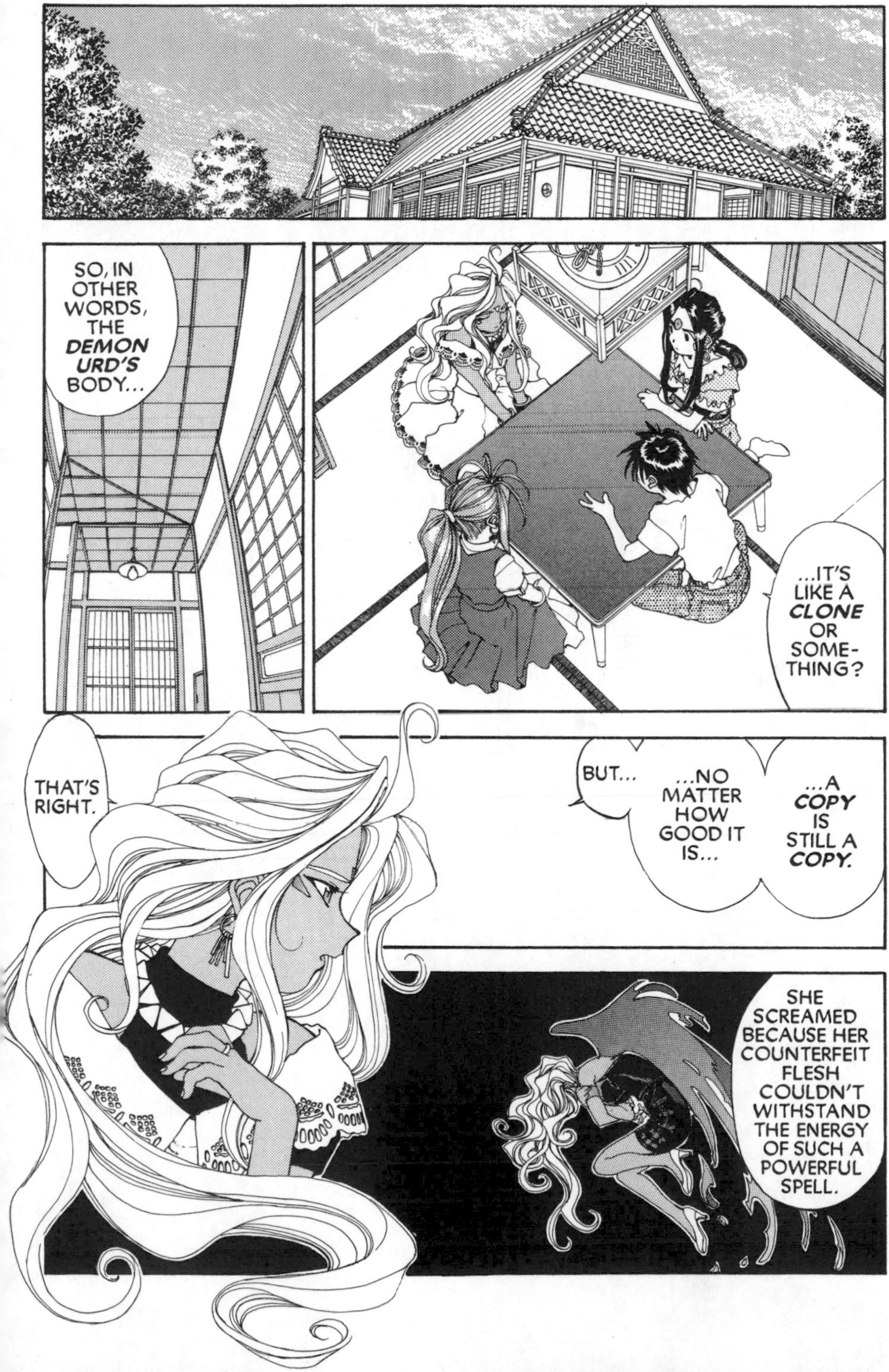

SO, IN OTHER WORDS, THE DEMON URD'S BODY...
...IT'S LIKE A CLONE OR SOME-THING?
THAT'S RIGHT.
BUT...
...NO MATTER HOW GOOD IT IS...
...A COPY IS STILL A COPY.
SHE SCREAMED BECAUSE HER COUNTERFEIT FLESH COULDN'T WITHSTAND THE ENERGY OF SUCH A POWERFUL SPELL.

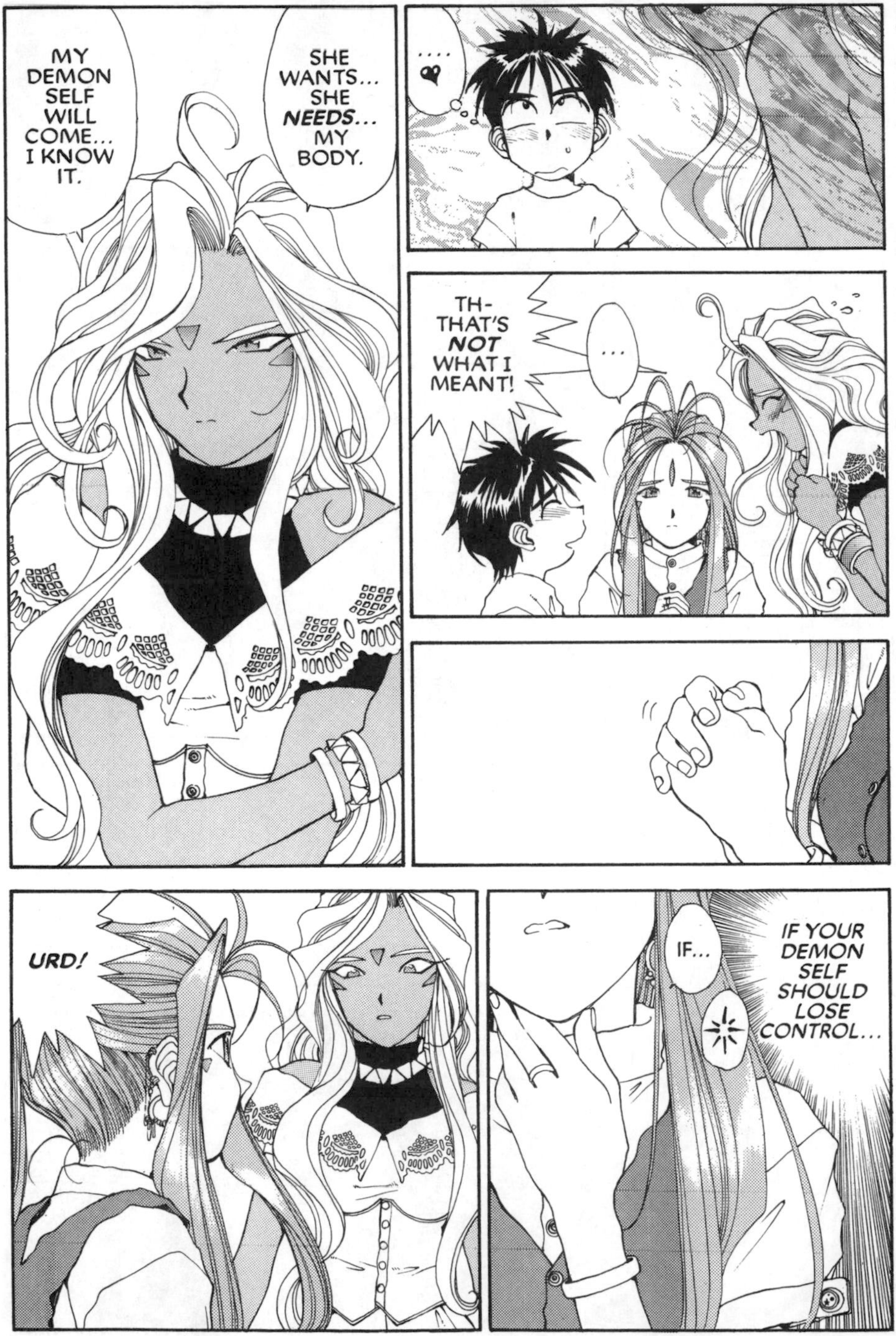
MY DEMON SELF WILL COME... I KNOW IT.
SHE WANTS... SHE ***NEEDS...*** MY BODY.
....
TH- THAT'S ***NOT*** WHAT I MEANT!
...
URD!
IF...
IF YOUR DEMON SELF SHOULD LOSE CONTROL...

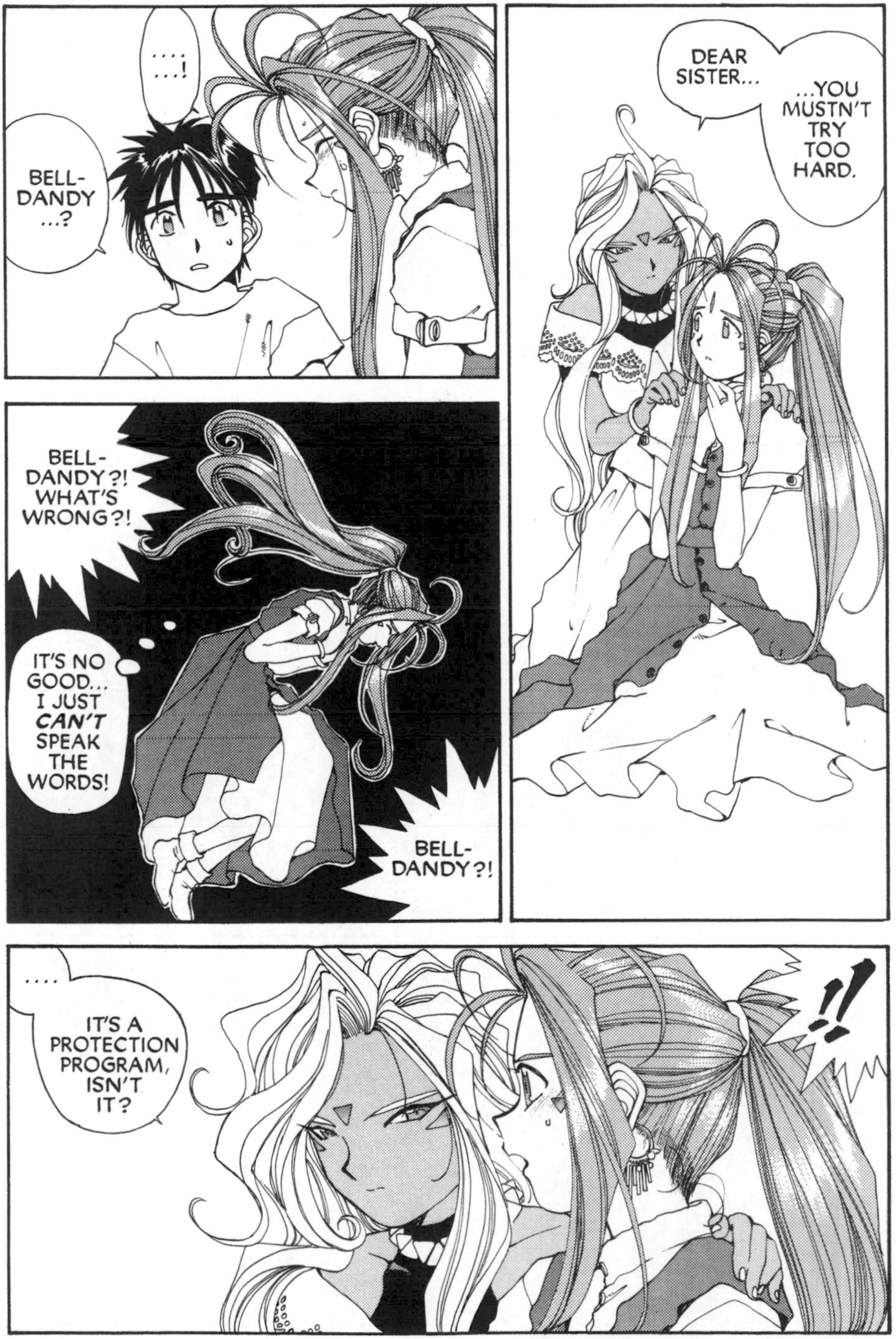
......!
BELL-DANDY ...?
BELL-DANDY?! WHAT'S WRONG?!
IT'S NO GOOD... I JUST *CAN'T* SPEAK THE WORDS!
BELL-DANDY?!
DEAR SISTER...
...YOU MUSTN'T TRY TOO HARD.
....
IT'S A PROTECTION PROGRAM, ISN'T IT?
!!

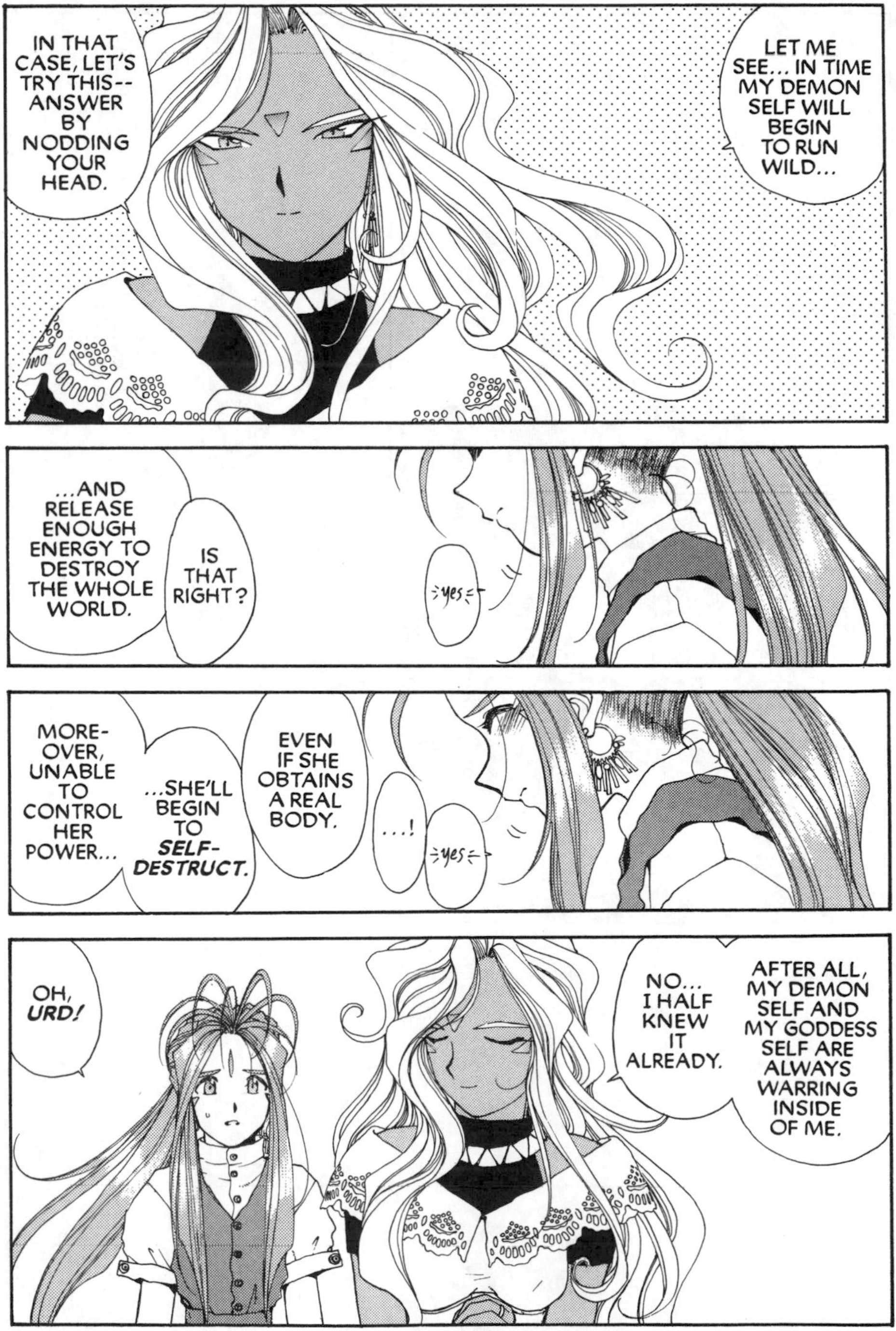
IN THAT CASE, LET'S TRY THIS-- ANSWER BY NODDING YOUR HEAD.
LET ME SEE... IN TIME MY DEMON SELF WILL BEGIN TO RUN WILD...
...AND RELEASE ENOUGH ENERGY TO DESTROY THE WHOLE WORLD.
IS THAT RIGHT?
yes
MORE-OVER, UNABLE TO CONTROL HER POWER...
...SHE'LL BEGIN TO ***SELF-DESTRUCT***.
EVEN IF SHE OBTAINS A REAL BODY.
...!
yes
OH, ***URD!***
NO... I HALF KNEW IT ALREADY.
AFTER ALL, MY DEMON SELF AND MY GODDESS SELF ARE ALWAYS WARRING INSIDE OF ME.

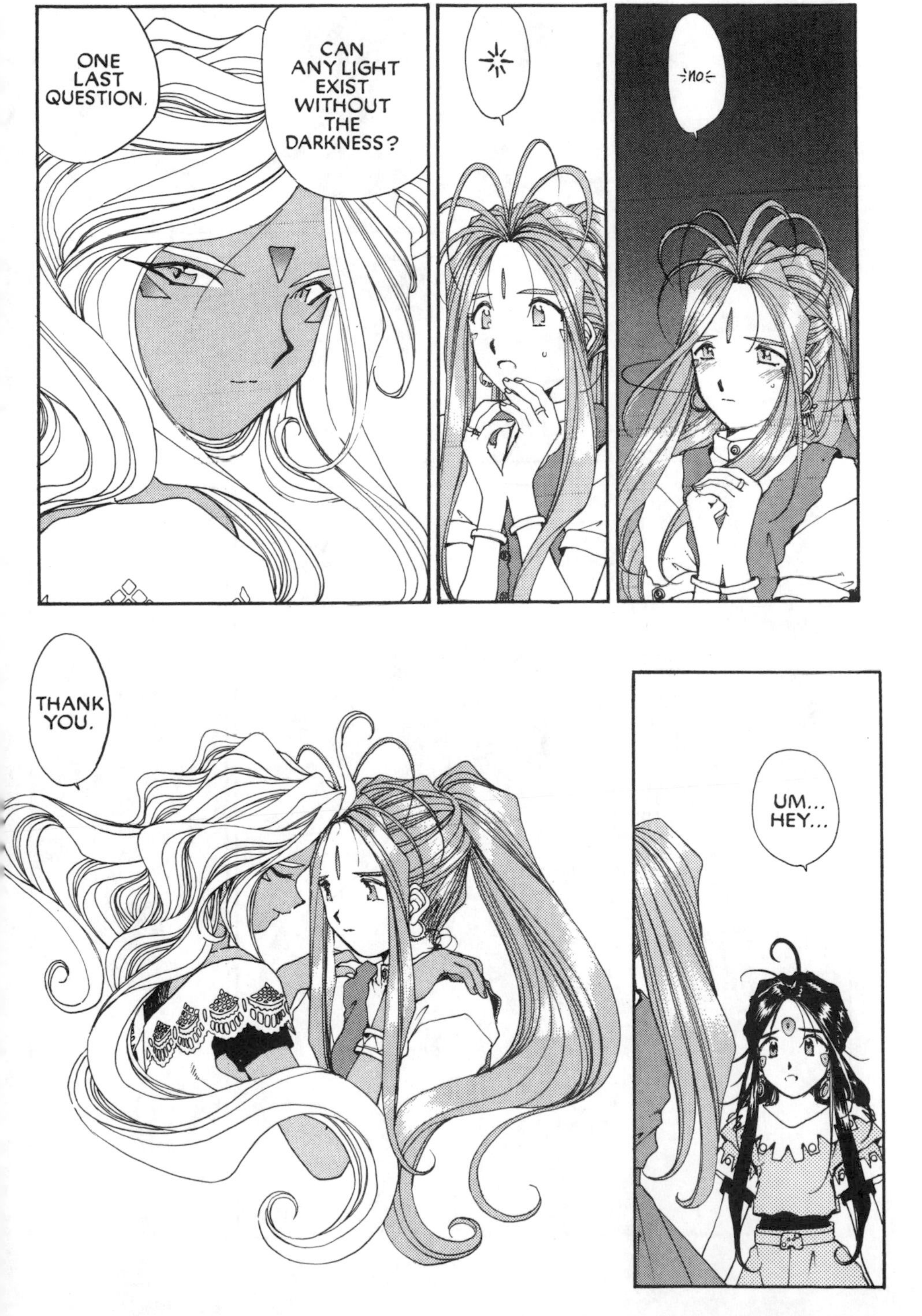
ONE LAST QUESTION.
CAN ANY LIGHT EXIST WITHOUT THE DARKNESS?
NO
THANK YOU.
UM... HEY...

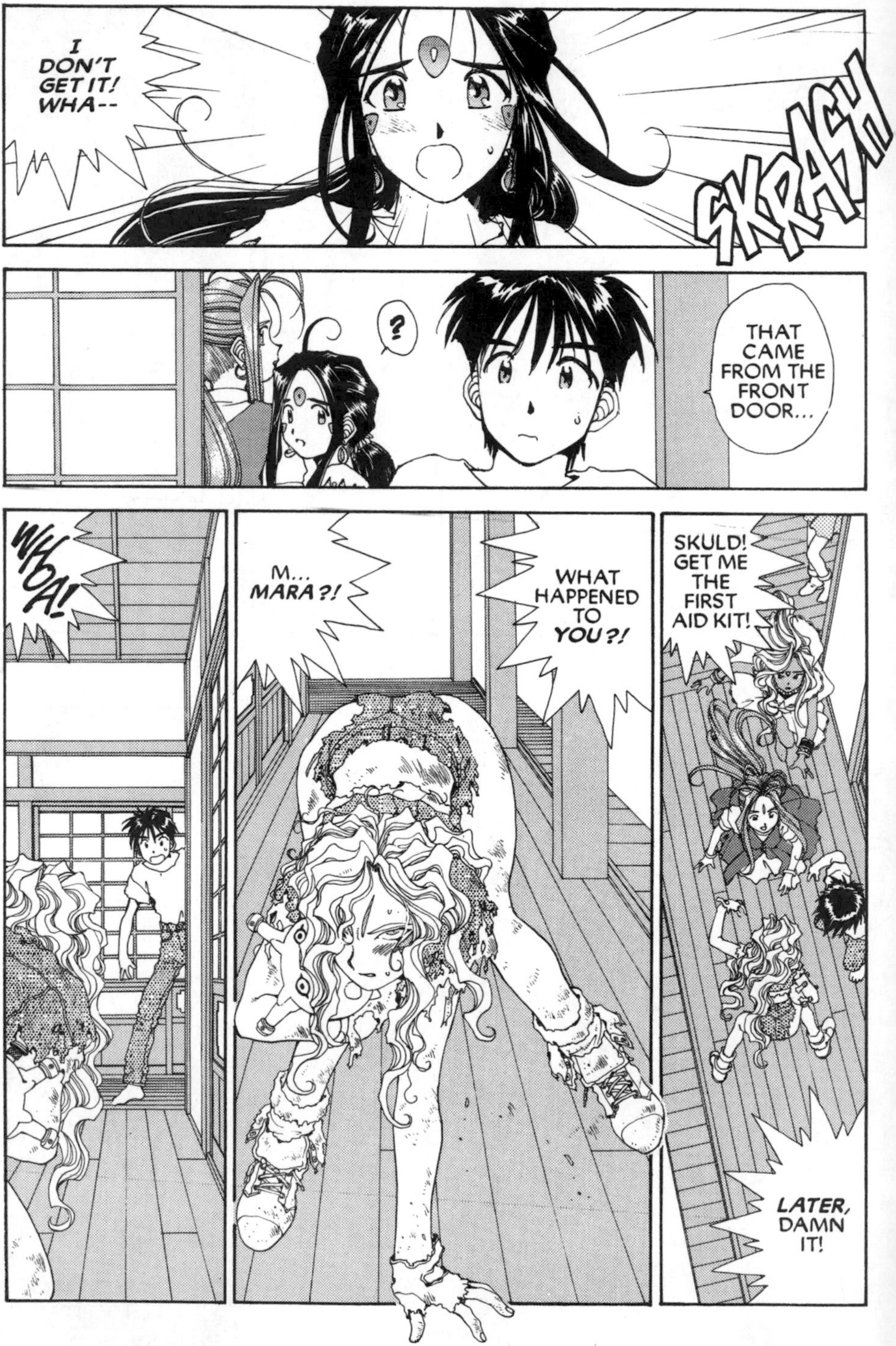
I DON'T GET IT! WHA--
SKRASH
?
THAT CAME FROM THE FRONT DOOR...
WHOA!
M... *MARA?!*
WHAT HAPPENED TO *YOU?!*
SKULD! GET ME THE FIRST AID KIT!
LATER, DAMN IT!

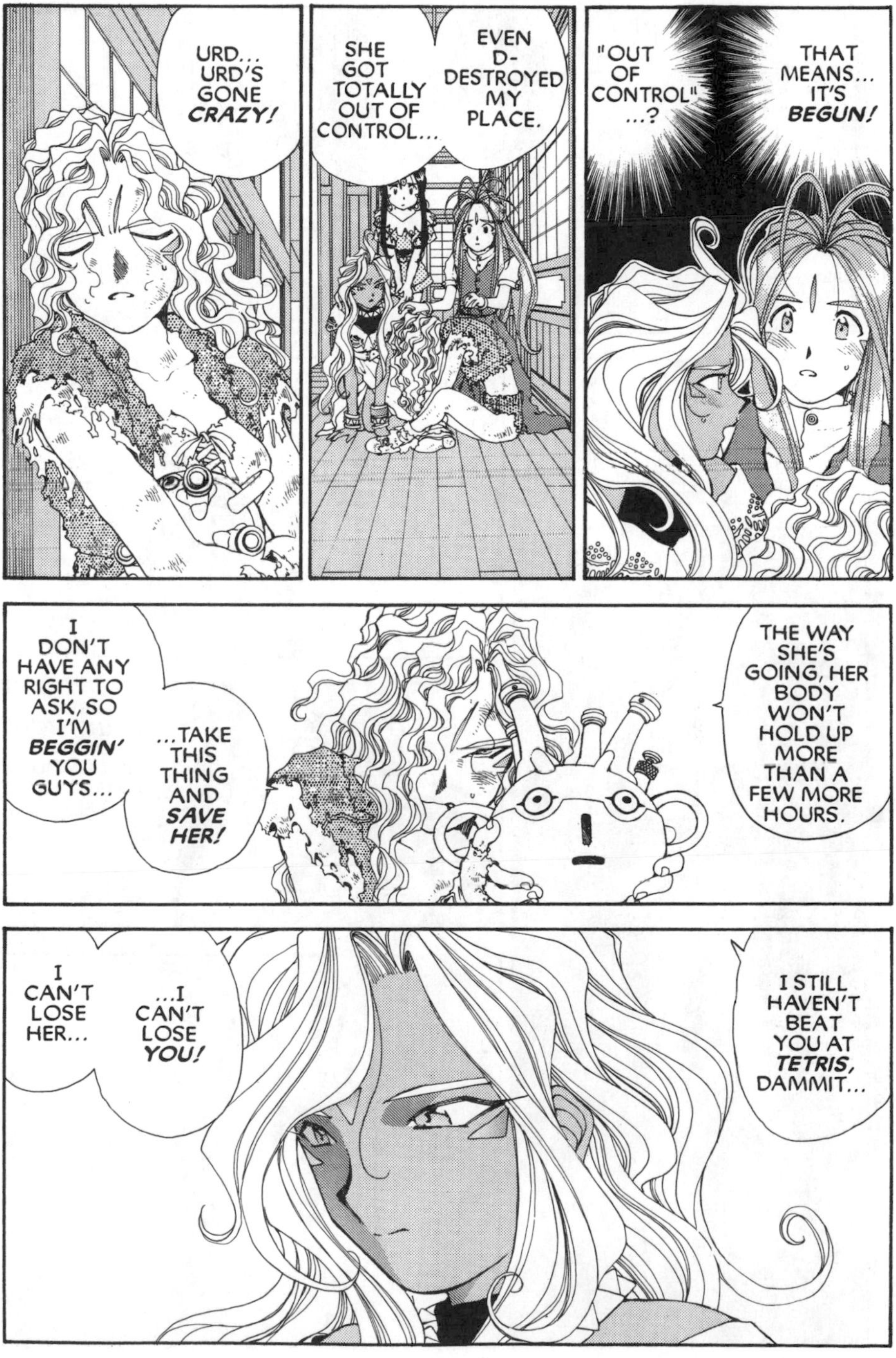
URD... URD'S GONE *CRAZY!*
SHE GOT TOTALLY OUT OF CONTROL...
EVEN D-DESTROYED MY PLACE.
"OUT OF CONTROL" ...?
THAT MEANS... IT'S *BEGUN!*
I DON'T HAVE ANY RIGHT TO ASK, SO I'M *BEGGIN'* YOU GUYS...
...TAKE THIS THING AND *SAVE HER!*
THE WAY SHE'S GOING, HER BODY WON'T HOLD UP MORE THAN A FEW MORE HOURS.
I CAN'T LOSE HER...
...I CAN'T LOSE *YOU!*
I STILL HAVEN'T BEAT YOU AT *TETRIS,* DAMMIT...

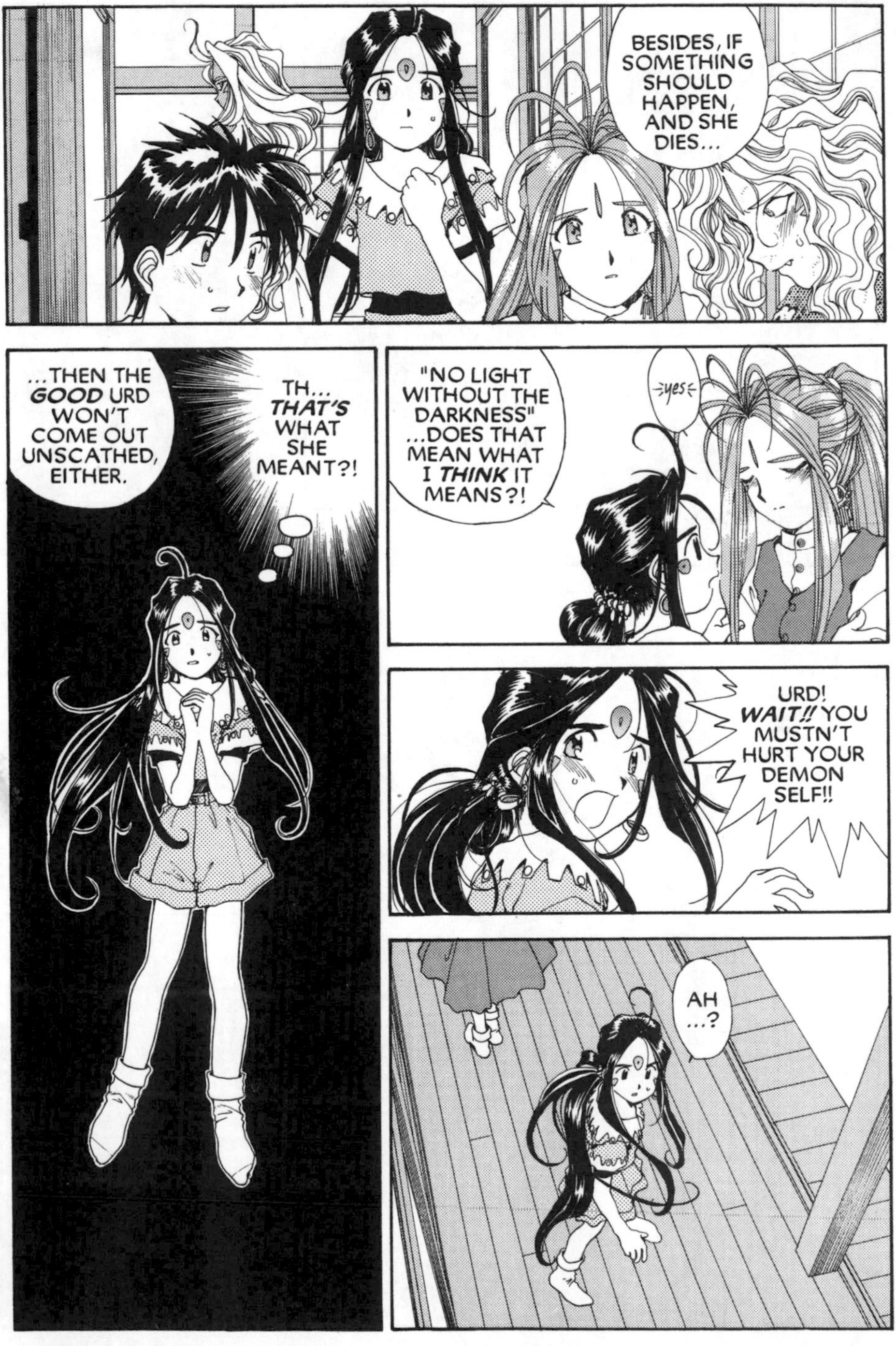
BESIDES, IF SOMETHING SHOULD HAPPEN, AND SHE DIES...
...THEN THE **GOOD** URD WON'T COME OUT UNSCATHED, EITHER.
TH... **THAT'S** WHAT SHE MEANT?!
"NO LIGHT WITHOUT THE DARKNESS" ...DOES THAT MEAN WHAT I **THINK** IT MEANS?!
yes
URD! **WAIT!!** YOU MUSTN'T HURT YOUR DEMON SELF!!
AH ...?

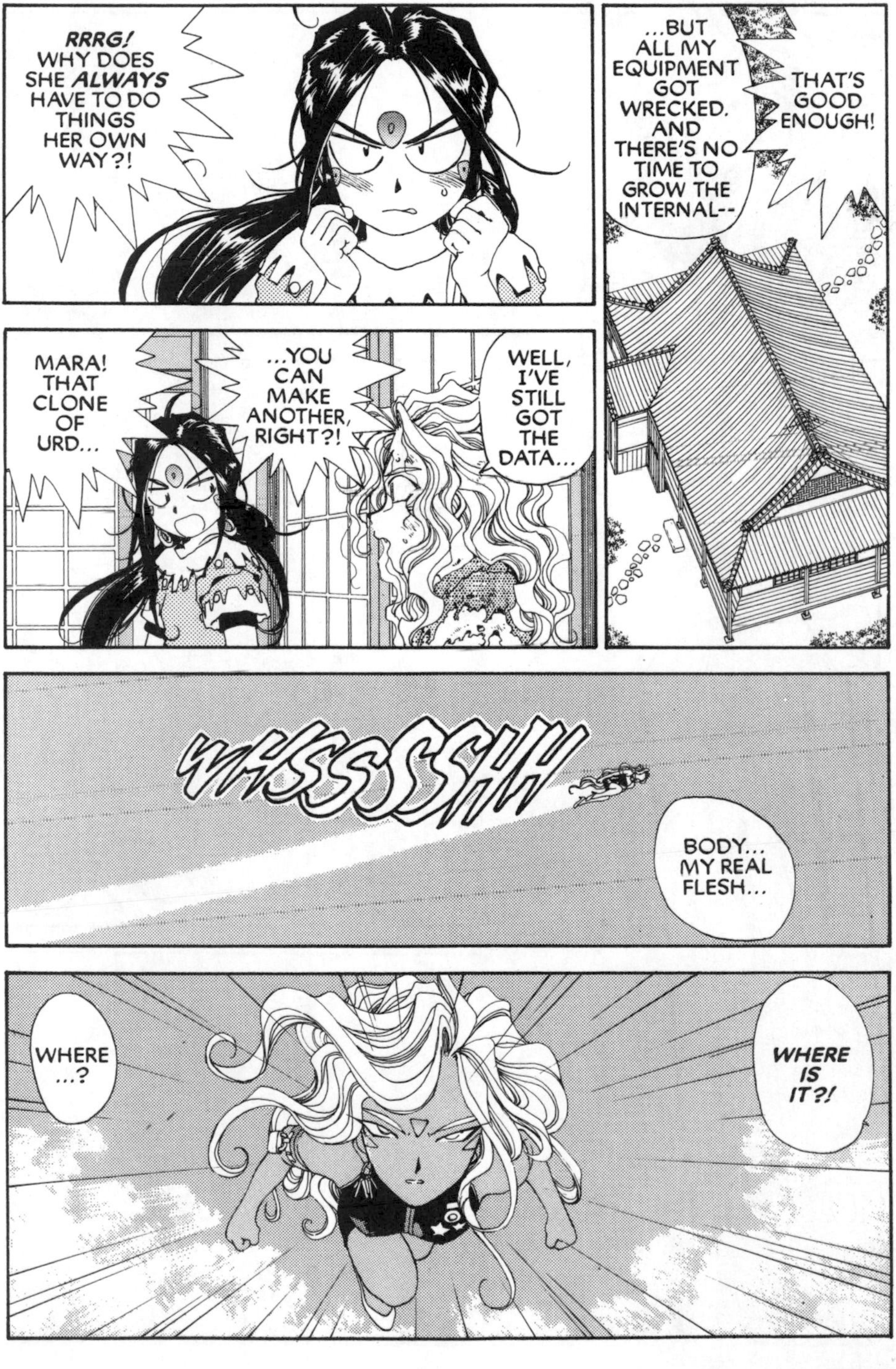
RRRG! WHY DOES SHE ALWAYS HAVE TO DO THINGS HER OWN WAY?!
MARA! THAT CLONE OF URD...
...YOU CAN MAKE ANOTHER, RIGHT?!
WELL, I'VE STILL GOT THE DATA...
...BUT ALL MY EQUIPMENT GOT WRECKED. AND THERE'S NO TIME TO GROW THE INTERNAL--
THAT'S GOOD ENOUGH!
WHSSSSHH
BODY... MY REAL FLESH...
WHERE ...?
WHERE IS IT?!

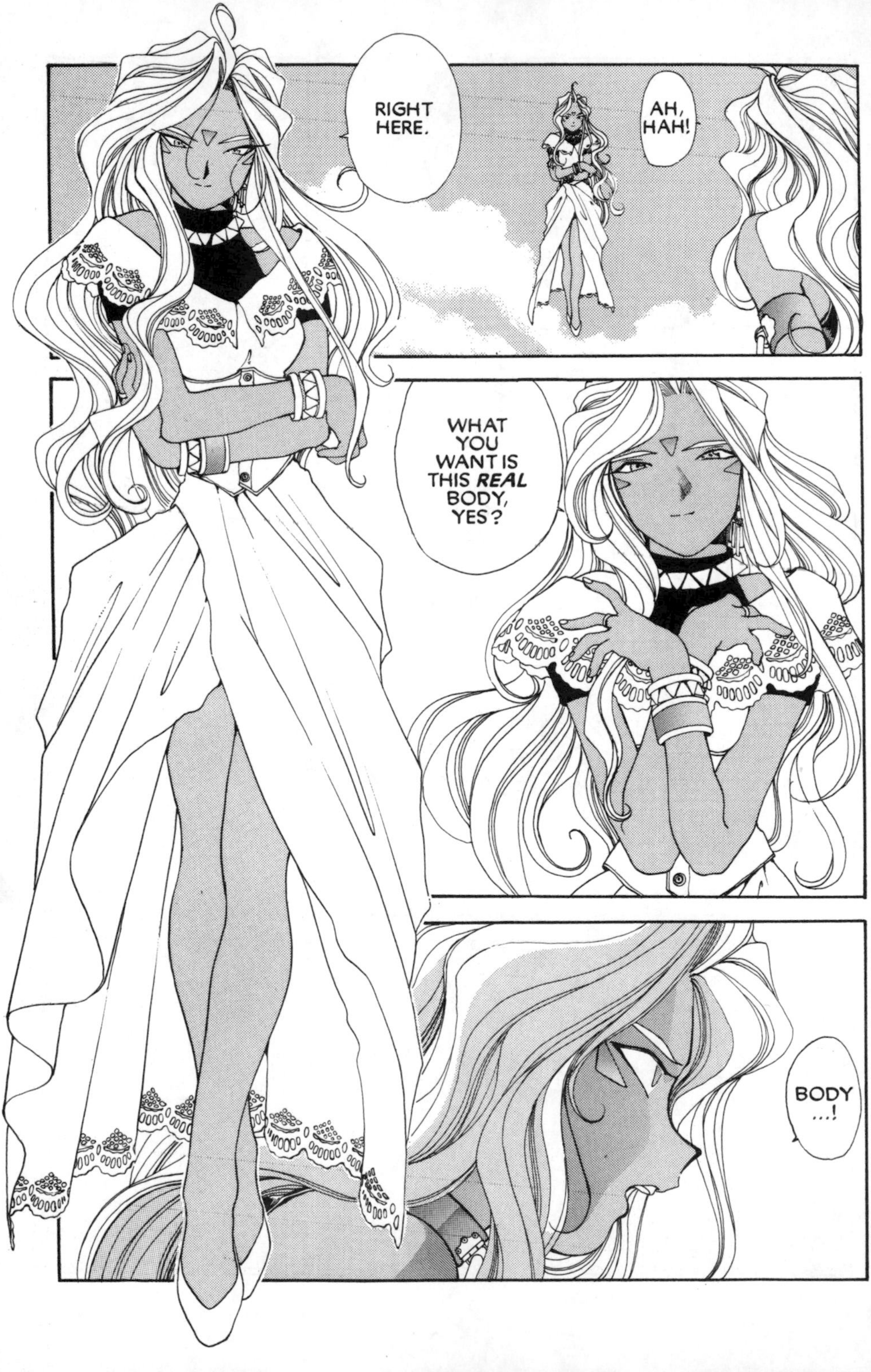
RIGHT HERE.
AH, HAH!
WHAT YOU WANT IS THIS REAL BODY, YES?
BODY ...!

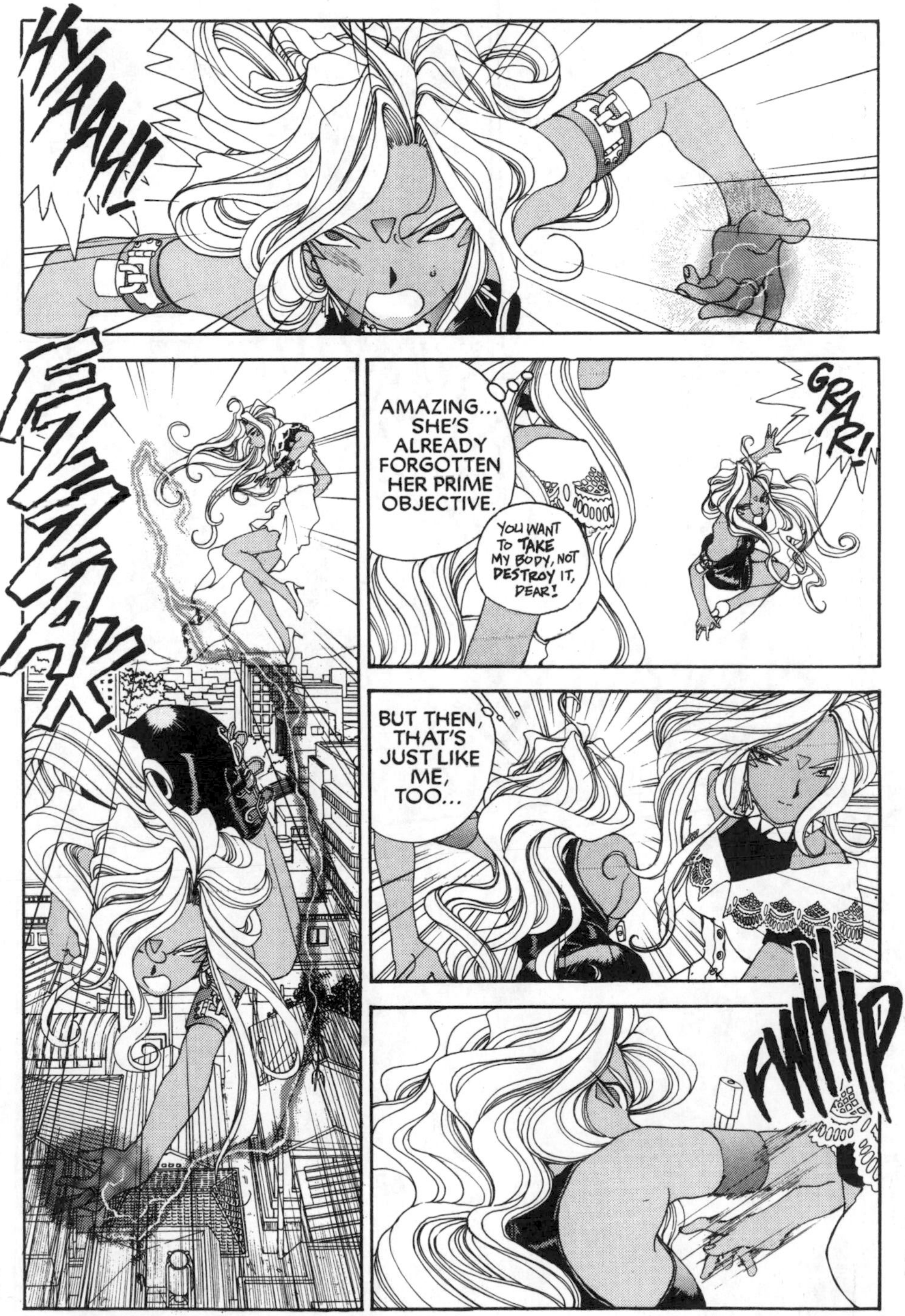
KYAAAH!
AMAZING... SHE'S ALREADY FORGOTTEN HER PRIME OBJECTIVE.
YOU WANT TO TAKE MY BODY, NOT DESTROY IT, DEAR!
GRAR!
BUT THEN, THAT'S JUST LIKE ME, TOO...
FWHIP

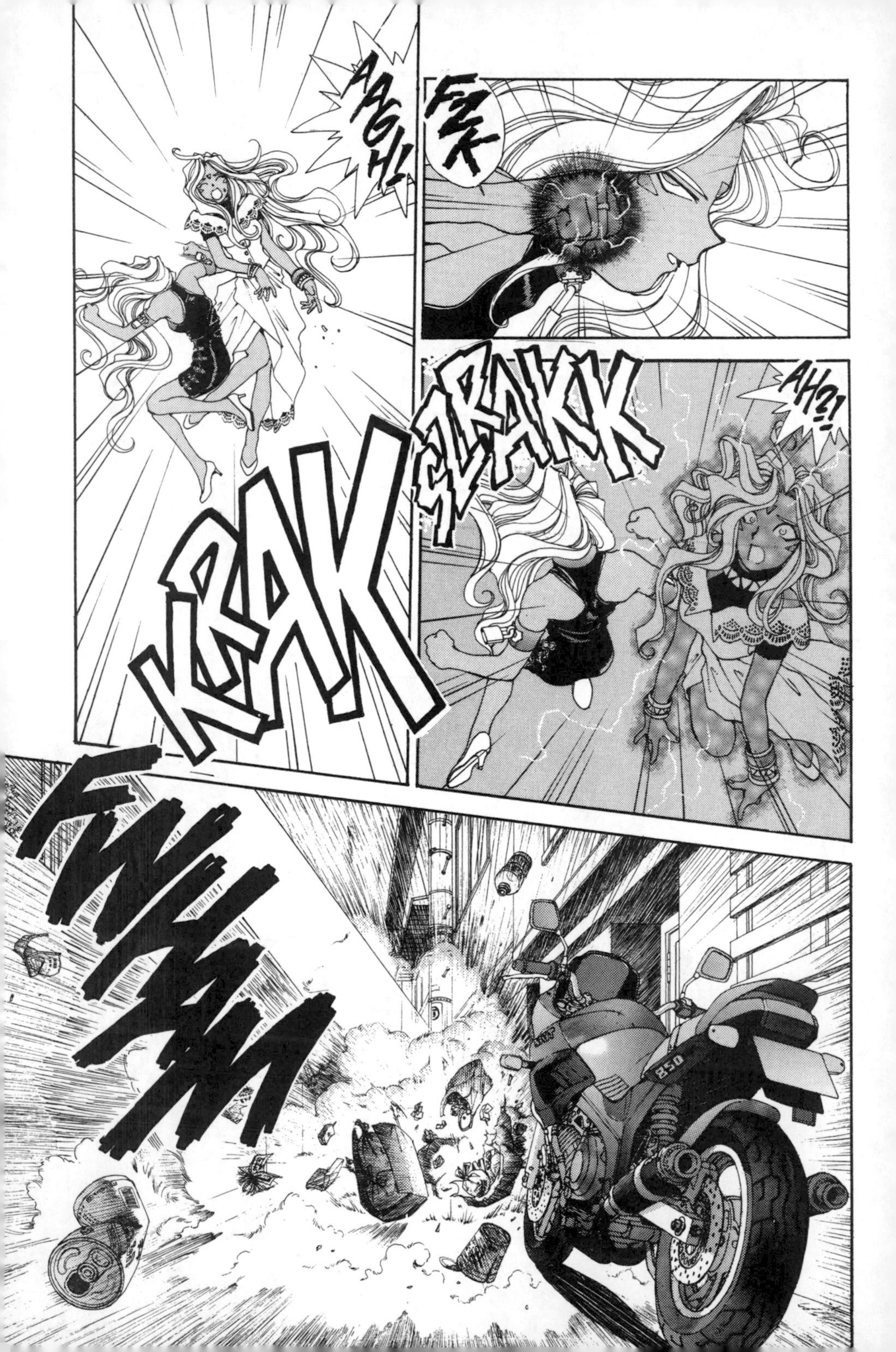
AAGH!
KRAK
FZZK
SZRAKK
AH?!

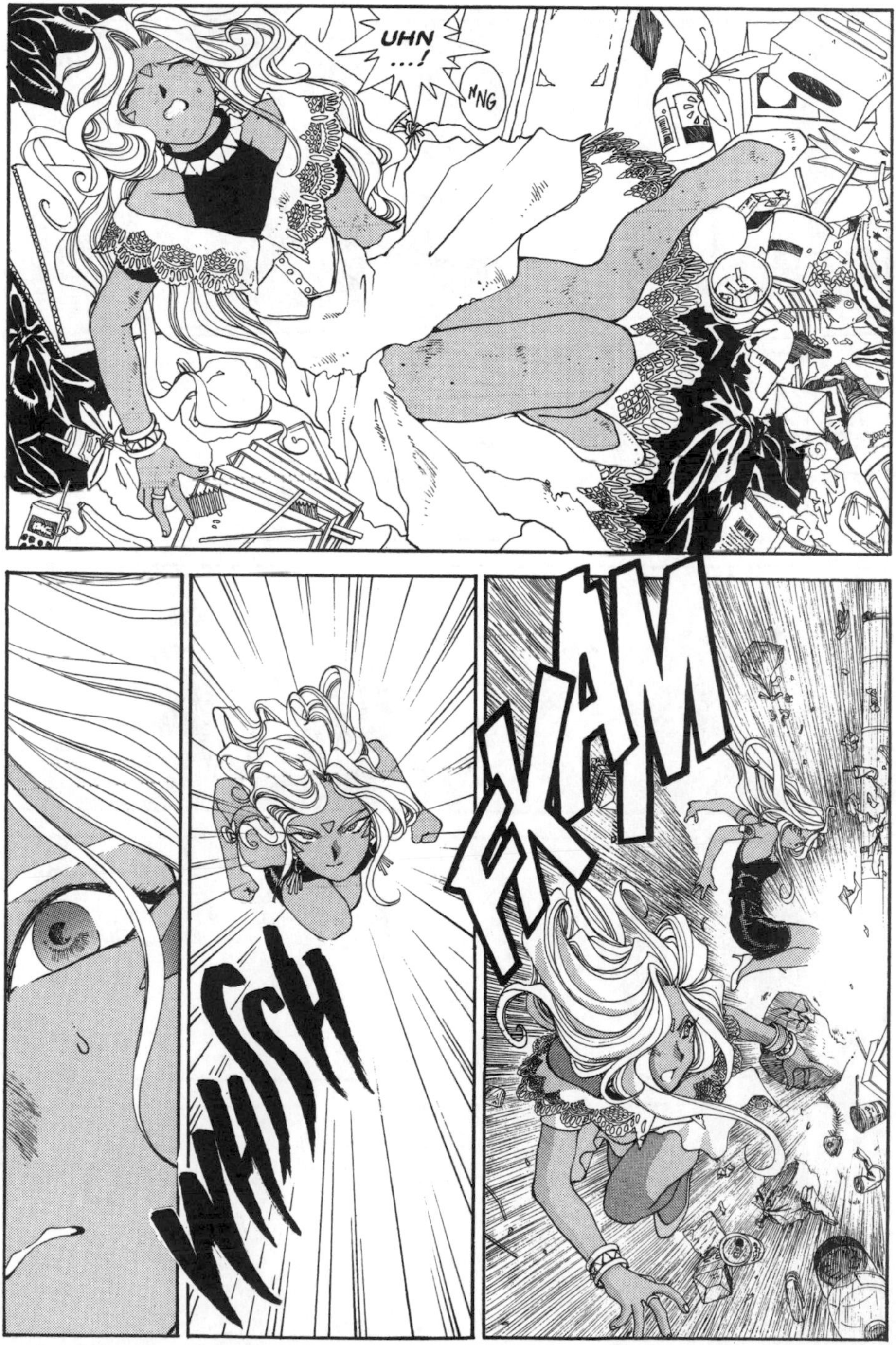
UHN ...!
NNG
WHISH
FKAM

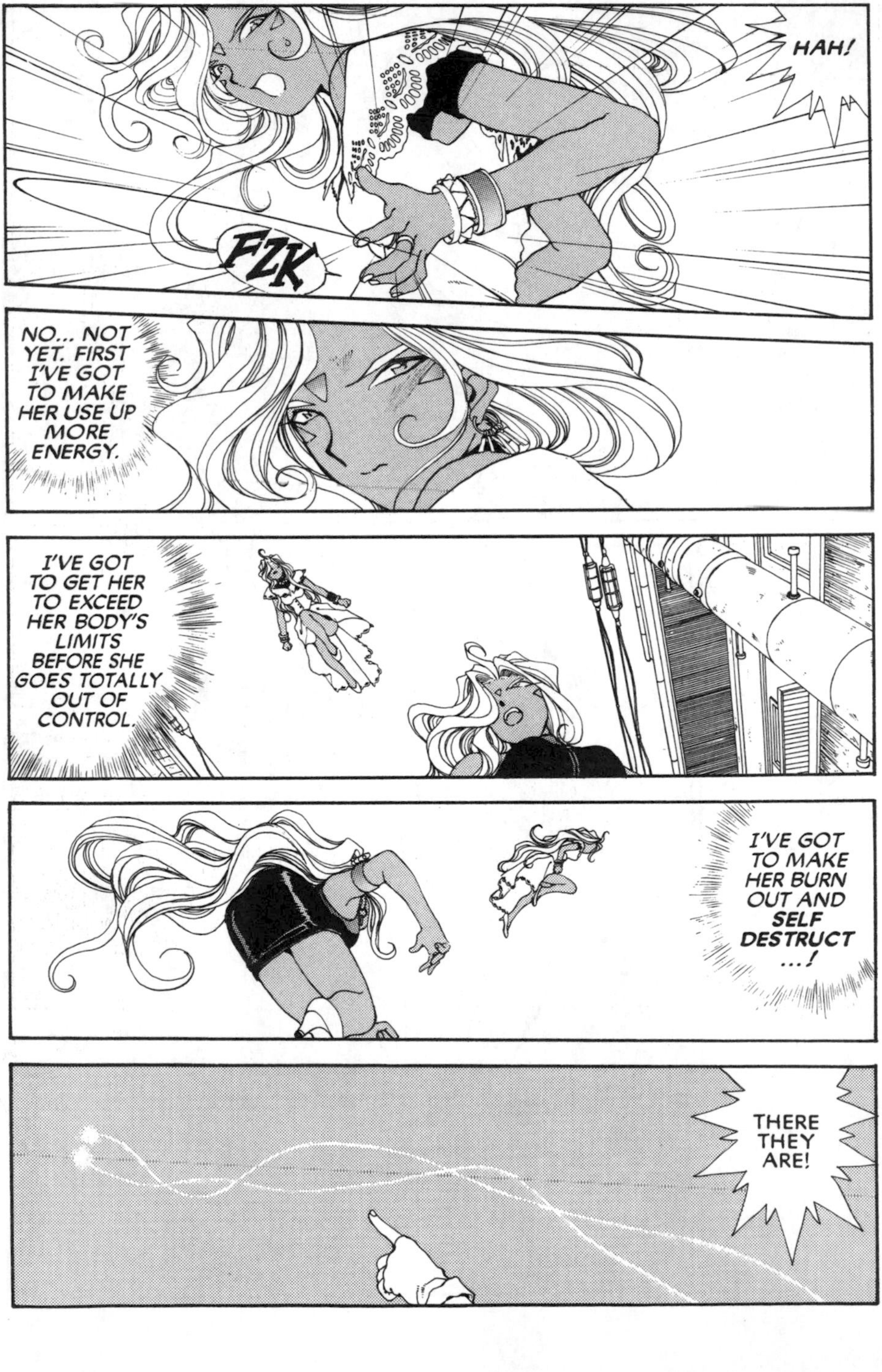
HAH!
FZK
NO... NOT YET. FIRST I'VE GOT TO MAKE HER USE UP MORE ENERGY.
I'VE GOT TO GET HER TO EXCEED HER BODY'S LIMITS BEFORE SHE GOES TOTALLY OUT OF CONTROL.
I'VE GOT TO MAKE HER BURN OUT AND SELF DESTRUCT ...!
THERE THEY ARE!

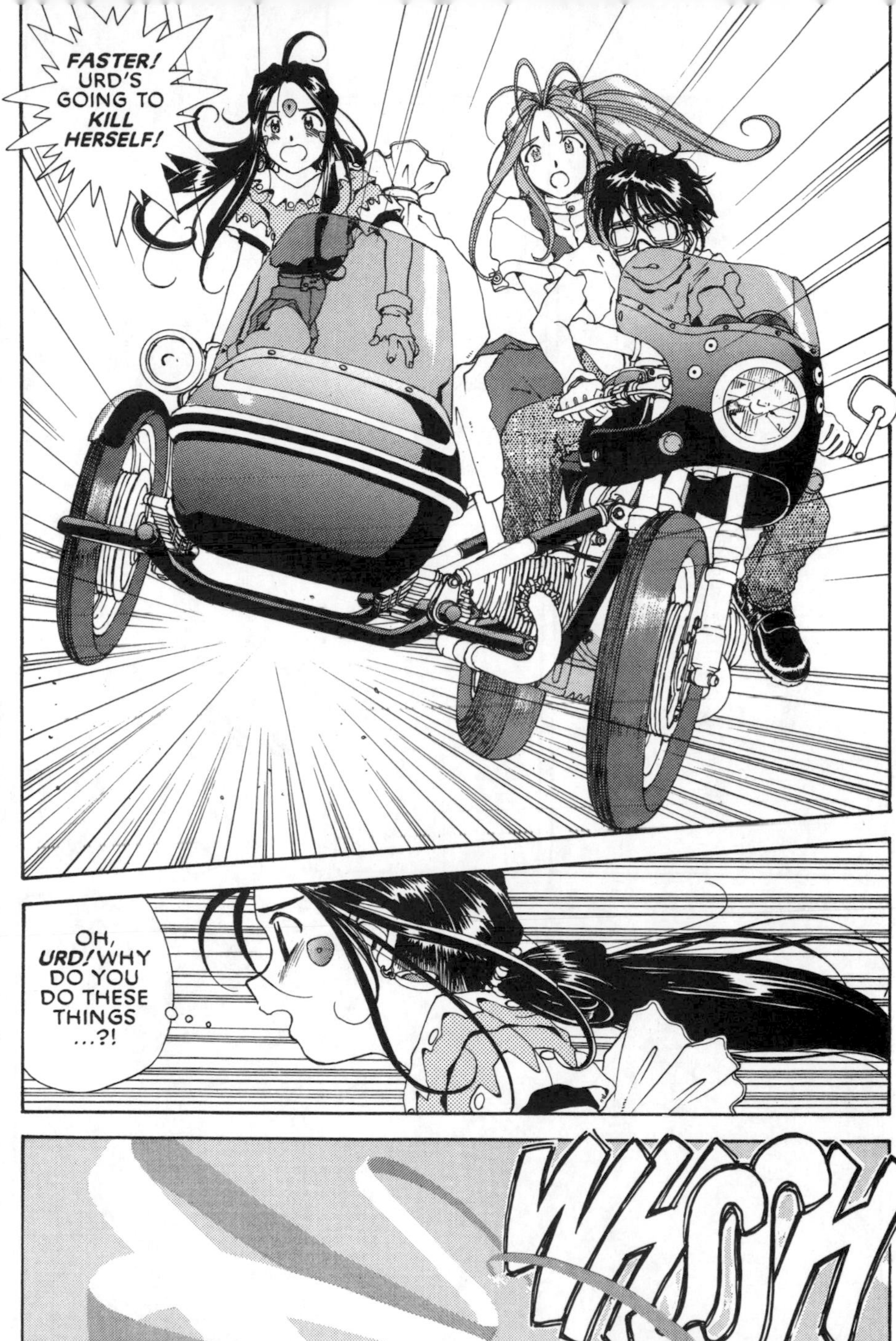
FASTER! URD'S GOING TO KILL HERSELF!
OH, URD! WHY DO YOU DO THESE THINGS ...?!
WHOOSH

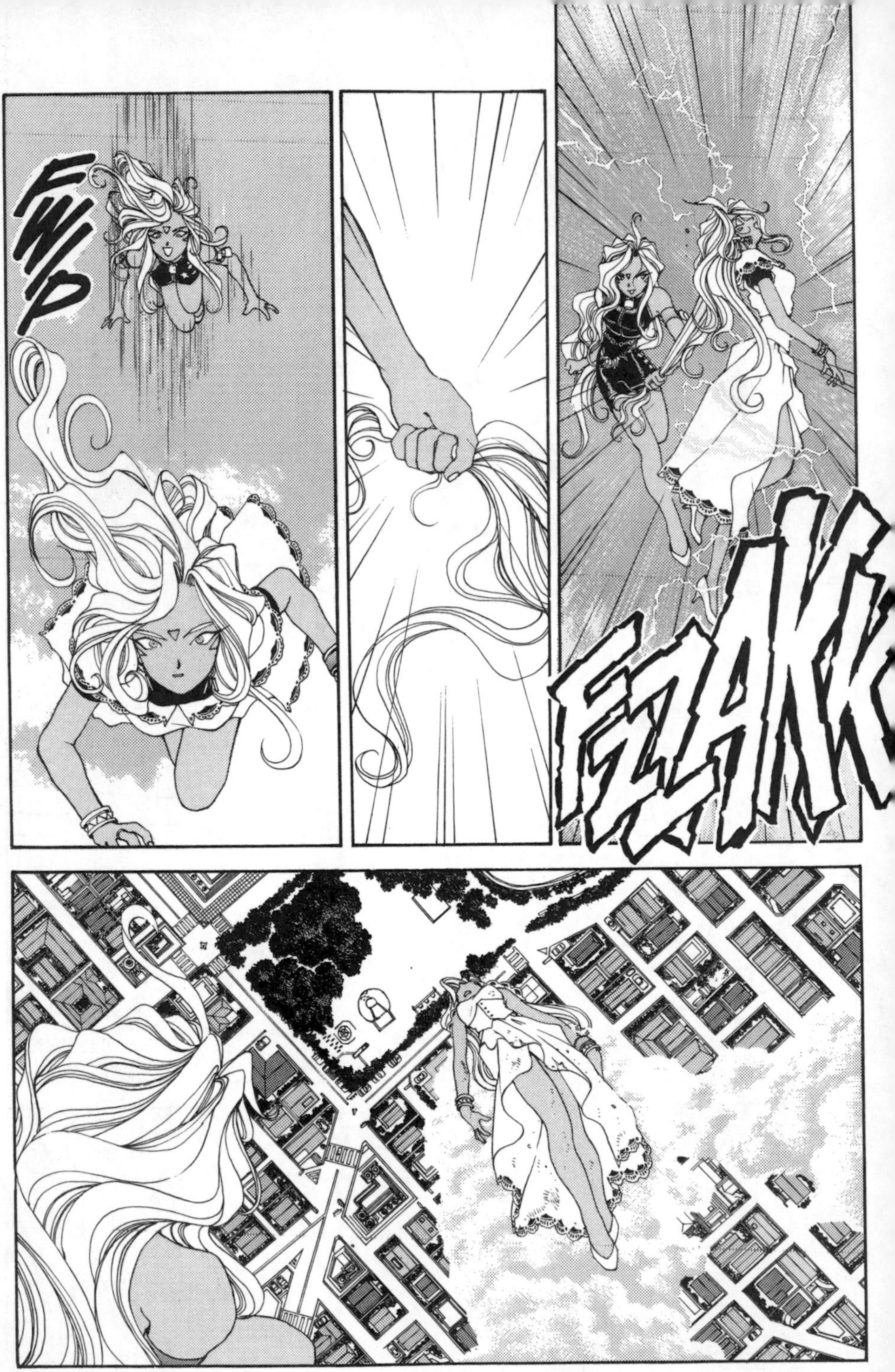
FWIP
FZAKK

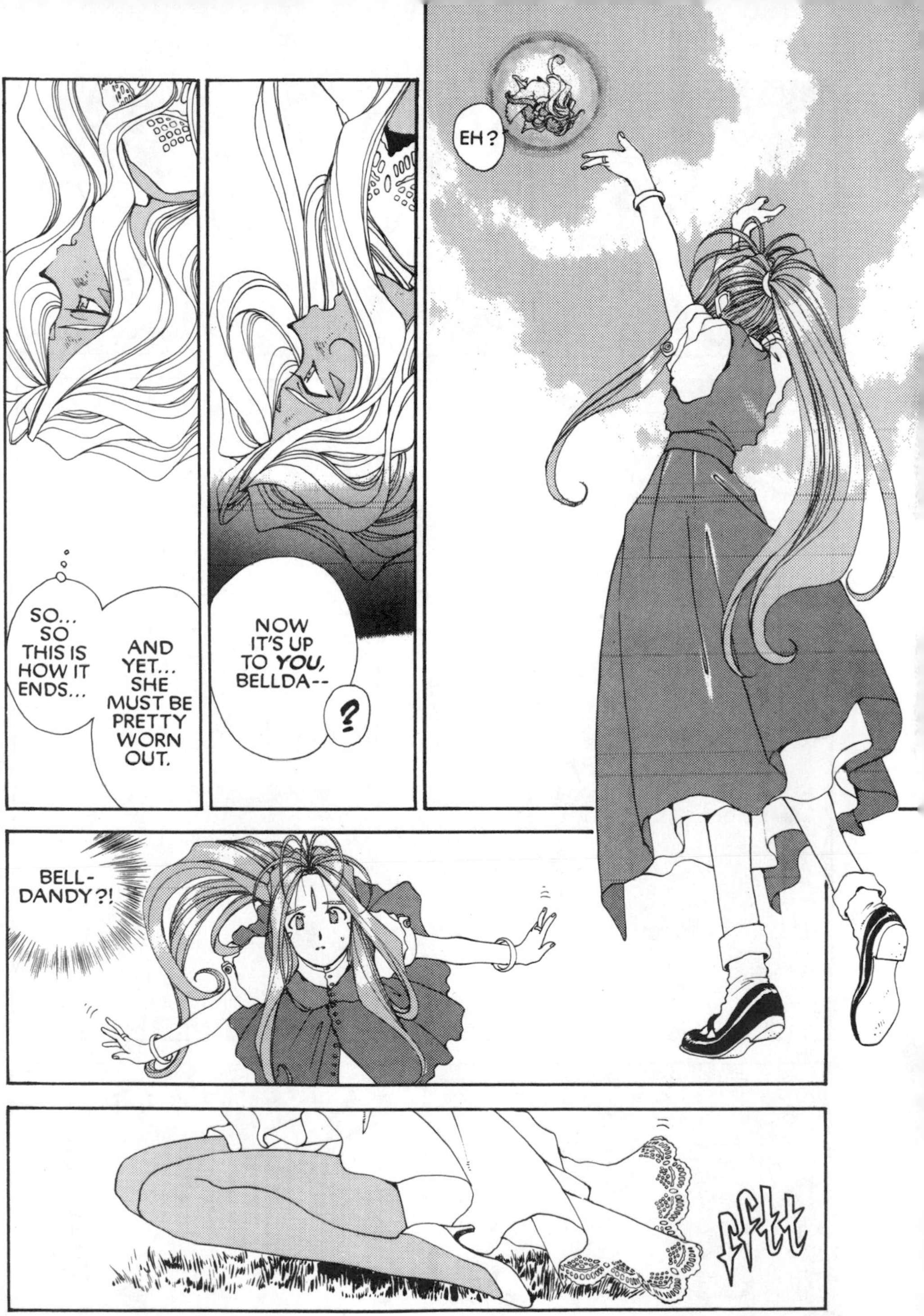
SO... SO THIS IS HOW IT ENDS...
AND YET... SHE MUST BE PRETTY WORN OUT.
NOW IT'S UP TO *YOU,* BELLDA--
?
EH?
BELL-DANDY?!
fftt

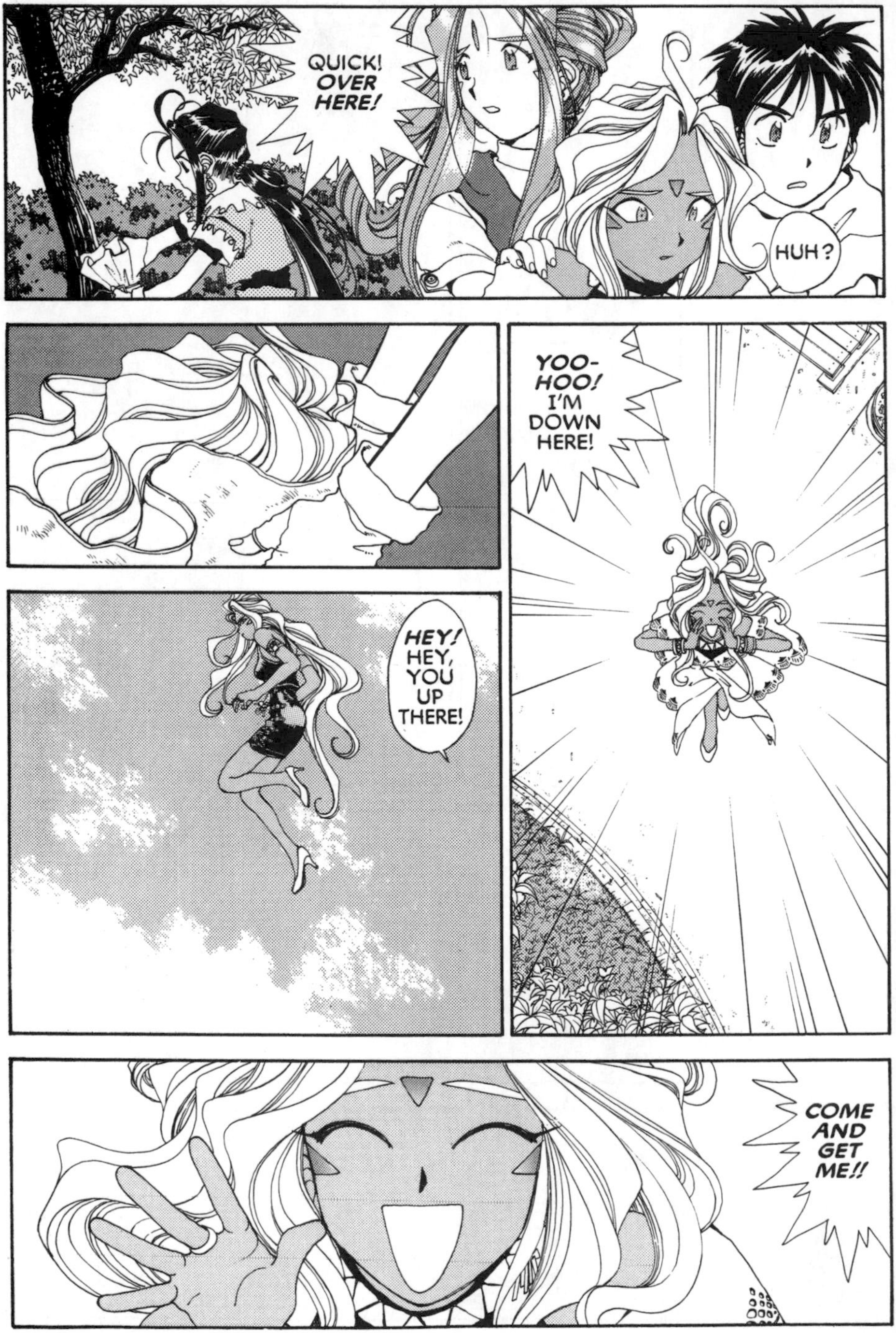
QUICK! OVER HERE!
HUH?
YOO-HOO! I'M DOWN HERE!
HEY! HEY, YOU UP THERE!
COME AND GET ME!!

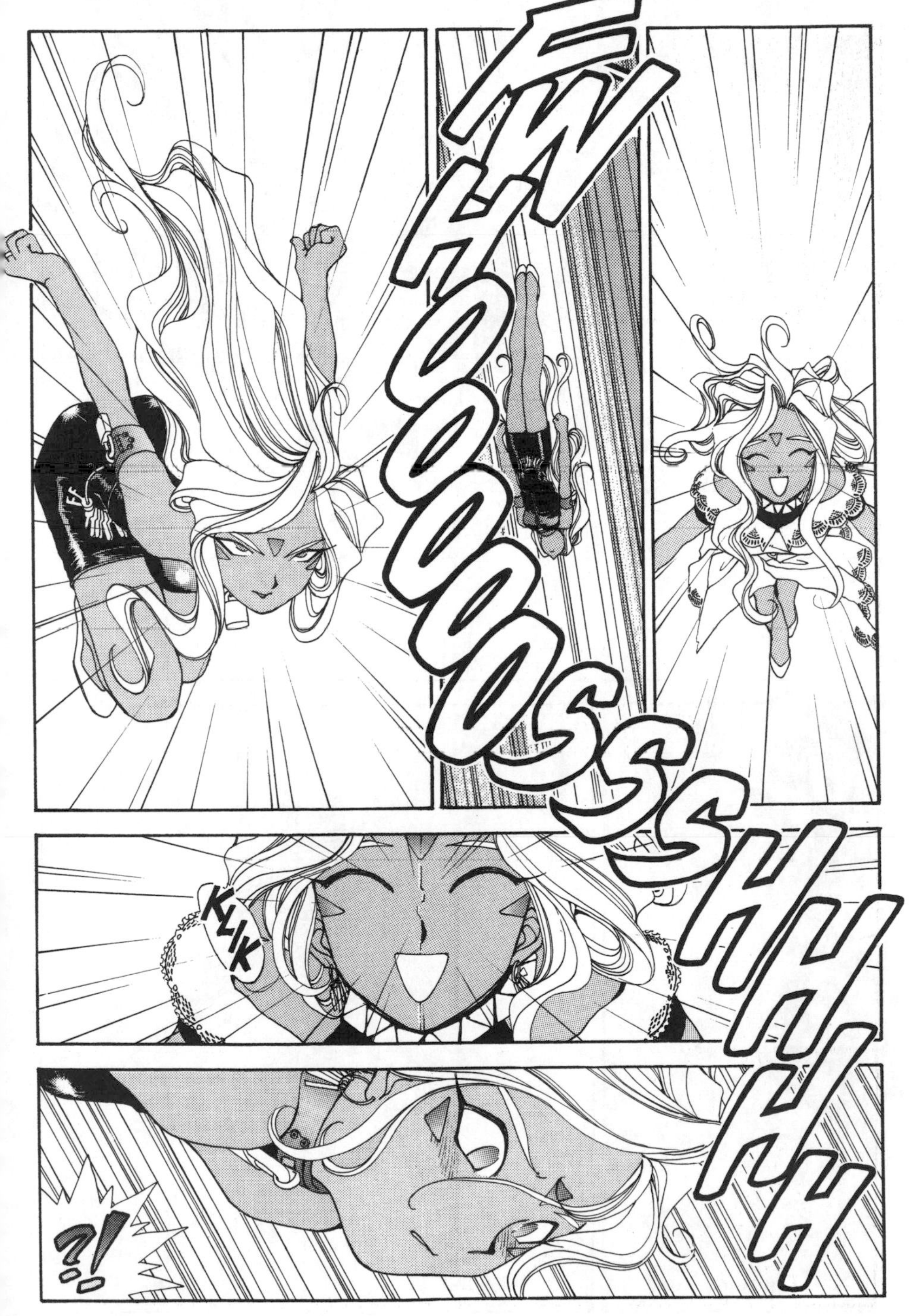
FWHOOOOOOSSSHHHHHH
KLIK
?!

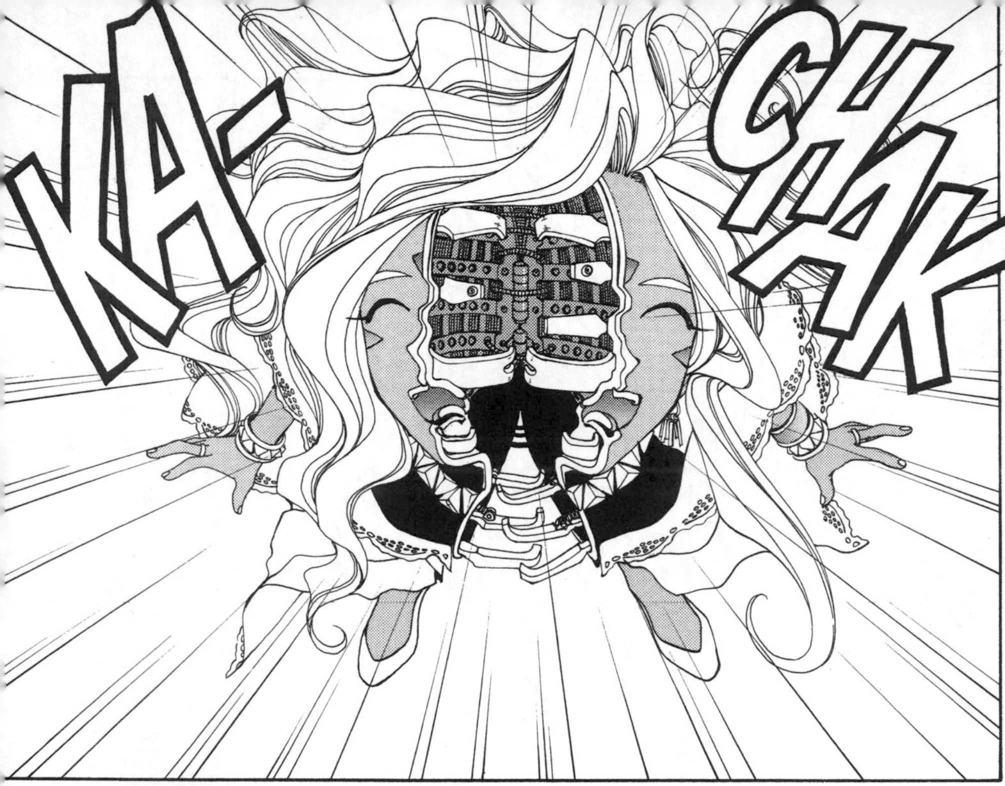
KA-
CHAK
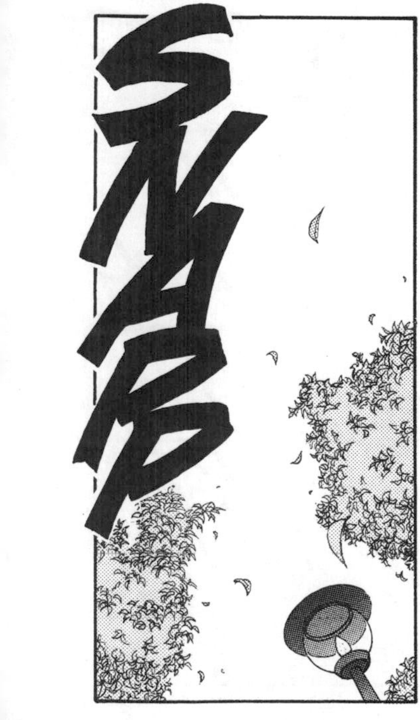
SNAP
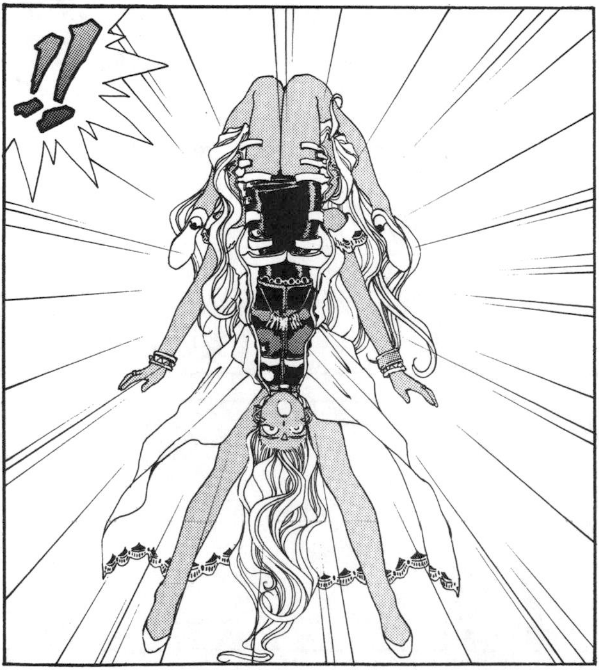
!!

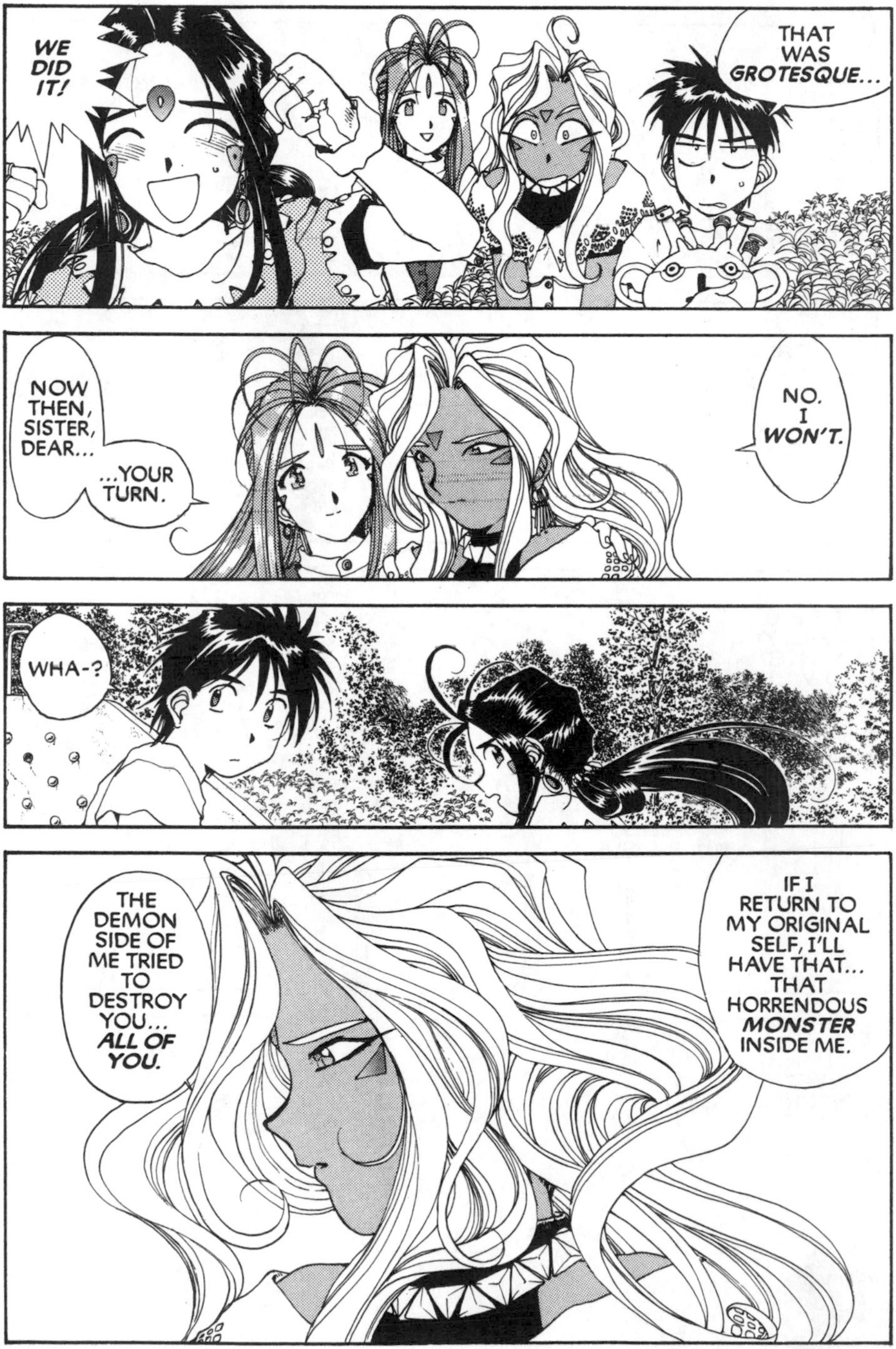
WE DID IT!
THAT WAS *GROTESQUE*...
NOW THEN, SISTER, DEAR...
...YOUR TURN.
NO. I *WON'T.*
WHA-?
THE DEMON SIDE OF ME TRIED TO DESTROY YOU... ***ALL OF YOU.***
IF I RETURN TO MY ORIGINAL SELF, I'LL HAVE THAT... THAT HORRENDOUS ***MONSTER*** INSIDE ME.

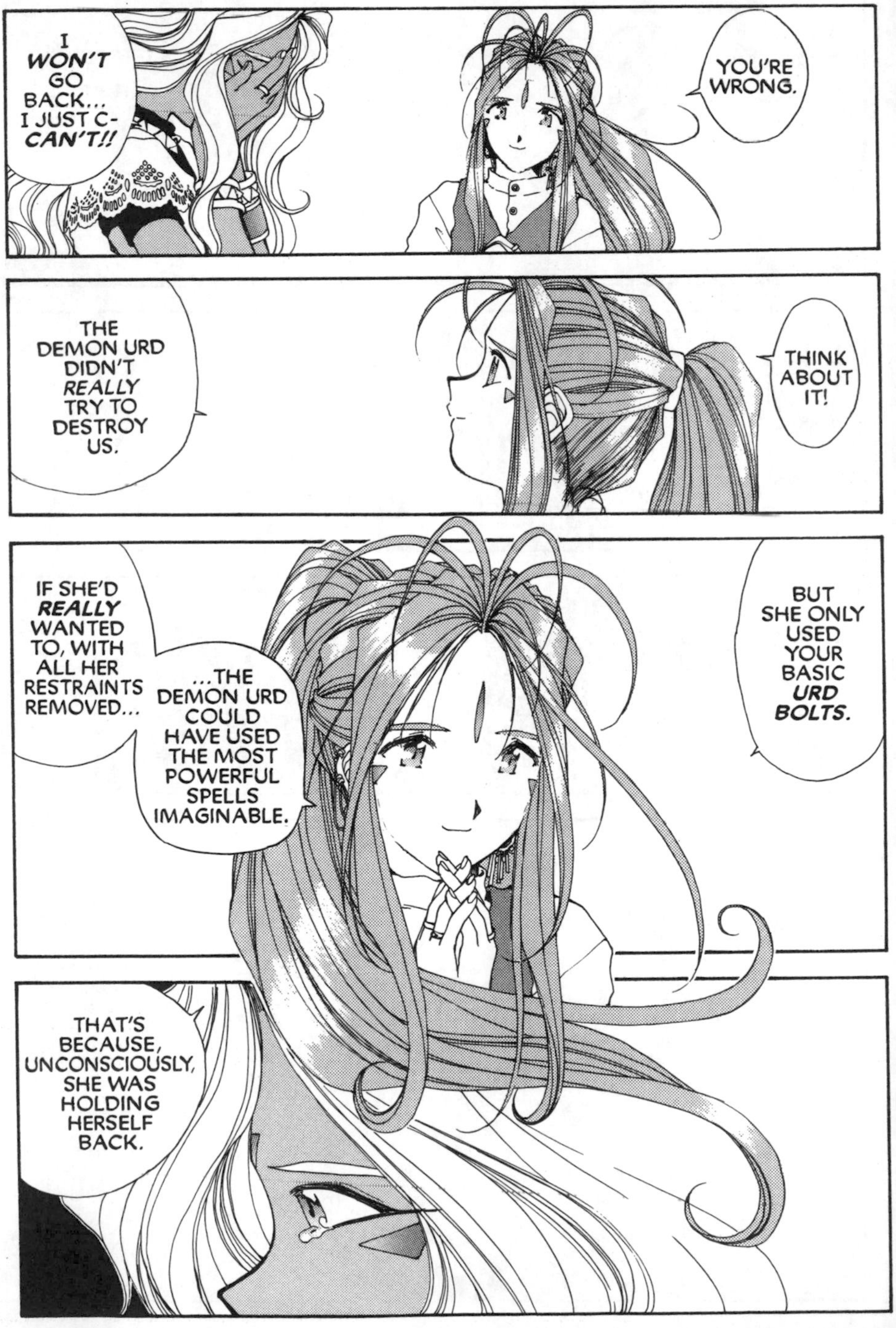
I *WON'T* GO BACK... I JUST C- *CAN'T!!*
YOU'RE WRONG.
THE DEMON URD DIDN'T *REALLY* TRY TO DESTROY US.
THINK ABOUT IT!
IF SHE'D *REALLY* WANTED TO, WITH ALL HER RESTRAINTS REMOVED...
...THE DEMON URD COULD HAVE USED THE MOST POWERFUL SPELLS IMAGINABLE.
BUT SHE ONLY USED YOUR BASIC *URD BOLTS.*
THAT'S BECAUSE, UNCONSCIOUSLY, SHE WAS HOLDING HERSELF BACK.

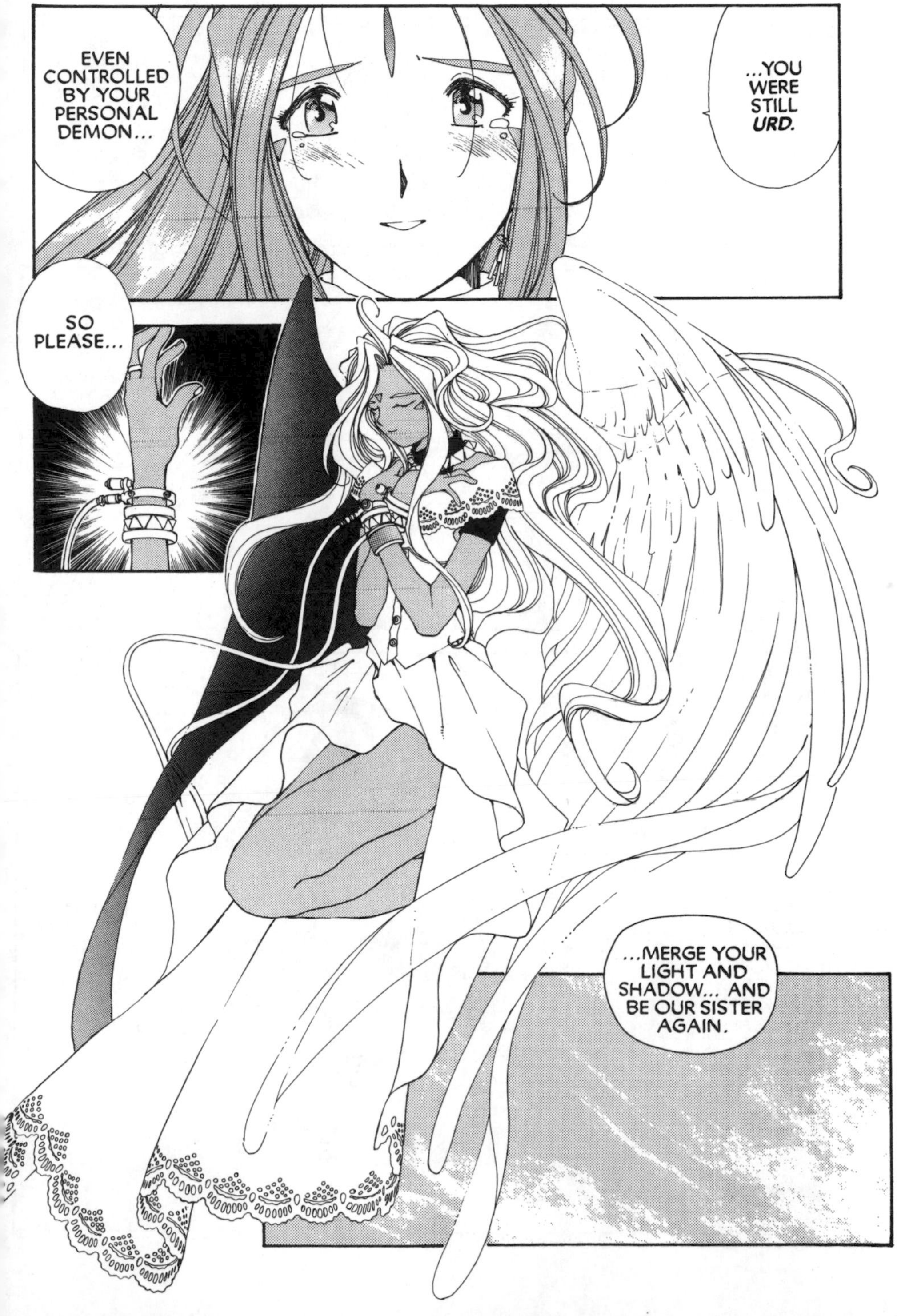
EVEN CONTROLLED BY YOUR PERSONAL DEMON...
...YOU WERE STILL *URD.*
SO PLEASE...
...MERGE YOUR LIGHT AND SHADOW... AND BE OUR SISTER AGAIN.

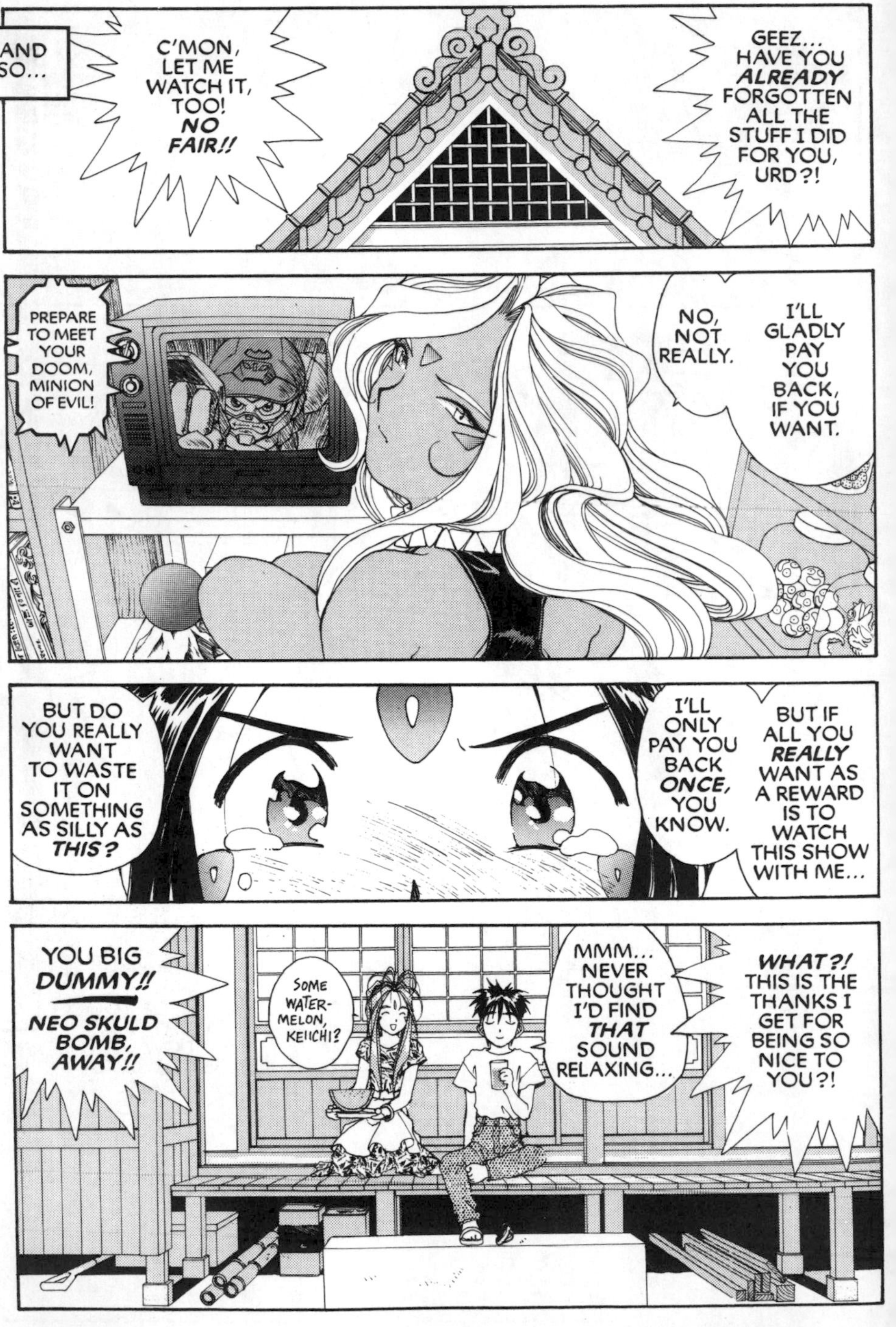
AND SO...
C'MON, LET ME WATCH IT, TOO! NO FAIR!!
GEEZ... HAVE YOU ALREADY FORGOTTEN ALL THE STUFF I DID FOR YOU, URD?!
PREPARE TO MEET YOUR DOOM, MINION OF EVIL!
NO, NOT REALLY.
I'LL GLADLY PAY YOU BACK, IF YOU WANT.
BUT DO YOU REALLY WANT TO WASTE IT ON SOMETHING AS SILLY AS THIS?
I'LL ONLY PAY YOU BACK ONCE, YOU KNOW.
BUT IF ALL YOU REALLY WANT AS A REWARD IS TO WATCH THIS SHOW WITH ME...
YOU BIG DUMMY!! NEO SKULD BOMB, AWAY!!
SOME WATER-MELON, KEIICHI?
MMM... NEVER THOUGHT I'D FIND THAT SOUND RELAXING...
WHAT?! THIS IS THE THANKS I GET FOR BEING SO NICE TO YOU?!

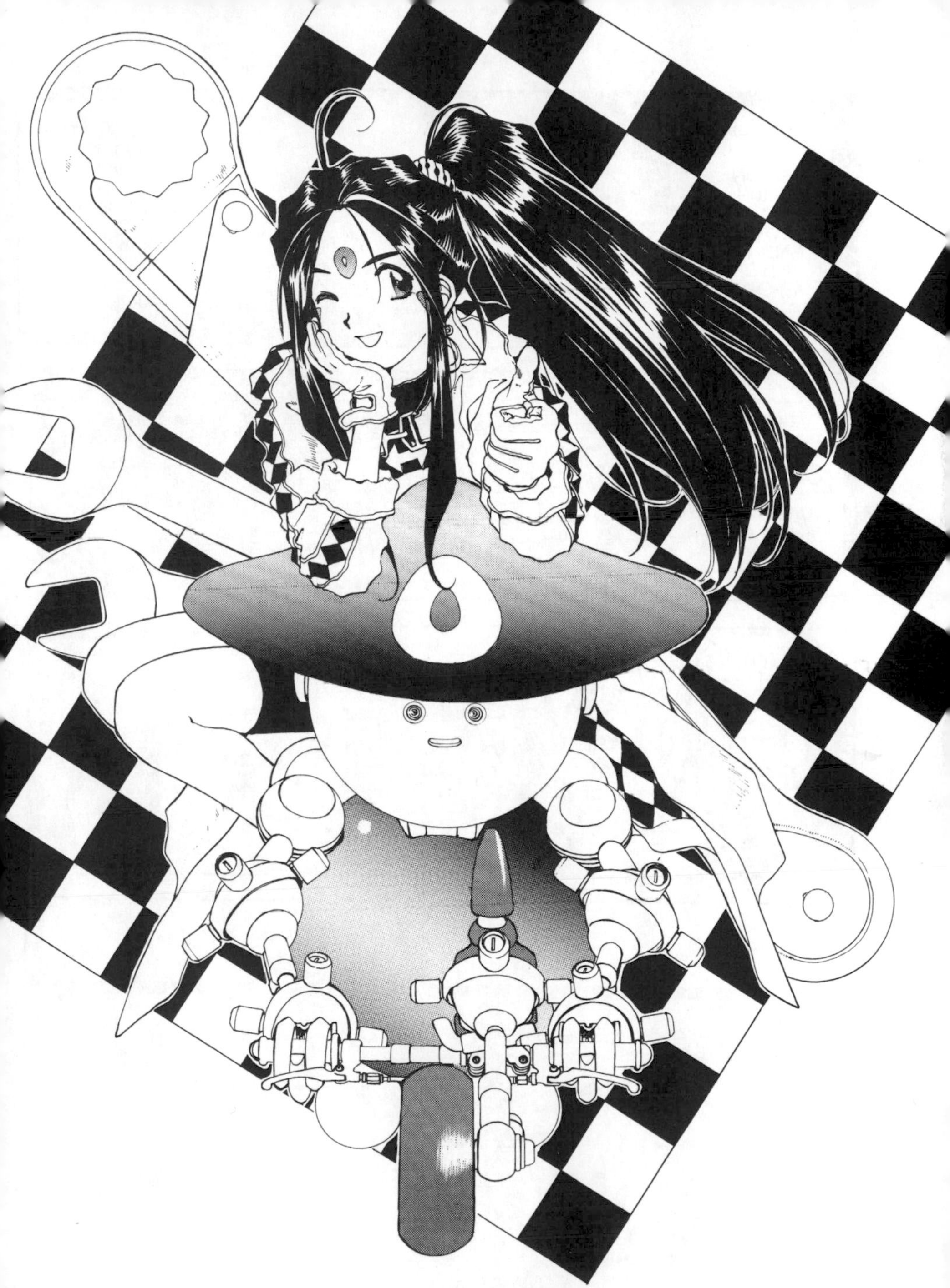

SUPERURD

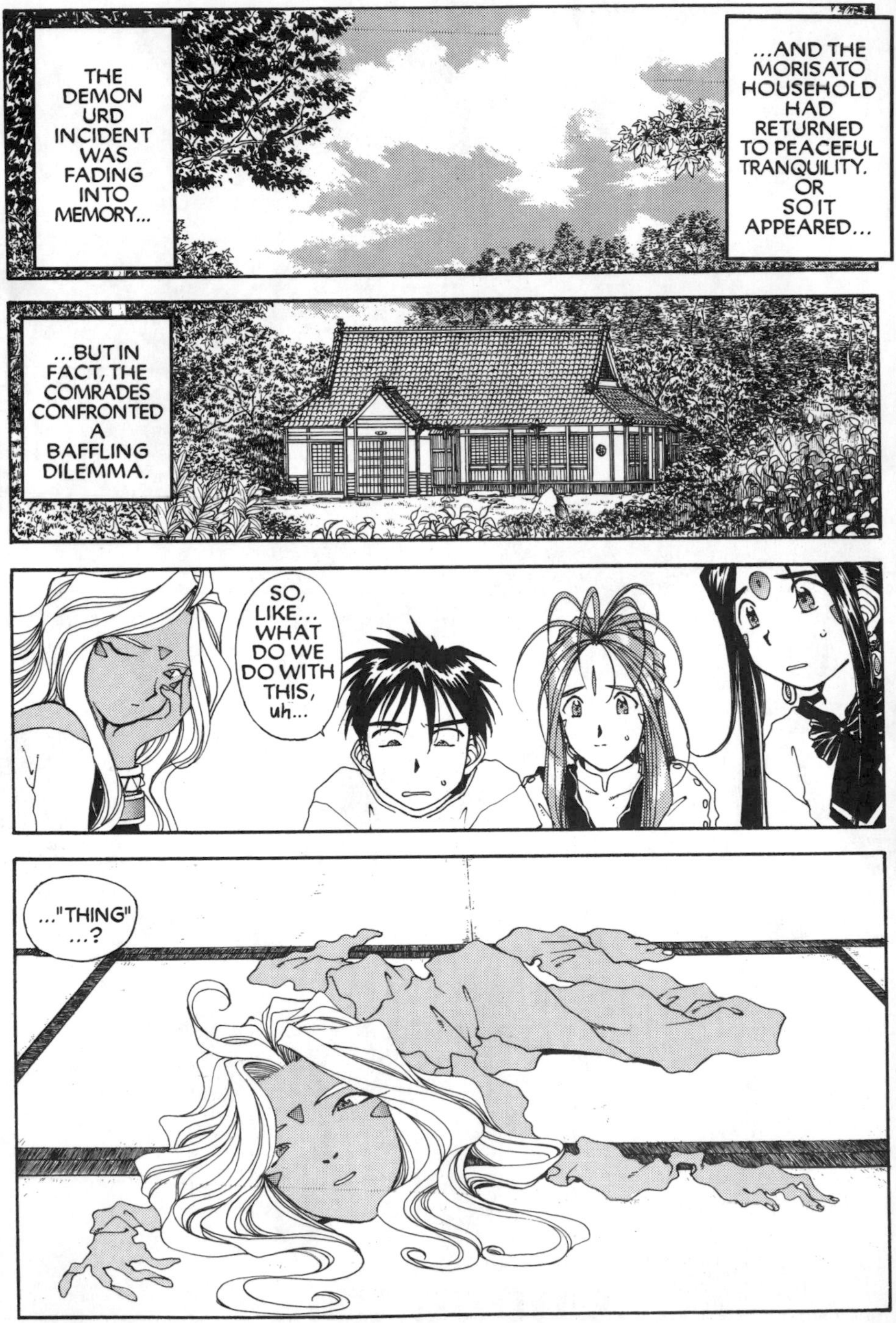
THE DEMON URD INCIDENT WAS FADING INTO MEMORY...
...AND THE MORISATO HOUSEHOLD HAD RETURNED TO PEACEFUL TRANQUILITY. OR SO IT APPEARED...
...BUT IN FACT, THE COMRADES CONFRONTED A BAFFLING DILEMMA.
SO, LIKE... WHAT DO WE DO WITH THIS, uh...
..."THING" ...?

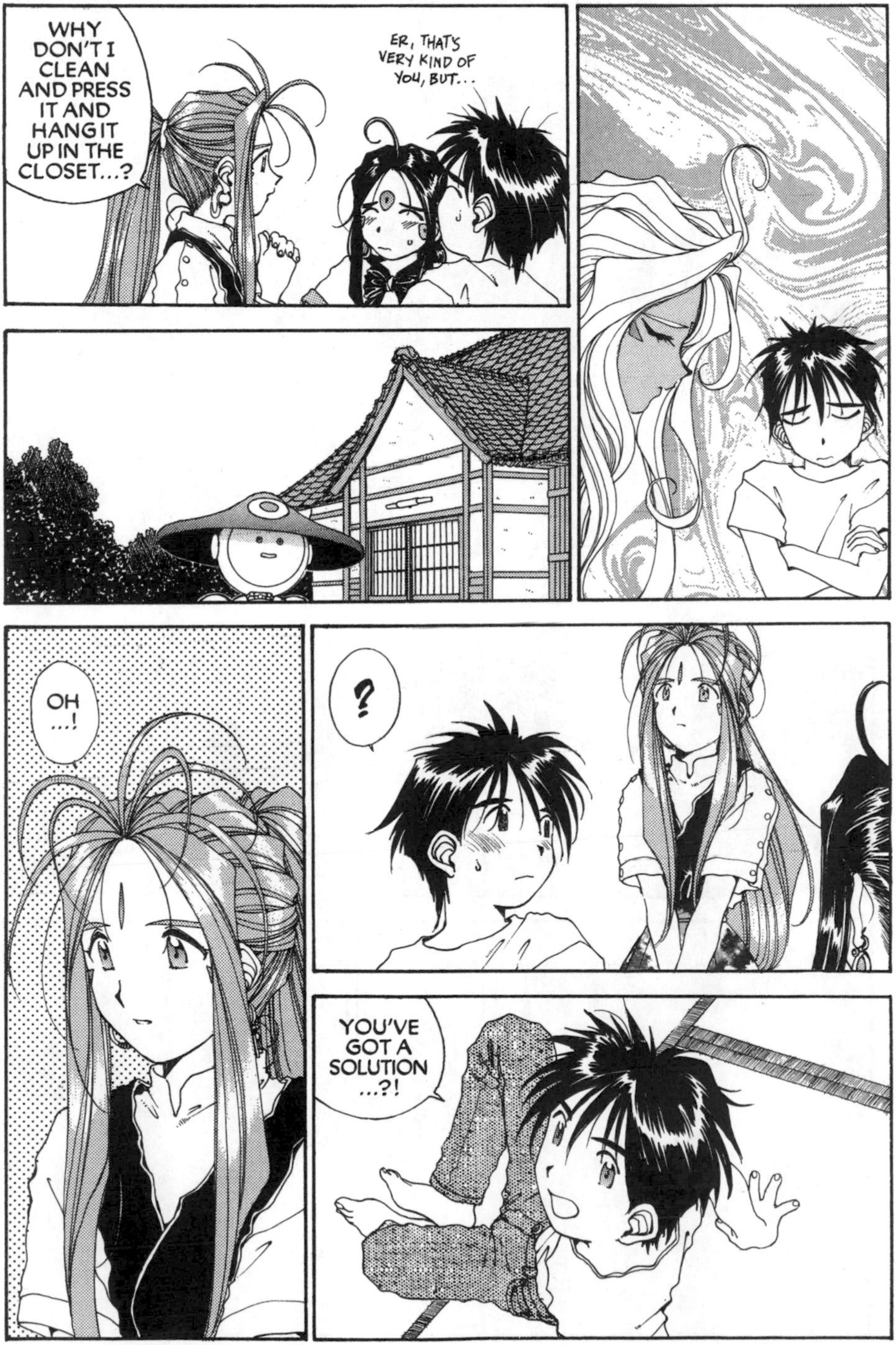
WHY DON'T I CLEAN AND PRESS IT AND HANG IT UP IN THE CLOSET...?
ER, THAT'S VERY KIND OF YOU, BUT...
OH ...!
?
YOU'VE GOT A SOLUTION ...?!

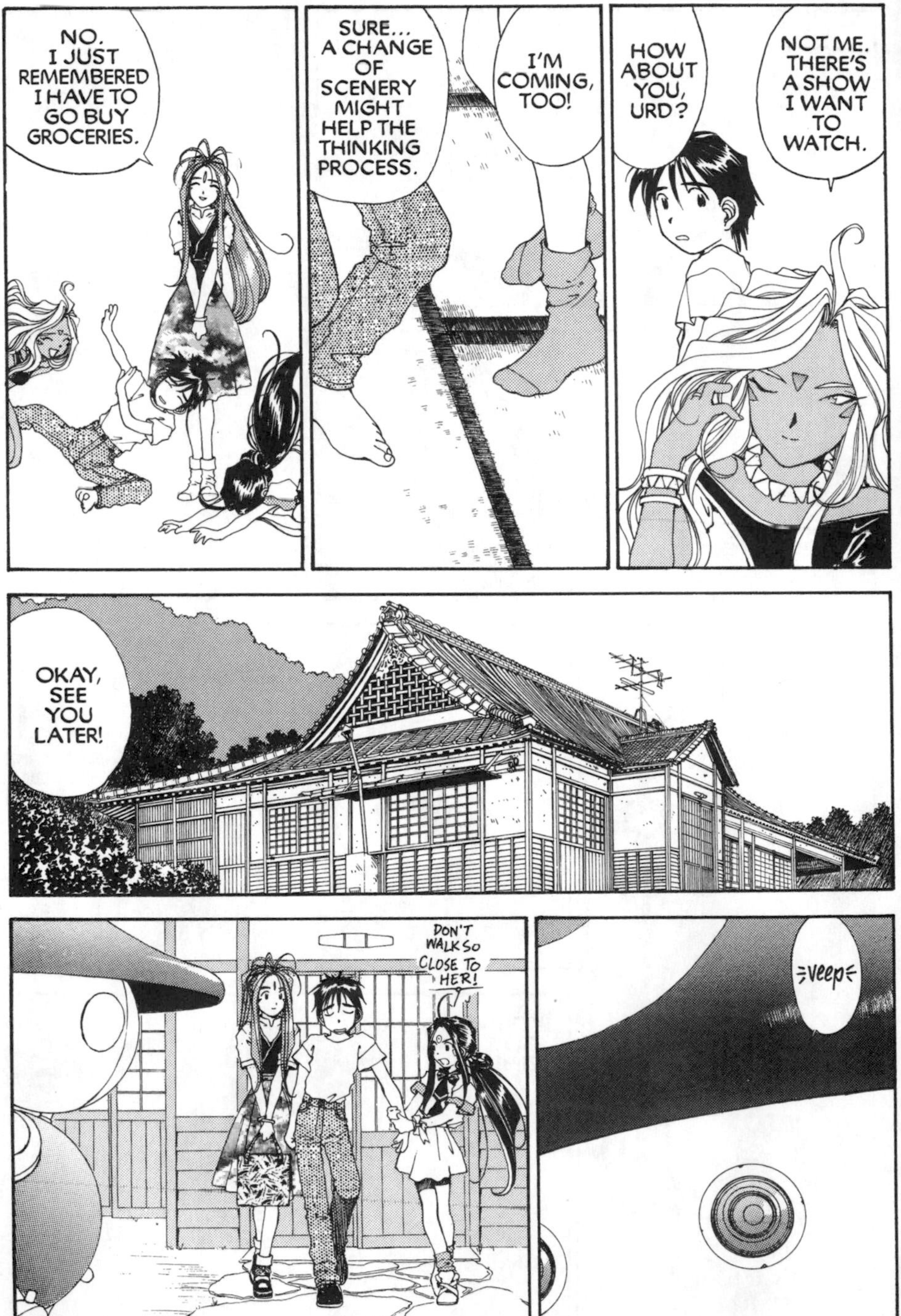
NO. I JUST REMEMBERED I HAVE TO GO BUY GROCERIES.
SURE... A CHANGE OF SCENERY MIGHT HELP THE THINKING PROCESS.
I'M COMING, TOO!
HOW ABOUT YOU, URD?
NOT ME. THERE'S A SHOW I WANT TO WATCH.
OKAY, SEE YOU LATER!
DON'T WALK SO CLOSE TO HER!
veep

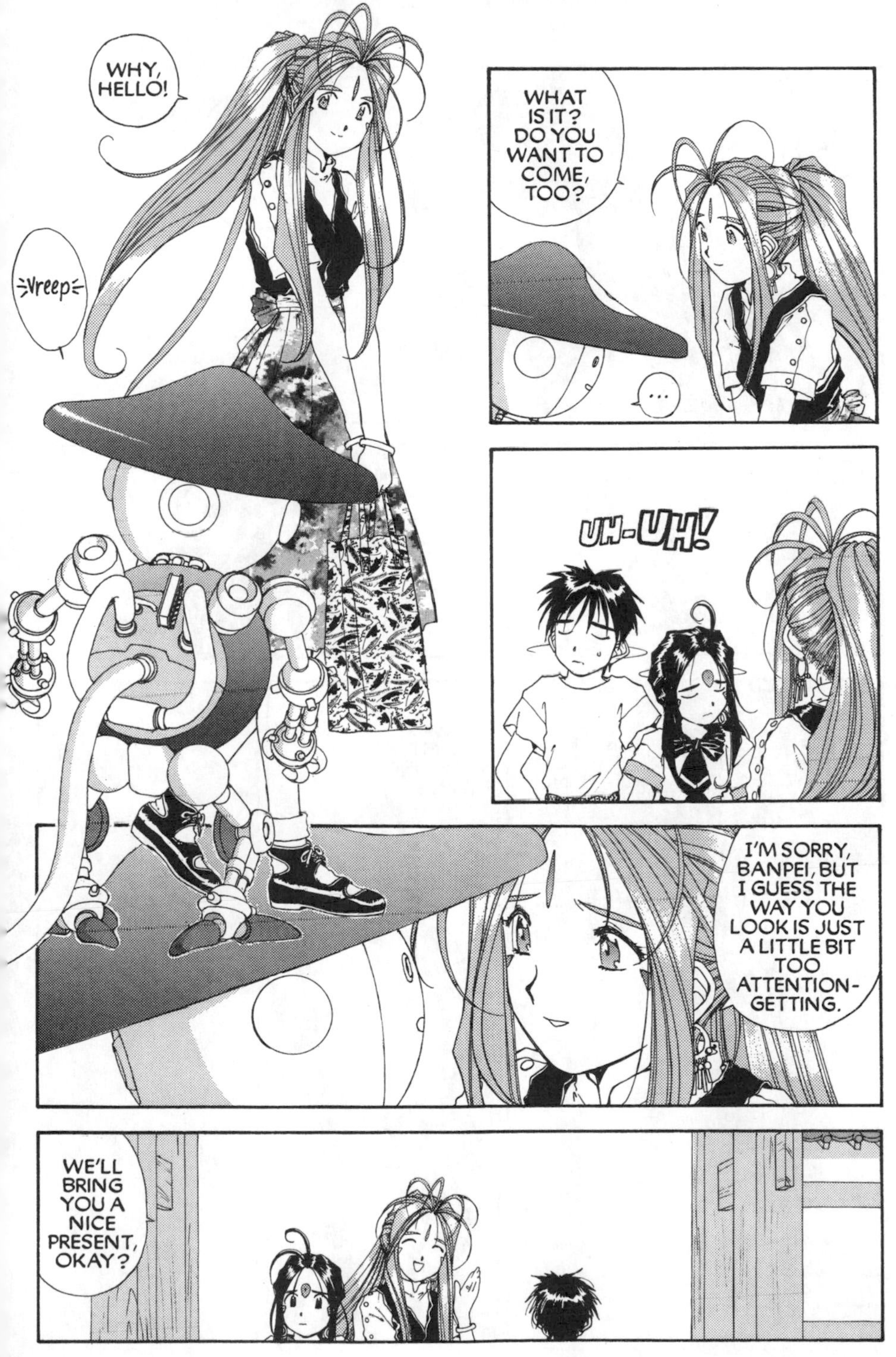
WHY, HELLO!
Vreep
WHAT IS IT? DO YOU WANT TO COME, TOO?
...
UH-UH!
I'M SORRY, BANPEI, BUT I GUESS THE WAY YOU LOOK IS JUST A LITTLE BIT TOO ATTENTION-GETTING.
WE'LL BRING YOU A NICE PRESENT, OKAY?

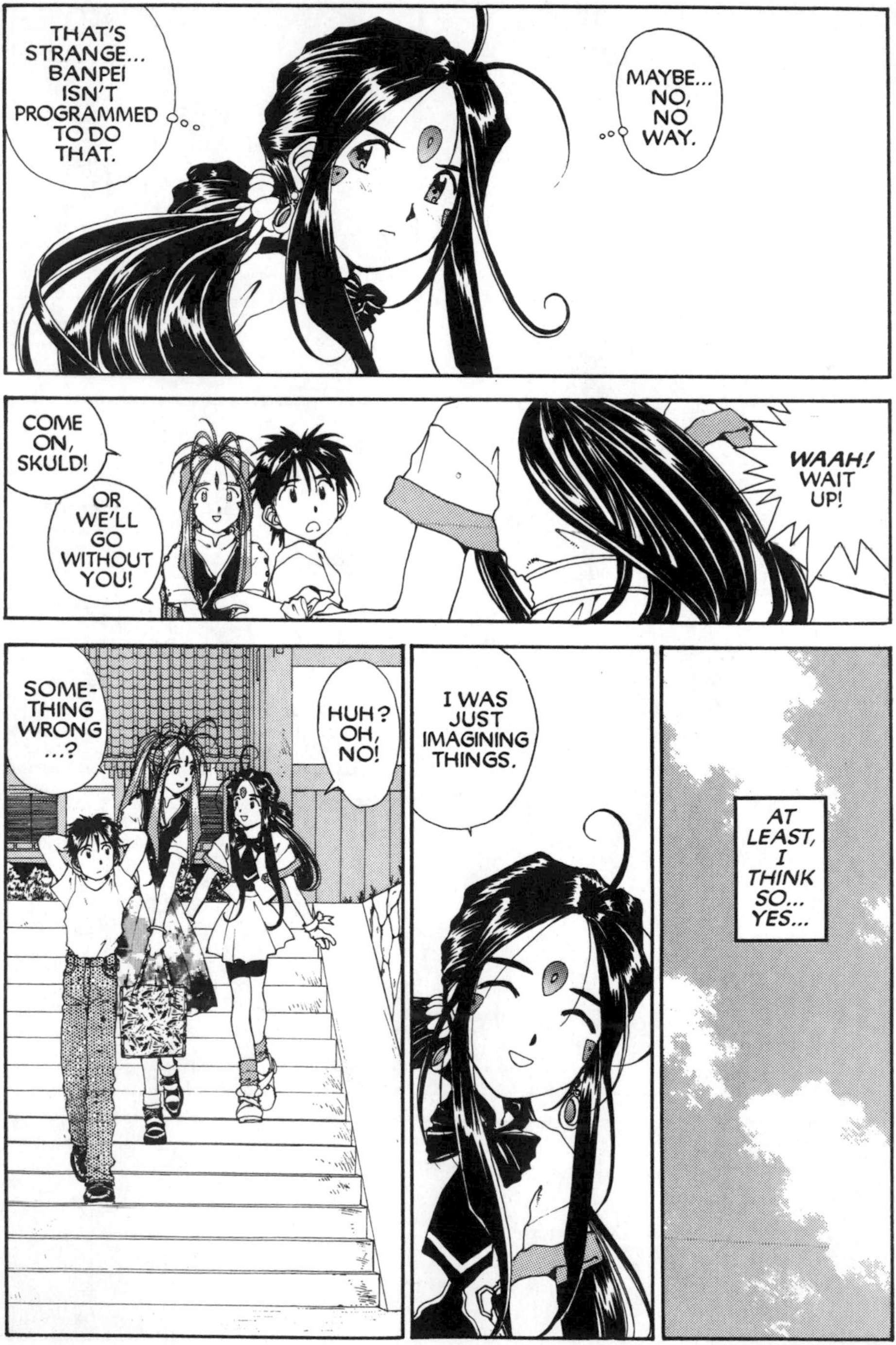
THAT'S STRANGE... BANPEI ISN'T PROGRAMMED TO DO THAT.
MAYBE... NO, NO WAY.
COME ON, SKULD!
OR WE'LL GO WITHOUT YOU!
WAAH! WAIT UP!
SOME-THING WRONG ...?
HUH? OH, NO!
I WAS JUST IMAGINING THINGS.
AT LEAST, I THINK SO... YES...

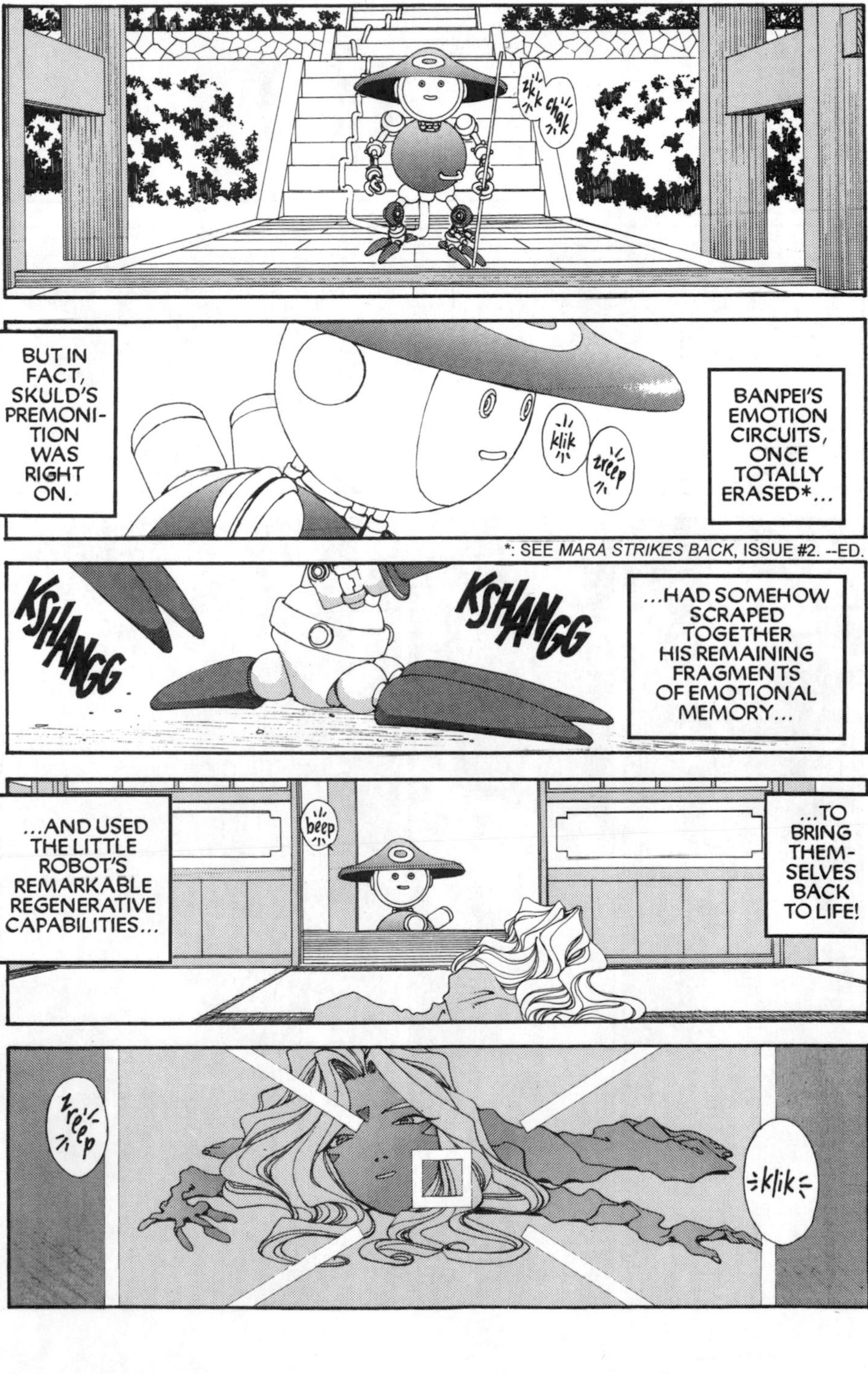
zikk chak
BUT IN FACT, SKULD'S PREMONITION WAS RIGHT ON.
klik
zreep
BANPEI'S EMOTION CIRCUITS, ONCE TOTALLY ERASED*...
*: SEE *MARA STRIKES BACK*, ISSUE #2. --ED.
KSHANGG
KSHANGG
...HAD SOMEHOW SCRAPED TOGETHER HIS REMAINING FRAGMENTS OF EMOTIONAL MEMORY...
...AND USED THE LITTLE ROBOT'S REMARKABLE REGENERATIVE CAPABILITIES...
beep
...TO BRING THEMSELVES BACK TO LIFE!
zreep
klik

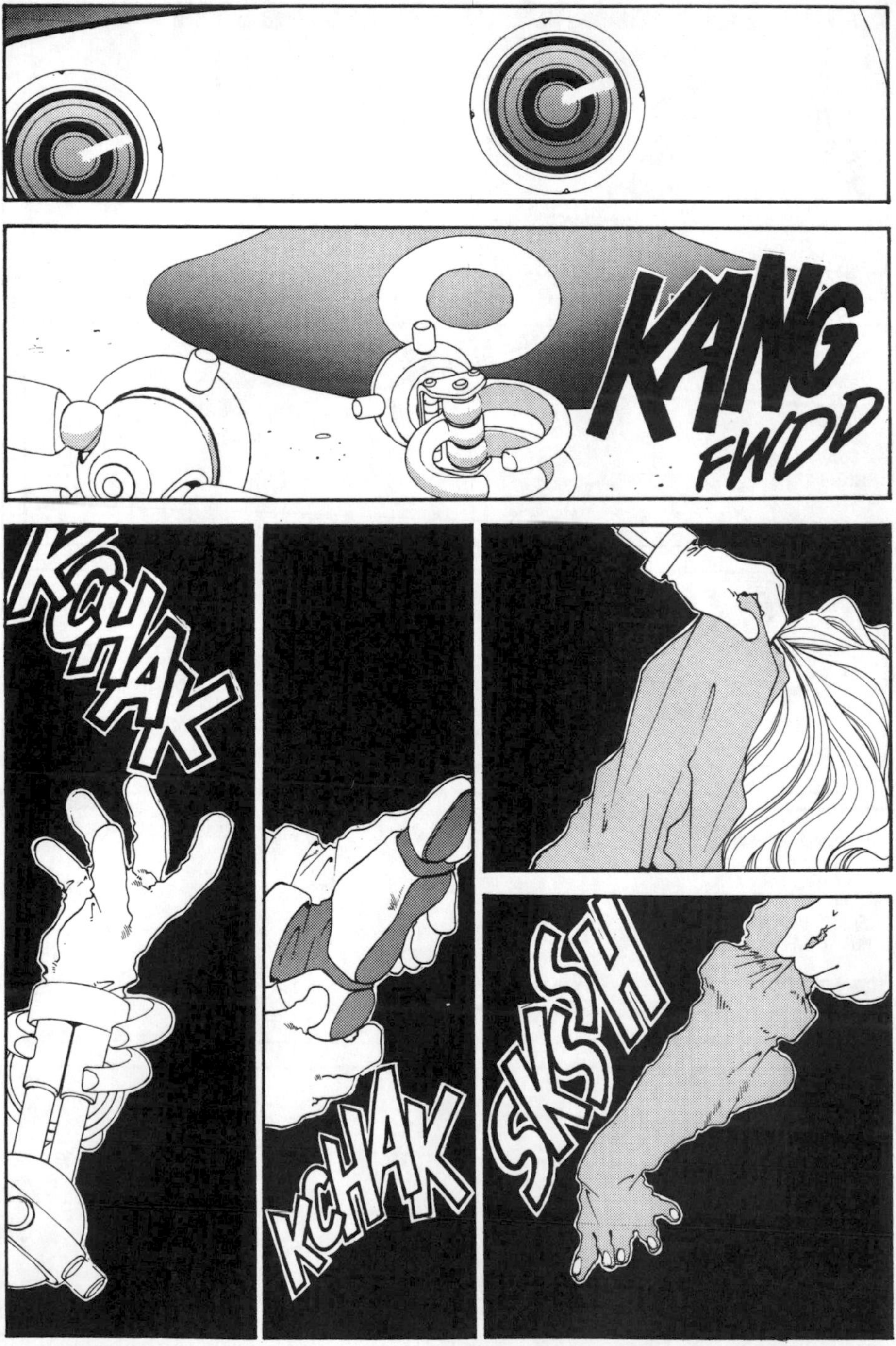
KANG
FWDD
KCHAK
KCHAK
SKSH

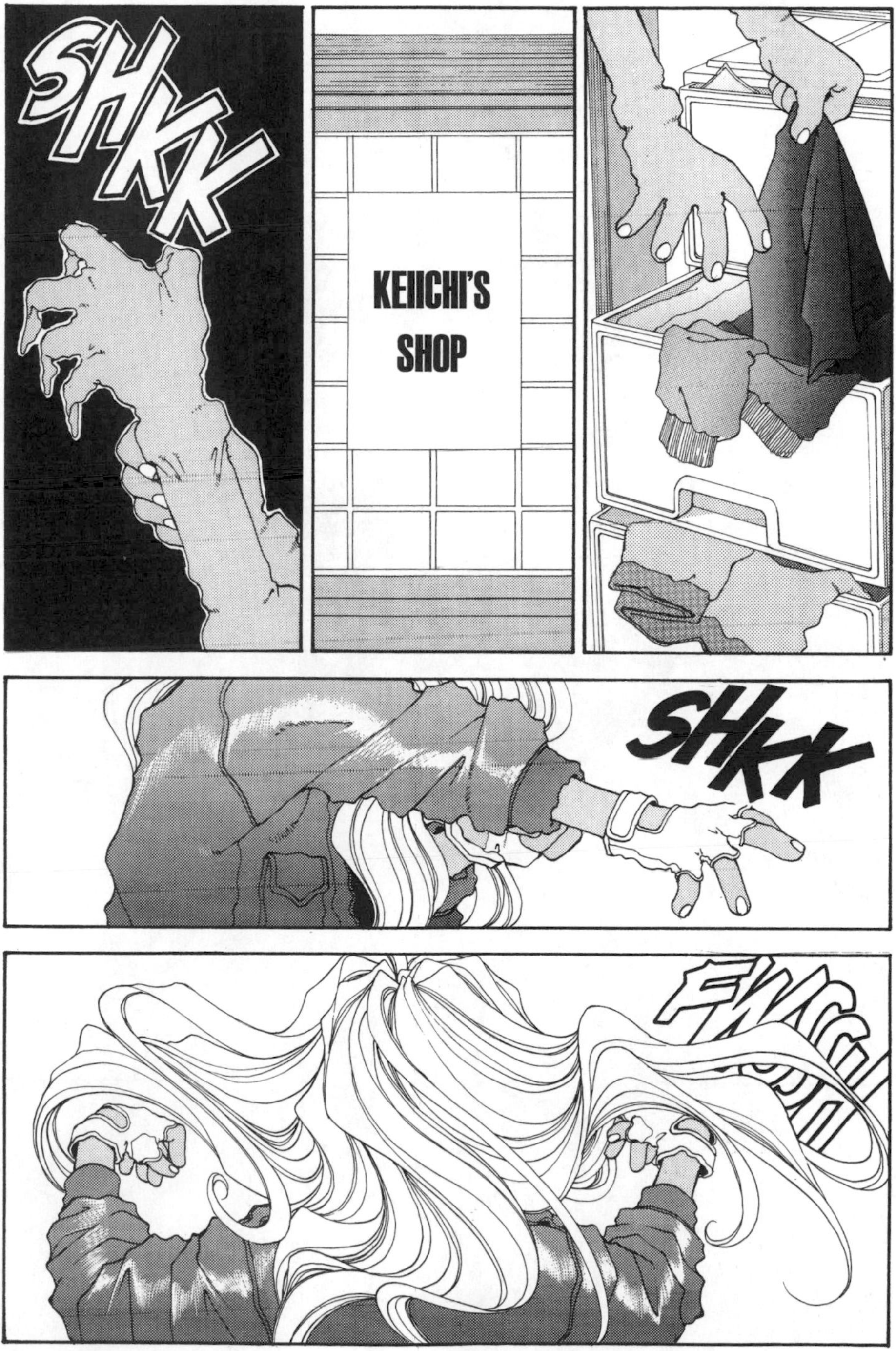
SHKK
KEIICHI'S SHOP
SHKK

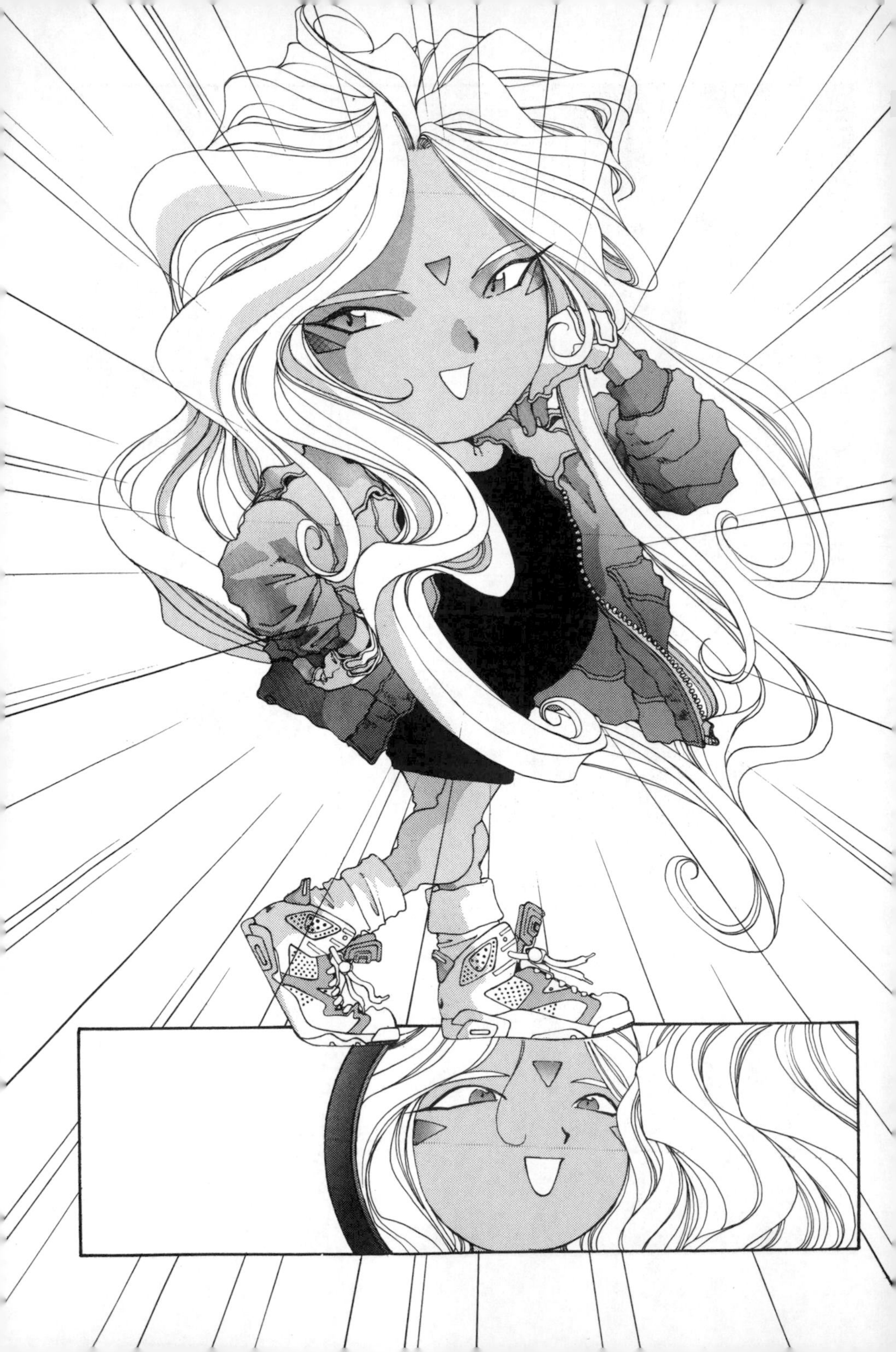

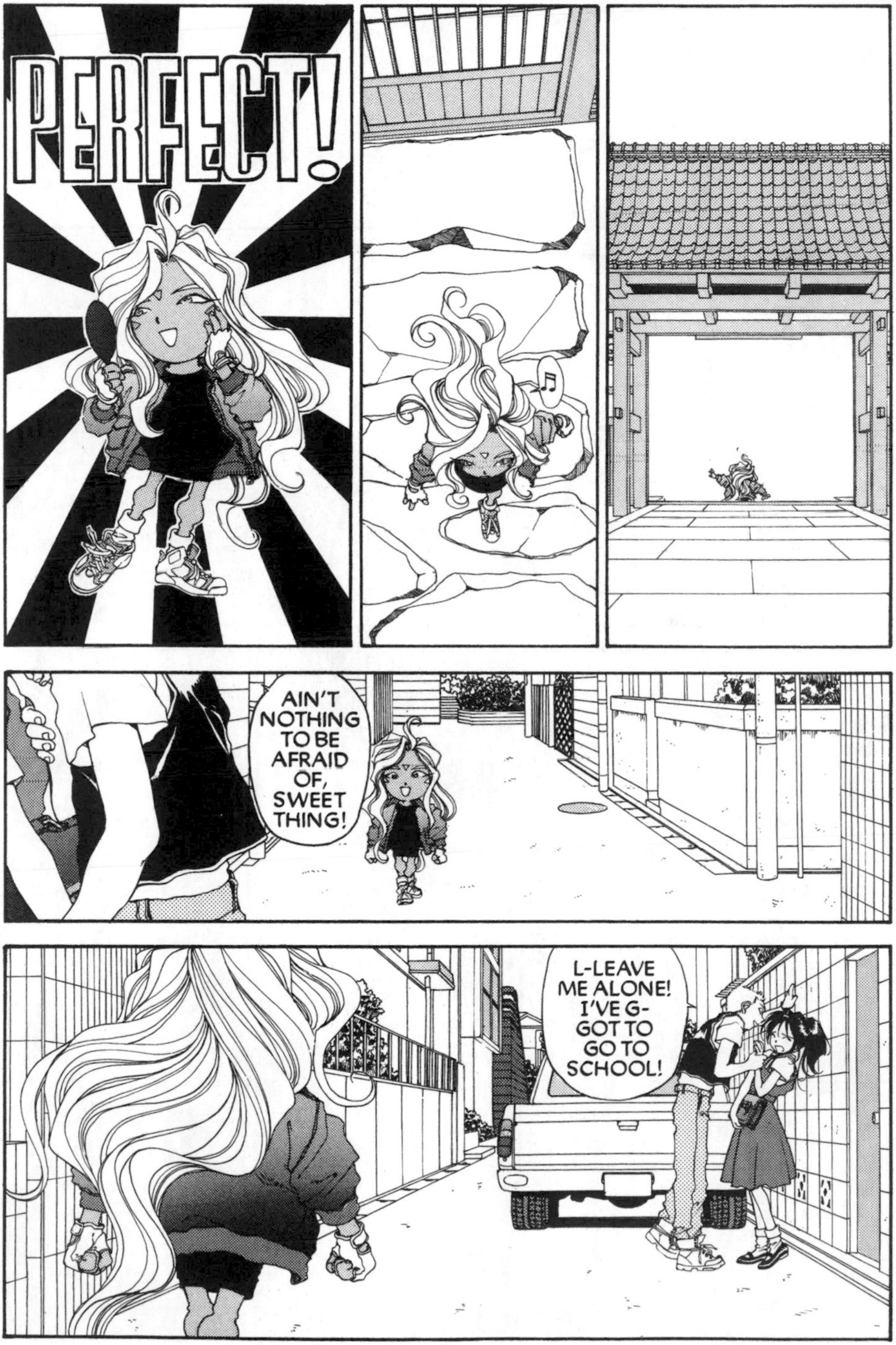
PERFECT!
AIN'T NOTHING TO BE AFRAID OF, SWEET THING!
L-LEAVE ME ALONE! I'VE G-GOT TO GO TO SCHOOL!

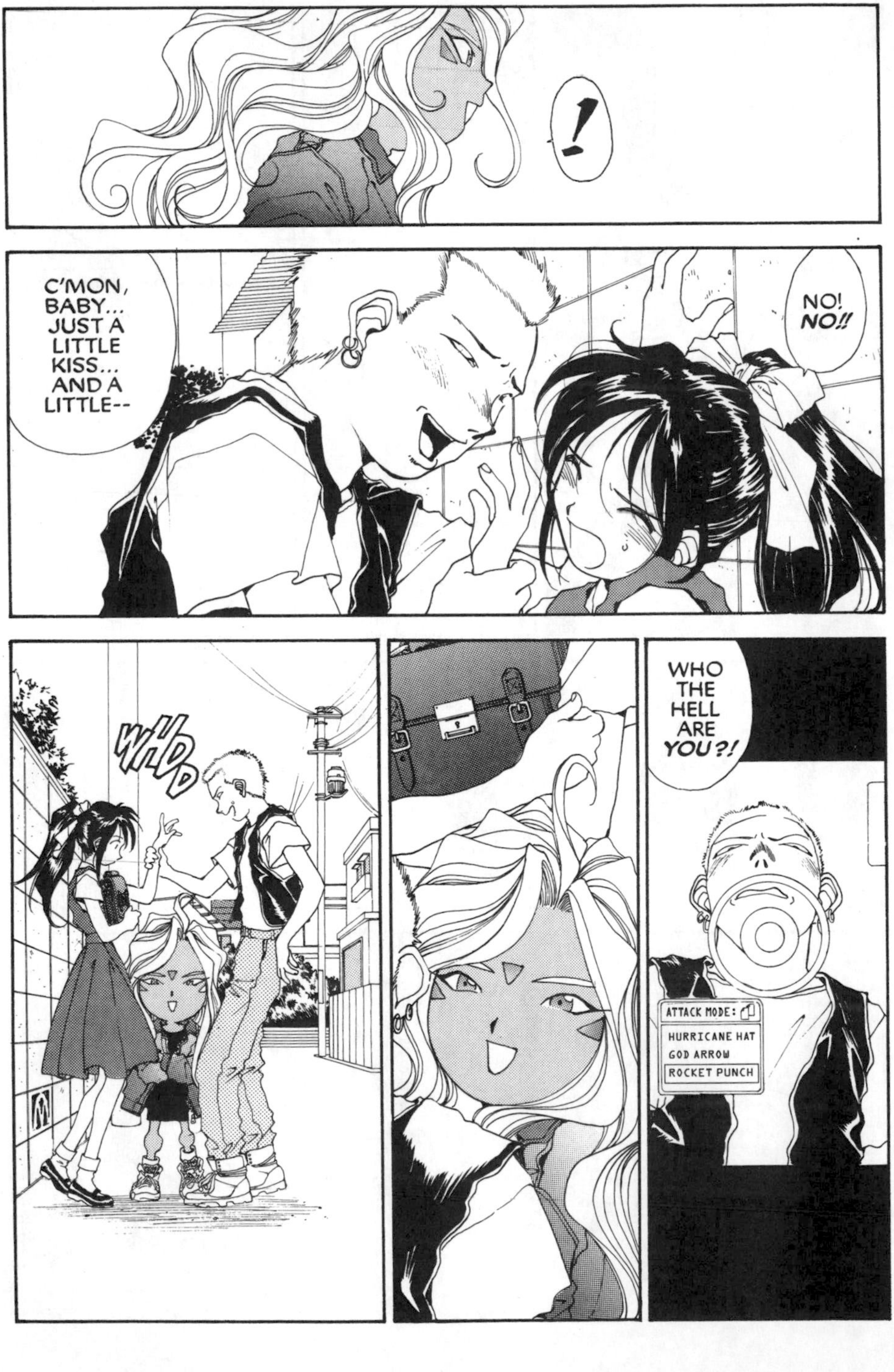
!
C'MON, BABY... JUST A LITTLE KISS... AND A LITTLE--
NO! *NO!!*
WHDD
WHO THE HELL ARE *YOU?!*
ATTACK MODE:
HURRICANE HAT
GOD ARROW
ROCKET PUNCH

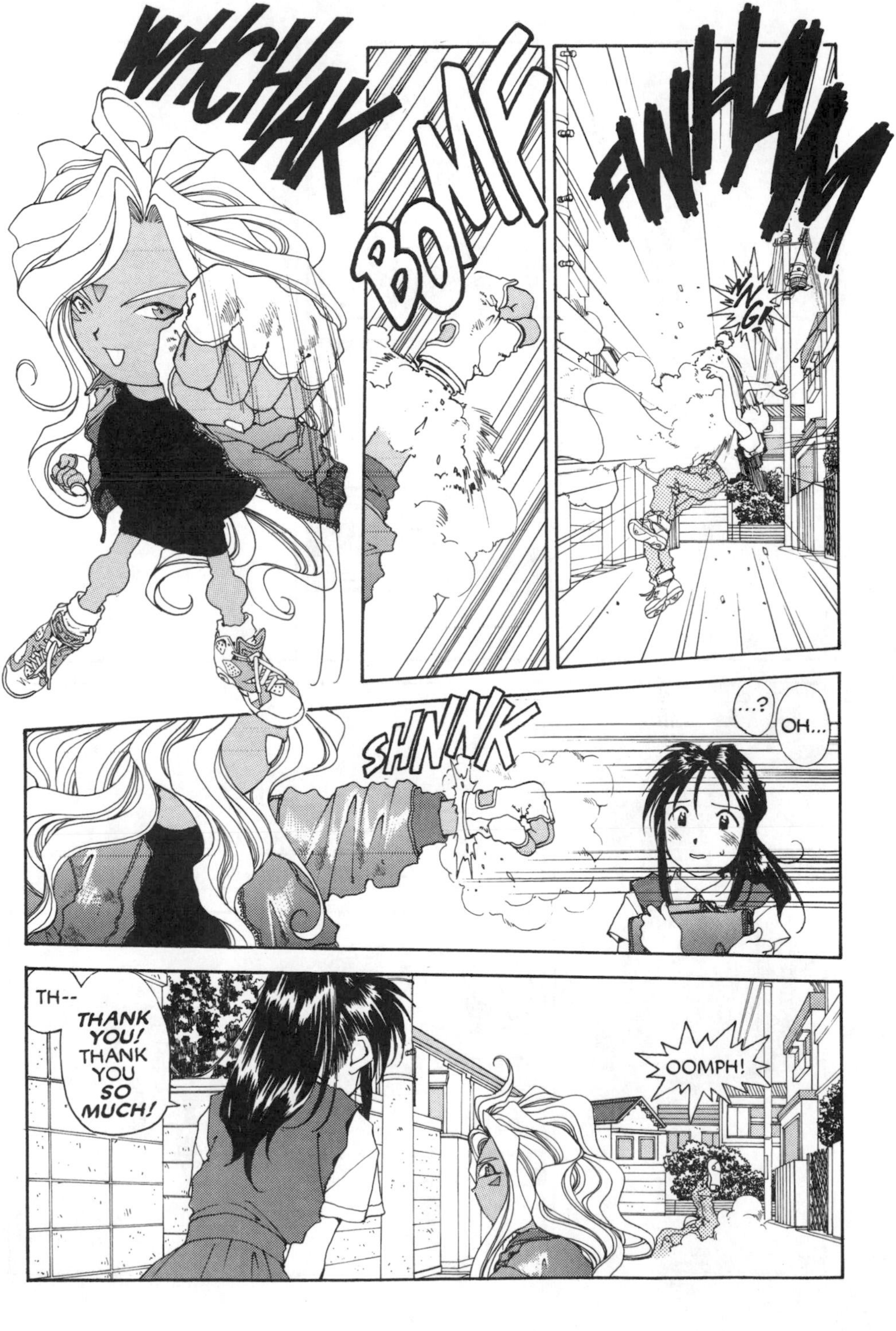
WHCHAK
BOMF
FWHAM
NNG!
SHNNK
...?
OH...
TH--
THANK YOU! THANK YOU SO MUCH!
OOMPH!

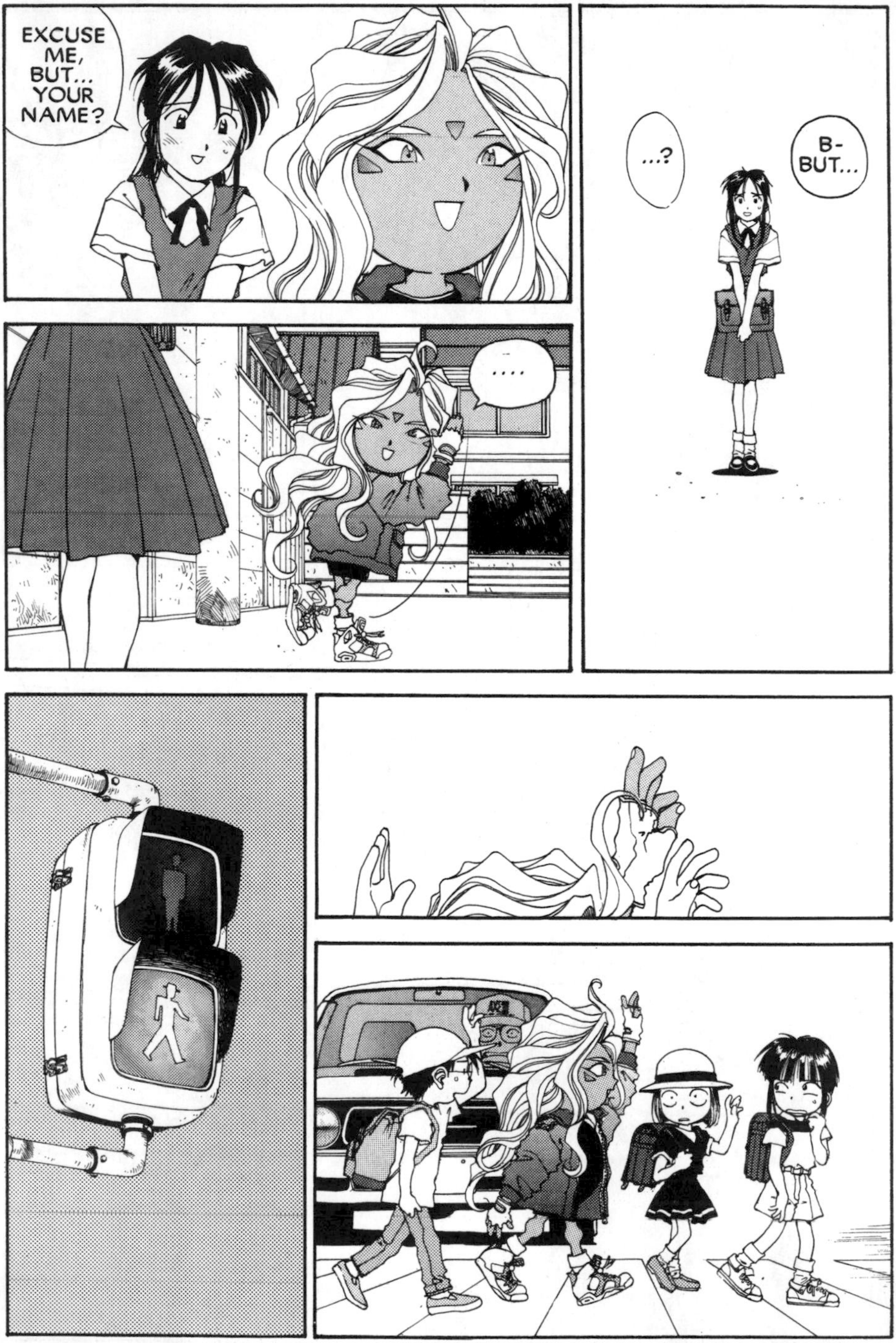
EXCUSE ME, BUT... YOUR NAME?
...?
B-BUT...
....

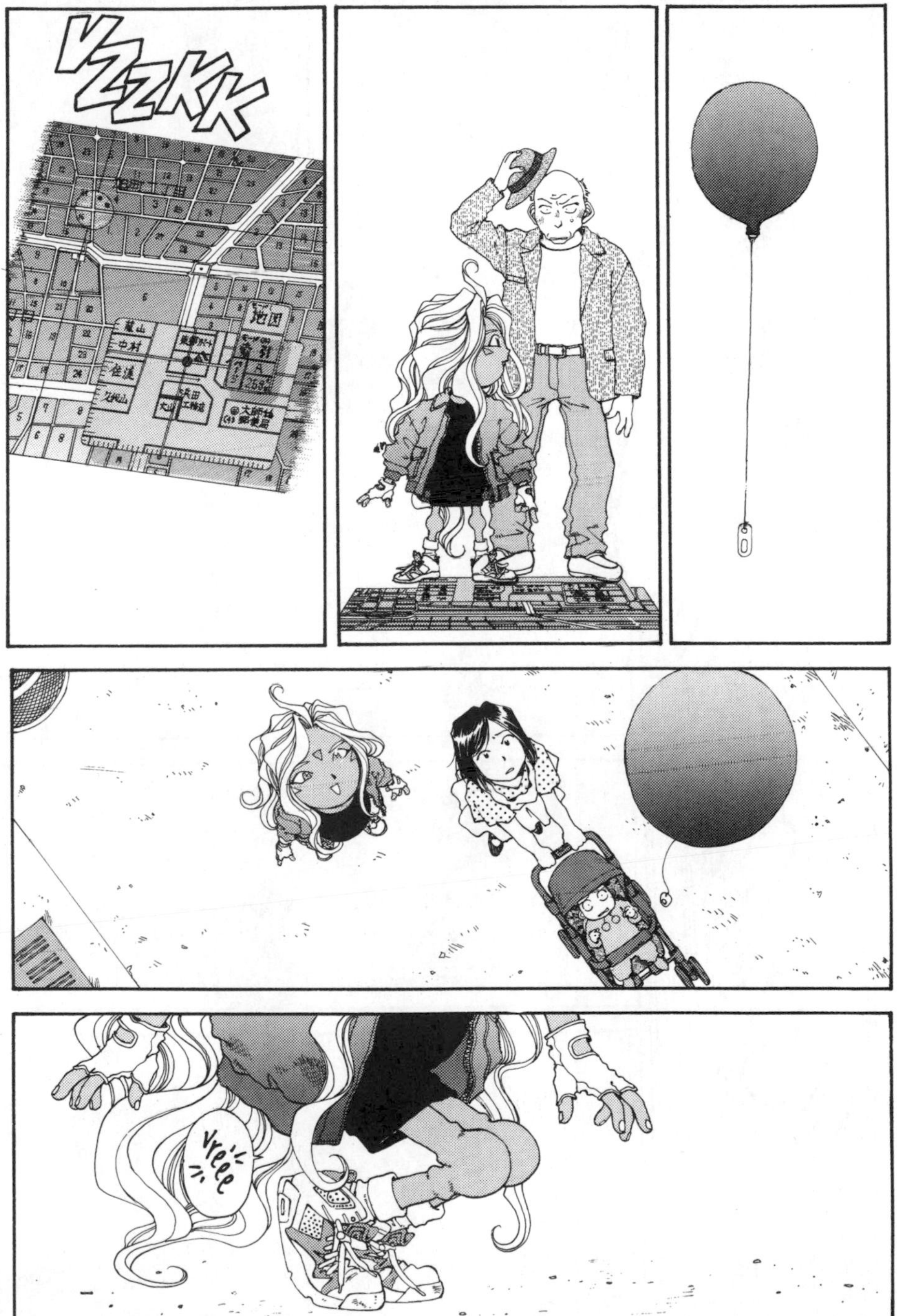
VZZKK
vreee

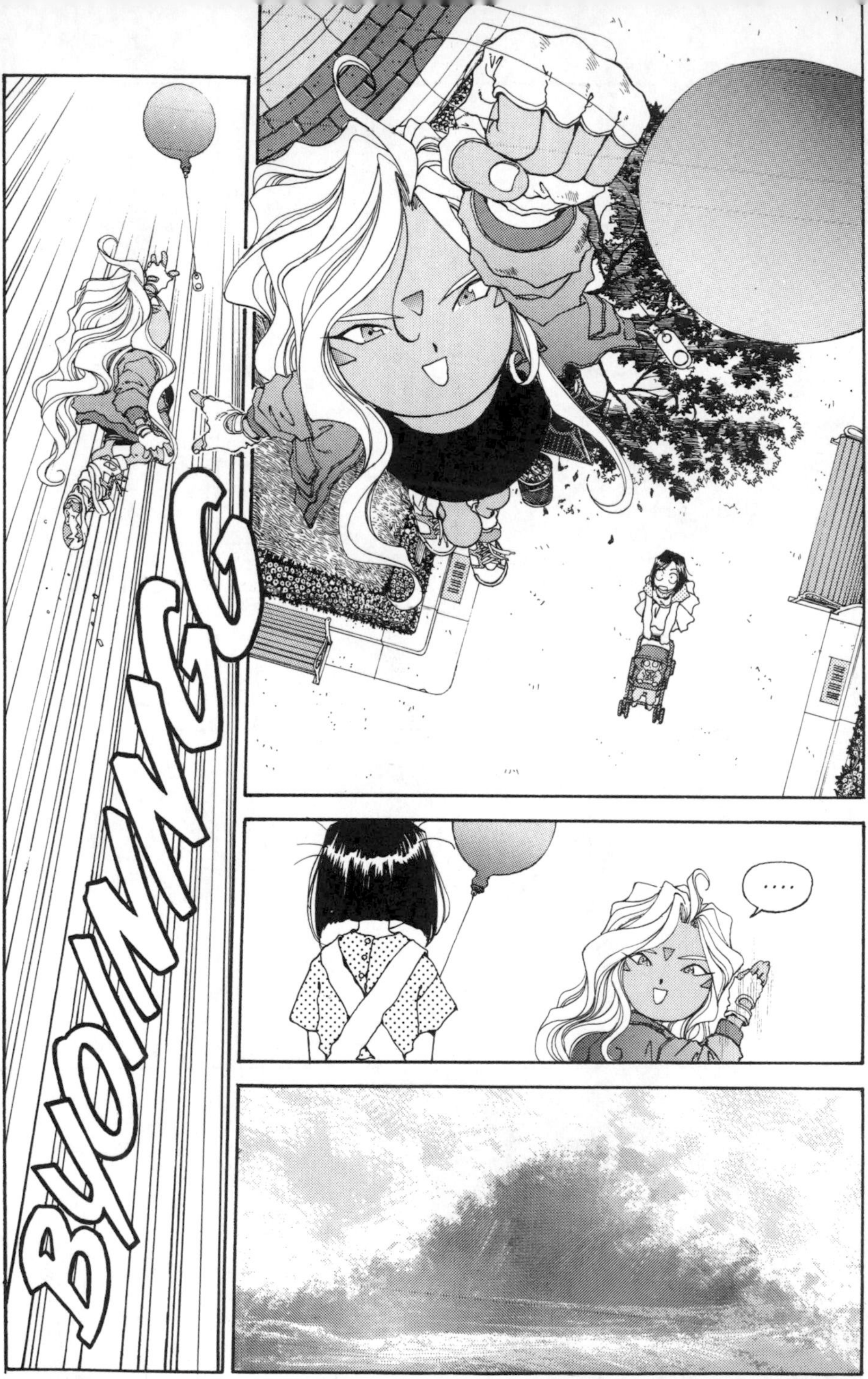
BYOINGG
....

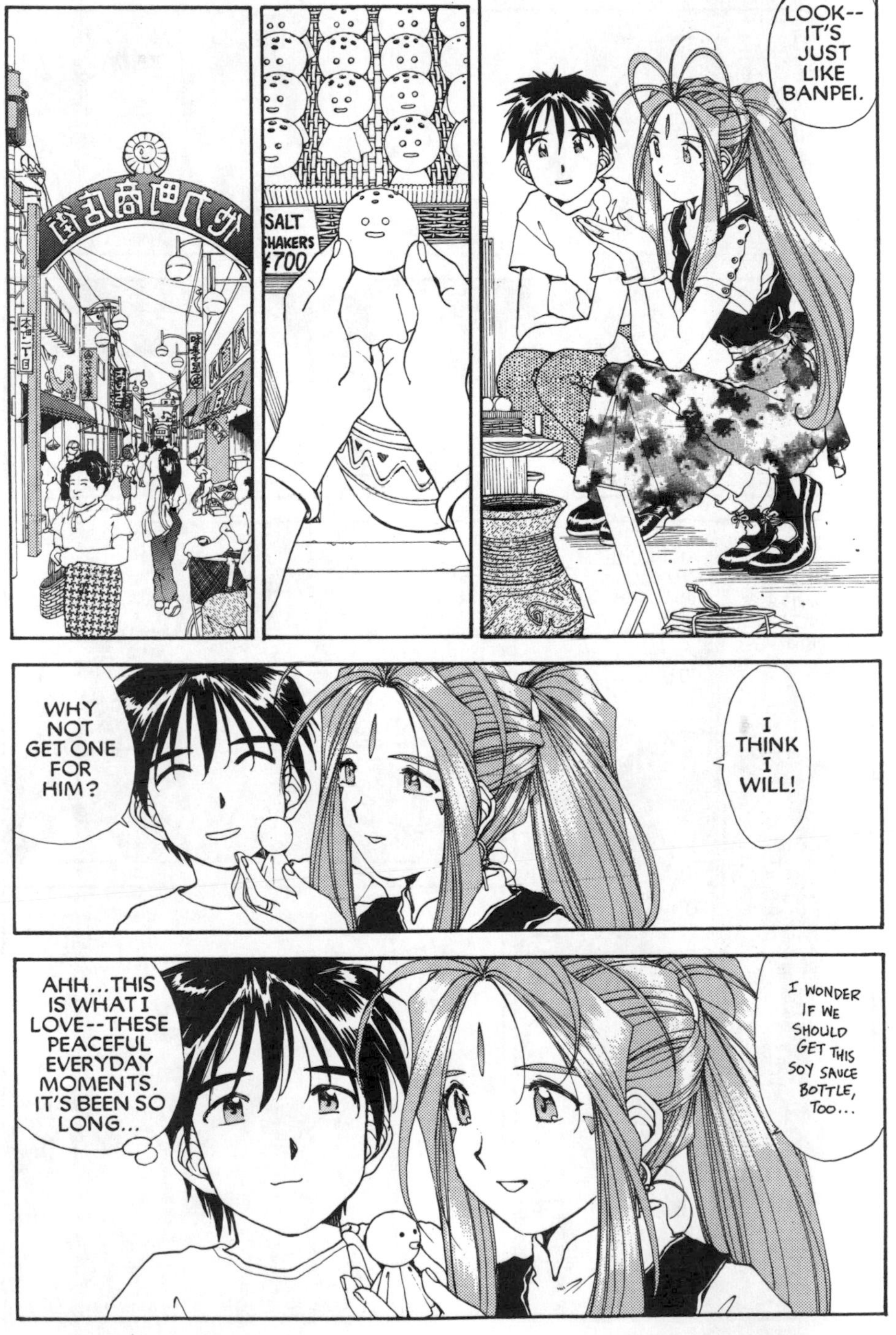
SALT SHAKERS ¥700
LOOK-- IT'S JUST LIKE BANPEI.
WHY NOT GET ONE FOR HIM?
I THINK I WILL!
AHH... THIS IS WHAT I LOVE--THESE PEACEFUL EVERYDAY MOMENTS. IT'S BEEN SO LONG...
I WONDER IF WE SHOULD GET THIS SOY SAUCE BOTTLE, TOO...

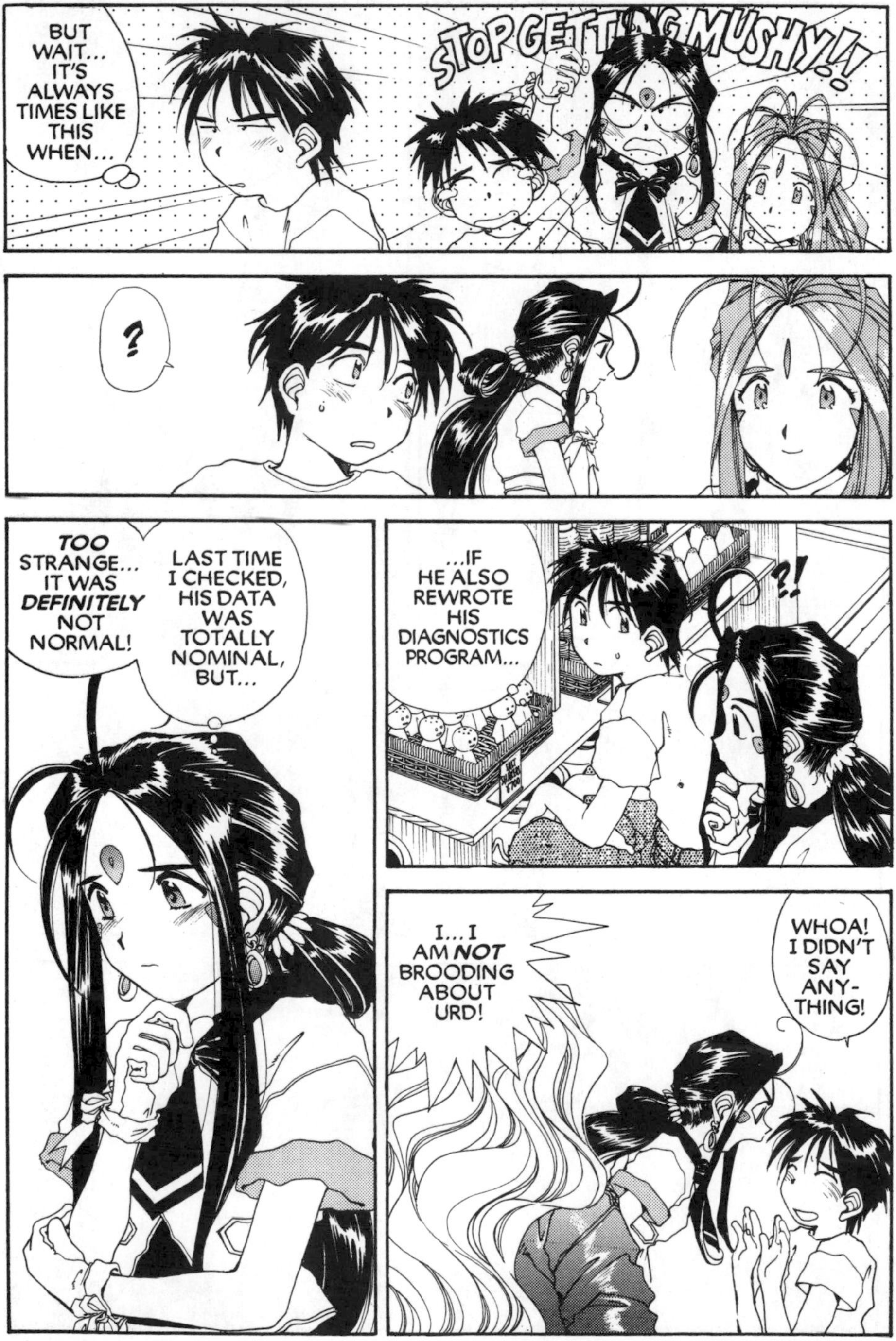
BUT WAIT... IT'S ALWAYS TIMES LIKE THIS WHEN...
STOP GETTING MUSHY!!
?
TOO STRANGE... IT WAS DEFINITELY NOT NORMAL!
LAST TIME I CHECKED, HIS DATA WAS TOTALLY NOMINAL, BUT...
...IF HE ALSO REWROTE HIS DIAGNOSTICS PROGRAM...
?!
I... I AM NOT BROODING ABOUT URD!
WHOA! I DIDN'T SAY ANY-THING!

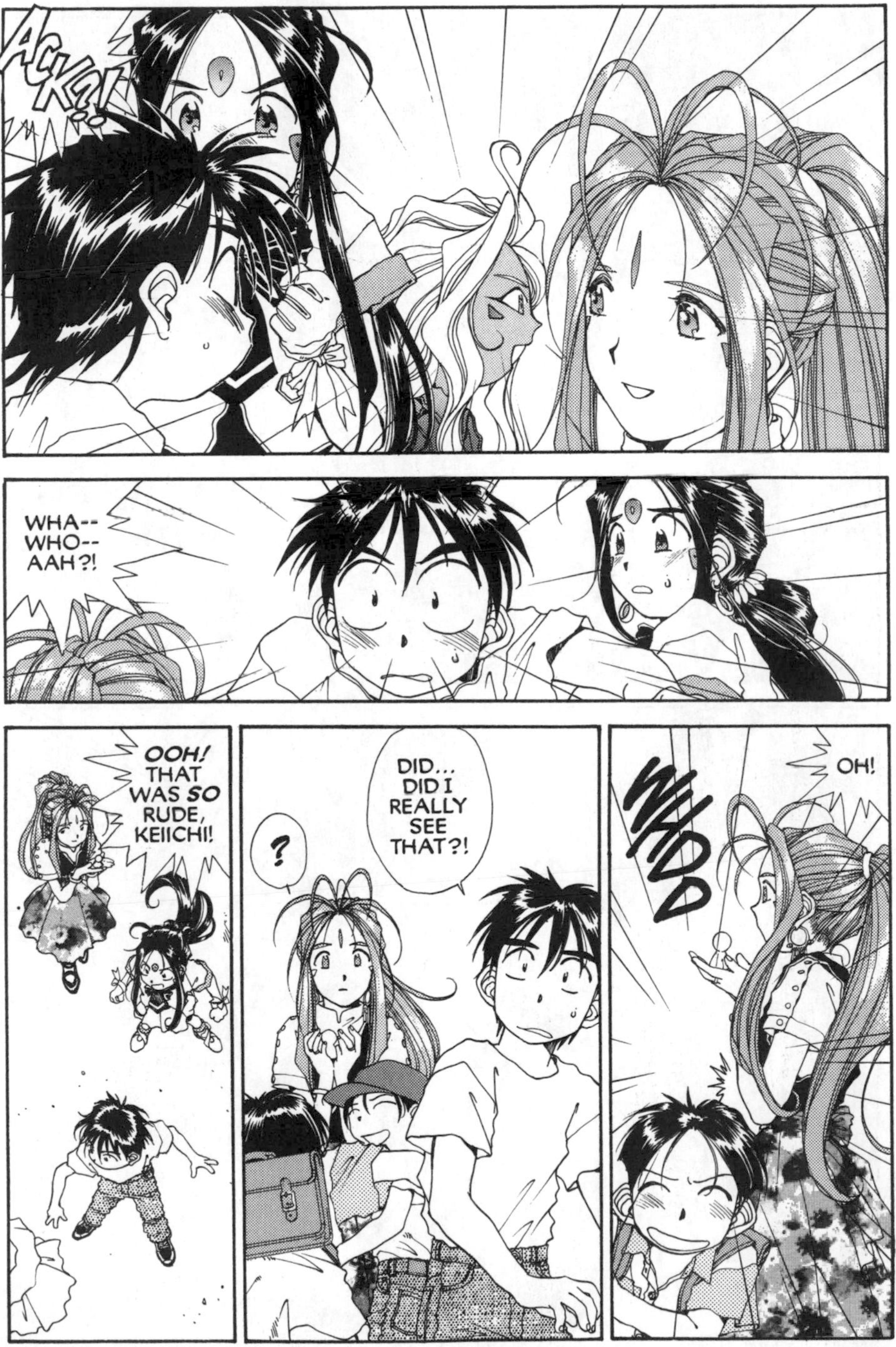
ACK?!
WHA-- WHO-- AAH?!
OOH! THAT WAS SO RUDE, KEIICHI!
?
DID... DID I REALLY SEE THAT?!
OH!

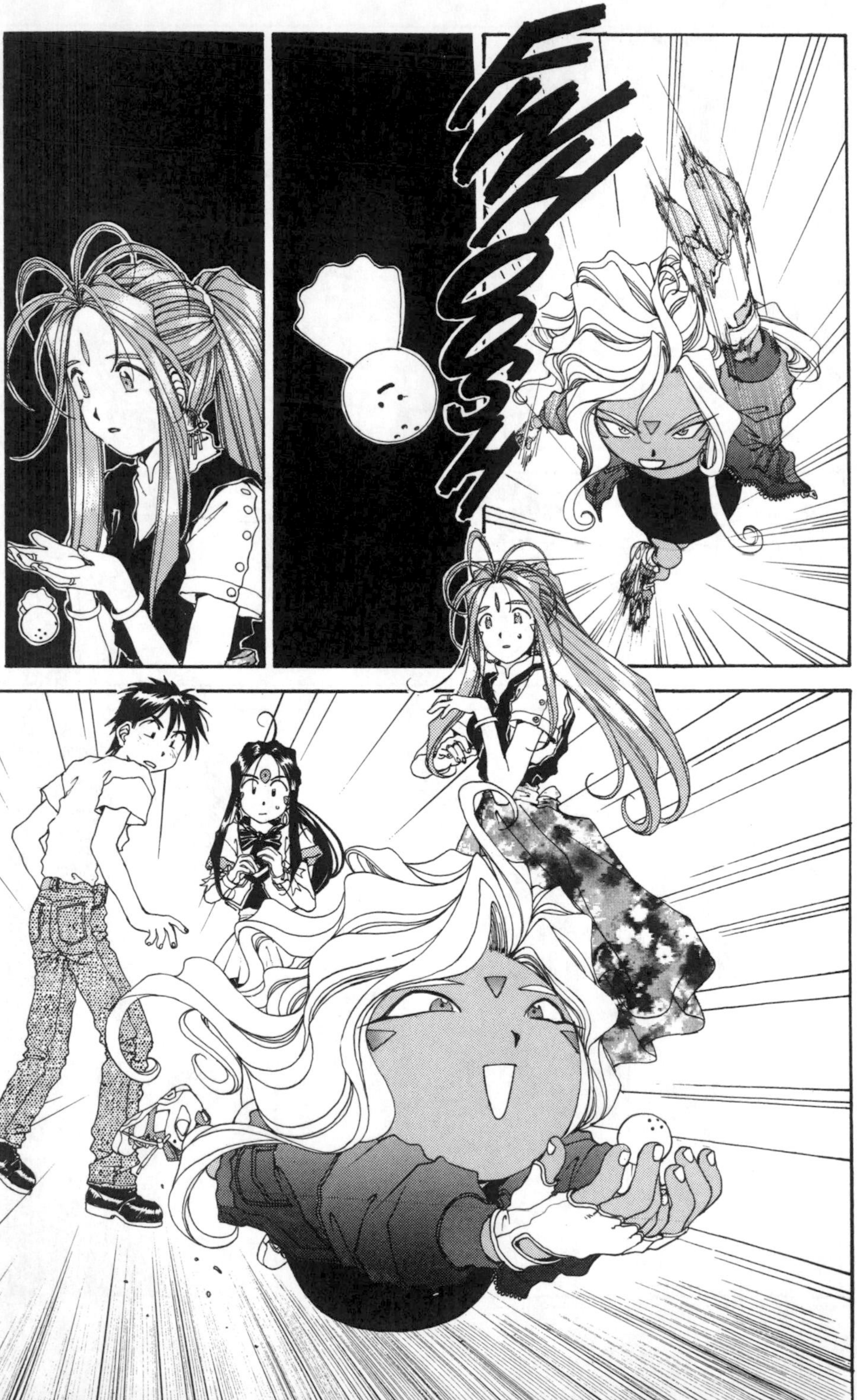

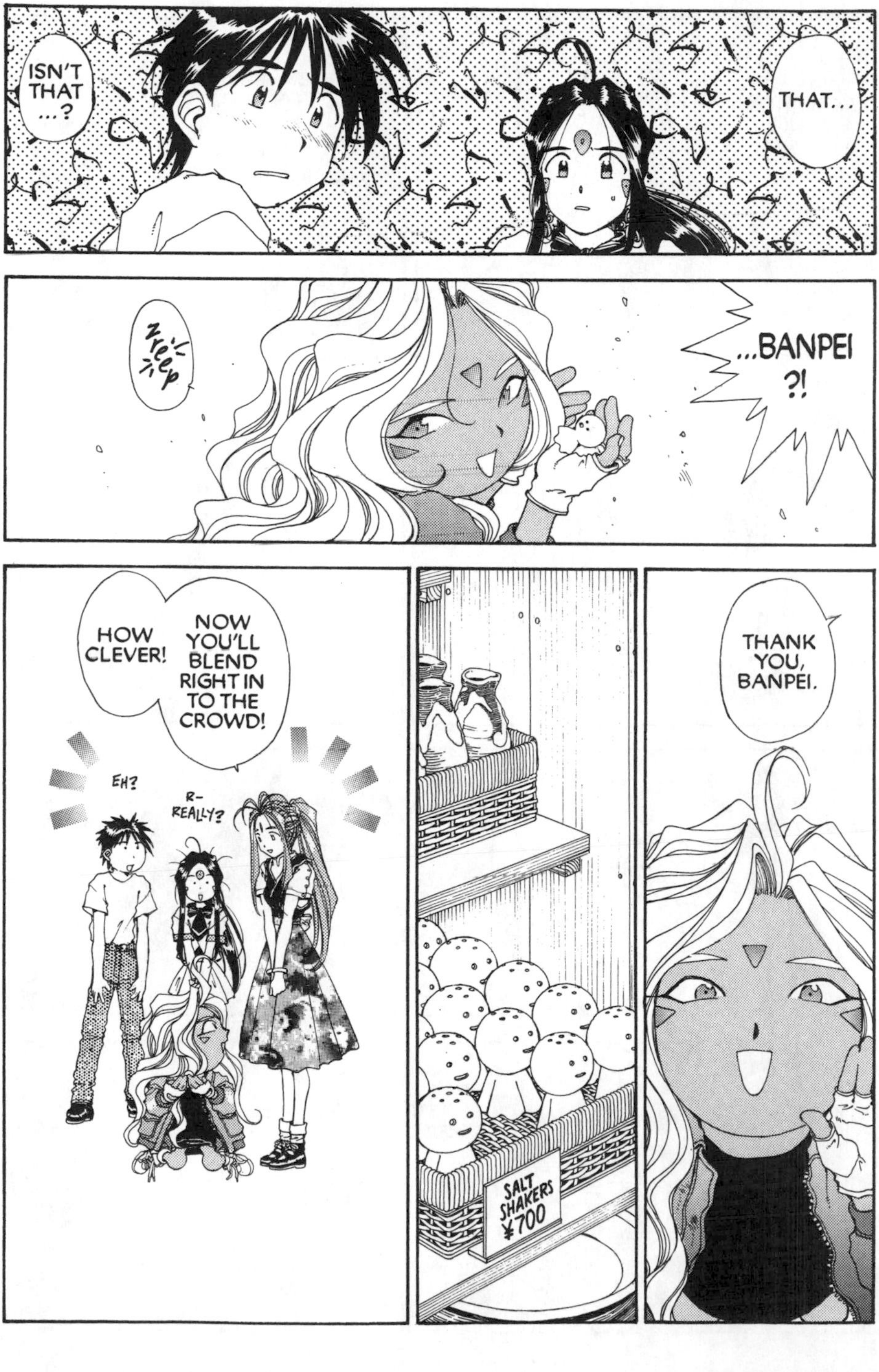
ISN'T THAT ...?
THAT...
zreep
...BANPEI ?!
HOW CLEVER!
NOW YOU'LL BLEND RIGHT IN TO THE CROWD!
EH?
R-REALLY?
SALT SHAKERS ¥700
THANK YOU, BANPEI.

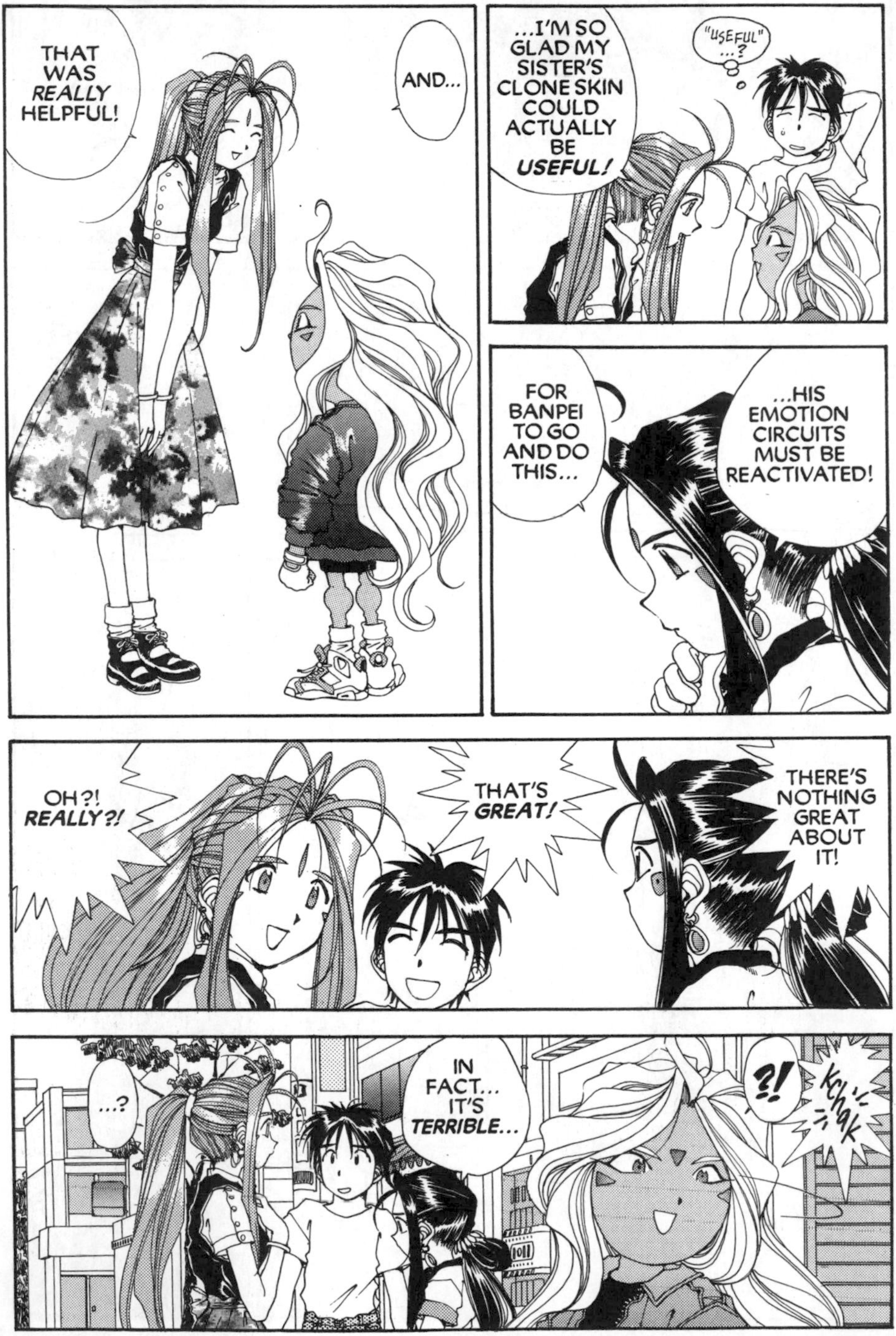
THAT WAS REALLY HELPFUL!
AND...
...I'M SO GLAD MY SISTER'S CLONE SKIN COULD ACTUALLY BE USEFUL!
"USEFUL" ...?
FOR BANPEI TO GO AND DO THIS...
...HIS EMOTION CIRCUITS MUST BE REACTIVATED!
OH?! REALLY?!
THAT'S GREAT!
THERE'S NOTHING GREAT ABOUT IT!
...?
IN FACT... IT'S TERRIBLE...
?!
KCHAK

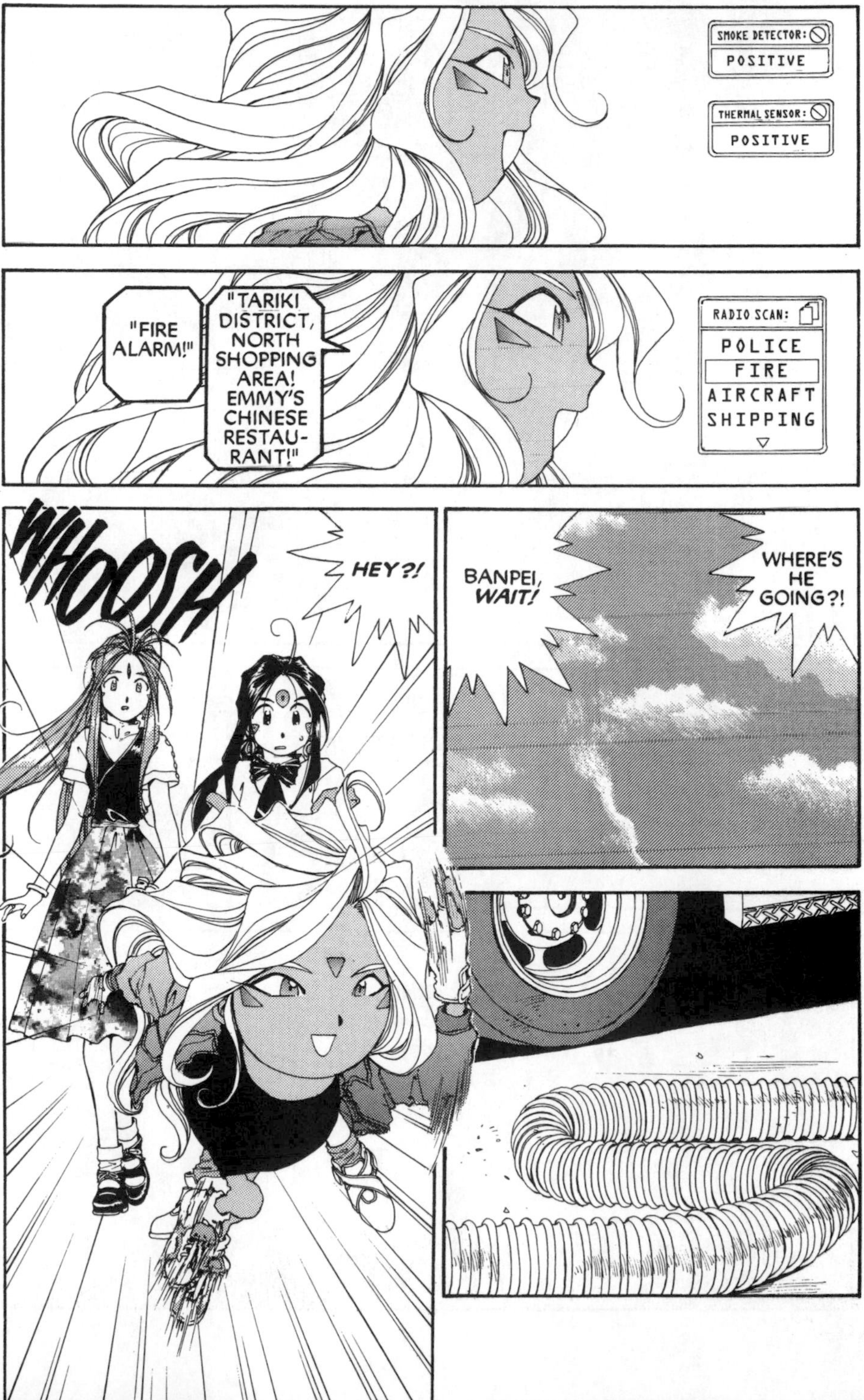
SMOKE DETECTOR:
POSITIVE
THERMAL SENSOR:
POSITIVE
"FIRE ALARM!"
"TARIKI DISTRICT, NORTH SHOPPING AREA! EMMY'S CHINESE RESTAU-RANT!"
RADIO SCAN:
POLICE
FIRE
AIRCRAFT
SHIPPING
WHOOSH
HEY?!
BANPEI, WAIT!
WHERE'S HE GOING?!

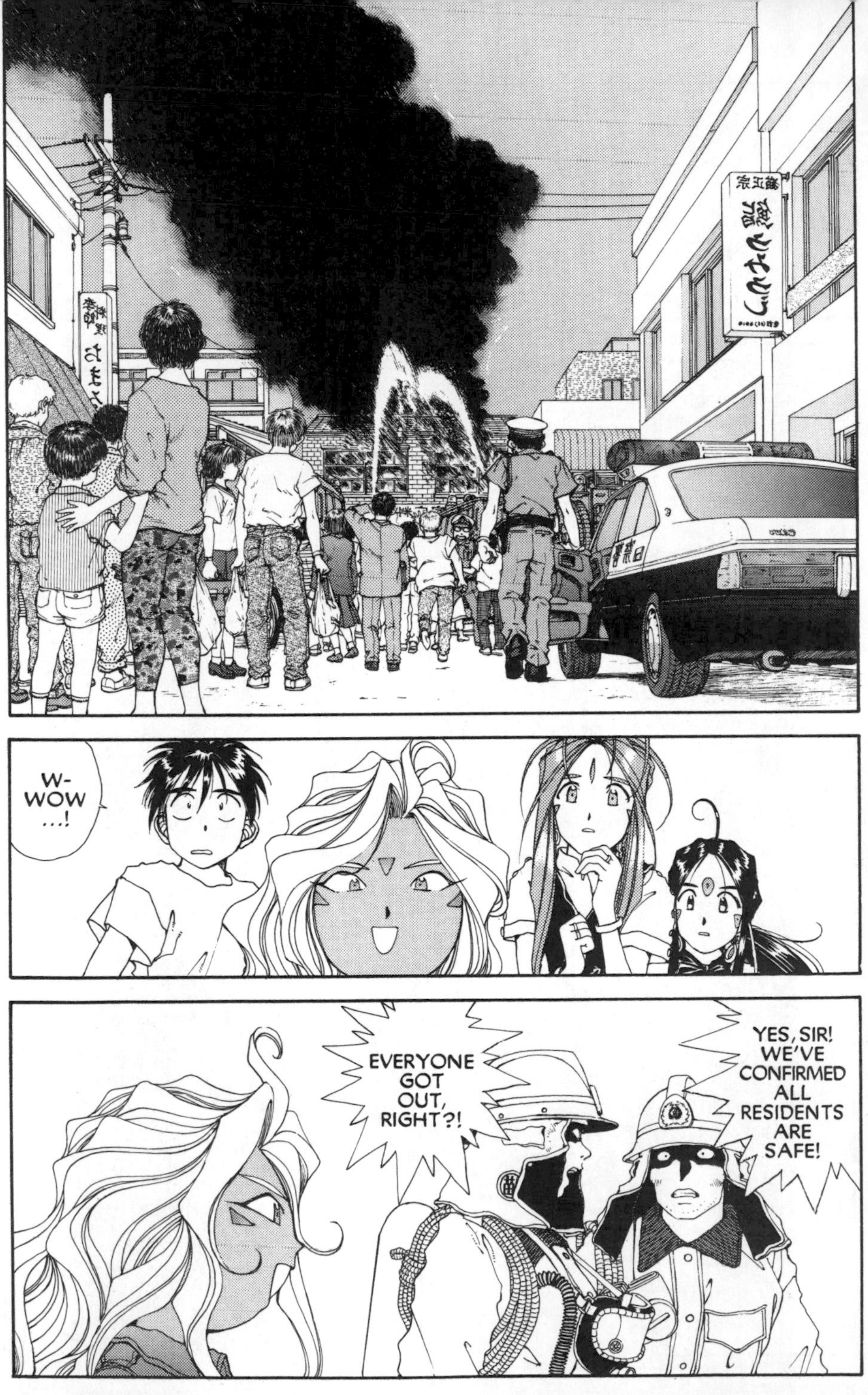
W-WOW ...!
EVERYONE GOT OUT, RIGHT?!
YES, SIR! WE'VE CONFIRMED ALL RESIDENTS ARE SAFE!

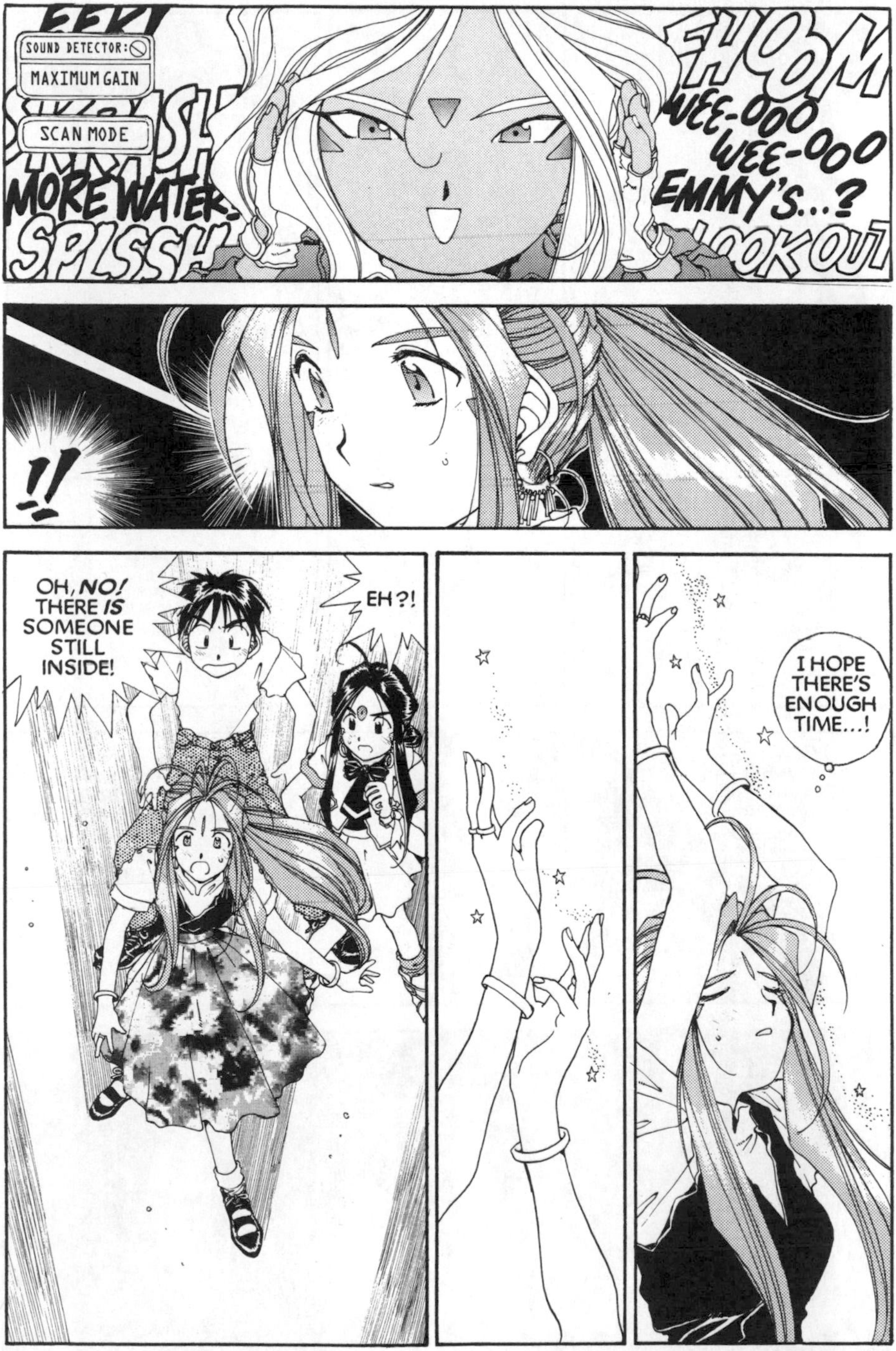
EEK!
SOUND DETECTOR:
MAXIMUM GAIN
SCAN MODE
SPLASH
MORE WATER-
SPLSSH
FWOOM
WEE-OOO
WEE-OOO
EMMY'S...?
LOOK OUT
!!
OH, NO! THERE IS SOMEONE STILL INSIDE!
EH?!
I HOPE THERE'S ENOUGH TIME...!

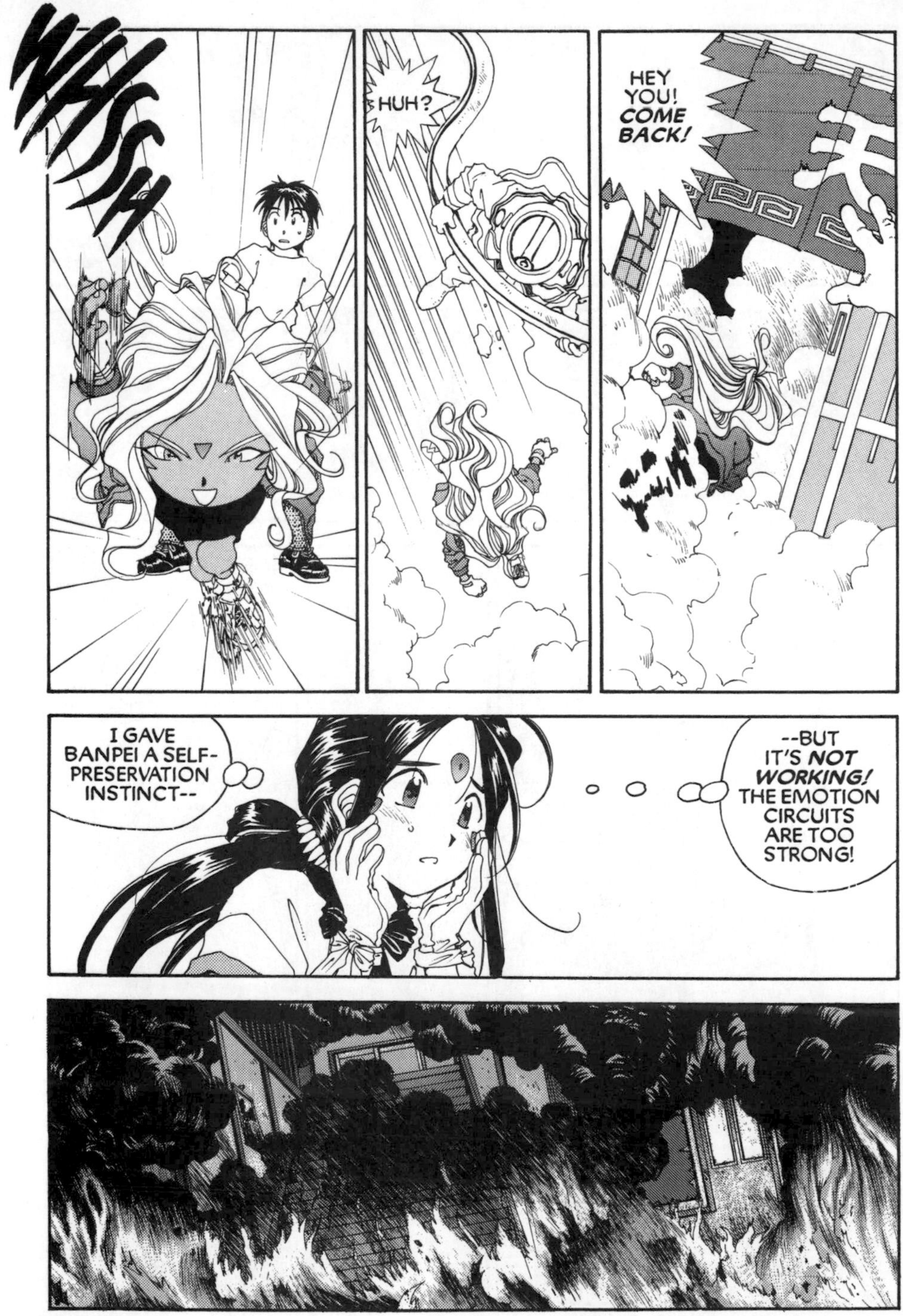
WHSSH
HUH?
HEY YOU! COME BACK!
I GAVE BANPEI A SELF-PRESERVATION INSTINCT--
--BUT IT'S NOT WORKING! THE EMOTION CIRCUITS ARE TOO STRONG!

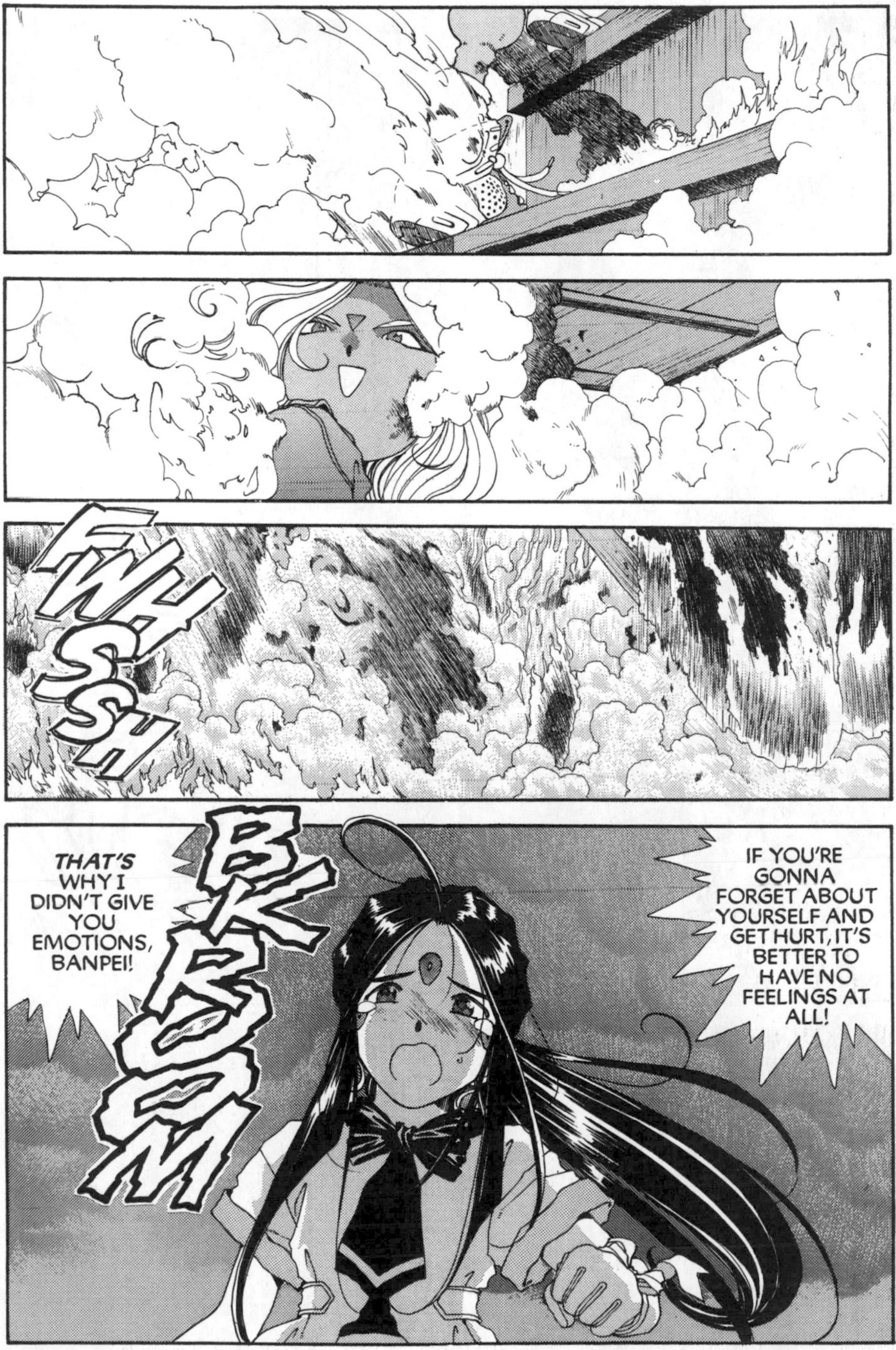
FWHSSH
THAT'S WHY I DIDN'T GIVE YOU EMOTIONS, BANPEI!
BKROOM
IF YOU'RE GONNA FORGET ABOUT YOURSELF AND GET HURT, IT'S BETTER TO HAVE NO FEELINGS AT ALL!

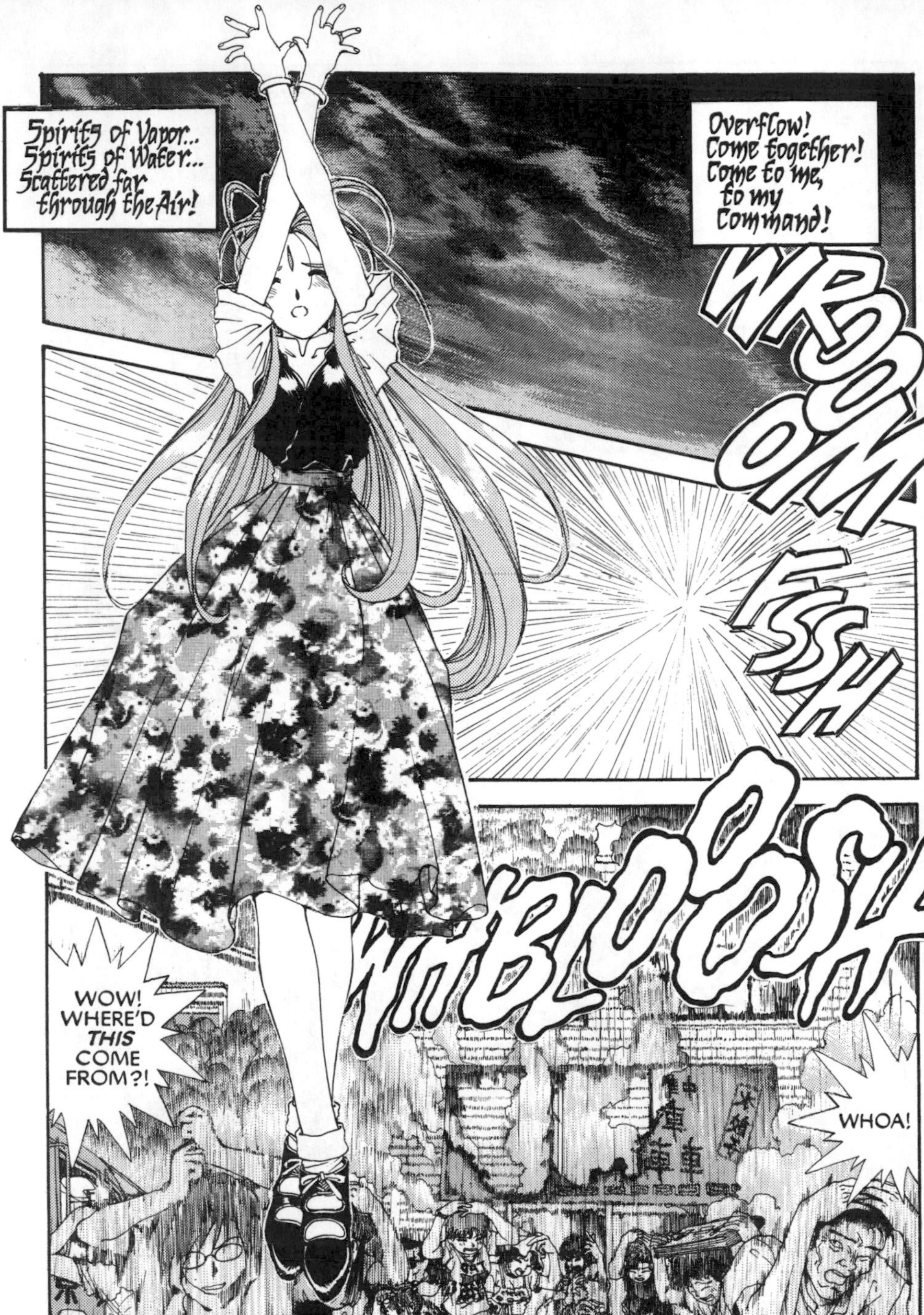
Spirits of Vapor...
Spirits of Water...
Scattered far through the Air!
Overflow! Come together! Come to me, to my Command!
WROOOOM
FSSH
WHBLOOOOSH
WOW! WHERE'D THIS COME FROM?!
WHOA!

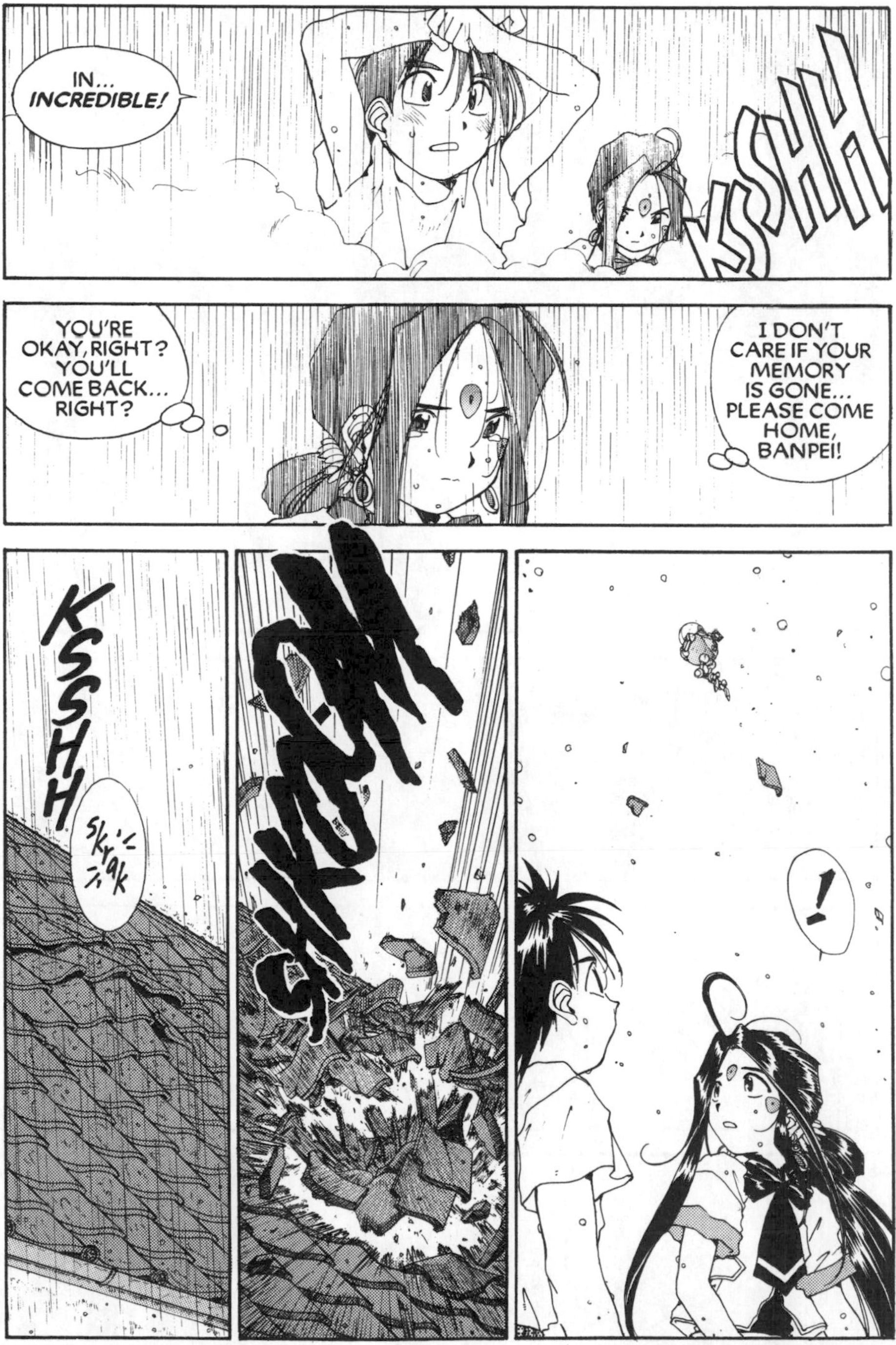
IN... INCREDIBLE!
KSSHH
YOU'RE OKAY, RIGHT? YOU'LL COME BACK... RIGHT?
I DON'T CARE IF YOUR MEMORY IS GONE... PLEASE COME HOME, BANPEI!
KSSHH
skrak
!

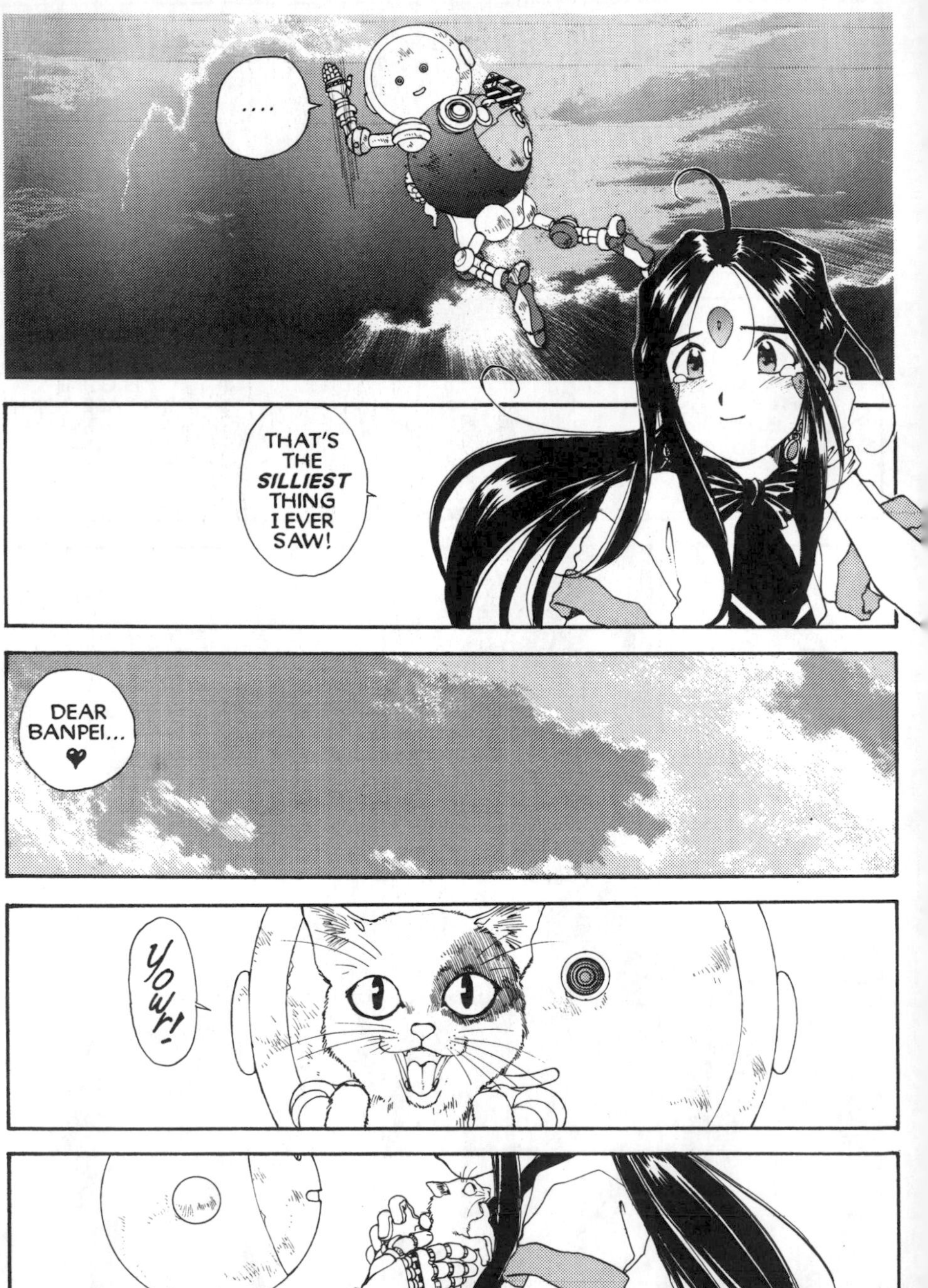
....
THAT'S THE *SILLIEST* THING I EVER SAW!
DEAR BANPEI... ♥
YOWR!

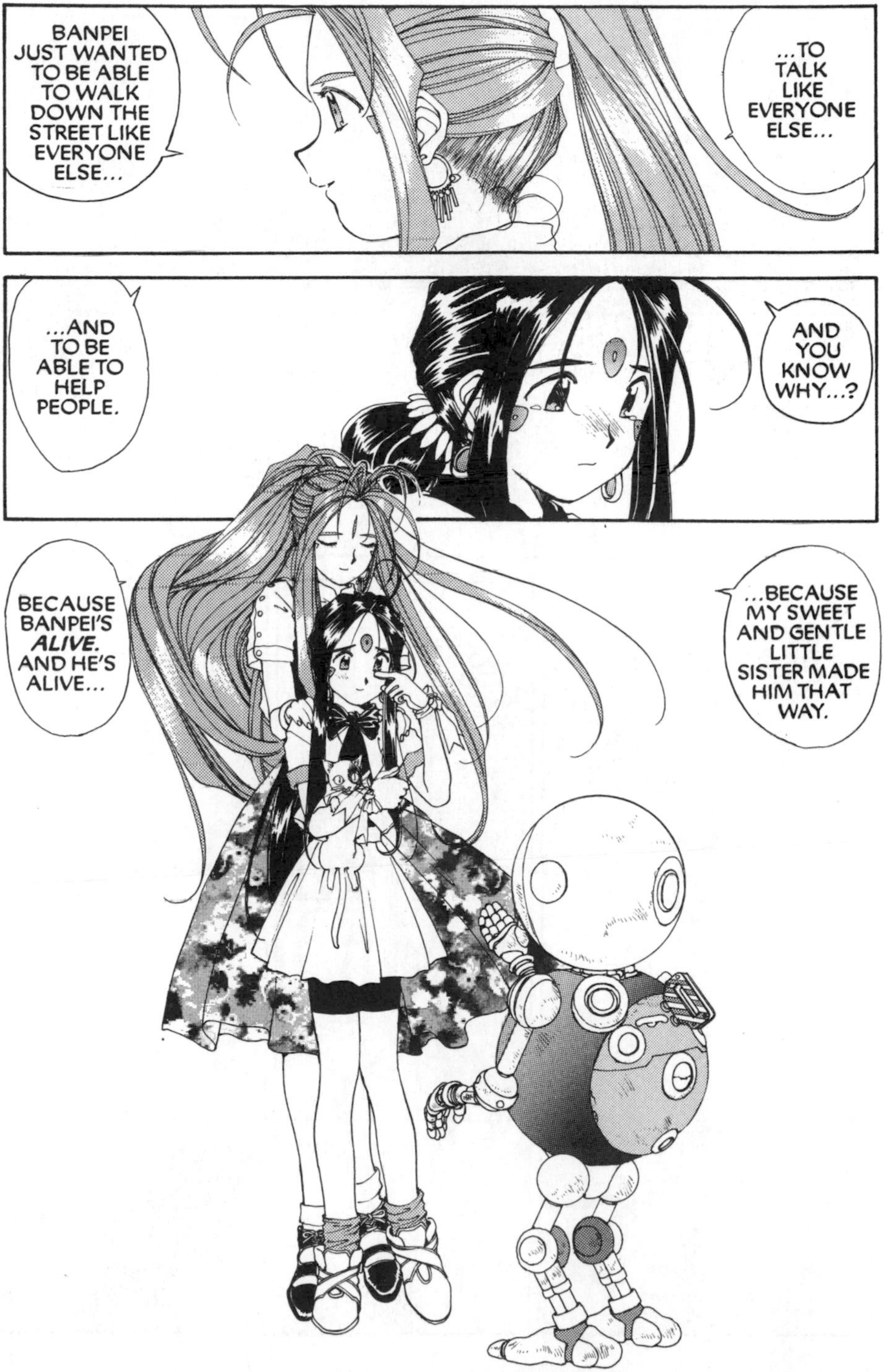
BANPEI JUST WANTED TO BE ABLE TO WALK DOWN THE STREET LIKE EVERYONE ELSE...
...TO TALK LIKE EVERYONE ELSE...
...AND TO BE ABLE TO HELP PEOPLE.
AND YOU KNOW WHY...?
BECAUSE BANPEI'S ALIVE. AND HE'S ALIVE...
...BECAUSE MY SWEET AND GENTLE LITTLE SISTER MADE HIM THAT WAY.

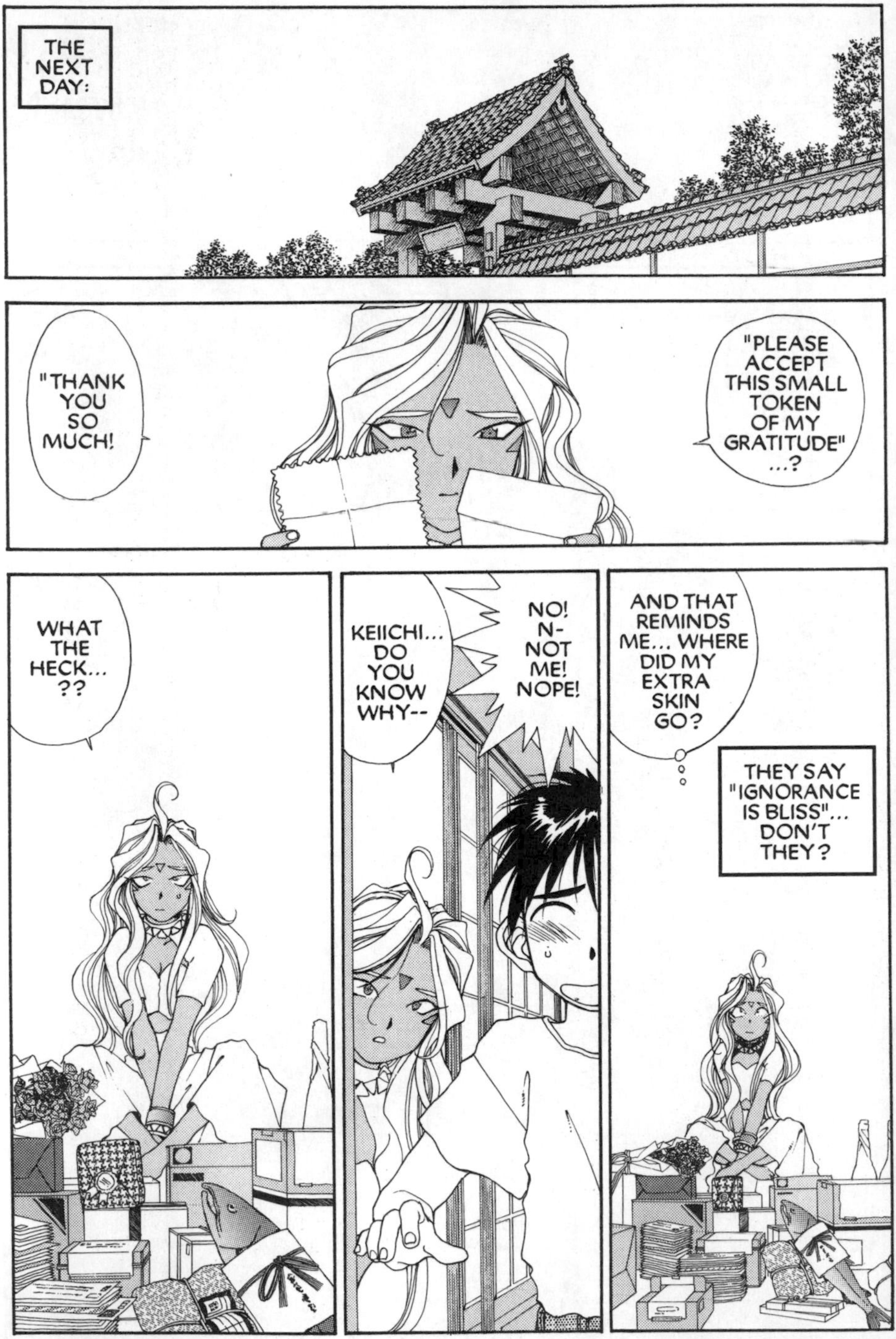
THE NEXT DAY:
"THANK YOU SO MUCH!
"PLEASE ACCEPT THIS SMALL TOKEN OF MY GRATITUDE" ...?
WHAT THE HECK... ??
KEIICHI... DO YOU KNOW WHY--
NO! N-NOT ME! NOPE!
AND THAT REMINDS ME... WHERE DID MY EXTRA SKIN GO?
THEY SAY "IGNORANCE IS BLISS"... DON'T THEY?